O9-CFS-936

THE TELEVISION GENRE BOOK

THE TELEVISION
GENRE BOOK

Edited by
Glen Creeber

Associate Editors
Toby Miller and John Tulloch

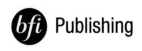 Publishing

FOR DANIEL AND ALEX

First published in 2001 by the
British Film Institute
21 Stephen Street, London W1T 1LN

The British Film Institute promotes greater understanding of,
and access to, film and moving image culture in the UK.

Cover design: Squid Inc./Jethro Clunies-Ross

Cover illustration: *The X-Files* (Chris Carter, USA, 1994–), Gillian Anderson and David Duchovny.

Set by Fakenham Photosetting, Norfolk
Printed by St Edmundsbury Press, Bury St Edmunds, Suffolk

British Library Cataloguing–in–Publication Data
A catalogue record for this book is available from the British Library
ISBN 0–85170–849–8 pbk
ISBN 0–85170–850–1 hbk

Contents

(Grey box case studies are indicated in brackets)

POPULAR ENTERTAINMENT

CHILDREN'S TELEVISION

NEWS

DOCUMENTARY

Preface

Some years ago I began a television based PhD at the University of East Anglia. Coming from a primarily literary background, I visited both the library and the university bookshop in the search of a general, accessible and up-to-date introduction to television studies. However, I was surprised to find few books that satisfied my needs. Although some important academic material had been published, I found few texts gave me the sort of clear and comprehensive outline to the subject (particularly its existing debates and criticism) that I needed or desired. When I began teaching television studies a few years later things had improved, but I found my students still complained that they lacked a solid and straightforward introduction to the subject or a clear summary of what had already been written on it. While things are clearly changing and students have a much better choice today than ever before, this book is really an attempt to write the sort of volume that I hoped to find in the bookshop or library when I first naively arrived at East Anglia.

As this suggests, *The Television Genre* book is aimed as an introduction to the study of television, in particular to the study of genre. As part of a series of books (which will finally make up *The Television Book*) it is loosely based on Pam Cook's *The Cinema Book* (BFI). This new venture aims to reflect and celebrate a growing confidence and maturity in the field of television studies, taking the opportunity to now emulate the BFI's originally ambitious format and apply to it the small screen. Like its predecessor, the book brings together overviews of the leading areas in subject of study by authorities in the field, placing emphasis on linking theoretical discussion to the concrete analysis of television programmes and specific critical debates (particularly through the apparatus of the 'grey boxes' that adorn the text throughout). Likewise there are recommendations for selected reading on a topic and a systematic bibliography presented in parallel to the main sections at the back.

As such, the book is aimed to be one of the first places of reference a student might turn to when they begin researching a particular TV genre, debate or programme. Whilst it has been impossible to cover every genre, every debate, every programme we might have desired (or in the detail we might have liked), the book clearly covers some of the most important, historical and recurrent areas of interest that occupy the study of television genre today. As Pam Cook put it to her 1985 introduction to *The Cinema Book*, 'This precept has informed the book's structure, which is intended to be open to many different kinds of reader'. Similarly, I hope the structure and the level of analysis that this book incorporates will provide both the newcomer and those more familiar with the subject an equal amount of interest and pleasure. Each separate contribution attempts not only to introduce the major debates of a particular genre (such as its institutional, textual and cultural context), but also provoke new areas of debate, dispute and discussion. Despite these aims, readers may be alerted to the relative absence of a longer historical context, of a broader and deeper discussion of theoretical models and methodologies, of a discussion of television as an industry and lastly as a medium facing a whole host of technological and cultural changes in a globalising and increasingly diversifying world. However, further volumes on *Television History*, *Television Studies*, *Television Industries* and *Contemporary Issues* will address these topics in more detail than we could ever provide here.

Needless to say, the generic sections we have chosen to concentrate on are always open to debate and interpretation. For example, chapters such as 'Popular Entertainment' are clearly less generic specific than say a section such as 'News' or 'Documentary' (although that is increasingly open to debate – see, for example, p. 118). However, we hope the reader will understand that genre (as many of the contributors are at pains to point out) does not always fit into neat and tidy categorisations for the discerning critic, student or viewer. 'Soap Opera', for instance, should clearly be part of the 'Drama' section, but to reflect both its institutional proliferation and historical significance in television studies, it seemed justified (and intensely practical) to grant it a section to itself. Similarly, the increasing hybridity of newer genres (such as the 'Docusoap' or 'Reality TV') means it is not always easy to decide what genres should go where and which ones should or should not be included in detail. Choices had to be made and I can only assure the reader they were taken purely on *practical* rather than any *hierarchical* considerations. A similarly practical consideration has meant that in the main the focus has been on Anglo-American genres and programmes. Honourable exceptions there are, including material on, for example, Brazilian Telenovelas (see p. 59), but television still travels much more unevenly over national boundaries than cinema, and it seemed, for our aims at least, important to retain a focus on the two dominant English language traditions, though retaining an awareness that this is only ever part of a much larger picture. The simple aim of this book has been to help the study of television (and that means *all* television) continue to get the critical attention it has so long deserved.

Glen Creeber, July 2001

Acknowledgments

My thanks must firstly go to Andrew Locket and Ann Simmonds at the BFI for their enormous help and support during the making of this book. I would also like to thank all the contributors for their time, effort and understanding; particularly John Hartley and my associate editors John Tulloch and Toby Miller for their continued help and encouragement. On a personal note, I would also like to thank Catrin, John, Valmai, Elen and Rowen for making it such an enjoyable experience – iechyd da! Finally, thanks to Jamie Sexton.

Notes on Contributors

William Boddy is a professor in the Department of Communication Studies at Baruch College and in the Certificate Program in Film Studies at the Graduate Center, both of the City University of New York. He is the author of *Fifties Television: The Industry and its Critics*, and is currently working on a social history of electronic media for Oxford University Press.

Dr Rod Brookes is a lecturer in the School of Journalism, Media and Cultural Studies at the University of Wales, Cardiff. His current research is on the relationship between media, sport and national identities, and is the author of *Representing Sport* (Arnold, 2001).

Dr Stella Bruzzi is Senior Lecturer at Royal Holloway, University of London. Recent publications include *Undressing Cinema* (Routledge,1997), *New Documentary* (Routledge, 2000) and, co-edited with Pamela Church Gibson, *Fashion Cultures* (Routledge, 2000).

Lez Cooke is Principal Lecturer in Media Studies at Staffordshire University. He has published widely on British cinema and television and is currently writing a history of British television drama for the British Film Institute.

John Corner is a professor in the School of Politics and Communication Studies, University of Liverpool. He is an editor of the journal *Media, Culture and Society* and has written widely on media topics. His recent books include *Studying the Media* (Edinburgh, 1998) and *Critical Ideas in Television Studies* (Oxford University Press, 1999). He is currently working on books on political culture and on the history of current affairs television.

Dr Glen Creeber is a research fellow in the School of Journalism, Media and Cultural Studies at the University of Wales, Cardiff. He is Reviews Editor for the *International Journal of Cultural Studies* and his publications include

Dennis Potter: Between Two Worlds, A Critical Reassessment (Macmillan 1998). As well as editor of *The Television Genre Book* he is currently researching *Serial Fictions: Television Drama in the Age of the Mini-Series*.

Dr Kevin Donnelly is a lecturer in Film, Television and Radio Studies at Staffordshire University. He is author of *Pop Music in British Cinema* (BFI, 2001) and editor of *Film Music* (Edinburgh University Press, 2001).

Jon Dovey is a writer, producer and lecturer in the School of Cultural Studies at the University of the West of England. He is the editor of *Fractal Dreams – New media in Social Context* (Lawrence & Wishart, 1996) and the author of *Freakshow – First Person Media and Factual TV* (Pluto Press, 2000).

Jane Feuer is Professor of English at the University of Pittsburgh. She is the author of *The Hollywood Musical* (IUP, 1993), *Seeing through the Eighties: Television and Reganism* (BFI, 1995) and the co-author of *MTM: Quality Television* (BFI, 1984).

Dr Jackie Harrison is a lecturer in the Department of Journalism at the University of Sheffield. She teaches and has published books and papers on television violence, European audiovisual policy, the culture of news production and the changing digital television environment. Her publications include *Terrestrial Television News in Britain: The Culture of Production* (Manchester University Press, 2000) and *The Changing Face of Television* (Garnet Publishing, 2000).

John Hartley is Professor and Dean of the Faculty of Creative Industries, Queensland University of Technology, Australia. Previously he was Head of the School of Journalism, Media and Cultural Studies at the University of Wales, Cardiff. He is author of many books and articles on

TV studies going back to the 1970s (*Reading Television*, with John Fiske [Routledge, 1978]). His most recent books are *Uses of Television* (Routledge, 1999), and with Alan McKee, *The Indigenous Public Sphere: The Reporting and Reception of Aboriginal Issues in the Australian Media* (with Alan McKee, Oxford University Press, 2000).

Dr Luke Hockley is Head of the Department of Media Arts at the University of Luton. His recent publications include *Cinematic Projections: The Analytical Psychology of C. G. Jung and Film Theory* (ULP, 2001) and 'Spectacle as Commodity: Special Effects in Feature Films' in Richard Wise (ed.), *Multimedia: a Critical Introduction* (Routledge, 2000).

Dr Jason Jacobs is Senior Lecturer in the School of Film, Media and Cultural Studies, Griffith University, Brisbane. He is author of *The Intimate Screen: Early British Television Drama* (Oxford University Press, 2000) and *Body Trauma TV: The New Hospital Dramas* (BFI, forthcoming). His research interests include television history, television aesthetics and issues of judgement and value in television studies.

Catherine Johnson is researching a PhD on television fantasy at the University of Warwick. She has published articles on factual television in Britain and on the *Quatermass* serials of the 1950s.

Justin Lewis is Professor of Communication and Cultural Industries at the University of Wales, Cardiff. He has written several books about media and culture. His particular interests are media influence, cultural policy and the ideological role of media in contemporary societies. His most recent book, *Contructing Public Opinion: How Elites Do What They Like and Why We Seem to Go Along With It* is an analysis of the media and public opinion (Columbia University Press, 2001).

Anna McCarthy is Assistant Professor of Cinema Studies at New York University. She is the author of *Ambient Television: Visual Culture and Public Space* (Duke University Press, 2001). Her current research is on the history of advertising and corporate speech in American television.

Dr Máire Messenger-Davies is Senior Lecturer in the School of Journalism, Media and Cultural Studies at the University of Wales, Cardiff. She is the author of *Television is Good for Your Kids* (Hilary Shipman, 1989) and '*Dear BBC': Children, Television Storytelling and the Public Sphere* (Cambridge University Press, 2001).

Toby Miller is Professor of Cultural Studies and Cultural Policy at New York University. He is the editor of the journal *Television and New Media*, co-editor of the journal *Social Text*, and author or editor of eight books.

Dr Brett Mills is a lecturer in Media and Cultural Studies at the University of Glamorgan, and Associate Tutor at the Centre for Mass Communication Research, University of Leicester. He co-edited *Critical Mass: Theory and Practice in Literary Studies*, and his *No Laughing Matter: the Constraints Upon Television Sitcom in Britain* is forthcoming.

Dr Rachel Moseley teaches film and television at the University of Warwick. She has published on both film and television and has a book forthcoming from Manchester University Press, *Growing Up with Audrey Hepburn: Text, Audience, Resonance*. She is now researching teen film and television.

Steve Neale is Research Professor in Film, Media and Communication Studies at Sheffield Hallam University. He is author of *Genre* (BFI, 1987) and *Genre and Hollywood* (Routledge, 2000), co-author of *Popular Film and Television Comedy* (Routledge) and co-editor of *Contemporary Hollywood Cinema* (Routledge).

Robin Nelson is Professor and Head of the Department of Contemporary Arts, Manchester Metropolitan University. He has broad research interests in the arts and media and his publications on TV drama include *Boys from the Blackstuff: The Making of TV Drama* (Comedia Pub. Group, 1986) and *TV Drama in Transition: Forms, Values and Cultural Change* (St Martin's Press, 1997).

Dr Adrian Page is Principal Lecturer in Media Arts at the University of Luton. He is the author of *Cracking Morse Code: Semiotics and Television Drama* (University of Luton Press, 2000) and is currently working on philosophical issues in television and film. He is also the editor of *The Death of the Playwright? Modern British Drama and Literary Theory* (Macmillan, 1992).

Jane Shattuc is an associate professor at Emerson College in Boston. Her publications include *Television, Tabloids, Tears: Fassbinder and Popular Culture* (University of Minnesota Press, 1995) and *The Talking Cure: Women and TV Talk Shows* (Routledge, 1997).

Thomas Tufte is Associate Research Professor at the Department of Film and Media Studies at the University of Copenhagen, Denmark. He is co-editor of the *Danish Journal of Communication* and has published work on telenovelas in Latin American, American and European journals and anthologies. Currently, he is working on a research project that explores the relationship between media use and identity formation among young ethnic minorities in Copenhagen.

John Tulloch is Professor of Media Communication and Head of the School of Journalism, Media and Cultural Studies at the University of Wales, Cardiff. His recent books include *Watching Television Audiences: Cultural Theories and Methods* (Arnold, 2000), *Performing Culture: Stories of Expertise and the Everyday* (Sage, 1999), and (with Deborah Lupton) *Television, AIDS and Risk* (Allen & Unwin, 1997).

Current theoretical areas of research interest are risk and the media, theories of performativity and 'artistic' events.

Graeme Turner is Professor of Cultural Studies and Director of the Centre for Critical and Cultural Studies at the University of Queensland, Brisbane, Australia. He has published widely on media and cultural studies topics. His most recent publications include (with Stuart Cunningham) *The Australian TV Book* (Allen & Unwin, 2000) and (with Frances Bonner and David Marshall) *Fame Games: The Production of Celebrity in Australia* (Cambridge University Press, 2000).

Paul Wells is Professor of Media and Cultural Studies at the University of Teeside, a radio and television programme-maker and the author of *Art and Animation* (1997) and *Understanding Animation* (Routledge, 1998).

INTRODUCTION: WHAT IS GENRE?

Studying Genre

'Genre' is a French word meaning 'type' or 'kind'. As such, it has played an important role in the study of literature, theatre, film, television and other art and media forms. It has long been recognised that output in each of these fields can be grouped into categories, and that each category or class is marked by a particular set of conventions, features and norms. Examples include epic poetry and the novel in literature; melodrama, comedy and tragedy in the theatre; Westerns, thrillers and musicals in the cinema; and sitcoms, news and soaps on television. However, among those who have studied genre in these and other fields, debates and disagreements of various kinds have arisen. Some are particular to individual fields (those concerning television will be discussed in more detail in the section on 'Genre and Television' below), but others are more general in nature or import. They concern the scope of genre as a concept and as a phenomenon, and they concern the role and the purpose of genre study.

Most theorists of genre argue that generic norms and conventions are recognised and shared not only by theorists themselves, but also by audiences, readers and viewers. The classification of texts is not just the province of academic specialists, it is a fundamental aspect of the way texts of all kinds are understood. Thus if a character walking down the street on screen suddenly bursts into song, audiences accustomed to the genre are likely to classify the film they are watching as a musical, to understand that this is the kind of thing that happens in this kind of film, and to anticipate that other instances of singing – perhaps accompanied by dancing – are likely to occur during the rest of the film. In many cases, of course, it is likely that audiences will have some idea in advance of the kind of film (or play or programme) they are going to watch. They will have made an active choice either to watch or, if their preferences dictate, to avoid it. They will have done so on the basis of information supplied by advertising, by reviews and previews, perhaps by a title (such as *Singin' in the Rain*) or by the presence of particular performers. They are therefore likely to bring with them a set of expectations, and to anticipate that these expectations will be met in one way or another.

Many theorists have recognised these aspects of genre, and have devised a number of terms to mark ,them. Drawing on the work of Todorov (1977, pp. 42–52, 80–8; 1981, pp. 118–19), Neale has written about forms of 'generic verisimilitude', the ways in which otherwise unlikely occurrences can properly and predictably occur in genres such as the musical (1980, pp. 36–41; 1990, pp. 46–8; 2000, pp. 31–9). Jauss (1982) has talked about the extent to which genres entail 'horizons of expectation'. Altman (1996, p. 280) has written about the 'generic audience' as a means of identifying those sectors of any population 'sufficiently familiar with the genre to participate in a fully genre-based viewing', as well as about 'generic frustration' as 'the emotion generated by . . . a failure to respect generic norms' – often the product of what he calls 'generic tension'. Roberts (1990, pp. 71–86) has stressed the extent to which audiences and readerships possess different degrees of generic knowledge and exhibit different degrees of generic preference, varying from 'exclusivists' and 'fans' to 'allergics', and Frith (1996, pp. 47–95) has discussed the role of groups of this kind within the field of popular music. Drawing on the work of Lukow and Ricci (1984), Neale (1990, pp. 48–52; 2000, pp. 39–43) has stressed the ways in which the 'intertextual relay' – the systems and forms of publicity, marketing and reviewing that each media institution possesses – plays a key role not only in generating expectations, but also in providing labels and names for its genres and thus a basis for grouping films, television programmes, or other works and texts together.

This last point is a point of disagreement. Altman (1984; 1987, pp. 5–15) has argued that institutions and their terms only provide a starting point for constructing generic 'corpuses' or groupings. For him, it is the job of 'the genre critic' to study such corpuses, to identify and to define their principal features, and to use these definitions as a means of deciding which works properly belong to each corpus and which do not. Only once this is done is it possible to construct the histories of genres and to theorise about the social and cultural roles these genres perform. For Altman (1996, pp. 283–5), genre history then becomes a matter of locating the 'semantic' and 'syntactic' components of a genre (broadly speaking, those items of setting, character and action that repeatedly mark them and the structures into which they are organised) and tracing the patterns of change and interaction among and between them. He divides sociocultural theories, meanwhile, into two basic kinds: 'ritual theories', which stress the extent to which the popularity of genres is an index of audience allegiance to the values they encode; and 'ideological theories', which stress the extent to which these values are imposed by the industries that produce them in the first place (1987, p. 94; 1996, p. 285. For examples of the former, see Cawelti, 1971, 1976; Schatz, 1981; Wright, 1975. For examples of the latter, see Hess, 1986; Neale, 1980, 1990 pp. 58–65, 2000 pp. 214–29). These approaches are however, too schematic. Altman argues that ritual and ideological theories alike tend to underplay the heterogeneity of audiences and their responses to genres themselves. Echoing Kapsis (1991), he argues that theory and history should take much more account of local institutional and sociocultural conditions.

These disagreements hinge on the role of the critic and theorist and on the ways in which genre itself is defined. As Feuer (1992, p. 139) has pointed out, theorists have often sought to define what she calls 'ideal types' – to specify what a genre should be rather than what it is – and have often tended to use these types as an evaluative tool (the same might be said, incidentally, of fans – see Jancovitch, forthcoming). For several centuries, it was the role of academies and other cultural institutions precisely to specify the generic norms and ideal types to which artists and writers were meant to adhere or aspire. Feuer also points out that what counts as a genre can vary in kind from one aesthetic field to another: 'literary categories are very broad ones. Such literary types as drama and lyric, tragedy, and comedy span numerous diverse works and numerous cultures and centuries. Film and television, however, are culturally specific and temporally limited'. In some cases, literary theorists have augmented these differences by constructing 'theoretical genres', categories modelled on the possible properties of literary modes (p. 140. For an example, see Todorov, 1975).

These differences have been noted by Ryall (1975/6, p. 27), by Williams (1984, p. 121) and by others. They reflect some of the historical and institutional differences between the fields in question. However, they also reflect a tendency to conceive of genres and fields as single, self-contained entities, and a corresponding tendency to limit the scope of the concept of genre itself. In so far as they do that, they reflect the history of the concept and of the uses to which it has often been put.

In English-speaking countries, the term 'genre' came to be applied to literary works during the nineteenth century, at a point in history at which art of all kinds began to be industrialised, mass-produced for a popular public (Cohen, 1986, p. 120). Genres came to be identified with

impersonal, formulaic, commercial forms and distinguished from individualised art. Ironically, this represented a reversal of previous characterisations, which saw 'high art' as rule-bound and ordered (as evident in genres like the sonnet and tragedy) and 'low art' as unconstrained by the rules of decorum (Threadgold, 1989, pp. 121–2). Nevertheless, this characterisation, and the distinction that underlies it, has continued to prevail, not only among those who sought to attack mass culture, but also among those who sought to defend it. It has given rise, for example, to the concept of the 'genre film', 'genre fiction' and the 'genre text', entities that differ from non-genre texts in so far as they are commercially formulaic, marked by norms and conventions, and presumed to cater to consumer demand and audience expectation (Neale, 2000, pp. 25–8).

Thus segregated, the genres recognised within each area of cultural production have been subject to further segregation, not only from one another but from other areas too. The degree of hybridity and overlap among and between genres and areas has all too often been underplayed. ('Comedy drama' in all its varieties has rarely if ever been discussed in studies of film, theatre, radio and television. 'News' is a genre that clearly plays a part in newspapers and magazines, in radio and television, and, though far less frequently now than it once did, in the cinema too.) Underplayed, too, has been the degree to which texts of all kinds necessarily 'participate' in genre (Derrida, 1990), and the extent to which they are likely to participate in more than one genre at once.

These last points emerge from the study of 'speech-acts' and other forms of communication in linguistics and philosophy (Blakemore, 1992; Davis, 1991; Pratt, 1977, 1981). The position here is that all instances of communication are framed in the light of particular norms and encounter, in context, a specific array of expectations, cued in various ways by various means. There is thus a generic aspect to all instances and forms of communication. Even instances designed to flaunt norms and expectations find themselves placed alongside others that do so as well (Freadman, 1988). In addition, more than one set of norms can be involved. Neale, for example, argues that 'both *Star Wars* (1977) and *Body Heat* (1981) participate in the genre "film", "fiction film", "Hollywood film" and "narrative feature film". The former also participates in the genre "science-fiction", and the latter in the genre "thriller"' (2000, p. 25; see also Altman, 1987, p. 123).

As a result, the category 'genre' expands beyond the confines established in traditional areas of study both within and across particular fields of cultural production. Quite apart from generic hybrids, instances in which genres occur in or cross over from one medium or art form to another (comedy, melodrama, science fiction, documentary and news, for example), it should be recognised that categories such as 'narrative' and 'fiction' – even 'film' and 'television' – are generic in nature, that there is a generic aspect to all instances of cultural production, and that these instances are usually multiple, not single, in kind.

These points serve to underline the multidimensional nature of genre itself: its numerous aspects, the numerous meanings it can have, and the numerous analytical uses to which it can be put. Genre can mean 'category' or 'class', generic can mean 'constructed or marked for commercial consumption'; genre can mean a 'corpus' or 'grouping', generic can mean 'conventionally comprehensible'; genre can mean 'formulaic', generic can mean 'those aspects of communication that entail expectation'; and so on. When thinking about genre and television, it is useful to bear all these dimensions in mind.

Steve Neale

Genre and Television

The study of genre and television has been conditioned not just by the formats and forms of television itself but also by the history of genre as a concept, the uses to which it has been put, and the other art and media forms to which it has been applied. The definitions and issues that have arisen as a consequence have also been heavily influenced by the fact that television has adopted and adapted formats and forms from a number of different sources since its inception. Radio, film, written fiction, theatre, journalism, music and other art and media forms have all played an important part in television and its history. The ways in which genre has figured in these forms, and in the theories and debates that have surrounded them, has had an important effect on theories and debates about genre and television itself. Several examples will be noted in the sections on individual genres in this book. The focus here will be on general theories and conceptions, and the ways in which they relate to some of the issues raised in this chapter.

A key issue here is that of definition. What counts as a genre? What counts as a genre in television? Lacey (2000, p. 133) argues that the 'repertoire of elements' that serve to identify genres consists of character types, setting, iconography, narrative and style. This definition derives from, and seeks to encompass, popular fiction and films as well as television. It is thus well suited to the study of Westerns, cop, detective and crime forms, melodrama, adventure and

science fiction, all of which can be found, though in some cases only intermittently or cyclically, in all three spheres of cultural production. However, in particular when it comes to more medium-specific genres with a less clear-cut narrative or fictional base, ambiguities can arise. Lacey looks at game shows (p. 206), and argues that they can be defined in terms of the repertoire mentioned above: there is a standard setting (the television studio), a standard set of characters (the studio audience, 'ordinary people', an 'avuncular host'), a narrative ('the questions or tasks [that] must be overcome to win the prizes'), an iconography ('a high-tech, glitzy set'), and a style ('basic "live" television'). However, both narrative and style here are either weakly defined or weakly specific. Is the overcoming of tasks a sufficient definition of narrative? Is 'basic "live" television' sufficiently marked as a style to constitute a particular generic ingredient? (For further discussion of these points, see the section headed 'The Quiz Show' on p. 79).

There are several even more ambiguous cases than this. Style is a strongly marked feature of advertisements and music videos, both of them staple ingredients of modern television. Yet styles vary from advert to advert, video to video. In addition, some adverts and videos are narrative in form and others are not, and most adverts and videos are presented in segments, blocks and programme contexts that lack any kind of narrative dimension. Like news programmes, variety shows, talk shows and most forms of religious programming, these contexts (popular music shows, teen magazine programmes, advertising segments, and so on) possess a structure, a time frame, and a set of basic ingredients. Some or all of them may involve the presentation of mini-narratives, but they are not themselves narrative in form (see 'Music on Television' on p. 89 and 'Advertising' on p. 94).

Does that mean, then, that they should not be considered as genres? For Lacey, for Selbey and Cowdery (1995) and for Feuer (who refers only to soap operas, crime shows and sitcoms in her 1992 essay) the answer might well be 'yes'. These writers are heavily influenced by film and literary theory, and therefore tend to focus on genres that have their parallels or origins in the cinema, on stage or in popular fiction. They thus tend to stress the importance of narrative forms and conventions. For others, however, the answer is 'no'. News programmes, talk shows, religious programmes and variety shows are all treated as genres in Rose (1985a). Although he acknowledges the lure and importance of narrative, Butler (1994) not only stresses the existence of 'non-narrative genres', but also discusses news programmes, sports programmes, 'non-narrative commercials', music television and, indeed, game shows as specific examples. Like Lacey and Selbey and Cowdery, Butler tends to distinguish between genres and other categories ('modes', 'formats', 'forms' and the like), and thus to underplay the extent to which multiple generic participation is as much a feature of television as it is of other media. (Just as *Friends* could be said to participate in the genres 'television programme', 'television series', 'fictional narrative', 'comedy', 'situation comedy' and so on, so most breakfast shows could be said to participate in the genres 'television programme', 'television magazine programme', 'actuality' and, depending on the nature of the programme, 'news' and/or 'topical variety' and perhaps even 'daytime' or 'morning' TV). However, his position is otherwise consonant with some of the broader conceptions of genre outlined in this chapter

The same is true of those who recognise or stress hybridity and overlap. Hoffer, Musburger and Nelson (1985), for instance, underline the hybrid nature of docudrama, Nordern (1985, p. 34) the extent to which 'the detective genre overlaps considerably with . . . cop shows, spy shows, lawyer shows, and even newspaper shows', and Edgerton (1985) the extent to which, as well as proliferating its own generic categories and types (telefeatures, docudramas and mini-series; biopics, family sagas, social problem dramas, and so on), the telefilm can be seen as combining elements of the Hollywood feature film, anthology drama, and television drama in general (see also Rose 1985b). In addition, and as a separate point, several commentators have noted the influence of soap opera and/or sitcom not only on medical dramas, cop shows and Westerns, but on game shows and talk shows as well (Alley, 1985, p. 82; Robards, 1985, pp. 20, 22; Barson, 1985, pp. 64–5; Goedkoop, 1985, pp. 8–9; Rose, 1985c, pp. 80–1). The recent advent of the 'docusoap' clearly confirms the pertinence of points such as these (see the section headed 'Docusoaps' on p. 132).

Meanwhile, the institutional aspects of genre and television – the relationship between genres and scheduling regimes, modes of production, the varying demands of advertisers and audiences, and developments in adjacent institutions of entertainment and in the media field as a whole – have been noted by most of those who have written on individual genres or on television and genre in general. The role of television's intertextual relay in the categorisation of programmes and in the generation of expectations has been discussed by Tolson (1996, pp. 97–105), who underlines the historicity of categories, genres and time slots. He also underlines the extent to which, for the *Radio Times* and the BBC at least, they have served as a means by which to cultivate a 'socially responsible, family-oriented, discriminating' viewership. As such he raises issues to do with the sociocultural roles performed both by television genres and by television institutions in general.

These issues are complex. They have been rendered even more complex by changes in the distribution and consumption of television programmes during the course of the last two decades. As Feuer points out (1992, p. 157), the advent of remote control and multichannel cable and satellite TV has helped generate a tendency to 'zap' from one channel to another. Along with the advent of video-recording, these developments have served to fragment and to customise the consumption of programmes and genres alike, making it difficult (especially at a time when 'classic' television is increasingly being recycled) to align ritual or ideological readings of programmes and genres with contemporary audiences and viewing populations. At the same time, the proliferation of generic channels like Comedy Central, the Sci-Fi Channel, MTV, CNN News and TCM alongside viewing practices such as zapping – which, as Feuer points out (1992, p. 158), entails the rapid deployment of genre-recognition skills suggests that genre, in each of its facets and dimensions, remains central to television, its organisations, and its viewers and consumers.

Steve Neale

RECOMMENDED READING

Butler, Jeremy G. (1994), *Television: Critical Methods and Applications*, Belmont: Wadsworth Publishing Company.

Neale, Steve (2000), *Genre and Hollywood*, London: Routledge.

Rose, Brian G. (ed.) (1985a), *TV Genres: A Handbook and Reference Guide*, Westport: Greenwood Press.

The Uses and Limitations of Genre

As it has been used within film and literary studies, genre is a means of constructing groups of texts and then discriminating between them. As Steve Neale points out in the first section of this book, for a critic such as Rick Altman this is a preliminary to the construction of a history of the genre concerned, itself a preliminary to understanding its social function (Altman, 1999). For others, particularly in literary study, it is an end in itself: the construction of a defensible definition of the genre (see Todorov, 1975).

Literary genres are routinely traced back to classical models (see Frye, 1957), so that it is deemed possible to determine if a contemporary play is properly a 'tragedy', for instance, by referring back to Aristotle's definition. In such a disciplinary context, generic structures are timeless and universal, carrying with them a cachet of authenticity and purity that is not easily replicated in the study of television. As popular cultural forms, television and film genres are much more historically, culturally and temporally contingent (see Feuer, 1992). Products, for the most part, of the commercial media, many television genres are also subject to market pressures that influence the shape of their texts.

Given such differences, how is the concept of genre used in relation to television? We can approach this question through thinking about the uses of genre for audiences, for academic researchers and critics, and for the television industry.

As is the case with film, genre operates as an important means of communicating information about the television text to prospective audiences. Through its inscription in publicity, in the listings in the TV guide, in the repertoires of cultural knowledge around individual personalities and other intertextual experiences, genre helps to frame audience expectations. For the television viewer, genre plays a major role in how television texts are classified, selected and understood.

For those who study television, genre is a means of managing TV's notorious extensiveness as a cultural form by breaking it up into more discrete or comprehensible segments. The diversity and variety of television programming, as well as television's modes of consumption, makes it very difficult to describe what 'television' is. From the beginning, television studies have approached the medium through the analysis of specific generic forms (see Newcomb, 1974): discussing news or soap opera rather than the whole of television. Researchers have found that to understand the characteristics, conventions and pleasures of a particular television genre is also to understand a great deal about television as a cultural form.

For those producing television, genre participates in the definition of a project by mapping its relation to other, similar, texts. Once we move from production to programming and transmission, genre becomes an even more important descriptor of the project. On pay or cable TV, whole channels are named after the genre to which their programming belongs. The development of pay TV, in fact, has been structured around niche-marketing to audience genre preferences for sports, music video, lifestyle programming, documentary and so on.

The component that is often left out of the conventional media industry/text/audience triangle is the programmer or scheduler: the person who places the programme within the channel or network schedule. There has been very little aca-

demic attention paid to the work of the programmer, but it would seem logical to assume that their practices – and thus TV schedules – are influenced by their understanding of genre. One would imagine that an understanding of the pattern of differences and similarities that help define the individual programme must be built into the strategic structuring of a schedule that will match the competition and maximise audience capture. These are the strategies, for instance, that have networks programming *Friends* against *Seinfeld* or *ER* against *Chicago Hope*, or deciding to produce *A Current Affair* rather than *Lateline*. However, it has to be said that there is not much evidence that the term 'genre' or any equivalent abstraction is actually used in this industrial process. In one of the most successful handbooks on programming currently in use in the USA (Vane and Gross, 1994), the word 'genre' does not appear at all and the commercial practices described are conceptualised almost entirely on a case-by-case basis. This suggests that, at the industry level at least, there may be practical limitations to the usefulness of the notion of genre.

Graeme Turner

ER: an example of an hybridised genre?

Genre, Hybridity and Mutation

As has already been suggested in this book, there are many that would argue that there are limitations to the usefulness of genre theory in general, let alone in relation to television. Debates within film theory, in particular, have been vigorous and continuing. A familiar complaint is that genre criticism is circular: the critic constructs their own, perhaps quite idiosyncratic, definition of the genre in question which then licenses them to dismiss texts that fail to conform to this definition. A further complaint is that genre criticism is prescriptive. Although some accounts are content to map changes in genres over time, more characteristic is the insistence on maintaining an ideal version of the genre and criticising any departures from this ideal (Tudor, 1976).

With television, such problems are multiplied. It is pointless to insist on generic purity in relation to television programmes (Feuer, 1992). Television genres and programming formats are notoriously hybridised (Allen, 1989) and becoming more so. John Ellis, in the first edition of *Visible Fictions* (1982), confidently outlined the difference between the series and the serial. One of the key differences, it seemed then, was the series' use of self-contained episodes with relatively autonomous plotlines as against the serial's use of continuing storylines with characters who learned from episode to episode. Today, there are elements of the serial in many of what the industry would regard as series: US sitcoms such as *Friends*, hospital dramas such as *ER*, and cop shows such as *NYPD Blue* (see 'The Mini-series', p. 35). In the UK, the self-contained, narratively low-key, realist format of the police series *The Bill* has given way to the continuing storylines and the focus on characters' private lives that is typical of soap opera.

The fact that such examples have mutated over time raises another important characteristic of television genres. Unlike the audiences for films or the readers of novels, the audiences for continuing television programmes respond to the texts they consume directly through ratings figures, phone calls to the network, talk radio and so on. Much television programming is produced either live or in relatively close proximity to its screening date. This is obvious in the case of news or current affairs, but it also affects comedy and drama series as well. Television producers change aspects of their programmes in response to audience feedback: characters can be killed off or foregrounded; presenters can be siphoned out of prime time into late night or weekends, or off-air altogether.

In some cases, the cumulative effect of repeated tweaking of the format and content amounts to a change in genre. The introduction of soap opera-like continuing domestic storylines has been a constant feature of Australian television drama, for instance, as series gradually mutate into serials. Often this shift is accompanied by a move downmarket, both in storylines and in production values.

Changes in technology have reinforced the direct nature of the relationship between viewers and programming. The introduction of alternatives to old-fashioned ratings surveys (replacing the ratings book with the people meter, for instance) has responded to networks' interest in detailed audience information by providing more finely grained, and more readily available, viewing figures (Ang, 1991, pp. 78–84). The increasing use of programme-based websites and e-mail addresses has also provided another means of recording audience interest in programmes or in particular aspects or segments of programmes. This may be reflected in the increased number of magazine-styled formats now found across the television schedule. In addition to the ratings information on such shows, which can record the viewers' choices every fifteen minutes, the success of specific segments can be deduced from such things as requests for recipes, building instructions or 'fact sheets'. In a cautious industry with few opportunities to take commercial decisions on the basis of hard evidence, the effect of these developments is significantly to influence content, format and, ultimately, genre.

Graeme Turner

Genre, Format and 'Live' Television

Television genres are not constructed in relation to an Aristotelian model; individual programmes may evolve out of an originating premise that can itself be revised or shelved without guilt or hesitation. Contemporary arguments over the changes in news values claimed to mark the decline in television news and current affairs reflect a shift from what was predominantly an information genre to one that is predominantly aimed at providing entertainment. Williams and Carpini (2000) argue that the Bill Clinton–Monica Lewinsky story was in fact kept alive by the entertainment rather than the news media – for its

Friends: transcending traditional generic categories

entertainment rather than its news value. From Russian television, recently, it has been reported that weather girls are performing a striptease while presenting the latest weather reports – certainly a shift in genre orientation (see 'The Infotainment Debate', p. 118).

Even the metaphor of evolution is perhaps too systemic to describe the promiscuous hybridity that informs the generation of programme formats. Consider the example of television make-over shows, a genre that has developed in recent years. Building on audience interest in specific segments within lifestyle, DIY home-decorating or other infotainment shows (as well as home decorating and fashion magazines in print) the make-over show such as the UK *Ground Force* or *Changing Rooms* has a richer generic origin than this. The characteristics of make-over programmes come from at least the following television genres: game shows, soap opera, reality-TV or 'fly-on-the-wall documentary', confessional talk shows, daytime product-based talk shows, and gardening advice programmes.

It is important to recognise here the importance of a related, in some ways competing, term – 'format'. Unlike genre, format is widely used within the industry and among consumers as a way of describing the kind of programme they are watching. Formats can be original and thus copyright, franchised under licence, and traded as a commercial property. Genres, by definition, are not original. Format is a production category with relatively rigid boundaries that are difficult to transgress without coming up with a new format. Genre is the product of a text- and audience-based negotiation activated by the viewer's expectations. Genre is the larger, more inclusive

category and can be used to describe programmes that use a number of related formats, such as the game show (see p. 79).

Finally, it has to be acknowledged that some television formats actively challenge the idea of genre. The 'liveness' of television, its investment in immediacy and provisionality, is in direct conflict with the regulated production imperatives implied by genre and format. Further, the cultural richness of the television message, its capacity to carry an excess of meaning for its viewing audience (Hartley, 1992, pp. 36–8), means that the television message is always difficult to control. A contradiction deeply embedded in television's function and appeal, television's probing of the boundaries between the 'produced' and the 'real' is built into television formats that include the potential for their own disruption. The most radical examples of this would include the Jerry Springer style of talk show, or the antics represented as disruptive in *World Championship Wrestling*. However, it is more extensive than this. What Adrian Martin has called 'stretch-TV' (see Turner, 1989) can range from the self-reflexive or deconstructive tactics used by the host or presenter, such as those used by David Letterman or Ruby Wax, to the deliberately unstructured format for the UK comedy series *Baddiel and Skinner Unplanned*. In such cases, the format/genre includes the attempt to create 'liveness' that is disruptive and immediate. There are even programmes that simulate this potential: *Funniest Home Videos*, or blooper and out-take shows. Although this may indicate the limits of the uses to which genre may be put, it is important to recognise that it would be very difficult to produce the above description without recourse to the notion of genre itself.

Graeme Turner

RECOMMENDED READING

Allen, Robert C. (1989), 'Bursting Bubbles: "Soap Opera", Audiences, and the limits of Genre' in Ellen Seiter, Hans Borchers, Gabriele Kreutzner and Eva-Maria Warth (eds), *Remote Control: Television, Audiences and Cultural Power*, London and New York: Routledge.

Feuer, Jane (1992), 'Genre and Television' in R. Allen (ed.) *Channels of Discourse, Reassembled: Television and Contemporary Criticism*, London and New York: Routledge.

Tudor, Andrew (1976), 'Genre and Critical Methodology' in Bill Nichols (ed.), *Movies and Methods: An Anthology*, Berkeley: University of California Press.

DRAMA

Studying Television Drama

Television drama studies has mixed origins and is yet to emerge as a domain in its own right to complement film studies. Nevertheless, as courses in media, cultural and communication studies have proliferated alongside those in performing arts and screen studies, interest in the analysis of TV drama has extended considerably. One reason why the study of drama on television has lagged behind film (in spite of television's relative predominance in our everyday lives) is that television programmes are short-lived. In addition, 'the box' is so commonplace as to pass almost unnoticed, at times even unwatched, despite being switched on. In the academic world, the content of television was for some time considered unworthy as an object of study. Whereas films might be viewed several times and have had some pretensions to art, TV dramas were dismissed as ephemeral diversions. Until the relatively recent arrival of videos recirculating TV favourites and repeats of past programmes on such channels as UK Gold, old TV programmes were consigned either to memory or oblivion.

In turn, academic writing about specific television programmes is limited by the time it takes to publish an article or book, by when (or so publishers think) the programmes themselves will be of little interest. Notwithstanding these hindrances, a considerable body of literature relating to drama on television has emerged and several teacher–researchers have made significant contributions to a changing field, two of whom (Brandt and Tulloch) are featured here in more detail (see box) since key shifts in the approach to TV drama studies are reflected in their work.

Bearing still the traces of its theatre origins, early TV drama typically took the form of the single play (see below). Even though the studio-based production and live distribution of these plays was an extremely complex multi-camera procedure, credit for the outcome was given to the playwright, as in theatre. Accordingly, early academic study tended to be literary and writer-centred (see Brandt, 1981). Subsequently, more theoretical debate about TV drama forms and functions reflected the 1970s dominance of 'screen theory' (see Tulloch, 1990, p. 11) in film studies. Drawing on Althusser, there was a tendency to privilege

textual form and its alleged capacity to position viewers. In the famous *Days of Hope* debate (see Bennett et al., 1981), the 'classic realist text' through its very form was alleged to fix subjectivity by drawing all viewers to a singular viewpoint consistent with that of 'the dominant ideology'. All potential contradiction between differing views was apparently resolved by a controlling 'meta-discourse', rendering viewers 'passive' subjects in ideology. The consequence of such a view was the advocacy of a formal experimentation more suited perhaps to avant-garde cinema than to television, but the non-naturalist work of Dennis Potter (see the box in the section headed 'The Single Play', p. 9, and the section 'The Mini-series' p. 35) might serve as a TV drama example.

A consonance may be noted between the formalist 'screen theory' view and that of Brandt, which tends to privilege the author–playwright as a guarantor of fixed meanings. To Brandt, the audience benefits by an author's insights into the human condition inscribed in the text and available to the discerning reader. It is perhaps ironic that, though different in their political affiliations, both 'screen theory' (coming from a Marxian left) and Brandt (coming from a centrist liberal tradition) invite academic interpretations of the scriptures to be passed down where a stable significance is allegedly fixed and transparent.

Partly in reaction to the textual determinism of 'screen theory' and partly in an attempt to rescue members of the mass audience from their construction as 'cultural dupes', cultural studies approaches turned their attentions to the audience. Conceiving the audience not as the homogeneous mass of earlier paradigms, ethnographers set about finding out how subgroups, or even individual members, of the audience, actually read the texts transmitted into their living rooms. Ang and Morley, in particular, established in their audience studies that a range of readings and pleasures is taken by different people engaging with texts from different positions in different ways (see 'Soap Operas and their Audiences', p. 55). In *Television Culture* (1987), an influential television studies primer, Fiske celebrates 'producerly texts' (p. 239), constructed in readings resistant to normative ideology or simply through the popular pleasures of subordinate groups. Where high-gloss, fast-moving, machine-made series and serials had been dismissed as inferior by commentators like Brandt, Fiske talked up what people did with them by way of evading social control (see 'The Populist Debate', p. 76).

Taken to its logical extension in the reception theory of Stanley Fish, there may be as many readings as there are readers. Indeed, Schroder (Skovmand and Schroder, 1992, p. 207) claims that: '[t]he text itself has no existence, no life, and therefore no quality until it is deciphered by an individual and triggers the meaning potential carried by this individual'. Thus, in the span of a decade between the late 1970s and late 1980s, the preferred model had been inverted from one of a stable text fixing the subjectivity of *passive* spectators to one of *active* readers negotiating their own meanings and pleasures in play with a slippery text. The influence of post-modern accounts of the unstable signifier and dialogic negotiations of meanings and pleasures between texts and readers are patently influential in this shift (see 'Post-modern Drama', p. 43).

An excessive emphasis on readers' freedom to play with texts began in time to be balanced by a sense of 'bounded knowledgeability' (see Tulloch, 1990, p. 13) and a renewed acceptance that the form of texts imposes some constraints. Nelson (1997) sustains a view, traceable back to aspects of Brandt, that the compositional principles of texts matter and tend to dispose some readings rather than others. His analysis of *Casualty* shows, however, how television's dominant 'flexi-narrative' has emerged as a relatively open dramatic form (see 'Hospital Drama', p. 23). Absorbing the insights of cultural studies approaches and post-modern theory, Nelson avoids a simple reassertion of Brandt's textual hierarchy. With Tulloch, he acknowledges that the writer is but one of many contributors to a complex industrial process that shapes the text. Indeed, in his account of the making of *Heartbeat*, he demonstrates how the focus group of modern market research may be used in a feedback loop to allow reception to influence 'authorship'.

Heartbeat: market research can allow reception to influence 'authorship'

Thus in television drama studies today, attention may usefully be paid to the production context (particularly the impact of new technologies), to the compositional principles of the text itself and to readers' active engagements with the text to produce various meanings and pleasures. The kinds of drama that form the object of study now range from the rare single play (see below) through to the most popular series/serial hybrid. Given the range of possibilities, it is necessary above all for scholars in the field to be self-reflexive about their approaches.

Robin Nelson

RECOMMENDED READING

Brandt, George (ed.) (1981) *British Television Drama*, Cambridge: Cambridge University Press.
Tulloch, John (1990), *TV Drama: Agency, Audience and Myth*, London: Routledge.
Nelson, Robin (1997), *TV Drama in Transition: Forms, Values and Cultural Change*, London: Macmillan.

The Single Play

The single play (or 'teleplay') has been through many mutations since it first became a staple ingredient of early television. From its origins in live, studio-bound drama, through to its increasing use of outside location, videotape, editing and film, it produced some of the landmark productions of television history. In its heyday in the 1950s and 1960s it was one of the most highly acclaimed and frequently controversial of genres, making a name for itself as a natural site for 'agitational' television (see Macmurraugh-Kavanagh, 1997, pp. 367–81) and the dramatic airing of topical issues (see box). Its early origins in the theatre and radio helped to establish this cultural reputation, with some critics conceiving it as almost 'literary' in its artistic themes and aspirations. It has subsequently tended to be conceived in high cultural regard, marketed and received differently from the likes of soap opera (see p. 47) or the drama series or mini-series (see p. 31), with a writer of a single play often perceived as its sole 'author' (for a discussion of this, see Creeber, 1998, pp. 19–24). This may partly explain why it has become a natural symbol for social commentators who wish to criticise the apparent 'dumbing-down' of contemporary television, presenting it (somewhat nostalgically) as representative of a 'golden age' when television was, in their view, still interested in challenging its audience's views and expectations.

Critics have tended to assume that, because many early

George Brandt, *British Television Drama* (1981) and John Tulloch, *Television Drama: Agency, Audience and Myth* (1990)

George W. Brandt helped to establish drama on television as an object worthy of study. The introduction to his first edited book of essays concludes with the assertion that: 'television drama matters. It is an important aspect of the culture of today. It merits critical attention' (1981, p. 35). To draw this attention, however, Brandt located TV drama in a discourse of 'quality' in a literary–theatrical tradition with a strong canonical sense of individual writers. Conscious of 'some bias in the book towards the single play', he claims, 'it is more a matter of convenience than dogma'. But his emphasis on 'the quality of the writing' (p. 30) leaves the impression (as subsequent commentators have read him) that quality resides in 'the "cultural high ground" of the single play' (Buckingham, 1987, p. 29). By Brandt's second review of British television (1993), not only was that discourse of 'quality' scarcely sustainable but the authored single play form had itself almost disappeared (see below). To Brandt (1993, p. 17), TV drama's 'brightest moments of glory in the eighties may prove to have been the golden glow of a setting sun'.

Tulloch does not share Brandt's pessimism. Locating himself in the cultural studies tradition emergent in the decade between Brandt's two essay collections, Tulloch sees not so much the rich complexity of the authored text as the complexity of the process of producing meanings and pleasures in culture. For him, it is a matter of what people do with texts at least as much as a matter of what texts do to people. Tulloch examines the functioning in culture of popular genres in series/serial formats writing extensively, for example, about science fiction (see below). Furthermore, he was among the first to see the need for an account of 'the audience and the notion of differential readings' (Tulloch and Alvarado 1983, p. 9). His later work explicitly examines the range of meanings and pleasures produced by viewers in engagements with a wide range of texts, though he is critically reflexive about audience study (see Tulloch and Jenkins, 1995 and 'Soap Operas and their Audiences' p. 55 below).

Despite their differences, however, there are correspondences between the contributions of Brandt and Tulloch. Brandt's (1981) introduction offers a useful summary of changes in television culture from its early days to the 1970s. The impact of institutional changes in Britain (the introduction of ITV and BBC2) are noted along with technological developments (colour, videotape, lightweight 16mm film cameras). In parallel, Tulloch's earlier work on *Doctor Who* takes

an 'extensive approach' conducting 'an investigation in terms of the industrial, institutional, narrative, generic, professional and other practices' (Tulloch and Alvarado, 1983, p. 2) shaping the series' twenty-year development. Both address the seminal debate about television naturalism, and Tulloch to some extent echoes Brandt in his (1981) concern with 'authored' and 'serious' drama. The naturalism debate (see Bennett et al., 1981, pp. 302–53) questioned whether 'progressive' drama could be mobilised in the allegedly compromised form of television naturalism. To a considerable extent the debate was overtaken by new approaches to understanding how television functions culturally in the cultural studies approach of people like Tulloch.

For Tulloch's overall approach to the study of TV drama ultimately differs from Brandt's methodologically and ideologically. Brandt (as Tulloch himself points out) celebrates the authored single play as the form affording ventilation of public issues through creativity in a liberal tradition of the distinctive individual voice in opposition to 'the popular historical series as carrier of national myth' (Tulloch, 1990, p. 3). Tulloch, in contrast, recognises that myth-circulation through popular television creates sites of struggle for meanings.

Tulloch's position is a thought-through and self-reflexive mix of practical consciousness with post-modern relativism. As a liberal-left academic, he allies himself with the audience ethnographers who celebrate resistant pleasures and readings, but he also finds 'analytic mutuality' with the agency of the avowedly left-wing writers, directors and producers (e.g. Griffiths, Loach and Garnett) who form a substantial part of his study. Thus he avoids capitulation to utter relativism. A key point, following Giddens, is that agency in the sense of active reproduction must be acknowledged in a range of production and reception spaces. Nor is this simply a matter of discursive practice. Citing Giddens, Tulloch explains that: '[w]hat agents know about what they do, and why they do it – their knowledgeability *as* agents – is largely carried out in practical consciousness' (Giddens, 1979, p. 250, cited in Tulloch, 1990, p. 11).

It is possible, then, for Tulloch to see potential in those 'machine-made' serials and series with high gloss so worrying to Brandt, since it is what people do with those texts that ultimately matters. At the same time he can hold reservations about Fiske's wilder celebrations of allegedly resistant pleasures through 'producerly texts' (1987, p. 239) because he recognises that the structuring principles of TV dramas may dispose some readings rather than others. Agency is thus afforded to writers and producers. In Tulloch's account, some writers – as familiar as their audiences with genre and form –

can mobilise a radical 'text' in their subtle re-working of conventions. He follows Janet Wolff in retrieving the author from the brink of death, but it is an author 'now understood as constituted in language, ideology and social relations . . . the author being the first person to fix meanings, which will of course subsequently be subject to redefinition and fixing by all future readers' (Wolff, 1981, p.136, cited in Tulloch, 1990, p. 17).

In this light it becomes important to research the institutional constraints on writers' and producers' agency, and Tulloch's book demonstrates the value of extending an ethnographic approach beyond audience to 'all those institutional, industrial, educational and leisure spaces where pleasures and meanings contest in the construction of TV drama "texts" ' (1990, pp. 20–1).

Tulloch readily acknowledges his debts to colleagues' development of parallel cultural studies approaches in other disciplines (e.g. Janice Radway in literature). His work serves here to mark a distinct shift from Brandt's more hierarchical and canonical approach and to show how self-reflection is important in an academic context where a range of possible approaches may make insightful contributions to understanding.

Robin Nelson

single plays were adapted from classical theatre and were broadcast live (early recording technology was both primitive and expensive), the *style* itself of those early transmissions was also inherently *theatrical*. According to Gardner and Wyver (1983, p. 115), early single plays were 'tediously broadcast from the theatre, or reconstructed in the studio, even down to intervals, prosceniums and curtains'. However, Jacobs (1998, p. 58; 2000) has recently argued that the early single play was already evolving a televisual style and aesthetic of its own, developing '*multi-camera studio drama*' that broke down the theatrical dynamics of the stage play. As writers began to produce original dramas for the small screen, so this style gradually became inherently televisual in its own right. 'The structure of these plays related to circumstances under which they were produced. Such problems as costume changes and ageing were unwelcome. This encouraged plays of a tight structure, attacking a story close to its climax – very different from the loose, multi-scene structure of films' (Barnouw, 1975, p. 160).

Certainly by the 1950s the single television play was beginning to distinguish itself radically from classical theatre, in terms of both content and style. In America, writers like Paddy Chayefsky (1923–81) began producing original single dramas for television that attracted both large audiences and huge critical acclaim. Chayefsky signed on for the Philco–Goodyear anthology series in 1952 where he wrote many of his most famous single plays, including *Holiday Song* (1953), *The Mother* (1954), *Bachelor's Party* (1955), *A Catered Affair* (1955) and *Marty* (1953).

Chayefsky's characters were usually from the lower middle class, the dialogue they spoke and the problems they encountered always reflecting everyday, personal dilemmas. It was this deceptively ordinary world that seemed so uniquely suited to the domestic dynamics and interior style of television drama at the time. 'The technical requirements of live broadcast were a good fit with Chayefsky's dramatic gestalt: cramped living rooms, small working-class bars, neighbourhood mom-and-pop stores. Car chases, big crowds, and location shots were strictly out of the question' (Marc and Thompson, 1992, p. 122). The most well known of his single plays is undoubtedly *Marty* (starring a young Rod Steiger), which is still remembered today for its moving portrayal of a lonely middle-aged man, living in quiet desperation with his domineering mother. Transmitted live, much of it in close-up, its understated method acting and long claustrophobic scenes helped to give shape to what Chayefsky famously termed, 'the marvellous world of the ordinary' (cited by Brandt, 1981, p. 15. See also Hey, 1983, pp. 124–33).

Despite strong editorial interference and heavy censorship from their sponsors (see Boddy, 1993, pp. 187–213), successful American single plays like Rod Serling's *Requiem for a Heavyweight* (1956), Gore Vidal's *Visit to a Small Planet* (1955) and Reginald Rose's *Thunder on Sycamore Street* (1954) continued to develop this new aesthetic, proving that the limitations of the live studio could still produce exciting and innovative drama. Although generally less celebrated than Chayefsky, Reginald Rose was no less significant in terms of his ability to utilise the specific power and dynamics of the small screen. In particular, his claustrophobic and powerful *Twelve Angry Men* (directed by Franklin Schaffner, 1954) was justifiably celebrated for the way in which it found large-scale drama in an extremely limited setting (the twelve jury members of a homicide case). Like *Marty*, it was later adapted for the big screen, the director Sidney Lumet turning it into a successful Hollywood movie starring Henry Fonda.

This style of single play soon caught on in the UK, particularly with the introduction of the new commercial channel in 1955. One of the significant figures of this time was

Marty: 'the marvelous world of the ordinary'

Sydney Newman (1917–97), a successful Canadian television producer brought to Britain to work for ABC (see box). Although British single plays like Ted Willis's *Woman in a Dressing Gown* (1956) were already tackling lower-class themes, Newman's influence was unmistakable. Under the title Armchair Theatre, he helped put together a startling collection of new and original single plays during the period 1958–63. Although classical playwrights such as Ibsen were favourites of the series, original plays (Alun Owen's *No Trams to Lime Street* (1959), Clive Exton's *Where I Live* (1960) and Harold Pinter's *A Night Out* (1960), for example), gradually placed working-class and regional accents to the forefront of the action. Despite the limitations of live drama, directors and set designers also became increasingly experimental in their attempts to produce a new form of 'realism', and cameras became more fluid as directors tried to create three-dimensional space, incorporating long tracking-shots that would weave in and out of intricate sets. Newman would later continue and develop this tradition at the BBC, under the title The Wednesday Play (see box).

By the 1970s the harsh economic realities of television put the future of the single play increasingly under threat.

In the USA, prime-time advertising rates became progressively expensive, making full sponsorship of an anthology series a rarity. Whereas a 'themed' series like The Twilight Zone (CBS, 1959–65 – see 'Science Fiction', p. 26) proved popular, the individual single play gradually became less desirable. As the networks rejected the genre, so writers like Chayefsky were forced to leave for Hollywood. Ironically, his most famous movie was *Network* (1976), a vicious satire on American television, directed by one of his earlier television collaborators, Sidney Lumet.

Although the single play survived longer in the UK (see box), the move towards long-form drama was inevitable, quickened by the relatively high costs of the genre in comparison with the series or serial. The eclectic style and content of each individual play also made it difficult to schedule, whereas the reassuring predictability of the drama series could quickly build up a large and loyal audience that tuned in week after week (see 'The Mini-series' p. 35). The single play was also seen as too 'idiosyncratic' and 'parochial' to attract foreign buyers or co-production money (see Gardner and Wyver, 1983, p. 118).

Such economic concerns became even more pressing

The Wednesday Play and Play for Today

Hoping to emulate the success of ITV's Armchair Theatre, the BBC 'poached' Sydney Newman in 1962 and appointed him Head of Drama. The Wednesday Play (1964–84) followed two years later with some plays left over from Peter Luke's Festival series. However, it is generally seen to have got properly under way on 6 January 1965 with *A Tap on the Shoulder*, written by James O'Connor. Although responsible for adapting many European classics, the series is now primarily remembered for broadcasting original, contemporary and often 'politicised' drama, reportedly provoking national discussion on a scale never witnessed before or since. Frequently dealing with controversial issues such as homelessness or the legalisation of homosexuality, the series ingeniously gave the BBC both cultural credibility and exciting drama, although the relationship between practitioners and institution was seldom an easy one (see Macmurraugh-Kavanagh, 1997, pp. 367–81). The series certainly signalled an important shift in television drama generally, with its reputation for 'social realism' aided by the introduction of new recording techniques, easier editing facilities and newer lightweight cameras. As the producer Tony Garnett remembers, 'The whole logic of the scripts we were getting was forcing us to use film and to shoot outside the studios on location' (cited by Hudson, 1972, p. 20).

Among some of the series' most well-known plays were Dennis Potter's *Vote, Vote, Vote for Nigel Barton* and its companion piece, *Stand Up, Nigel Barton* (director Gareth Davies, 1965), David Mercer's *And Did Those Feet?* (director Don Taylor, 1965) and Jeremy Sandford's ground-breaking *Cathy Come Home* (director Ken Loach, 1966 – see 'Drama–Documentary', p. 31). Although generally less celebrated than *Cathy*, Nell Dunn's *Up the Junction* (1965) was both controversial and innovative in terms of its own radical style and subject matter. Also directed by Ken Loach, this single play dealt with the harsh realities of working-class life in and around London's Clapham Junction. Constructed around a number of loosely connecting storylines (adapted by Dunn from her own book of short stories), Loach's 'documentary' style of film-making gave a harsh realism to the drama's graphic depiction of unwanted pregnancy and back-street abortion. Utilising the new improvements in technology, *Up the Junction* was one of a number of dramas that helped produce a new aesthetic for television. Mixing elements of montage, voice-over and location filming, it built on and helped to establish the medium's 'unique capabilities for the representation of the social real' (Caughie, 2000, p.122).

The series was renamed Play for Today in 1970. Single plays such as Mike Leigh's suburban tragi-comedy, *Abigail's Party* (devised by Mike Leigh, 1977), Jim Allen's politically committed *The Rank and File* (director, Ken Loach, 1971) and Jack Rosenthal's *Bar Mitzvah Boy* (director, Michael Tuchner, 1976) seemed to continue the radical remit of the earlier series. Employing many of the same writers, directors and producers as before, the writer Dennis Potter is perhaps the consummate example of a creative force whose talent was nurtured and sustained by the series as a whole (see also 'The Mini-series' p. 35). Frequently provocative, Potter's *Blue Remembered Hills* (director, Brian Bibson, 1979) was an award-winning ensemble piece that consisted entirely of adult actors dressed as children. However, the series' uneasy relationship with the BBC continued and both Potter's *Brimstone and Treacle* (director, Barry Davis, 1976) and Roy Minton's *Scum* (director, Alan Clarke, 1979) were banned by an institution that had become increasingly paranoid (see Hollingsworth and Norton-Taylor, 1988, p. 116). Both plays were later transferred to the big screen before finally being transmitted a decade later on television. The series finally came to the end of its long and celebrated run in 1984.

Glen Creeber

with the arrival of satellite and cable in the 1980s. In the USA, the 'made-for-TV movie' became increasingly popular, while in the UK Channel Four Films ingeniously pioneered the way for commissioned drama to be made with both the big screen and the small screen in mind (a TV broadcast coming only after its cinematic release). Developments in technology and the success of films like *Angel* (1982) and *My Beautiful Laundrette* (1985) meant that single television drama had now become virtually indistinguishable from its big-screen rival.

More recently, critics have argued that the soap opera (see p. 47) is now helping to keep 'quality drama' alive, with some episodes of *EastEnders* worthy of being called single plays in their own right (see Tulloch, 1990, p. 3). However, other critics have complained that there are now virtually no opportunities left for new writers to experiment and take chances with the medium as there were in the 1950s and 1960s. The single television 'play' is now almost a rarity, apparently confined to that period of television history that was continually breaking new ground as its drama strove to define an aesthetic, style and content of its own. Ironically, that process would finally reject the very genre that gradually enabled it to come of age.

Glen Creeber

RECOMMENDED READING

Gardner, Carl and Wyver, John (1983), 'The Single Play: From Reithian Reverence to Cost-accounting and Censorship, *Screen*, vol. 24, no. 4–5.

Hey, Kenneth (1983), '*Marty*: Aesthetics vs. Medium in Early TV Drama', in Leslie Fishbein (ed.), *American History/American Television: Interpreting the Video Past*, New York: Frederick Ungar.

Shubik, Irene (1975), *Play for Today: The Evolution of Television Drama*, London: Davis-Poynter.

The Western

In many ways, the conventions of the Western genre would seem to make it uniquely suited to the demands of episodic television, balancing the need for narrative novelty within the production and promotional constraints of recurring characters and situations. The TV Western's nomadic hero, whether the hired gunslinger of *Have Gun, Will Travel* (CBS, 1957–63), the trail boss of *Wagon Train* (NBC, 1957–62; ABC, 1962–5), or the professional gambler of *Maverick* (ABC, 1957–63), allowed for a variety of plot situations, guest stars and incomplete resolutions, to the degree that many TV Westerns became near-anthology programmes in disguise. The Western genre on television also seemed robust enough to spawn several generic hybrids, including the domestic Western of *Bonanza* (NBC, 1959–73), comedies like *F Troop* (ABC, 1965–7), and even a nineteenth-century espionage Western, *The Wild, Wild West* (CBS, 1965–9).

The lone protagonist of the TV Western links the genre most directly to that of television's private eye, so much so that *Maverick* creator Roy Huggins recycled several story-lines from his Western series into his subsequent private-detective shows *77 Sunset Strip* (ABC, 1958–64) and *The Rockford Files* (NBC, 1974–80) (see 'The Action Series', p. 17, and and 'The Police Series', p. 19). Over its history, the TV Western has been represented by everything from low-budget juvenile programmes in fringe time, a range of thirty- and sixty-minute prime-time action-adventures, to the first ninety-minute series, *The Virginian* (NBC, 1962–70) and a number of made-for-TV movies and mini-series (see p. 17). Whereas the genre on television depended less upon the dramatic treatment of the Western landscape typical of Western feature films, due to the near-prohibitive expense of extensive location shooting and the medium's proclivity for close-ups, the TV Western has drawn upon the Western feature for its iconography, historical settings, and character-isations.

At the same time, the case of the Western genre on television contradicts the conventional notion that prime-time programme genres are historically relatively stable in popularity and form. Even compared with the uneven fortunes of the Western at the theatrical box office over the past four decades, the Western genre seems to have enjoyed a remarkably circumscribed life span on US television network prime time, roughly encompassing the decade between the launch of the so-called 'adult Western' in 1955 and the mid-1960s, when only a pair of long-running Western series lingered in the list of the top twenty prime-time shows. Indeed, the spectacular rise of the TV Western in the late 1950s, a time of traumatic change throughout the television industry, briefly transformed the genre into the subject of intense and sometimes hyperbolic critical scrutiny. Perhaps inevitably, the TV Western became the lens through which larger changes in American television were debated within and outside the industry. More than any other genre, the Western was the vehicle for the integration of the Hollywood studios and network television in the second half of the 1950s, and the early years of the genre feature the work of both veteran directors (including Budd Boetticher, Lewis Milestone, Sam Fuller and Tay Garnett) and an emerging generation of directors, including Sam Peckinpah and Robert Altman.

Although at the height of the genre's popularity, between 1957 and 1959, nearly one-third of network prime time consisted of Westerns, the decline of the TV Western only a few years later was precipitous and nearly permanent. Since the 1960s, the Western genre has been barely represented in the hundreds of TV movies, mini-series, and episodic series aired in network prime time, and many of the most popular TV Westerns of the past are almost unknown in the domestic and international syndication markets. For a genre that once dominated both network programme schedules and general critical debates over commercial television, the TV Western has all but disappeared in popular memory. More than for any other genre, the case of the television Western invites a consideration of the specific historical circumstances associated with both its sudden flourishing and its abrupt near-disappearance.

Like many other television genres, the TV Western has roots in earlier media, including popular fiction, Hollywood film-making, and network radio. Indeed, some of the earliest television successes, including the immensely popular *Hopalong Cassidy* (NBC, 1949–51, syndicated 1952–4), involved the repackaging for television of Western shorts and B-films from Hollywood's Poverty Row studios

Bonanza: the family- and domestic-centred Western

of the 1930s and 1940s. The remarkable success of *Davy Crockett* (an occasional episodic series within ABC's 1954 anthology show Disneyland) not only inspired a flood of new prime-time Westerns, but also marked the entrance of the Hollywood studios into the network television market. The following season saw the launch of four so-called 'adult Westerns' on television, which the networks took pains to distinguish from previous Westerns; *Gunsmoke*, for example, used actor John Wayne to introduce its first episode in order to distinguish the programme from its juvenile precursors.

Besides the long-running *Gunsmoke*, the other major TV Western introduced in the 1955/56 season was *Cheyenne*, produced by Roy Huggins at Warner Bros. for ABC, the producer, studio, and network most associated with the early success of the genre. Within two years Huggins helped launch *Colt 45* (ABC, 1957–60) and

Maverick, and the popularity of the new Warner Bros. Western and crime dramas brought ABC into genuine prime-time competition with the larger two networks for the first time in its history. By the end of the 1958/59 season ABC had four of television's top ten programmes, and ABC devoted 30 per cent of its autumn 1959 prime-time schedule to Warner Bros.-produced programmes. The two larger networks soon followed ABC's move to the prime-time Western, and there were fifteen new Western series in the 1957/58 season alone; the growing number of Westerns also reflected the collapse of the popular quiz show programmes at NBC and CBS following the revelations of widespread fraud in 1958 (see 'The Quiz Show', p. 79). The following season there were twenty-four Western series in prime time, and in 1959/60 the genre reached a peak with twenty-eight Western programmes. Whereas in the 1959/60 season both ABC and NBC offered eleven different

Alias Smith and Jones

As one of the few TV Western series introduced on US prime-time television since the mid-1960s to survive more than a single season, *Alias Smith and Jones* (ABC, 1971–3) occupies an unusual place in the history of the genre. Dismissed by many critics at the time as derivative of the 1969 Hollywood hit *Butch Cassidy and the Sundance Kid*, the series in fact owes more to television's *Maverick* (ABC, 1957–63), produced by *Alias Smith and Jones*'s executive producer Roy Huggins. Huggins, under the pseudonym John Thomas James, received exclusive or joint writer or story credit on forty-five of the fifty episodes of *Alias Smith and Jones*, and the series represents the last of many TV Westerns on which Huggins worked, beginning with the opening season of *Cheyenne* (ABC, 1955–63), one of the first so-called 'adult Westerns'.

Alias Smith and Jones continued the anti-heroic tone of Huggins's *Maverick*, for which he served as producer and frequent writer in its first two seasons. Glen A. Larson, the creator and producer of *Alias Smith and Jones*, had worked with Huggins as writer and producer on *The Virginian* (NBC, 1962–71) and *Run for Your Life* (NBC, 1965–8); Larson went on to create and produce several successful, if undistinguished, series, including *The Six Million Dollar Man* (ABC, 1974–8), *The Fall Guy* (ABC, 1981–8), and *Knight Rider* (NBC, 1982–6).

The self-conscious and ironic tone of *Alias Smith and Jones* was established in the opening narration of the ninety-minute pilot: 'Into the West came many men. Some were good men and some were bad men. Some were good men with some bad in them, and some were bad men with some good in them. This is the story of two pretty good bad men.' The series went on to recount the adventures of Hannibal Hayes (Pete Duel/Roger Davis) and Kid Curry (Ben Murphy), leaders of a gang of train and bank robbers who, faced with increasingly

sophisticated safes and determined posses, decide to take up a Western Governor's general offer of amnesty. However, the Governor's amnesty offer is secret, and contingent upon the pair staying out of trouble for one year, so the two outlaws take on the aliases of Smith and Jones and attempt to dodge assorted bounty hunters, former gang members and lawmen who seek to arrest them for past crimes or entice them into new ones. The heroes' uncertain legal situation and their ambivalence about repudiating their criminal pasts suggest their links to a line of nomadic anti-heroes of 1960s television, from *Route 66* to *The Fugitive*, and the picaresque possibilities of the Western allowed the programme to challenge occasionally the genre's traditional masculine hero.

Alias Smith and Jones was launched at a time of unusual volatility in network prime-time schedules and had the misfortune of being scheduled against two emerging hits on rival networks, the number-two rated *Flip Wilson Show* in *Alias Smith and Jones*'s first season and the number-one rated *All in the Family* in the Western's second season (see Situation Comedy, p. 61). Even for the third-ranked ABC, the ratings for *Alias Smith and Jones* were disappointing, declining from thirty-eighth among all network prime-time shows in the first season to sixty-fifth of sixty-five network shows in the second season. Some critics argued that the show was hurt by the loss of co-star Pete Duel, who committed suicide after only sixteen completed episodes; Duel was quickly replaced by Roger Davis, who had been the narrator on earlier episodes. Duel's death has contributed to the subsequent semi-cult status of *Alias Smith and Jones*; despite its relatively brief run, the series has enjoyed intermittent revivals in both domestic and international syndication and has generated a number of fan groups, Internet sites, and works of slash fiction and viewing pleasure.

William Boddy

Westerns in prime time, over the next two seasons NBC actually aired more Westerns than did ABC. Thus, although ABC and Warner Bros. remained associated with the early success of the genre, the TV Western quickly became an important part of the prime-time schedules of all three networks.

If the rise of the prime-time Western in the late 1950s was precipitous, the decline of the genre only a few years later was nearly as abrupt. By 1962 Warner Bros. Television was laying off 25 per cent of its staff; between the 1961/62 and 1963/64 seasons, the number of Westerns in TV's top ten programmes declined from four to three to one. As the studio and network most committed to the genre, Warner

Bros. and ABC suffered the most, as other production companies and networks shifted to a new generation of rural sitcoms, so-called 'magic sitcoms', spy dramas and variety shows. The nature of the surviving TV Westerns in 1960s prime time began to change as well, moving away from the unattached nomadic hero towards the increasingly family- and domestic-centred narratives of *Gunsmoke* and *Bonanza*. As well as the inevitable effects of a surfeit of nearly indistinguishable Western series at the beginning of the decade, other circumstances worked to diminish the appeal of the genre for networks and advertisers, if not necessarily for audiences.

One contributor to the TV Western's decline in the early

1960s was the initiation of a nearly continuous decade-long string of Congressional hearings and government reports about the harmful effects of TV violence. The first rounds of hearings, led by Senator Thomas Dodd between 1960 and 1963, brought several prominent TV Western actors, writers and producers (as well as network and other industry officials) before the Subcommittee on Juvenile Delinquency to respond to screenings of committee-assembled violent excerpts of popular Western programmes. Although inconclusive in terms of legislation, the extended series of Congressional hearings on television violence encouraged networks and sponsors to seek out less potentially controversial programme fare. By the time the second round of Congressional anti-violence probes rolled out in the late-1960s, the television Western, like the Hollywood Western, seemed nearly irrelevant to American culture. With the exception of *Alias Smith and Jones* (ABC, 1971–3 – see box, p. 16), no prime-time Western launched since the mid-1960s managed to survive more than a single season and, despite the occasional TV movie, mini-series and quickly cancelled episodic series, the TV Western has virtually disappeared from network prime time.

William Boddy

RECOMMENDED READING

Anderson, Christopher (1994), *Hollywood TV: The Studio System in the Fifties,* Austin: University of Texas Press.

Barson, Michale (1985), 'The TV Western', in Brian Rose (ed.), *TV Genres,* Westport: Greenwood Press.

MacDonald, Fred J. (1987), *Who Shot the Sheriff? The Rise and Fall of the Television Western,* New York: Praeger.

The Action Series

Several genres within US and UK TV drama focus on action rather than character, in keeping with the history of the medium and its social intertexts. There are some obvious examples: police programmes that feature violence rather than detection (*The Sweeney*, ITV, 1974–8 – see 'The Police Series' p. 19), war shows that stress fighting over politics (*Combat* , ABC, 1962–7), and action-packed historical (*Robin Hood*, UK, 1955–9) and science-fiction (*Xena: Warrior Princess*, US, 1995–) epics. Then there are espionage series (*Mission: Impossible*, CBS, 1966–73, 1988–9), off-beat buddy shows (*The A-Team*, US, 1983–7), cyborg/superhuman series (*Lois and Clark*, US, 1993–7), Westerns (*Gunsmoke*, US,

1955–75 – see 'The Western', p. 14), and spoofs (*Get Smart*, US, 1965–70, 1993).

We can identify these genres with particular historical moments and ideological preoccupations. For example, *The Sweeney* combines British social realism with US-style violence in a bitter account of working-class strife (see 'The Police Series' p. 19). *Combat* represents the Second World War celebration of returning heroes. *Robin Hood* stands for the 1950s investment by British commercial producers in swordplay and costume history as a potential export commodity via fantasy reconstructions that embody a heroic age where the ruling class can romantically represent peasant interests. *Xena* is a millennial celebration of girl power with a lesbian subtext. *Mission: Impossible* rises and falls with the high moment of covert action by US spy agencies, before Watergate de-glamourises breaking the law in the name of security. *The A-Team* calls to mind the privatisation and machismo of the Reagan presidency. *Lois and Clark* is the fleeting hope that the Clintons-as-power-couple might revive the rule of truth, justice and the remainder. *Gunsmoke*'s longevity straddles the birth and death of the TV Western, its ubiquity undermined by network desires for youthful audiences (see 'The Western', p. 14). And *Get Smart* embodies both the 1960s popularity of stylish espionage, as per James Bond, and TV's proclivity to parody its own genres.

Despite this polysemous quality, the action-adventure category is largely over as far as broadcast TV is concerned. The genre once took up perhaps a fifth of North American prime time on the main networks, but by the mid-1990s action series occupied only about 1 per cent of the schedule. Infotainment (see p. 118) grew from virtually nowhere in 1990 to earn US $1 billion *per annum* by 1994. An hour of reality television (see p. 133) at that time cost US $700,000, as opposed to US $1.3–2 million for action and US $1 million for studio-based drama. Infotainment is excellent prime-time cost-cutting. Cheap or rerun action series survive on cable networks and satellite services dedicated to particular genres or periods of television.

I focus here on perhaps the high-point of the genre – the 1960s – and its most memorable subcategories – espionage and detection. The late 1950s and early 1960s on US network TV had been characterised by male action adventure (*77 Sunset Strip, Hawaiian Eye, Bourbon Street Beat, Peter Gunn, Burke's Law, Checkmate, Michael Shayne, Route 66, Follow the Sun* and *Adventures in Paradise*), frequently in dyadic form.

The mid-1960s on American TV were, however, rather like the mid-1990s: full of situation comedy (see p. 61), which was cheap to produce and, when the networks or production houses colluded, a neat way of roadblocking viewers who might switch channels. Thirty years ago, life was stable for NBC, ABC and CBS. But matters changed suddenly with the 1965/66 TV spy craze, when eight espionage programmes appeared, spread across each network. Some were hastily made-over cop shows (see 'The Police Series', p. 19). The networks had wrested control of programme production from sponsors in the wake of the 1950s quiz-show scandals (see p. 79). This made it possible to diversify commercial sources, which made programming less susceptible to such 'active audiences' as the hysterical anti-Soviet lobby group, Aware Inc.

The stylish commodity/sex motifs of the 1960s meant that although spy-theme storylines often clearly bifurcated good from evil, which recreated the structural opposition of West and East, this narrative tendency was moderated by their visual style. Once an accomplice to straight, unstylish, empiricist but ideological policing in the 1950s, the 1960s focused on a hip, modern look that privileged individuation and commodity fun over group identity and uniformity. Storylines allegorised, cars and clothes diverted, and satire displaced didactic ideology. Ironically, a very peaceful era in American imperialism, the mid- to late 1950s, had produced a stuffy and stiff action genre, whereas the hyper violent Vietnam years saw series that were self-consciously quirky.

What of the detective programme? Classically, detection has meant the identification and defeat of wrongdoers, by applying reason to explain events that are irregular and socially undesirable. Both villains and detectives lose their individual identities through cloaks of substitution, commodity changes of costume, task, face, voice and history that free them from the traces of origin. Identity is assumed and discarded, in keeping with the self-actualising, transcendent subject of urban modernity who can move with ease across time and space. The villain and the detective depend on each other through an overarching third term: the law and its embodiment in the state, which one must elude and the other convince that justice be meted out. This nexus of violence and vacuousness leads critics of the crime genre to blame it for modelling anti-social conduct, heroising the capitalist state, or delighting in base consumerism (see 'The Police Series' p. 19).

Most detective shows on TV connect their officers of the law to the quotidian, ever-vigilant and ready to deal with infringements of order. Typically working in couples, they may not be equals, but the police need togetherness to survive rather than utility-maximising individualism. This affective bond allows protagonists to maintain a sense of self as they are sent into situations that frequently bear no relationship to their own existence. When the police move

onto a case, they often become involved in its detail and its people: informers, criminals, business proprietors or the ruling class. The narrative generally involves the following: the law is violated; the state finds out about it; the heroes try to find out why and how this happened and who was responsible; they encounter informants (some useful, others dangerous) and have initial struggles with the enemy; the villain is revealed and defeated in a fight sequence; and a coda restores equilibrium.

In both subgenres, heroes are forced to deal with elemental fears, most notably a personal, professional and frequently physical claustrophobia. Because open space is central to much action TV, when protagonists are restricted the spaces they occupy illustrate the impossibility of ever truly relaxing as a spy or police officer: inevitably, they will find themselves somewhere that emblematises the gruesome interiority and tension of their profession. Other typical ingredients include sexual conflict and spectacle, following a particular formula: attractive travellers, often in disguise but with ultimately stereotyped national characteristics, meet and pass information. Despite the openness of their good looks, their secret identities bespeak an untrustworthy world where threats are not just personal. They pose risks to the very fabric of society, so misrecognition, an effect of deception, is endemic, and the very act of travel shows that the apparently eternal verities and loyalties of blood and soil may be compromised. The great ability of the protagonists is to see through the fictions of others and uncover the truth.

For conservatives, the success of 1960s action series showed that citizens approved of their governments acting covertly or brutally in the interest of state security. For other watchers, the appeal lay in the romance of citizenship: within the norms of governance, viewers test and enjoy to the limit cases presented by life outside, in the comparative anarchy of international relations or crime, where loyalty and patriotism (even the mundanity of public employment) are suddenly reforged as a play with death and doom. They are equally associated with the fate of the individual 'under' technologisation and bureaucratisation, an existential dilemma that is not about an abstract absurdity, but material relations that are part of the everyday (as per overt commercial surveillance). This reliance on the banal as both an underpinning and an 'other' for action series sums up the quaint dependencies of a genre often associated with rugged individualism.

Author's note: My thanks to Marie Leger for her comments.
Toby Miller

RECOMMENDED READING

D'Acci, Julie (1994), *Defining Women: Television and the Case of Cagney and Lacey*, Chapel Hill: University of North Carolina Press.

Miller, Jeffrey S. (2000), *Something Completely Different: British Television and American Culture*, Minneapolis: University of Minnesota Press.

Miller, Toby (1997), *The Avengers*, London: British Film Institute; Bloomington: Indiana University Press.

The Police Series

For more than five decades the police series has been one of the most popular genres on television, with some series proving so successful that they have retained a presence in the schedules for ten years or more. In recent years, as the television companies compete for a diminishing share of the audience, there has been a proliferation of police, detective and crime drama (see 'The Action Series', p. 17), with endless variations and reworkings of a basic formula in which society is protected and the status quo maintained by the forces of law and order.

In the mid-1950s the tradition was established in Britain by the parochial and reassuring *Dixon of Dock Green* (BBC, 1955–76). George Dixon (Jack Warner) was an ordinary 'bobby on the beat', working close to the people and on their behalf against the occasional anti-social elements that dared to disturb the comfortable consensus of post-war Britain. He first began life as a character in the 1949 Ealing Studios film *The Blue Lamp*, where he was shot and killed by Dirk Bogarde's ruthless juvenile delinquent. Seeking a replacement for *Fabian of Scotland Yard* (BBC, 1954–6), the BBC persuaded Ted Willis (Dixon's creator) to resurrect the character for a new police series. Jack Warner returned to play the part of Dixon for the remainder of his career, until the series finally came to an end in 1976 (by which time Warner was eighty years old and Dixon had retired from the force).

In the early days the series was transmitted live from the BBC studios and featured little in the way of action, crimes usually being resolved with barely more than a minor tussle. Each episode dealt with one main story, introduced by George in a trademark address to camera at the beginning, which was matched by a similar coda at the end. This provided George with the opportunity to point out the moral of the story and, in so doing, deliver the ideological message: that the police were working for the common good of society at large.

When it was first introduced *Dixon of Dock Green* was lauded for its realism, largely because it focused on an ordinary, working-class policeman on the beat, rather than the more idealised detectives of other crime dramas (see 'The Action Series', p. 17). It had been preceded by *Fabian of Scotland Yard*, the first British drama series to be shot on film, which enabled it to achieve a faster narrative pace than the studio-bound *Dixon*, adding a surface realism that the latter lacked. But *Fabian* – like the subsequent *No Hiding Place* (Associated Rediffusion, 1959–67) and *Gideon's Way* (ATV, 1965–6) – focused on Scotland Yard detectives (rather than ordinary policemen) who used their analytical skills to solve the crime, as opposed to the more intuitive and common-sense attitudes of Dixon.

These two approaches to the police series – the ordinary uniformed policeman on the one hand, the skilled plain-clothes police detective on the other – set a pattern for the genre that has prevailed throughout its history. However, in 1962 the 'gritty' *Z Cars* (BBC, 1962–78) burst on to British television screens, exploding the cosy myth of its predecessors. In devising the series, writer Troy Kennedy Martin and director John McGrath were influenced by the pioneering American police series *Highway Patrol* (ITV, 1955–9), wishing to combine the faster narrative pace of that series with the social realism popular in Britain at the time (see Laing, 1991).

The setting for *Z Cars* was the fictional Newtown (based on Kirkby, Liverpool), and the 'documentary' impulse behind the series was used to explore changes in British society at the beginning of the 1960s. Rather than being named after an individual, it took its title from the new police cars that were being introduced into British policing, as Britain moved away from the older tradition of the

Z Cars moved away from the individual policeman

The Man from UNCLE and The Avengers

For many people, *The Man from UNCLE* (1964–8) represents the nadir of the TV spy genre, full of improbable plots, cheap sets, cliché gadgets taken from Bond-like prototypes (pens that were two-way radios, pistols that became machine guns, a Piranha sports coupé with rockets and machine guns), and amateur-hour performances below camp. In short, US television discovered how to make Bond blandly suitable to the cold war. But from another perspective, *UNCLE.* ushered in a productive era of programmes prepared to poke fun at the military–industrial complex. They were very different from their stiffly right-wing predecessors.

After a shaky start, the series was a huge ratings success in 1965 and 1966, at times receiving 10,000 fan letters a week. It was sold in sixty countries, and merchandising included twenty-three books, countless toys, comics, bubblegum cards, a lunch box of which I was very proud, and three records, plus the spin-off *Girl from UNCLE.* and eight movies, mostly designed for release outside the USA and made from newly filmed 'adult' material and TV episodes. Today there are many zines, feminist slash literature, fan conventions and Internet discussion groups.

It was an American form of pop, dedicated to requiring us all to be up with the times, to get onside with new technology. The fact that the principal enemy, THRUSH, was a multinational corporation, is also significant. One of the show's creators, Sam Rolfe, referred to UNCLE. as an 'international organisation that had no cold war philosophical differences to contend with'. To underscore the point, 'The Jingle Bells Affair' episode featured a Soviet politician shopping in New York and speaking on peace at the UN.

Even hipper, *The Avengers* ran on British TV from 1961 to 1969 and was exported to scores of other nations. It was the first (and still the only) UK show that aired during prime-time sweeps on the US networks. A hybrid of espionage and thriller, the program was notable for its lead characters. John Steed (Patrick MacNee) was a dandyish gentleman who embodied both a foppish style harking back to the Regency and modish 1960s chic. The successive women leads, Catherine Gale (Honor Blackman) and Emma Peel (Diana Rigg) personified modernity *tout court*: hip, leggy, sexy, brilliant, physically competent women who took nonsense from no man and were Steed's superiors intellectually and his equal in combat. Gale and Peel were single women who flirted with Steed, but could live without him. Each drew appreciative female audiences as a consequence. Perhaps women viewers witnessing uninhibited female stars who dressed for success through power saw the flip side to the uncompromising but sexy figures that leapt out to male fans.

Along with issues of gender, the once and doomed empire is ever-present in *The Avengers*. What looked like escapist spy television was also an allegory that resonated with progressive political practice and viewing protocols. The series materialised a transcendent new world, after patriarchy (or at least on the way there, via a Utopian alternative universe) and after empire (an unfurling narrative – TV series 1961–9, independence of Britain's 'possessions' 1957 onwards). As well as being figures of high modernity, reacting against and with the constraints of femininity even as they played with them, Mrs Gale and Mrs Peel were also representatives of a ruling-class white background from the former Empire, with 'winds of change' blowing through their political and domestic lives. Steed sat on the cross-benches of tradition and modernity, a playboy who destabilised conventional masculinity and simultaneously signified a disappearing genteel world and a new, brash one.

The programme garnered ratings and acclaim as both a harbinger of feminism and a sign that action television could be stylish and knowing as well as popular. It continues to fascinate. In the 1990s, Diana Rigg was still getting letters from

Man from UNCLE: a spy drama for the small screen

20   DRAMA

women for whom Mrs Peel had been an icon, and in 2000 the programme could be seen on the US Mystery cable channel, Radio Canada, Foxtel cable in Australia and TF1 in France, as *Agenti Speciali* on Italy's satellite Channel Jimmy, and as *Los Vengadores* in Argentina on Uniseries. The Web is sticky with related sites.   *Toby Miller*

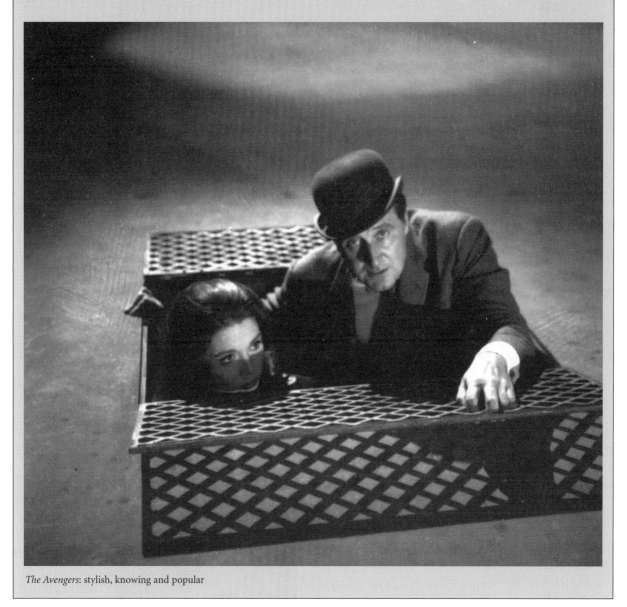

The Avengers: stylish, knowing and popular

policeman on the beat (a part of the community) towards a more depersonalised form of policing.

Concern to get the details of modern policing methods right (and to accurately reproduce the local dialect) was part of the documentary attention to detail of the series. This documentary research, as well as the decision to show violence as a routine fact of life, contributed to its repu-

tation for being more 'realistic' than other police dramas. However, the intention of Martin and McGrath was not to focus exclusively on the police. Instead, they wanted to use the police as a means to explore the lives of ordinary people living in the north-west of England.

Originally transmitted live, early episodes of *Z Cars* used an unusually large number of filmed inserts in order to give the drama a presence in the real world, thus increasing its documentary veracity. In this respect it marked a departure from previous series and helped to pave the way for the breakthrough into filmed drama that Tony Garnett was to achieve on The Wednesday Play (see 'The Single Play', p. 9) in the mid-1960s. The narrative pace of some of the early episodes was very fast, and Kennedy Martin, in particular, specialised in interweaving a number of different stories in each episode, thereby increasing the complexity of the narrative structure and maximising audience interest and involvement with a range of different characters and stories. To a large extent episodes were character-driven, rather than plot-driven, all part of the original objective of using the police series to explore the reality of people's lives. Originally conceived as a thirteen-part series, Z Cars proved an immediate success, with audiences increasing from nine million to fourteen million within eight weeks (Hurd, 1981; Laing, 1991).

In the 1970s the emphasis in police series shifted once again to individual policemen, this time rather more colourful (literally, as the series were now filmed in colour) and aggressive than the likes of Dixon and Fabian. In America, Kojak (BBC 1, 1974–8) and Starsky and Hutch (BBC 1, 1976–81) championed the police detective as fashionable and charismatic heroes, while in Britain a new, more ruthless breed of police detective was introduced in The Sweeney (Thames TV, 1975–8 – see 'The Action Series' p. 17). What all of these 1970s police detectives had in common was a self-righteous belief in the validity of their own methods, even if those methods involved a degree of violence and a bending of the rules. In a decade in which the social consensus of the post-war years was breaking down, the old, gentlemanly codes exercised by Dixon and Fabian no longer applied. Now the ends justified the (often illegal) means. In an increasingly lawless society extreme tactics were sometimes needed by these fictional policemen in the performance of their 'duty'. In the 'law and order' decade of the 1970s, television police series became an arena where the ideological and coercive work of the police was foregrounded as never before (Clarke, 1986, 1992; Donald, 1985; Hurd, 1981).

In Britain this tendency was controversially highlighted in a four-part drama series Law and Order (BBC 1, 1978), which foregrounded issues of police and judicial corruption in a naturalistic, vérité style (see 'Observational Documentary' p. 129). The documentary approach of the series offered a verisimilistic counterpart to the action sequences and stylised violence of The Sweeney and Starsky and Hutch and in doing so introduced a new realism into British police drama at the end of the 1970s.

Similarly, the ground-breaking American police series Hill Street Blues (MTM/NBC, 1981–9) sought to be more realistic in the early 1980s. A significant element of Hill Street was the more prominent role the series gave to women and ethnic minorities. Admittedly the men in its large ensemble cast still outnumbered the women, but at least the female cast had gained a significant presence as never before (see box). The 1980s, in fact, saw a significant reaction against the machismo of series like The Sweeney and Starsky and Hutch, with The Gentle Touch (LWT, 1980–4) and Juliet Bravo (BBC 1, 1980–5) in Britain, and Cagney and Lacey (BBC 1, 1982–8) in America, emerging to challenge the masculine hegemony of the past (see D'Acci, 1987).

The 1990s also saw a significant development in the portrayal of policewomen with the appearance of Detective Chief Inspector (later Superintendent) Jane Tennison (Helen Mirren) in Prime Suspect (Granada, 1991–5) (see Eaton, 1995; Brunsdon, 1998; Creeber, 2001b). More a crime drama than a police series, Prime Suspect, along with Cracker (Granada, 1993–), NYPD Blue (ABC, 1993–) and Homicide: Life on the Streets (NBC, 1993–) was part of a diversification of the police series in the 1990s as the genre

Cagney and Lacey: a reaction against the male hegemony of the police series

Hill Street Blues

The appearance of *Hill Street Blues* on NBC in 1981 was a landmark in the history of American television, breaking all the rules of series drama. It used a large ensemble cast of thirteen to fourteen central characters, overlapping dialogue, multiple narrative strands with a lack of resolution to many of the storylines, documentary-style camerawork, a multi-ethnic cast and strong female characters, and took a liberal attitude towards policing and social issues.

The series was a product of MTM, an independent company, and was screened on one of the main US networks, NBC. However, it was not an immediate success. In fact, the ratings were poor for the first series, but it received favourable reviews and it gradually attracted a loyal and dedicated audience. Inspired by the vérité style of *The Police Tapes*, a documentary series shown on the US Public Broadcasting System in 1976, *Hill Street* replicated the hand-held, observational style of that series in its morning roll call (see 'Observational Documentary' p. 129), and ended with the now famous warning: 'And hey, let's be careful out there.'

This traditional opening to each episode established a realistic and authentic ambience from the outset. The complex narrative structure – moving from one character, or pair of characters, to another, and from one storyline to another as the episode developed, with dialogue often overlapping as a consequence of the ensemble interplay and the interweaving of storylines – was all part of the objective of establishing a new *realism* in drama as a whole (see Nelson, 1997, pp. 30–9). The series was as far removed from *Kojak* and *Starsky and Hutch* as those series were from *Highway Patrol*.

It was a mark of the radicalism of *Hill Street Blues* that writer/producer Steve Bochco fought numerous battles with NBC's Broadcast Standards Department over what was permissible in the series. From the outset he and co-creator Michael Kozoll set out to break all the rules of the TV cop show, and they fought battles all along the way to get the series on the screen in the form and style that they wanted. The 'difference' of *Hill Street* was immediately apparent and its bold and innovative approach paved the way for *NYPD Blue, Homicide: Life On The Streets* and numerous subsequent series, within and outside of the police genre (see Jenkins, 1984; Kerr, 1984; Thompson, 1996). *Lez Cooke*

reinvented itself in a more hybrid form (police/detective/crime drama) in an attempt to maximise and retain audiences in an increasingly competitive television market (Brunsdon, 1998; Eaton, 1995).

Although traditional, romantic, individualistic, and typically English police detectives such as Morse, Dalgleish, Frost and Wexford remain popular on television, they appear to be a dying breed, being replaced by younger, trendier, female and ethnic counterparts (see Pines, 1995; Sparks, 1993; Thomas, 1997). Yet the ensemble-based, uniformed police series shows no signs of disappearing, with Britain's long-running *The Bill* (Thames TV, 1984– , see p. 6) still going strong, and new series, such as *City Central* (BBC 1, 1998–) and *Brooklyn South* (CBS, 1997) bearing witness to the perennial popular appeal of the genre.

Moreover, while *NYPD Blue* and *Homicide* have followed in *Hill Street Blues*' footsteps, being both experimental in style and progressive in content, two British series, *Between the Lines* (BBC 1, 1992–4) and *The Cops* (BBC 2, 1998), have shown that American television does not have a monopoly on the production of innovative, socially conscious police drama. The vérité style of *The Cops*, in particular, with its depiction of the police as 'ordinary human beings', with their own problems and flaws, demonstrates that the potential for using the police series to ask ques-

tions about the role of the police in contemporary society still survives (Eaton, 1995; MacMurraugh-Kavanagh, 2000; Nelson, 1997; Wayne, 1998).

Lez Cooke

RECOMMENDED READING

Brunsdon, Charlotte (1998), 'Structure of Anxiety: Recent British Television Crime Fiction', *Screen*, vol. 39: no.3.

Clarke, Alan (1992), ' "You're Nicked!": Television Police Series and the Fictional Representation of Law and Order', in Dominic Strinati and Stephen Wagg (eds), *Come On Down? Popular Media Culture in Post-War Britain*, London: Routledge.

Jenkins, Steve (1984), 'Hill Street Blues', in Jane Feuer, Paul Kerr and Tise Vahimagi (eds), *MTM – 'Quality Television'*, London: British Film Institute.

Hospital Drama

In the mid-1990s a common observation made by critics and commentators was that the proliferation of television medical dramas had reached epidemic proportions. As one critic put it, 'At the moment there are so many medi-

cal series and serials being aired that if you watch a clev-
erly planned selection, you will soon be able to conduct
your own operations' (Moir, 1996). Hospital dramas such
as *ER*, *Casualty*, and *Chicago Hope* were at the forefront of
this explosion of television's interest in medicine – which
included documentaries (see p. 124), docusoaps (see p.
132), science-fiction (see p. 26), and daytime magazine
programmes (see p. 92). Such dramas were also part of a
wider growth in the depiction of professional working life
on television (*NYPD Blue* (see 'The Police Series' p. 19),
The Bill, *London's Burning*, *This Life*). The advantage of the
hospital setting is that it is a ready-made receptacle for a
variety of dramatic situations: as the creator of *Cardiac
Arrest* commented, 'anything can walk through the door –
although they don't often walk' (*Radio Times*, 15–21 April
1995).

The 1950s saw the emergence of the first instances of
what was to become the staple hospital drama formula,
exemplified in shows such as *Medic* (US, 1954–5) and
Emergency – Ward 10 (UK, 1957–67). These shows were
based around an anthology format with self-contained
weekly episodes and regular central characters; they were
respectful of the growing power and authority of the medical institutions and took care to show that, whatever the
outcome in individual cases, medical progress was inex-

orable. The shows were paternal in the sense that they
sought to augment public trust in the medical profession,
largely through the 'stamp of quality' provided by medical
authorities such as the American Medical Association and
British Medical Association, which supplied medical advis-
ers who would check scripts for 'medical accuracy', and
who had a vested interest in making sure that their profession was represented positively.

It was important for these authorities that the shows did
not encourage anxiety and hypochondria, but instead reas-
sured the public. Reassurance was personified in the figure
of the infallible, capable doctor – Kildare, Welby, Finlay. In
the early shows the focus was on the individual doctor's
central role in healing people; typically, the doctors were
white males and the centre of authority in the hospital.
Early hospital dramas aimed for realism and accuracy in
their depiction of medical procedure (within the constraints of censorship and taste), balancing this against the
gravitational pull of melodrama (understood by the
industry as mere 'soap opera' – see p. 47).

By the 1960s the hospital doctor was seen as working as
part of a team, usually shown through a paternal relationship between the young doctor and more experienced
teacher. The touchstone in the development of such hospital dramas was *Dr Kildare* (NBC, 1961–6), which presented

---

ER

The creator of *ER* (1994–), Michael Crichton – himself
trained as a doctor at Massachussetts General Hospital –
waited twenty years for his idea for the show to be taken
seriously. *ER* (standing for Emergency Room) is the most successful and expensive hospital drama to date, at the time of
writing in its seventh season. It won eight Emmys in its first
year (matched only by *Hill Street Blues* – see 'The Police Series',
p. 19) and its directors have included Quentin Tarantino.
Despite the occasional (nostalgic) gesture towards the Utopian
view of medicine, it is unremittingly despairing. As two critics
noted approvingly, 'The programme is as much about disillu-
sionment as miracle surgery. It often ends on a downbeat,
reflective note about personal and medical failures as well as
the larger failures of American society . . . [the medical staff
are rendered] gratifyingly as flawed human beings' (Cassidy
and Taylor, 1997).

ER is an ensemble hospital drama, usually weaving three
or four plot strands per episode, each continuing the development of the characters. It inherits many of the concerns and
iconography of earlier instances of the genre – Mark Greene

(Anthony Edwards) inhabits the 'Hawkeye' role as the ban-
jaxed humanist in a war zone; John Carter (Noah Wyle) is an
idealistic Kildare to Peter Benton's (Eriq LaSalle) less than
avuncular Gillespie; Doug Ross (George Clooney) plays the
handsome but rebellious paediatrician bucking authority for
the sake of his infant patients.

However, what makes *ER* stand out is the way in which
complex character development is paced with the same
urgency as the medical treatment itself. As one critic has put
it, 'it's channel surfing without pressing the button, as scenarios and stories' progress 'through the ER room . . . at
dizzying speed' (Lewis and Stempel, 1999, p. 120). The stylish pace and fluidity of *ER*'s camerawork is clearly intended
to be expressive of the contemporary world as well as the
emergency room – a world that is risky, uncertain, and dangerous. Some have described its frenetic pace as excessive
(perhaps a recognition of the way in which the show has
modernised the melodramatic tendency of the genre), not
in opposition to realism, but as an acknowledgement of a
medicalised public sphere that is increasingly concerned
with the dramatic potency of the traumatised human body.

Jason Jacobs

the memorable 'father–son' relationship between Kildare (Richard Chamberlain) and his mentor and superior, Dr Gillespie (Raymond Massey). Set in a teaching hospital, it established the senior-to-junior doctor relationship as a nurturing one, where wisdom and knowledge were passed down without conflict. This was an important aspect of the genre: the education of a young, idealistic doctor was both instructional for the viewer and a way of showing how the eternal values of medical care and wisdom were reproduced in action. The show also situated Kildare not as an aloof member of a medical priesthood, but as a modern professional – committed, sincere, caring. *Kildare* also consolidated what was to become a pattern of later shows: patients (and their illnesses) were vehicles for the exploration of particular issues and topics.

By the late 1960s the figure of the individual doctor as infallible and godlike was becoming untenable. Although shows such as *Marcus Welby, MD* (ABC, 1967–75) restated many of the concerns of *Kildare*, it was possible to see changes in hospital drama that reflected a wider loss of confidence in medical institutions, medical science and doctors. This was also the period of an increasingly visible counter-culture populated by young people who defined themselves in conflict with the old establishment and its personifications. Television networks also needed to harvest the unpredictable youth demographic. *Medical Center* (CBS, 1971) can be seen as a response to these wider societal changes: it modifies the paternal teaching relationship to one of 'mutual respect' between senior and junior doctor. This show, like other hospital dramas of the 1970s, included frequent explicitness in the discussion of medical and social 'problems': abortion, homosexuality, rape, drug addiction, artificial insemination, venereal disease. Nonetheless, illness and injury continued to be catalysts for the exploration of human relationships, emotions, desires and morals.

Another generic change was from the single-doctor star (supported by older parental figures such as Dr Gillespie) to ward-based ensemble dramas. It was as if the impact of particular medical crises and their moral ramifications could no longer be credibly healed by one infallible figure.

M*A*S*H (1973–82), one of the most successful television shows of all time and marketed as a sitcom (see p. 65), depicts the abandonment of the consensus-based depictions of medical care. Here, for the first time, we see doctors with no control over their environment, in a war zone healing patients so that they could go back to war and kill or be killed. *M*A*S*H* revitalised the form, by mixing black comedy with the humanist despair of Hawkeye (Alan Alda) so that the comedy had an ironic and desperate edge, exemplified in the title song, 'Suicide is Painless'. The doctors

were no longer fighting against abstract forces of disease or the contingency of accidental injuries: their environment (including the regularly wounded patients) were part of the problem, and contributed to their (comic, absurd) despair.

This focus on medical staff facing the negative impact of a hostile environment was continued in the UK with Paula Milne's gritty *Angels* (BBC, 1975–83), which followed the chaotic lives of student nurses, and G.K. Newman's *The Nation's Health* (UK, 1984), which sought to expose a corrupt and failing National Health Service.

These downbeat generic concerns were the focus in the two key hospital dramas of the 1980s: *St Elsewhere* (NBC, 1982–7) and *Casualty* (BBC, 1986–). *St Elsewhere* was set in an under-funded Boston teaching hospital, St Eligius, and was heavily influenced by the visual and narrative style of *Hill Street Blues* (NBC, 1981– , see box p. 23). The medical staff were less potent than ever, neither heroic nor cool under pressure, and they were also the primary focus: the patients were rapidly becoming background devices for the development of the central characters where we see a mainstreaming of 'existential issues' (yuppie angst) such as the spiritual burden of doing a high-pressure job: doctors were not only more fragile, but more introspective about their failing potency.

The BBC's *Casualty* is an ensemble hospital drama that began with a campaigning tone in relation to the UK welfare cuts of the 1980s; however, from the beginning it also maintained an overtly moralistic tone in relation to its patients. Inheriting the sense of the emergency ward of the hospital as a war zone, the creators of *Casualty* (originally called *The Front Line*) wanted the staff in the ward to wear military-style fatigues: the battle was with 'immoral' patients and a pernicious cost-cutting bureaucracy.

Both series showcased their sensitivity in relation to controversial issues (AIDS, homosexuality, organ donation, euthanasia) and both were dress rehearsals for the speedier dramas of the mid-1990s. They also exemplify the different styles of UK and US television: *St Elsewhere* relied on a cinematic house style that emphasised chaos and complexity, underwritten by solid acting and writing. *Casualty*'s writing was weaker, and it exemplified British cinema and television's obsession with montage as a preferred dramatic technique, using teasing vignettes of potential casualties and cross-cutting between them and the casualty ward into which they would soon (perhaps) be delivered. Both flaunted a visceral explicitness in the depiction of injury and in relation to controversial issues. At the same time the medical staff were also rendered as fragile workers caught between a rigid bureaucracy and the contingent violence of everyday life.

The 1990s represented an unprecedented intensification of the medicalisation of everyday life: regular health scares, the theorisation of the 'risk society', the state promotion of 'healthy living' as a moral as much as a medical imperative all contributed to a popular engagement with the fictional depiction of hospital life. At the same time, with the collapse of the old distinctions between Left and Right, and the narrowing of politics to a managerial role, any sense of social change became collapsed on to the body itself: 'The intense social concern about health is closely related to the cult of the body [fitness fads, body-building, dieting, piercing, plastic surgery]: once you give up on any prospect of achieving progress in society, your horizons are reduced to securing your own physical survival' (Fitzpatrick, 2000, p.160). The sense of humanist despair and impotence in the face of illness, disease and injury hinted at in *M*A*S*H* became normalised as an everyday feature of the genre. As Susan Sontag argues, 'A permanent modern scenario: apocalypse looms ... and it doesn't occur. And it still looms . . . Apocalypse is now a long-running serial: not "Apocalypse Now" but "Apocalypse From Now On" ' (Sontag, 1991, p.173).

Medical dramas of the mid-1990s engaged and developed this new apocalyptic ideology of health, as well as inheriting many of the generic concerns and interests of previous instances, setting them to a faster beat. In 1990s hospital dramas there is a rapid alternation between scenes of action – emergency medical treatment – and those of reflection and introspection. The 'action mode' foregrounds the radical contingency of accidents and the 'sudden turn for the worse' that can befall patients. This is typically rendered in a fluid, restless visual style, complemented by medical technobabble that overlays the confusing immediacy of injury and treatment. These scenes alternate with moments of reflection, where characters assess the consequences of a medical procedure, for the patients and, more importantly, for themselves.

Cardiac Arrest (BBC, 1994–6) represents a shift of attention in the genre from a concern with the patient and nation as victims of welfare cuts, to a concern with junior doctors as victims of a pernicious healthcare system who also suffer the weight of their depoliticised 'grunge' generation. The main characters, in their early to mid-twenties, are confronted by monstrous senior doctors (who represent a corrupt macho medical profession), sleep deprivation, debt and the tyranny of their bleepers. They are also faced with hospital managers interfering with their medical judgement, fuelled by the ideology and management-speak of the business sector from which they were recruited. In *Cardiac Arrest* the medical/moral education exemplified in

the interaction of Gillespie and Kildare is banished to the realms of naive Utopianism.

Jason Jacobs

RECOMMENDED READING
Jacobs, Jason (2001), *Body Trauma: New Television Medical Dramas*, London: British Film Institute.
Karpf, Anne (1988), *Doctoring the Media*, London: Routledge.
Turow, Joseph (1989), *Playing Doctor: Television, Storytelling and Medical Power*, Oxford: Oxford University Press.

Science Fiction

Like much television drama, the earliest science fiction (SF) television was based on novels or stage plays. Despite these origins, science fiction television is not generally regarded as a high-culture form; instead, it has tended to be seen as popular entertainment (see p. 76), perhaps because of its association with aliens and special effects (see Baxter, 1970). The studio-bound setting of early television, and shooting on film for location work, imposed their own restrictions, and special effects work was time-consuming and expensive. However, the advent of location video in the 1970s and 1980, gave programme-makers more flexibility, with forests and disused quarries becoming favourite stand-ins for alien landscapes (this was particularly the case at the BBC).

More significantly, the arrival of relatively affordable digital technology in the 1990s gave rise to higher production values and the opportunity for more elegant special effects. Underneath its unusual and often slightly flashy *mise-en-scène*, science fiction television has a track record of addressing moral, ethical, political and philosophical themes – what Sobchack refers to as the 'intellectual development of an abstract premise' (1987, p. 25). In this respect, science fiction on television is, at best, notably different from many, although not all, of its special effects-driven counterparts in the cinema (see Hockley, 2000). For example, *Doctor Who* (1963) had an explicitly educational mission (see p. 28; *Star Trek* (US, 1966; BBC, 1969) tackled, on a weekly basis, problems of good and evil, the unreliable nature of technology and the potentially disastrous consequences of careless time travel (see box, and Hanely, 1997); and *Babylon 5* (1994) has more recently explored the intricate world of political intrigue.

Science fiction television has tended to be an underanalysed, and under-theorised area of academic study. Perhaps one of the reasons for this is that it eludes neat

Dr. Who challenged assumptions around the 'popular/serious' debate

classification (see Sobchack, 1987, for a good survey of attempts to define the science fiction genre film). Significantly what science fiction television does, like its counterpart in the cinema, is to reflect contemporary social and political concerns. The genre developed dramatically after the bombing of Hiroshima and during the cold war period, giving rise to a mix of technological Utopias and dystopias. For example, *V* (1983) and *Star Trek* (particularly in its depiction of the Klingons) suggests the continual fear of 'the Other', a fear that continues in *Star Trek: The Next Generation* and *Voyager* as a fear of assimilation into the 'Borg' collective (see Gregory, 2000, and the 'Star Trek' box).

British science fiction television started life with two BBC one-off plays. The first was adapted from Karel Čapek's philosophical drama about robots, *RUR* (1937). The second was H.G. Wells's *The Time Machine* (1949). These introduced what were to become two key themes in science fiction television, time travel and technologically produced human simulacra, and prepared the way for the first British science fiction television serial, *Stranger from*

Space (1951). Made for children, this was broadcast fortnightly and, showing that interactive television is nothing new, viewers were asked to write in with suggestions about how the story might develop. In 1953, the BBC returned to adult science fiction and transmitted the first of its three serials featuring the rocket scientist Quatermass (the fourth *Quatermass* serial in 1979 was produced by Euston Films, a subsidiary of Thames Television). The next attempt to produce a science fiction series for adults in the UK came with *A for Andromeda* (1961) and its sequel *The Andromeda Breakthrough* (1962). It is a testament to the strength of these narratives (which explore cloning, environmental and cold war issues) that they remain of interest today. However, as Joy Leman points out (1991, p. 123), they can never quite escape the historical moment in which they were made:

> Whilst science fiction would seem to take us outside of [the] structuring elements of class and gender by a discourse of fantasy and futurism, the metaphorical transformations always speak about the historical time in

which the production took place. The science fiction serials of the 1950s and 60s offered innovative possibilities both in form and content, but were finally limited to the dominant constructions of class and gender of their time.

1963 saw the start of the BBC's *Doctor Who* series, which became a British science fiction classic and the longest-running television science fiction series. It was created by Sydney Newman (see 'The Single Play', p. 9), who had come from ABC Television, where he had produced the sci-fi series *Target Luna* (1960) and its sequel *Pathfinders* (1960). The central character, referred to just as 'The Doctor', is a Time Lord who uses the TARDIS to travel through time and space; in a typically quirky British move this vehicle was disguised as a police telephone box. There have been eight television Doctors, and each has been played by a different actor ('The Doctor' can conveniently 'regenerate' his body up to thirteen times).

Star Trek

In many ways *Star Trek*, in all its incarnations, is what people think of as science fiction television. The first episode was transmitted in the USA on 8 September 1966 and had a run of three seasons with a total of seventy-nine, fifty-minute episodes. It came to the UK some three years later, by which point the series had been axed in America. The NBC network had put considerable pressure on the creator of the series, Gene Roddenberry, to downplay some of its more unconventional aspects. But it was the multiracial (and indeed multispecies) crew and the exploration of themes such as racism, colonialism, and human psychology that won the support of fans (see Jenkins, 1992; and Tulloch and Jenkins, 1995).

Although Captain James T. Kirk (William Shatner) was a full-blooded American, some critics argue that the series broke new ground in being explicitly multicultural with the female African-American Lt Uhura (Nichelle Nichols), the Japanese Mr Sulu (George Takei), the Russian Mr Chekov (Walter Koenig), the Scottish Montgomery 'Scotty' Scott (James Doohan) and the alien (or Vulcan) Mr Spock (Leonard Nimoy) on the bridge of the Starship *Enterprise*. However, as one might expect, its view of race is far from unproblematic (see, for instance, Barrett and Barrett, 2001). Indeed, some commentators have suggested that the alien species encountered in the series also represent racial caricatures – versions, for instance, of the Soviets (Klingons), Arabs (Cardassians) and Chinese (Romulans) (see Bernardi, 1998; Worland, 1998).

Largely as a result of fan pressure, a new series, *Star Trek: The Next Generation,* was commissioned in the USA in 1987 (UK, 1990). This was followed by two related series, *Star Trek: Deep Space Nine* (1993) and *Star Trek: Voyager* (1995). This amounts to 522 episodes and it is still growing. Typically, *Star Trek* is characterised as optimistic and progressive in its tone. As Kavanagh (1990, p. 74) puts it, 'Spock and Kirk are the most familiar recent mass-cultural version of [a] humanist ideological couple reconstructed in signifying practice'. But this also masks a reactionary strand to the series. For example, the Federation's apparent willingness to make treaties with 'fascistic' regimes suggests a degree of conservatism, not unlike J. F. Kennedy's liberal domestic reforms, which contrasted with his essentially conservative foreign policy (Gregory, 2000). The colonial overtones of the imperative to 'seek out new life and new civilisations' that open every episode of *Star Trek* and *The Next Generation* cannot help but evoke some uneasy references to our history as colonisers and conquerors.

The Next Generation appears to perpetuate the omnipresence of the Federation (to which all 'right-thinking' planets belong), and reflects a particular hostility towards species that work and live as a collective, such as the Borgs. The Borgs were introduced as a genderless cyborg (part machine, part flesh) but have subsequently acquired a gender, and even a Borg Queen to lead them. They were originally intended as an evil vision of technological progress (the fear of being assimilated into the Collective), and the series thus self-consciously plays with notions of the ideal subject, subjectivity and gender (see Harrison et al., 1996; Harraway, 1995).

Originally, *Star Trek* was less than progressive in the revealing costumes it provided for female crew members: 'Uhura was little more than an intergalactic receptionist and no less than seventeen women died for the love of Kirk' (Lewis and Stempel, 1999, p. 324). The predominant sexual orientation remains heterosexual and the female crew members still have to be as attractive as they are effective. The first series to have a female captain was *Voyager*; however, even Captain Janeway (Kate Mulgrew) has been the subject of nude bathing scenes (see Penley, 1997; and Roberts, 1999).

Suggesting a post-modern self-reflexivity (see 'Post-modern Drama', p. 43), *The Next Generation* has a number of episodes that are parodies of other genres: 'The Big Goodbye' (film noir), 'Elementary Dear Data' (detective), 'A Fistful of Datas' (Western), 'Qpid' (Robin Hood) and 'Disaster' (disaster movie) (see Gregory, 2000). There is now an animated series, seven feature films and numerous novels; as such, it seems that *Star Trek*'s universe is inherently intertextual and forever expanding (see Epstein, 1996).

Luke Hockley

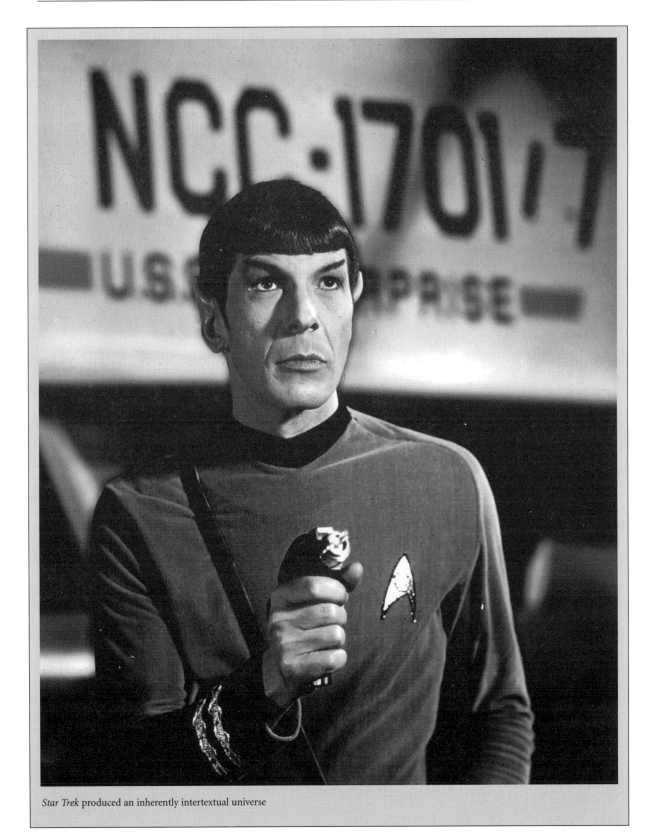

Star Trek produced an inherently intertextual universe

The X-Files

Moving away from the space operas of the *Star Trek* (see box) franchise, *The X-Files* (Fox/10:13, 1993–) situates its paranormal detective narratives within the contemporary reality of modern-day America. The series follows the investigations of two young FBI agents, Fox Mulder (David Duchovney) and Dana Scully (Gillian Anderson), into inexplicable cases of supernatural phenomena rejected by the bureau mainstream. Each episode depicts a different case, allowing the series to skirt between a number of interrelated genres: horror, detective, science fiction, thriller and comedy. The series integrates these self-contained narratives into a convoluted ongoing plot concerning a government conspiracy to conceal the presence of aliens from the general public, enabling it to combine an appeal to the loyal and the casual viewer.

The X-Files was produced by the then nascent Fox network, which was attempting to monopolise on the threat posed by cable and satellite to the three major networks that had dominated American television production from the late 1950s. At this point, Fox wanted to build on its reputation for comedies and teenage dramas by moving into drama production that would extend its demographic range into the 18–49 age group (see 'The Teen Series', p. 41). Manipulating the generic fluidity of science fiction television, the series attempted to integrate the basic structure of the detective genre (which was particularly successful in the early 1990s) with elements of horror and science fiction that were relatively absent from the network schedules at that time. The series became hugely successful both in America and internationally, spawning extensive marketing, a vociferous fan network and a spin-off film (*The X-Files: Fight the Future*, Rob Bowman, 1998), securing Fox's position as the fourth major network in American television broadcasting and reinvigorating the science fiction genre during the 1990s.

The X-Files depicts an uncertain world in which the inability of its protagonists to prove the existence of the paranormal undermines the stability of truth and reality. This is complemented by a cinematic style, which takes advantage of the developments in film stock and digital technology to create a mysterious and foreboding visual landscape where nothing is quite what it seems. Academic attempts to address the signifi-

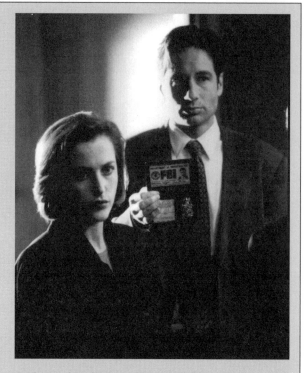

X Files: searching for meaning in an uncertain world

cance of what has since been called a 'popular culture phenomenon' (McLean, 1998, p. 4) have primarily focused on analysing the series' relevance to contemporary culture. *The X-Files*' conspiracy narratives of paranormal investigations have been associated with pre-millennial tension and the surge of interest and belief in alien abduction (Lavery et al., 1996; Dean, 1997). Post-modern theorists have argued that its treatment of history and multiplication of the truth exemplifies the ontological and epistemological crises in contemporary society (Kellner, 1999), whereas others argue for a modernist reading of the series, claiming that it maintains at its heart a belief that 'the truth is out there', to borrow from the series' oft-quoted catch-phrase (McLean, 1998). These studies tend to concentrate on *The X-Files*' narrative and thematic treatment of contemporary anxiety, arguing that its success lies in its dark and unresolved storylines, which engage with a pervasive malaise in late-twentieth-century America.

Catherine Johnson

Each of 'The Doctors' has also had a different 'Assistant', normally female. These ploys, along with the TARDIS, ensured a variety of locations and actors (see Tulloch and Alvarado, 1983). Aliens, such as the Daleks and the Cybermen, were less psychological or political than their

Star Trek counterparts and tended to pose a direct physical threat to 'The Doctor' or his Assistant, or indeed to Earth itself. However, like *Star Trek* it has dedicated fans that have exerted considerable pressure on the BBC to ensure the longevity of 'their' series (see Tulloch and Jenkins, 1995; for a more subversive use by fans of *Star Trek*, see Penley, 1997). Part of its attraction was clearly its unique ability to transcend a number of generic categories. According to Tulloch and Alvarado (1990, p. 311; originally published, 1983):

> As a popular series, *Doctor Who* is inescapably wedded to ratings and stardom. And yet the 'popular/serious' opposition is clouded by two considerations: the origins of the programme as 'education' as well as 'entertaining' and 'adult' as well as 'children's' drama, so that a considerable 'serious' audience has been built up over the years; and more importantly, by the fact that SF as a genre challenges the 'popular/serious' interface of the culture industries.

The 1960s also saw ITV commission a clutch of children's science fiction puppet shows. They were created by Gerry and Sylvia Anderson and developed the techniques established in their previous series *Supercar* (1961) and *Fireball XL5* (1962). *Stingray* (1964), *Thunderbirds* (1965), *Captain Scarlet and the Mysterons* (1967), and *Joe 90* (1968) all acquired a cult following. The quirky puppetry, which Anderson dubbed 'supermarionation', the special effects that were overseen by Derek Meddings, and the visual novelty of the programmes ensured the popularity of the series. However, in America, science fiction was taking a rather different route, with higher production values and narratives that were explicitly moral in their message – none more so than The Twilight Zone (US, 1959; UK, 1964), which explored a mixture of science fiction, fantasy and psychological themes, including psychic premonitions, alien invasions, abductions and time travel. Some of the cast of *Star Trek,* including William Shatner (Captain Kirk) and Leonard Nimoy (Mr Spock), made guest appearances on the show. As Jeffrey Scounce (1997, p. 1454) points out, science fiction narratives were usually employed by the series simply in an attempt to create morally informed story lines:

> The Twilight Zone was an anthology series that, while not exclusively based in science fiction, frequently turned to the genre to frame allegorical tales of the human condition and America's national character. Some of the most memorable episodes of the series used science fiction to defamiliarize and question the conformist values of postwar suburbia as well as the rising paranoia of Cold War confrontation.

In 1978 Terry Nation (inventor of the Daleks in *Dr Who*) created the BBC's *Blake's 7*. Strong characters, but typically bad props and sets (the use of quarries and forests as locations continued) gave the series a familiar feel that endeared it to many viewers. One of the more innovative programmes produced by the BBC was the unlikely *Hitch-Hiker's Guide to the Galaxy* (1981). The series, which started on the BBC's Radio 4, developed a dedicated following, with its mixture of comedy, philosophical musing and aurally rich backgrounds. Given the budget of the television version, it is perhaps not surprising that the appearance of a two-headed Zaphod Beeblebrox (Mark Wing-Davey) and Marvin (David Learner), a paranoid android, were not entirely successful in their costumes or make-up. However, the quality of the writing, by Douglas Adams (an earlier writer for *Doctor Who*), and the computer graphics for the book ensured that the series was consistently funny and visually appealing. In part, the series prepared the way for the science fiction parody *Red Dwarf* (1988), which became BBC2's longest-running comedy (see p. 69).

The 1990s saw the start of a vast number of new science fiction series. Some were unsuccessful, like Gerry Anderson's blend of live action and puppetry in *Space Precinct* (1995). Others, such as the children's *Mighty Morphin Power Rangers* (1993) with its bizarre blend of martial arts and monsters, have been a success with viewers (if not critics). Derived from the film of the same title, *Stargate SG-1* (1998) has emphasised special effects over narrative interest, while *Babylon 5* (1994) has introduced new levels of sophistication to special effects with its digitally generated spaceships against which it sets its own political narratives.

Luke Hockley

RECOMMENDED READING

Fulton, Roger and Betancourt, John (2000) *Encyclopedia of TV Science Fiction*, London: Boxtree.

Harrison, Taylor, Projansky, Sarah, Ono, Kent and Helford, Elyce (eds) (1996), *Enterprise Zones: Critical Positions on 'Star Trek'*, Oxford: Westview Press.

Lavery, David, Hague, Angela and Cartwright, Marla, (eds) (1996), *Deny All Knowledge: Reading* 'The X-Files', London: Faber and Faber.

Drama–Documentary

'Drama–documentary' is the label most often used in Britain and parts of Europe to indicate the combination of dramatic and documentary elements in a programme. In the United States, the term 'docudrama' has been the preferred term. Rather than a distinct subgenre of programme, it is best to see the classification as pointing to a very wide range of different mixtures.

Drama–documentary has been a controversial area of work, one around which a good deal of analysis and debate has developed (Paget (1998) is an essential critical commentary). Quite apart from whatever specific issue it raises in relation to chosen topics and themes, it presents us with some central questions about the nature of audiovisual representation. Some academic critics have found it problematic to separate in the first place the two 'sides' that drama–documentary brings together. They have seen 'documentary' to be a narrative form relying extensively on different kinds of artifice. Conversely, they have also seen much 'drama' to be grounded in real circumstances, carrying a commitment to the exploration of real problems. By contrast, many commentators in the press and many public figures have regarded any kind of fusion of the two modes as an unacceptable blurring of boundaries, likely to misinform and mislead the public.

It makes some sense, certainly within the British and European tradition of practice, to draw a rough division between two kinds of work. There is that work that has developed as a documentary project, with degrees of dramatisation (through scripting and acting) added to give it stronger projection. Then, there is work that has developed very much in the conventional manner of a play (a script emerging largely from individual creative work, which is then cast and shot) but that has employed some of the looks and sounds of documentary material to deliver a more 'realist' impact. Within British television, the first kind of project has often been called 'dramatised documentary' whereas the second has been referred to as 'documentary drama'.

Examples of the 'dramatising' of documentary projects can be found in the pioneer television of the 1950s. The main reason for dramatisation here was the inaccessibility of so many different areas of social life to the cumbersome technology of television at that stage of its development. Thus dramatisation was to a degree a necessity for a good range of documentary engagement, although the added popularity of presenting character and action in this way was not lost on producers. Early examples of the 'documentarisation' of drama also exist: for instance, a number of British films made in the Second World War set their fictional occurences within a very firm context of documentary-style footage. Corner (1996, pp. 35–8) gives a brief account of this earlier filmic and televisual history, with examples.

There is no doubt that it becomes quite difficult to place some works into the right category, whereas others are more easily seen as belonging to the one or the other. A good general principle is to separate off questions of *reference* from questions of *depiction*, even if this is sometimes hard to do. Questions of reference concern how a particular programme relates itself to the real world, with what degree of specificity as to people, places, times, events and actions. There is a spectrum here, running all the way from the loose 'based on a real incident' model through to the tightly researched reconstruction of, say, a trial (where transcripts are available upon which to ground the dialogue). Knowing just what the relations of reference are in any given 'drama–documentary' sometimes poses a problem, particularly since these relations often shift from scene to scene. Strong referential claims clearly raise questions about the scale and strength of the evidence that supports them and therefore about the quality of the research lying behind the depiction. In general, and not surprisingly, programmes constructed from a documentary base have a more specific, reconstructive character than those emerging directly from playscripts.

Questions of depiction concern the extent to which the audiovisual depiction follows the 'rules' either of dramatic or documentary representation. For instance, is voice-over commentary used? Do certain scenes appear to be straight actuality footage? In what ways are we asked to relate to the characters as real people appearing before the camera rather than as acted roles? It is worth noting here that, whereas 'dramatised documentary' might include conventional documentary material alongside the dramatised sequences, it is likely that, with the exception of brief scenes from archive footage, most of a documentary–drama will be the product of full directorial management of scripted action and speech.

The biggest single issue in public discussion of drama–documentary (of both kinds outlined above) is that of possible confusion among the audience. In fact, a confusion about the fundamental status of what is being watched (is it really happening or is being acted out?) is far less likely than a confusion about how what is dramatically depicted relates to what did actually happen or, more loosely, what might well have happened. It is the way in which drama–documentary stimulates and sometimes shocks the social and historical imagination of the audience that has been at the core of concern. Where the topic is itself already a sensitive one (raising questions, for instance, of national history, social inequality or injustice or misuse of official or corporate power), then a 'dramatisation' will often serve to cause a controversy to flare up.

In Britain during the 1960s and 70s, a number of writers, directors and producers used the 'documentary

Cathy Come Home

Cathy Come Home (written by Jeremy Sandford, directed by Ken Loach, produced by Tony Garnett) was screened by BBC1 on 16 November 1966 within the regular Wednesday Play slot (see 'The Single Play', p. 9). It is a 'drama–documentary' concerning homelessness and its effect upon families (Corner, 1996, pp. 90–108, gives it a full critical appraisal). The programme has become a British TV 'classic', regularly referred to by critics and researchers. Part of the status accorded to *Cathy* is undoubtedly owing to its particular qualities of scripting, direction and acting, but part follows from the way in which it has been seen to focus and exemplify questions about the mixing of dramatic with documentary material and, more generally, about the public power of television.

Cathy is organised as a narrative about a young woman who marries, has children and who then, following an accident to her husband that results in his loss of job and family poverty, suffers various states of homelessness in poor or temporary accommodation until her children are taken into care by the social services. The programme adopts an episodic structure, depicting the stages in the decline of Cathy and her family across a number of years. It is held together by the commentary of Cathy herself, a commentary that is given in a self-reflective past tense and that not only introduces and ends the programme but is heard regularly throughout it, providing a bridge between episodes and a source of additional explanation to that obtained by watching events unfold. Cathy both tells us more about what is happening and keeps us closer to it by her subjectively involved recounting.

The 'documentary' element of *Cathy* is partly a matter of depictive style and partly a matter of the amount of time the script gives to portraying aspects of the general problem of homelessness in addition to advancing its storyline.

Stylistically, the programme has a number of scenes that are shot in the documentary mode of action-led camera, with events appearing to develop spontaneously and to be caught by the filming. The resulting effect is one of high immediacy values, providing the viewer with a strong sense of 'witness'. A documentarist element is more directly present in the use of commentary and brief 'viewpoint' voice-over at several points in the film, offering statistics on the housing situation and allowing various perspectives on it to be heard in a manner that follows conventional documentary practice.

Most of the newspaper critics recognised the impact and quality of the programme. Public discussion of it tended to circulate around two issues: the possibility of the audience being deceived into according to it a greater truth than was warranted by its fictional status, and the way in which the account was a 'biased' one, depicting officials as uncaring and often hostile in a manner that would have been unacceptable in a conventional documentary.

It is hard to imagine any viewer believing that *Cathy* was actuality footage, so extensively is it conceived of in terms of narrative fiction. However, doubt clearly existed in some viewers' minds as to whether it was a story based directly on a real incident, or whether (as was actually the case) Cathy's tale was a construction developed from a range of researched instances. The legitimacy of combining dramatic licence with the documentary requirement to be 'impartial' was queried by several commentators, not for the first time nor the last (Goodwin et al. (1983) offer several useful extracts from the contemporary debate).

Against these complaints, other critics defended the programme-makers' right to use emotional tactics in order to engage the viewer with public issues, and pointed to the way in which the programme's view of officialdom was essentially the view of Cathy herself – in their eyes, a perfectly proper use of character viewpoint from which audience members could measure their own distance.

John Corner

drama' format precisely to generate this kind of debate around questions that had, in their view, been neglected and that had escaped the scrutiny of orthodox documentary programmes because of the timidity of programme-makers, the elusiveness of the material or its historical non-availability. Such an approach fitted well with the contemporary form of the 'realist' play, taking a theme from ordinary life and giving it a provocative realisation in which story and background were both given weight. Indeed, classic forms of the 'documentary drama' blur into the forms of television realist drama (this is certainly the case with *Cathy Come Home* (see the box headed 'The Wednesday Play', p. 13 and the box in this section). On the whole, the strand of 'dramatised documentary' offers less fluent, less fully rendered and less aesthetically satisfying depictions, partly because it is still interested in carrying out a job of reporting and analysis alongside, and underneath, its more dramatic business.

It is interesting that dramatic reconstruction has found its way into a variety of documentary formats in recent years, including the newer 'reality TV' shows (see p. 134 – this application is usefully explored by Kilborn and Izod, 1997). Rarely, however, is it used as the only mode of depiction within the programme. So the 'dramatised

The Day After

The Day After (ABC TV, 1983, written by Edward Hume, directed by Nicholas Meyer, produced by Robert Papazian), a drama–documentary about nuclear war and its aftermath, was screened across the United States in November 1983 and on the British ITV network some three weeks later. It gained huge ratings in America, being watched by an estimated half of the adult population. The British audience was a moderately sized one, with the film receiving a cool reception from many newspaper critics, who saw it as lacking the aesthetic discipline that the subject required.

The theme of the disastrous consequences of nuclear war had been treated in Britain almost twenty years earlier in Peter Watkin's classic *The War Game* (BBC, 1965), a film that was banned from broadcast transmission at the time (ostensibly because of its frightening nature, although it is now clear that its implications for government defence policy were seen to be unacceptable).

The Day After incorporates key features from both the American soap opera (see p. 47) and the Hollywood disaster movie, as well as containing other generic elements. By shadowing familiar generic forms it gains increased emotional power and popular accessibility. However, such a generic project shifts it away from a 'social realist' plausibility of character, action and setting that many British audiences and critics are more used to in the handling of a major public issue on screen.

The narrative of the film involves a lengthy period of build-up, as a superpower confrontation in Europe becomes increasingly dangerous. A nuclear strike on the town of Lawrence, Kansas, is chosen as the focus for the story, and a 'community' of people working on the site of the University of Kansas provides an inner grouping of victims/survivors. To these are added others, including a group of serviceman on duty at a nearby missile silo. There is a clear 'lead' role, a medical academic, played by a well-known actor, Jason Robards. His experience and feelings provide a centre for the account, one to which it regularly returns.

In her excellent discussion of the film, Susan Boyd-Bowman notes how American drama–documentary 'privileges the dramatic fiction over the factual documentation' (1984, p. 85). This is certainly true, despite sequences of documentary-style footage, including library film of bombers and missiles. She also makes the cogent case that the interweaving of generic discourses finally becomes unsatisfactory across the different components of soap opera (see p. 47), melodrama, science fiction (see p. 26), horror, disaster movie, documentary (see

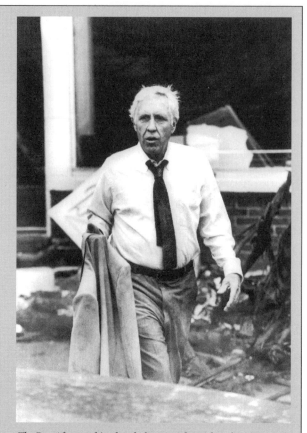

The Day After combined melodrama and social exploration

p. 124) and 'art television' (the latter strand manifest in the elegant and self-consciously symbolic styling frequently employed).

It is possible to argue, nevertheless, that this pulling together of different modes, although it might look messy to critics, was a key factor in making the film continuously watchable, powerful and effective for the huge audience. In order to understand it properly, perhaps a certain sympathetic contact has to be made with the popular meanings and values of 'America' as these might be threatened and destroyed by the events we witness. There is, for instance, a sentimental play on the rural landscape (farms and livestock) and on the honest and Christian virtues of hard work and family life. But there is also some serious exploration of underlying tensions within the family unit and, indeed, of broader tensions within the social order.

This combination of melodrama with social exploration as well as issue-focused shock is familiar to us from many of the best American films, and it would be wrong to underestimate the sheer cumulative force of *The Day After*'s recipe of ingredients. The ending of the film offers little hope – the Jason

Robards character stumbles through a scene of devastation and debris and is sorrowfully embraced by a fellow survivor, both sinking down on their knees. In its use of popular tropes and narrative devices to engage an American audience with a crucial issue of national policy and, indeed, national destiny, *The Day After* deserves to be seen as a major television achievement.

John Corner

documentary' continues, if mostly in part- rather than whole-programme usage. What of the documentary–drama? This continues too, as an occasional item, but it is much more likely now to organise its looks and sounds in relation to established fictional genres (such as thriller or disaster movie) rather than to imitate documentary appearance. This is partly because of the way in which the terms of realism in television fiction have moved away from that convergence with the codes of documentary that was so apparent in the 1960s.

The manner in which television narratives can relate both to the imaginative realm of fiction and the real historical world continues to be a topic of public interest and critical fascination. As well as Paget (1998), there is an excellent collection of articles in Rosenthal (1999). The history of 'drama–documentary' is one of the most interesting strands in the whole history of television as a public medium. The questions of motive, method and form that work in this strand have posed deserve the scholarly attention that they will continue to receive.

John Corner

RECOMMENDED READING

Paget, D. (1998), *No Other Way to Tell It: Dramadoc/Docudrama on Television*, Manchester: Manchester University Press.

Rosenthal, A. (ed.) (1999), *Why Docudrama?*, Carbondale and Edwardsville: Southern Illinois University Press.

Corner, J. (1996), *The Art of Record*, Manchester: Manchester University Press.

The Mini-Series

The increased serialisation and complexity of television drama means that it has become increasingly difficult to make clear distinctions between the series, serial and mini-series (see 'The Uses and Limitations of Genre', p. 4). However, as a crude guide, a *series* like *The Avengers* (1961–9 – see p. 20), *Cagney and Lacey* (1982–8 – see p. 22) and *Charlie's Angels* (1979–82) are generally made up of a separate number of episodes that are usually self-con-

tained with 'no final resolution' (Butler, 1994, p. 29). As John Ellis puts it, 'the series implies the form of the dilemma rather than that of resolution and closure' (1989, p. 135). This broad definition can also include an 'anthology' series like The Twilight Zone (1959–65 – see p. 31) or *Boys from the Blackstuff* (1982), 'a group of separate plays linked together by a theme and title' (Self, 1984, p. 25).

In contrast, the storyline within a *serial* is usually carried *over* from one instalment to another. This explains Newcomb's suggestion that they can also be referred to as 'cumulative narratives' or 'arch' shows (cited by Feuer, 1995, pp. 111–12). The serial itself can be further divided into those shows that are specifically engineered to run continuously and those that are designed to reach a final conclusion. So whereas a *continuous* serial such as *Dallas* (see p. 52) and *ER* (see p. 24) are commissioned to run indefinitely (see Geraghty, 1987, pp. 9–26), a *finite* or 'closed' serial such as *Prime Suspect* (see p. 22), *Murder One* (1996) and *The Sopranos* (1999) has a fixed and *limited* number of episodes that (discounting sequels) are generally intended to reach some form of closure (however loose) in the final instalment. As Sarah Kozloff puts it (1992, pp. 90–1):

Series refers to those shows whose characteristics and settings are recycled, but the story concludes in each individual episode. By contrast, in a *serial* the story and discourse do not come to a conclusion during an episode, and the threads are picked up again after an hiatus. A series is thus similar to an anthology of short stories, while a serial is like a serialized Victorian Novel. Serials can be further divided into those that do eventually end (despite the misnomer, miniseries belong in this category) and those, such as soap opera, that maybe canceled but never reach a conclusion, a new equilibrium.

Whereas the continuous or never-ending serial is frequently associated with soap opera (see p. 47), the finite serial or *mini-series* (a term originating from its heyday in 1970s America) has sometimes been linked with less 'formulaic' drama. Because of its inbuilt narrative arch, it is arguable that characters and storylines are frequently given more room to change, evolve and develop. As Patricia Holland (1997. p. 114) explains, its movement towards a

Roots

This landmark television mini-series (first shown in 1977 and subtitled *Triumph of an American Family*) began life as Alex Hayley's work of 'faction', a novel that dramatised his own family tree, tracing his Negro descendants back to Africa. In order to raise money while writing it, Hayley sold the rights to legendary television producer David Wolper, who apparently convinced him that a 'two-hour theatrical film would cut too much of the plot' (cited by Stark, 1997, p. 200). Running twelve hours long, the decision to broadcast it over eight successive nights was made as much out of caution as courage. As Wolper puts it: 'ABC was a little nervous about it so they put on all the shows in one week so if it was a disaster they'd get rid of it all in one week' (cited by Wheen, 1985, p. 152; see also Fishbein, 1983, pp. 279–80). Indeed, there was some reason for caution, as ABC's Fred Silverman later put it: 'Here's a twelve-hour story where the whites are the villains and the blacks are the heroes in a country that is 85 per cent white. It doesn't sound like a good idea at first blush' (cited by Stark, 1997, p. 200). This partly explains the inclusion of some well-known black faces such as Maya Angelou and even O.J. Simpson in the cast: an attempt to limit the alienation of white audiences.

However, the mini-series (directed by Marvin J. Chomsky, David Green and Gilbert Moses) became one of the most popular television dramas in American history, the last episode being watched by 80 million people. Although its version of history was regarded by many as dubiously sensational (see Ross, 1996, pp. 97–8), *Roots* clearly touched the guilty heart of America in its bicentennial year. Despite its complex dramatisation of various generations – beginning with Kunta Kinte (Le Var Burton) in 1700s Gambia and his horrific shipment to America; the story of his daughter Kizzy (Leslie Uggans), raped by a white plantation owner, and her son, Chicken George (Ben Vereen); finally ending with Tom Harvey's (Georg Stanford Brown) emancipation – the story proved powerfully addictive. It seemed that the intensity of the scheduling produced an almost 'soap-like' (see p. 47) familiarity with characters and events. Occasional cliffhangers also

Roots touched the guilty heart of America

kept viewers in suspense, eagerly awaiting the next dramatic installment.

In 1979, ABC aired its sequel *Roots: The Next Generation*, taking the story from the Civil War to the present day. It also inspired a whole host of other mini-series (frequently scheduled over consecutive nights), most notably *Holocaust* (1978), a four-part mini-series that controversially dramatised Hitler's extermination of the Jews. Wolper would later say that a successful mini-series should either be based on a best-selling novel, have 'sociological significance' or be a family saga (see Stark, 1997, p. 202). *Roots*, to its credit, had all three.

Glen Creeber

final resolution is 'in many ways an expansion of the creative coherence of the single play'. As a result, a 'mini-series' like *Edge of Darkness* (1985), *The Singing Detective* (1986 – see box) and *Twin Peaks* (1991 – see p. 44) have given the genre a reputation for frequently producing innovative, challenging and hugely popular drama.

As well as being considerably cheaper to produce than the single play (see p. 9), it could be argued that the mini-series more successfully exploits the fundamental dynamics of television consumption. In particular, they tend to encourage intense audience involvement through the use of multi-narrative cumulative storylines that (with the help of conventional cliffhangers) tends to bring back audiences week after week. However, like the single play, they are occasionally marketed around the name of a single writer (Lynda La Plante's *Prime Suspect* – see p. 22) or director

The Singing Detective

Originally a writer of single plays (see p. 9), Dennis Potter (1935–1994) apparently came reluctantly to the serial form. However, by the time he wrote *Pennies from Heaven* (1978), his six-part serial set in the 1930s (which famously included characters suddenly bursting (or 'lip-synching') into song), he seemed to relish the freedom and breadth of vision offered by the cumulative narrative. Eight years later, a similar sort of innovation and commitment helped produce *The Singing Detective* (1986), 'one of the major works of post-war British culture' (Caughie, 2000, pp. 27–8). Co-produced by his long-term collaborator Kenith Trodd, Potter's six-part 'mini-series' is essentially a first-person narrative, its famously convoluted storyline taking place primarily inside the head of Philip Marlow (Michael Gambon). A writer of 'cheap detective thrillers' (Stead, 1993, p. 108), Marlow is bedridden in a London hospital suffering from an acute case of psoriatic arthropathy, a debilitating skin and joint disease suffered by Potter himself (see Purser, 1981, p. 172; Fuller, 1993, pp. 12–13; Carpenter, 1998, pp. 125–6). During this enforced process of self-reflection he looks back on his life and childhood, retreats into a world of pulp fantasy, rages against an unjust universe and reluctantly endures therapy. In doing so, the serial takes the viewer on a remarkably complex psychological journey, gradually and teasingly revealing insights into his unstable, unhealthy and frequently unreliable mind.

Marlow's interior landscape is 'entertainingly' played out through a number of different and conflicting narrative levels, all competing for prominence and comprehension in his sick, acerbic and unmistakably Freudian mind (see Delaney, 1988, pp. 511–21; Lichenstein, 1990, pp. 168–72; Creeber, 1998, pp. 166–178). Hospital sitcom (see p. 23), lip-synching hallucinations, childhood flashbacks, film noir detective stories and misogynistic fantasies create a heady, extraordinary and frequently breathtaking mixture of narrative/generic techniques that finally forces him to face up to his personal demons (see Hilfer, 2000). The serial form proved to be a perfect vehicle for such a complex narrative structure, forcing audiences to come back week after week, desperate (perhaps like Marlow himself) to slowly piece together the shattered fragments of his troubled life. So unusual were many of Potter's techniques that it led some critics to define the serial as essentially 'modernist' (see Cook, 1995, p. 144; Creeber, 1996, pp. 501–8; Caughie, 2000, pp. 168–71), while others preferred to interpret it as quintessentially 'post-modern' (see Corrigan, 1991, pp. 179–93; Bondebjerg, 1992, pp. 161–80; Gras, 2000, pp. 95–108. See also 'Post-modern Drama', p. 43).

Many critics and journalists have tended to conceive

The Singing Detective: a complex psychological journey

Potter's 'serial masterpiece' (Day-Lewis, 1998, p. 24) as essentially biographical and its production as an almost solitary expression of a tortured artist (for discussion see Coward, 1987, pp. 79–87; Creeber, 1998:, pp. 11–24). However, Joost Hunningher was one of the first critics to reveal the long and collaborative process that finally brought the serial to the screen. Notoriously overlooked by commentators at the time, its director Jon Amiel not only had enormous influence on how it would finally look, but even demanded that Potter rewrite important areas of the script before shooting (Hunningher, 1993, pp. 243–5; see also Gilbert, 1995, pp. 267–72; Cook, 1995, pp. 217–22; Nelson, 1997, pp. 204–6; Carpenter, 1998, pp. 447–54). The construction of probably the most famous of all Potter scenes, the sequence when the doctors and nurses suddenly begin singing and dancing to 'Dry Bones', actually came about through intense collaboration between Amiel, Quinny Sacks (the choreographer) and Jim Clay (the designer). However, what is clear is that the final product has become a benchmark against which some critics would argue that 'quality television' is now judged. It certainly utilised all the strengths of serialisation, taking narrative, thematic and character development way beyond what Potter had produced in the past or would sadly achieve in the future.

Glen Creeber

(David Lynch's *Twin Peaks* – see p. 44), delivering the prestige of authorship seldom attributed to the series or soap opera (see p. 47). So while the series and continuous serial are often equated with the lower end of the quality divide, the mini-series has frequently (although not always) achieved a higher cultural status, sometimes compared with the serialised Victorian novel.

Not surprisingly, classic literary adaptations such as *I, Claudius* (1976*), Brideshead Revisited* (1981) and *Middlemarch* (1994) have found their natural home in the finite serial form (see 'Costume Drama', below). Such drama has frequently sold worldwide, enhancing its reputation as both an immensely popular and lucrative genre. Less prestigious but no less successful, *Rich Man, Poor Man* (directors, David Greene and Boris Sagal, 1975) was arguably television's first hit mini-series. Adapted from Irwin Shaw's 1970 blockbuster and originally shown in nine weekly instalments, it averaged 40 million viewers and won three Emmy awards. Other hugely successful adaptations of contemporary melodrama included *Bouquet of Barbed Wire* (1976), *The Thorn Birds* (1984) and *North and South* (1986). Meanwhile, adaptations of contemporary novels such as *Tinker, Tailor, Soldier, Spy* (1979), *The Lives and Loves of a She Devil* (1986) and *Lonesome Dove* (1988) have continued to win the genre both large audiences and considerable critical acclaim.

The mini-series has also proved an unusually successful genre for dramatising large historical narratives. Whereas *Days of Hope* (1975), *Edward and Mrs Simpson* (1978) and *Kennedy* (1983) took on specific historical events, others – *The Winds of War* (1983), *The Fortunes of War* (1987) and *Our Friends in the North* (1997), for example, – tended to use history as a rich and epic background (see Caldwell, 1995). In particular, a mini-series such as *Roots* (1976 – see box), *Holocaust* (1978), *Das Boot* (Germany, 1982) and *Heimat* (Germany, 1984) have sometimes been criticised for turning complex historical debates into little more than soap opera fare. In contrast, critics such as Creeber have argued that the serial's personalisation of the past creates a complex *Alltagsgeschichte* ('a history of the everyday'), providing a large and multilayered form of historical discourse rarely equalled by the single-text dynamics of either the cinema or theatre (Creeber, 2001a). Whether it resides in the form of the literary adaptation or the original screenplay, the mini-series or finite serial certainly seems to provide an important space for more complex issues and stylistic innovation than either the series or continuous serial can provide alone.

Glen Creeber

RECOMMENDED READING

Butler, Jeremy G. (1994), 'Narrative Structure: Television Stories', in Jeremy G. Butler, (ed.), *Television: Critical Methods and Applications*, Belmont: Wadsworth.

Caldwell, John Thornton (1995), 'Excessive Discourse in the Mini-Series' in John Thornton Caldwell, *Televisuality: Style, Crisis, and Authority in American Television*, New Brunswick and New Jersey: Rutgers University Press.

Feuer, Jane (1995), 'Serial Form, Melodrama, and Reaganite Ideology in Eighties TV', in Jane Feuer, *Seeing Through the Eighties: Television and Reaganism*, London: British Film Institute.

Costume Drama

Though period adaptations of historical novels have long been a tradition of British television, 'costume drama' might be seen as a more recent phenomenon. As designer Gerry Scott observes, 'BBC classic drama used to be a studio production, mainly broadcast on Sunday afternoons at children's teatime, and seen largely as being educational' (cited in *BBC Education*, 1994, p. 30 – see also 'Educational TV', p. 137). Today, costume dramas are big-budget, sumptuous productions shot on film for an audience approaching ten million in the UK alone. Though the production phenomenon seems peculiarly British, costume dramas reach a world market. Indeed, without co-production funding, the budgets required for a multipart serialisation are unlikely to be realized.

An abstract of a 'costume drama' based on a classic novel might cite dashing heroes and attractive young women, perhaps dancing in colourful costumes, and above all a love story. There would be fine houses in verdant parklands, horses and carriages, romance and ultimately a wedding. Andrew Davies's 1995 BBC adaptation of *Pride and Prejudice* ('Jane Austen Adaptations', p. 40) illustrates all of these generic characteristics. To unpack the broad, transnational appeal of contemporary costume drama is to reveal insights into the genre and the various meanings and pleasures it offers to a diverse audience.

The mainspring of costume drama is the classic English novel established in the canon of English literature. Though a canonical approach to both literature and television has been called in question, adaptations of Jane Austen, George Eliot, the Brontë sisters, Hardy, Trollope and Dickens continue to carry cultural capital. Other notable examples of the genre, for example *The Jewel in the Crown, Brideshead Revisited, Fortunes of War* (see 'The

Mini-series', p. 35) and, more recently *Gormenghast*, derive from substantial modern novels and often evoke moments of British 'greatness'. Drawing on Bourdieu's account of the aspirant new middle class (1979, translation 1992, pp. 11–18), it might be surmised that some viewers are buying into cultural capital with the greatest ease when they watch *Middlemarch* or *Pride and Prejudice* on television in preference to reading the novels. A process of popularisation might indeed account in part for the appeal of adaptations beyond a traditional high-culture audience. But this is just one way of experiencing costume drama.

Extending, in marked contrast, the pleasures of sensual luxury in the spectacular, other segments of a plural audience might delight primarily in the sumptuousness of the costumes and sets. From Richard Dyer's viewpoint (1992, p. 36), '*Fortunes of War* would have been worth it for Harriet's cardigans and tea-cups alone'. Stately homes typically provide the settings for the frocks and bonnets of costume dramas, affording wide-angle establishing shots of magnificent parks and buildings. A kind of 'star system' is evident in the casting of established actors (Michael Hordern, Robert Hardy, Michael Redgrave, Peter Jeffrey) with that peculiarly British upper-class acting style, while the new generation (Emma Thompson, Kate Winslet, Gwyneth Paltrow, Hugh Grant, Colin Firth, Alan Rickman) increasingly suffuse 'costume dramas' with a patina of the Hollywoodesque.

Narrative accessibility and followability are vital to popular television, and romance is at the heart of the central stories. With its convention of setbacks keeping the hero and heroine apart but leading ultimately to comedic resolution, the narrative code of romance has a strong drive motivating both characters and viewers. It also allows, however, for the breakdown of the story into serial-length sections with 'cliffhangers' (see 'The Mini-series', p. 35). Indeed, many of the novels were originally published in instalments, but the process of selection in adaptations for television of period novels is typically one of reduction of scope and modification of structure to suit the needs of the medium.

The inevitable selectivity in compression, and the need to shorten long narrative sections for the fast intercutting of stories in popular television's 'flexi-narrative' form (see Nelson, 1997, pp. 24 ff.), has its impact on context. Personal relationships in close-ups of domestic situations – the very stuff of television's staple dramatic mode, the soap (see p. 47) – tend to be foregrounded in costume dramas to the detriment of the broader scope of higher ideals (Dorothea's and Lydgate's aspirations to improve the world in *Middlemarch*) or of world events (the end of the British

Empire in *The Jewel in the Crown*). There is, at least, a tension between the narrative pulse of the romance code and the complications of broader historical circumstances. In television adaptations, the latter tend to be reduced merely to obstacles to the hero and heroine's consummation. This may point to a significant difference between the mediums of popular television and the Realist novel (see Dyer, 1992, pp. 36–9, and Nelson, 1997, pp. 142–8, for contrasting accounts).

Another attraction of costume dramas is their production values. This 'quality' is at once the presumed virtue of British costume drama production and of artefacts from the times past that they represent, a pre-obsolescence culture when things were made to last. For a segment of the audience, there may indeed be a richly conservative self-satisfaction at its own appreciation of things well done. As the accompanying, '*The making of . . .*' documentaries suggest, there is considerable viewer interest in the crafting of the serials themselves, in how the illusion of historical reality, the conviction of authenticity, was achieved. Some may even take pleasure in the cultural myth of 'Englishness', of tradition, stability and fair play constructed by some costume dramas. The rural sleepiness of the opening sequence of *Middlemarch* (BBC, 1994), underscored by Vaughan Williams's adaptation of Thomas Tallis, connotes an England that exists outside TV drama only in the historic imaginary. To non-Brits, particularly perhaps Americans and Australians who form the substantial part of the anglophone overseas television market, period costume dramas may appear to tap into deep history. That what they offer is constructs for cultural consumption, however, is evidenced in the need for clean fingernails for the American market (see Nelson, 1997, p. 150).

In sum, costume dramas today differ from their children's serial predecessors in pursuing less a commitment to fidelity to the instigating novel (*werktreue*, as the Germans put it), or to the historical circumstances in which it is set, than an attractive heritage package of signifiers. Freed from denotational responsibility, other than to construct an internally convincing world, production teams may broaden the appeal to build a large audience conceived not as a mass but as a post-modern conflation of microcultures (see 'Post-modern Drama', p. 43). The hybrid of traditional narrative romance form and heritage splendour perhaps accounts for the effusion of costume dramas in the mid-1990s and their undoubted success.

Robin Nelson

Jane Austen Adaptations

There have been numerous televisual and cinematic adaptations of Jane Austen's novels over the years, but in 1995/6 alone there were *Pride and Prejudice*, *Persuasion*, *Sense and Sensibility* and two versions of *Emma*. Austen's work patently resonated somehow with the 1990s but, in the market context noted, television adaptations can appeal on different grounds to a range of readers.

Austen adaptations are not identical. They range from the 'mannered watercolour prettiness of the Lee/Thompson *Sense and Sensibility*' (Matthews, 1996, p. 40) to 'Roger Michell's social realist *Persuasion*' (Fuller, 1996, p. 21). The extent to which a book's characteristics determine the nature of the adaptation is evidently as variable as those credited for the outcome (see Giddings, 1990). Although the process of adaptation is ultimately a collective one steered perhaps by the producer, director and screen playwright, television has historically credited the writer. But writers vary. Fay Weldon's 1970 television version of *Pride and Prejudice* (director Jonathan Powell), though scrupulously faithful to the book, lacks the verve and visual style that Andrew Davies (BBC, 1995) aimed to capture.

To Davies, *Pride and Prejudice*'s narrative structure needed just minor modification to lend televisual shape with episode 'cliffhangers'. The novel contains much well-crafted dialogue requiring only editing for the screen. The real challenge was catching Jane Austen's famous 'ironic style': the authorial voice must somehow be transposed into images and sounds. Davies adds a number of small but significant scenes to give access to everyday vitality beneath social form. The younger Bennet girls are frequently heard bickering. In Part 2, Lydia *en déshabillé* collides on the landing with the ponderous Mr Collins to peals of off-screen laughter. Davies delights in visualising an ironic gap between the surface manners of polite society and the animated bustle beneath. When, in Part 6, Bingley arrives at Longbourn finally to propose to Jane, all the girls hurry to dress. This highly energised scene (pulsed by Colin Davis's theme tune soundtrack that seems successfully to combine Mozart with the Keystone Cops) cuts a moment later to the drawing room where a particularly stilted exchange of pleasantries marks the ironic contrast.

Directed by Simon Langton, another feature of this adaptation involves the humanising, if not sexualising, of the otherwise formal Mr Darcy. Davies was aware (see BBC, 1995) that for the first half of the novel, its romantic hero seems an overwhelmingly proud man, partly because his image is mediated through Elizabeth Bennet's prejudice. To soften this image and make Darcy (played with an increasingly smouldering sensuality by Colin Firth) more attractive to viewers, Davies scripts brief scenes of him taking a bath (Part 1),

fencing (Part 4) and finally emerging after an impromptu dip in the pond on his return to Pemberley (Part 4). Some Austen purists resent any additions to the novel, but the above are genuine transpositions, of authorial tone in the first instance, and narrative followability on television in the second. Where the production overall evidences a commercial disposition to heritage splendour is in the treatment of material wealth itself.

In the novel, Jane Austen is interested in clothes and houses only as markers of status. Descriptions of both are remarkably limited and confined to characters the novel invites us to ridicule. Mr Collins is satirised for telling everybody of the £800 fireplace and sixty-four windows at Lady Catherine de Bourgh's Rosings Park. Preoccupation with bonnets and costume materials is part of the prattle of Mrs Bennet and her sillier daughters, Kitty and Lydia. In Davies/Langton's televisual 'costume drama', however, all material texture is captured by the camera from the embroidered peach silk folds of the titles' backdrop to the virtual catwalks of the balls and drawing rooms.

'Costume drama' treats the revelation of buildings as a dimension of narrative suspense. Though Davies's *Pride and Prejudice* opens with Bingley and Darcy riding to view Netherfield, viewers are not afforded a full-frontal mid-shot until Mrs Bennet arrives to fetch Jane home from her convalescence there (late Part 1). In the interim even the 'modest' Longbourn, home of the Bennets, looks like something from *Homes and Gardens*. In Part 3, we move up the stately home league to the grandeur of Lady Catherine's Rosings Park, shot from a number of angles. The best, Darcy's mansion, is kept to last. The audience finally sees the much-vaunted Pemberley with Elizabeth Bennet in Part 4 as her aunt's carriage sweeps up the drive and she is smitten by the panorama of the house across the lake.

Romance, however, remains the heart of the matter, but in this mid-1990s TV 'costume drama', a modern sexual chemistry is required to be anachronistically displayed through casting, costuming, location and cinematography. The décolletage revealing Jennifer Ehle's ample bosom as Elizabeth Bennett in *Pride and Prejudice* has more perhaps to do with the anticipated viewing pleasures of a heterosexual male segment of the contemporary audience than Regency English manners. Likewise, Firth/Darcy's dip in the lake had a strong appeal to heterosexual women.

In the final close-up, freeze frame on the Darcy/Elizabeth kiss as the open wedding carriage takes them to their narrative destiny, it may even be that Davies and the production team capture something of Jane Austen's irony. A viewer disposed to romance might exhale a deep sigh of satisfaction; while a postmodern reader (see p. 43) might delight in the ironic play with a worn romantic trope (see BBC, 1995).   *Robin Nelson*

RECOMMENDED READING

BBC Education (1994), *Middlemarch: A Viewer's Guide*, London: BBC Education.

Dyer, Richard (1992), *Only Entertainment*, London: Routledge.

Nelson, Robin (1997), *TV Drama in Transition: Forms, Values and Cultural Change*, London: Macmillan.

The Teen Series

The teenage audience has been increasingly important to the film industry since the 1950s, and programming aimed at a teenage audience occupies a growing sector of the television schedules. There is a significant history of programming featuring and addressing teenagers and teenageness in the anglophone television landscape, beginning with the introduction of television pop music coverage. In the British context this strand of programming in the 1950s played an important part in offering breadth of provision with shows such as *Oh Boy!* (ITV, 1958–9) and *Six-Five Special* (BBC, 1957–9), and has continued to occupy a significant place in British broadcasting. In the United States, *The Monkees* (US, 1966–8) was an interesting precursor of contemporary teen television series. A thirty-minute crossover pop music/sitcom inspired by the Beatles' *Hard Day's Night* (Richard Lester, 1964), *The Monkees* centred on the band's comic antics, and combined adventure and showcase musical performances with an energetic visual style. This hybrid pop/sitcom format was reworked in the 1990s, in UK–US co-productions centring on the adventures of British pop band S Club 7 (*Miami 7* (UK, 1999); *LA 7* (USA, 2000); *S Club 7: Artistic Differences* (UK, 2000)) (see 'Music Television', p. 89).

Situation comedies, particularly those centred on family relationships, have frequently featured teenagers, such as *The Brady Bunch* (US, 1969–74) and *The Partridge Family* (US, 1970–4). The teen sitcom centred on the lives, loves and adventures of teenage characters and directly addressed to a younger teenage audience, however, has been a significant form of teen television programming since the 1980s. The popular series *Saved by the Bell* (US, 1989–93) followed six archetypal teen characters familiar from successful early 80s teenpics like *The Breakfast Club* (John Hughes, 1985) – the preppy type, the jock, the nerd, the fashion queen, the cheerleader, the A-grade student – through high school, and in later seasons (*Saved by the Bell: The College Years* (1993–); *Saved by the Bell: Wedding in Las Vegas* (1994)) into college and marriage. Recently, the teen sitcom has become a primary form of television teen pro-

gramming, with series set primarily in the high school and/or the family home, such as *California Dreams* (1992–7), *Boy Meets World* (US, 1993–2000), *Sweet Valley High* (1994), *The Secret World of Alice Mack* (US, 1994–8), *Sister, Sister* (US, 1994–9), *Sabrina the Teenage Witch* (US, 1996) and *Malibu* (US, 1998), forming the basis of narrowcasting for a young teenage audience on satellite, cable and digital through channels like the US-based Nickelodeon and the UK's Trouble TV (see 'Situation Comedy' p. 61).

Soap opera has increasingly revolved around teenage characters and is a significant context for understanding the development of contemporary teen drama. Popular Australian soaps *Neighbours* (1985–) and *Home and Away* (1988–) have always prominently featured teenage characters, and British soaps *Coronation Street* (1960–), *Brookside* (1982–) and *EastEnders* (1985–) have increasingly highlighted teen issues including truancy, pregnancy and drug addiction in their address to the everyday conflicts of family and community. More recently, Channel 4's early-evening teen soap *Hollyoaks* (UK, 1995–) has taken its place alongside the American teen fare (for example, *Malibu*, *Dawson's Creek*) offered on the channel's Sunday morning teen slot T4. *Melrose Place* (US, 1992–9) began as a spin-off from popular teen drama *Beverly Hills 90210* (US, 1999–2000) (see the chapter entitled 'Soap Opera', p. 47).

CONTEMPORARY TEEN DRAMA

With these precursors and companions, the quality teen television drama series appeared, developed and flourished in the 1990s, which have also seen a vigorous return of the teen film with movies such as *Clueless* (Amy Heckerling, 1995), *She's All That* (Robert Iscove, 1999), *10 Things I Hate About You* (Gil Junger, 1999), *Cruel Intentions* (Roger Kumble, 1999). Key shows have been *Beverly Hills 90210*, *Party of Five* (US, 1994–2000), *My So-Called Life* (1994–5), *Heartbreak High* (Aus., 1994–9), *Buffy the Vampire Slayer* (Fox, 1997–), *Dawson's Creek* (Warner Bros., 1998–), *Charmed* (US, 1998–), *Buffy* spin-off *Angel* (US, 1999–), *Popular* (US, 1999–) and *Roswell High* (US, 1999–).

Some contemporary teen drama, though sometimes introducing and resolving a plot line in a single forty-five- to sixty-minute episode, can be understood in relation to the long-running serial form in their emphasis on repetition and deferral of resolution, and in this respect are close to soap opera in narrative organisation (see p. 47). At the imaginative centre of the teen drama, as in soap, are place, character and relationships, and emotional drama is often heightened through the use of close-up and (generally

Buffy the Vampire Slayer

With the articulate dialogue and playful irony characteristic of
1990s teen dramas such as *Dawson's Creek* (Warner Bros.,
1998) and *Clueless* (UPN, 1996-9), *Buffy the Vampire Slayer*
(Fox/Kuzui/Sandollar/Mutant Enemy, 1997–) depicts its
eponymous heroine as she struggles to juggle her sacred
birthright as a demon-slayer and the everyday demands of
adolescent life. Assisted by her friends Willow (Alyson
Hannigan) and Xander (Nicholas Brendon), and Giles
(Anthony Stewart Head), her 'Watcher', Buffy (Sarah Michelle
Gellar) encounters a different demonic foe each week, defeat-
ing them with a combination of archaic investigation, high-
school savvy and impressive fighting skills. These
single-episode storylines act as metaphors for the 'real' anxieties of *Buffy*'s teen protagonists, and are integrated into a
continuous narrative that follows them from high school to
college (in the fourth season) as they gain sexual awareness
and increasing freedom from parental and institutional authority.

A spin-off from the film of the same title (Fran Rubel
Kuzui, 1992), *Buffy the Vampire Slayer* was produced as part of
the Warner Bros. network's move into prime-time hour-long
drama, helping to solidify its signature as the 'family' network
(De Moras, 1997, p. 11) with a strong teen appeal. As such it
reflects the American networks' growing interest over the
1990s in the adolescent market as a valuable niche demographic. This appeal to a teen audience is combined with the
high production values associated with quality prime-time
television. The series' sophisticated scripts address with wit
and sincerity the enormity of growing up in contemporary
America, complemented by a glossy visual style, fluid camerawork and artistically choreographed fight sequences.

Much of the series' drama (and comedy) stems from the
incongruity of Buffy's position, as she wisecracks her way
through fights with vampires twice her size while dressed in
heels and a party dress. Her concern that she will ruin her hair
or break a nail is combined with a painful awareness of the
responsibilities and dangers of her powerful position. As such,
Buffy the Vampire Slayer combines the female address of earlier
series such as *Bewitched* (ABC, 1964–72) and *I Dream of
Jeannie* (NBC, 1965–70) that attempted to explore the social

Buffy the Vampire Slayer: dealing with adolescent anxieties

contradictions for 'powerful' women through the introduction
of fantasy into the domestic sphere (Spigel, 1991), with the
potentially titillating representation of highly feminised action
heroes in series like *Charlie's Angels* (ABC, 1976–81) and
Wonder Woman (ABC, 1976–7; CBS, 1977–9).

While *Buffy* provides men with a position from which
they 'can safely indulge the male fantasy of the dominatrix
and combine it with the Lolita fixation' (Forest, 1998, p. 6),
it also 'offers transgressive possibilities for re-imagining gendered relations and modernist American ideologies' (Owen,
1999, p. 24). Broadly post-feminist in its address, the series
attempts to create spaces in which women can be powerful,
vulnerable and feminine, and to explore the consequences of
this regendering for traditional masculine roles. In its self-
conscious and playful inversion of the conventions of the
horror genre, *Buffy the Vampire Slayer* engages with a perceived crisis both in gendered relationships and in the place
of the adolescent in contemporary American society.

Catherine Johnson

romantic pop) scoring (for example, *My So-Called Life* and
Dawson's Creek), further pointing to the melodramatic
nature of the genre. In these respects, teen drama can be
considered usefully in relation to quality American prime-
time soaps such as *Dallas* (US, 1978–91) and *Dynasty* (US,

1981–9), the address having shifted to a teenage audience
(see the chapter entitled 'Soap Opera', p. 47). Teenageness is
a significant 'in-between' period, and teen drama deals with
the stuff of adolescent anxiety: friendship, love, sex and
impending adulthood.

Many of these shows deal with questions of difference, otherness, increased power and the impact of these on personal and community relationships: a significant number of them draw on other cult television forms, using supernatural power as a motif through which to explore these concerns. Many shows give the sense that to be a teenager is to be not quite human. In *Charmed* (characters in their twenties, but addressing the teen audience), the Halliwell sisters discover that they have inherited the power of witchcraft (as does Sabrina Spellman in *Sabrina the Teenage Witch*); cheerleader Buffy Summers discovers that she is 'the chosen one' in *Buffy the Vampire Slayer*, and four of the main characters are teenage human/alien hybrids (see box).

Dawson's Creek, created and written by Kevin Williamson, has been particularly successful, and at the time of writing the show is in its fourth season. Williamson has been responsible for a number of playfully self-conscious and intertextual teenpics of the 1990s, writing *Scream* (Wes Craven, 1996), *Scream 2* (Wes Craven, 1997), the characters in *Scream 3* (Wes Craven, 2000), the screenplays for *The Faculty* (Robert Rodriguez, 1998) and *I Know What You Did last Summer* (1997), and writing and directing *Teaching Mrs Tingle* (1999). *Dawson's Creek*, similarly, has featured episodes based on *The Breakfast Club*, *Risky Business* (Paul Brickman, 1983), *The Blair Witch Project* (Daniel Myrick and Eduardo Sánchez, 1999) and *The Perfect Storm* (Wolfgang Petersen, 2000), and is highly self-referential with characters discussing the melodramatic plot-lines and elevated, analytical dialogue that characterise their lives in Capeside, Massachusetts. In its combination of self-consciousness and intense emotionality, *Dawson's Creek*, like many teen television dramas, offers a broad address in which both engagement with the melodramatic/emotional and knowing distance can be accommodated. Given the intense nostalgia that surrounds the teenager and teenageness in contemporary culture, the audience for the teen drama may exceed the teenage years. What is certain, though, is that the teenager remains profoundly American.

Rachel Moseley

RECOMMENDED READING

Felperin, Leslie (1999) 'Genre: Teenpics', in P. Cook and M. Bernink (eds) *The Cinema Book* (2nd edn), London: British Film Institute.

Owen, Susan A. (1999), '*Buffy the Vampire Slayer*: Vampires, Postmodernity and Postfeminism', *Journal of Popular Film and Television*, 27(2).

Spigel, Lynn (1991), 'From Domestic Space to Outer Space: The 1960s Fantastic Family Sitcom', in Constance Penley et al. (eds), *Close Encounters: Film, Feminism, and Science Fiction*, Minneapolis: University of Minneapolis Press.

Post-modern Drama

Post-modern television drama is almost the antithesis of naturalism. Whereas naturalistic drama tends to offer an authentic-looking impression of social events in a style that seems to show the inevitable consequences of certain actions, post-modern drama adopts Lyotard's scepticism towards the 'master-narratives', which make such conclusions seem inevitable. The major world views such as Marxism or Christianity, which offer comprehensive explanations of social change, are rejected by post-modern thinkers who tend not to believe in 'final truths' and prefer to think of reality as endlessly open to further interpretation. Thus post-modern drama tends to reject historical authenticity, mixes styles and genres of television using the technique of *bricolage*, and even draws attention to its own constructedness like Brechtian theatre in order to frustrate the temptation to derive meaning from an open text (see Nelson, 1997, pp. 235–48).

Post-modernism is founded on the belief that signs are arbitrary and that their conventional meanings can always be abandoned and substituted. Genres are, therefore, no longer stable and can be continually reinterpreted. Hence, the value of post-modern drama is a matter of intense debate. For Baudrillard (1988), post-modern phenomena such as drama have become an interplay of simulacra, or signs that mimic reality and yield no profound meaning, but for others such as Linda Hutcheon (1989) the post-modern dissolution of conventional meanings is a politically progressive gesture. Hutcheon argues that in deconstructing conventional wisdom such as that found in naturalism, mythologies are exposed and their influence is overcome. In post-modern drama, however, the act of deconstruction calls for a considerable effort on the part of the viewer, who has to find meanings in texts that aim to be inscrutable.

The first generation of television dramatists who could be labelled post-modern were the playwrights who belonged to what Martin Esslin (1961) labelled the 'Theatre of the Absurd'. The absurdist tradition is one where drama shows the world to be devoid of dependable values and seeks what little consolation can be found. Samuel Beckett, whose play *Waiting for Godot* is sometimes identified as a founding text of post-modernism, wrote drama for

Twin Peaks

In his essay 'The Author as Producer', Walter Benjamin (1977) wrote that 'The revolutionary strength of Dadaism consisted in testing art for its authenticity.' *Twin Peaks* (1989) has generally been seen as a post-modern drama that at its most effective compels viewers to re-evaluate traditional genres using techniques that are often as bizarre as Dadaism. Masterminded by the film director David Lynch (although he actually only directed five episodes and co-wrote four with its principal writer Mark Frost), the series mixes the detective genre and the mythical quest with elements of soap opera (see p. 47) and other genres to create a bewildering, intertextual parody of them all which quickly achieved cult status. As David Lavery puts it (1995, pp. 6–7):

> *Twin Peaks* seems generated from, spun out of (cloned from?) precedent texts and thus cultic in origin, authority and appeal. A large part of the series' appeal to aficionados . . . was tracking its intertextual, allusionary quotations: the many actors and actresses reborn from the never-never land of old TV and movies, the red herring evocations of old movies, allusions to previous Lynch films, numerous inside jokes, cameos by Lynch (as Gordon Cole), Frost (as a newscaster in the first episode of the second season), and even Lynch's son Austin (as Mrs Tremond's magical grandson, Pierre). These and many other facets of *Twin Peaks* invited fanatic, cultic participation, generating discourse about discourse.

As this suggests, its convoluted narrative presents the most unexpected developments for viewers familiar with traditional genres. When FBI agent Dale Cooper (Kyle MacLachlan) investigates the death of Laura Palmer (Sheryl Lee) in the town of Twin Peaks, he resorts to dreams and intuitive methods of detection borrowed from Tibetan Buddhism. The abandonment of the hypothetical and deductive reasoning that is a necessary feature of the detective genre is the source of much of the drama's humour, but may also contain serious elements. The other characters, for instance, fail to register surprise at these bizarre events and the drama itself has a dream-like quality, heightened by its slow pace, its hypnotic music and its

Twin Peaks subverted traditional genres

sometimes startling images. Sub-plots that offer red herrings multiply confusingly.

Unlike detective drama, however, the solution of Laura's murder (which we are not given a fair chance to guess at until halfway through), does not conclude the narrative. A deeper underlying struggle with evil (which appears to have transmigrated from one character to another in a reversal of Buddhist philosophy) continues and Cooper has to save his lover Annie (Heather Graham) from the Red Room, where some of the coded warnings he has received from Laura and others in dreams suggest that he is really battling an omnipresent evil. Motive has little meaning for the bizarre extremes of personality that are encountered here. The warnings hinted at by, among others, the Log Lady (Catherine Coulson), who introduced the series with gnomic statements to help us 'read' the text, suggest that the search for human motives may not only be fruitless but also extremely dangerous.

The Red Room promises to hold the key to the mysterious events, but here Cooper may discover that, as the Log Lady says, 'all the characters in a dream may be yourself'. Cooper's former partner turned murderer, Windon Earle (Kenneth Welsh), may therefore possess Cooper himself in a way that turns the Red Room into a psychoanalytic (re)enactment. When Josie is killed, 'Coop' is taunted by a non-realistic vision of Bob (Frank Silva). If the viewer is also implicated and equally unable to stand apart from his or her own deep involvement in the action, the notion of truth itself is questioned and the conclusive revelations of other drama series may seem far too glib in comparison.   *Adrian Page*

television in the 1960s and 1970s such as *Eh, Joe* (1966) and *Ghost Trio* (1977). These characteristically bleak and difficult dramas display the futility of human expectations in a world that cannot promise any ultimate fulfilment.

The absurdist tradition was taken up in the 1960s cult television series *The Prisoner* (1967–8), starring and directed by Patrick McGoohan. Here a secret agent is about to resign when he is abducted and finds himself a prisoner

Ally McBeal

Ally McBeal has been dubbed a 'dramedy' since it is a genre
hybrid embracing aspects of sitcom (see p. 65), soap opera
(see p. 47), courtroom drama and MTV (see p. 91). Its narrative structure, however, is relatively conventional among
series–serial hybrids. Ongoing stories of the interrelationships
between the partners in the Fishman & Cage law firm are
intercut with episode-contained lawsuit cases undertaken by
one or more of the partners. Typically, however, the courtroom dramas address a topical social issue from an unusual
angle, subverting (on many occasions inverting) dominant
social values. 'Silver Bells', for example, advocates the legitimacy of a *ménage à trois,* a new model perhaps for the
American family. In another episode, Fish vigorously defends
the case of a female litigant charging harassment against her
boss because he had seduced all the women in the office
except her. The main characters are themselves idiosyncratic.
Beneath the opulent veneer of their legal practice, Cage's lack
of confidence is manifest in several nervous tics and Fish has a
shoe fetish.

A range of compositional devices prevents viewers from
believing too deeply in the fictional world, opening up spaces
with critical potential. Taken as sign, Ally McBeal (Calista
Flockhart) is herself double-coded, at once an independent
professional woman in charge of her destiny and a vulnerable,
waif-like figure waiting for 'Mr Right' to come along. The play
of these two images (and the divided response it has generated
from feminists and post-feminists) suggests a productive tension. By exaggerating glamorous character types familiar in
American television, and by parodying familiar televisual
tropes, *Ally McBeal* draws attention to its compositional principles and exploits the double-coded post-modern irony of
simultaneous affirmation and subversion. Digital technologies
serve to break the frame by visually distorting the physical
world. Ally's tongue pokes out and extends grossly when she
dislikes somebody. Advised to 'think lips' when she needs to be
romantically confident, Ally puckers her lips till they expand
fleshily with a pink lipgloss.

Additional appeal to the 'now' generation is made by use of
popular music. Vonda Shepherd features regularly in the bar
where each episode ends up below the Fish & Cage family
home–workplace. But the music is used in interesting ways. At

Ally McBeal combined elements of the sitcom, soap opera and
MTV

times, it marks a dramatic moment, not so much by under-
scoring but by musical mood and lyric offering a counterpoint.
On other occasions, music is used directly to comment on the
action. Ally, and some of the other main characters such as
Cage, have their own private theme song. On advice from her
psychoanalyst (Tracey Ullman), Ally thinks Gladys Knight and
the Pips when she needs a boost of confidence, and they duly
appear digitised on screen as if both in and out of her head.
Thus the use of music expressionistically to articulate a character's interior thoughts and feeling has a new take.

The overall result is a multilayered, self-conscious post-
modern text. Its multi-tracked *bricolage* of televisual and
musical styles affords a range of sheer pleasures to be taken.
But it also offers a provocation seriously to consider contemporary social issues by transgressing normative codes to disturb traditional sureties and invite quizzical – if not outright
oppositional – readings (see Nelson, 2000).

Robin Nelson

in a mysterious village where every attempt is made to
encourage him to surrender his autonomy and conform.
The series tested the idea that the human spirit could resist
the futuristic scenario where social control had reached its

ultimate technological perfection. All efforts by the prisoner to discover the identity of Number One, the supreme
controller of the Village, are unsuccessful until finally he
appears to discover that *he* is Number One. The issue of

whether social control is maintained by coercion or by our own consciousness remains open and relevant in the final episode. Chris Gregory (1997) traces strong similarities between these early dramas, *The Prisoner* and *Twin Peaks* (see box, p. 44).

Such an interpretation of *The Prisoner*, however, runs the risk of sounding more like a *modernist* reading of the series, since it still seems to hold out the prospect of making sense of the world we know. To be truly post-modern, television drama must suggest multiple ironic readings, which undermine the stability of all our contemporary certainties. Thus, rather than categorising a specific set of dramas as post-modern, it may be more appropriate to trace the post-modern tendency of familiar genres to invite alternative readings. Dominic Strinati (1995), for example, has argued that the 1980s cop series *Miami Vice* is 'post-modern' because it drew attention to the aspects of popular culture of which it was composed. John Caughie (2000, p. 164) has also argued that the mode of irony he calls 'suspensive' is found in post-modern drama, where 'a radical vision of multiplicity, randomness, contingency and even absurdity, abandons the quest for paradise altogether'.

Post-modernism also tends to dissolve the distinction between 'popular' and 'highbrow' genres. In particular, post-modern drama often involves a central character's quest for truth in a world saturated with 'semiotic excess' (Collins, 1992, p. 331). In *Northern Exposure* (1990–5), for instance, allusions to 'high' art, literature and philosophy are frequently mixed with everyday references to television, Hollywood movies and pop music. Joel Fleischmann (Rob Morrow) may dream of a failed love affair in terms of 'old black-and-white Hollywood films' (ibid., p. 332), but he also 'encounters' great figures of the twentieth century such as the founder of modern psychoanalysis, Sigmund Freud. In one heated debate, Freud even dismisses criticism of his doctrines with the ironic sentence, 'It's only a theory.' In this way, *Northern Exposure* creates comedy from the paradoxes that a search for authenticity leads to in a post-modern environment. As Jim Collins has pointed out, following Umberto Eco's ideas, the post-modern sign is 'always already said' (ibid., p. 333). The sign that is reused must be quoted knowingly in order to endow it with additional meaning.

However, *Northern Exposure* may also be an example of what Fredric Jameson (1993) argues is post-modernism's assimilation by capitalism. The endlessly unfolding questions may represent no more than an infinitely extendable 'product' whose lack of closure simply ensures continued audiences and increased revenue. Phillip Hayward (1990) suggests that this might be particularly true of a series like *Moonlighting*:

> Instead of dreams of radical, analytically deconstructive television the media mutation of the late Eighties has followed hot on the prophecy of theory and witnessed an eclectic pillaging of once esoteric formal devices, pressing them into forms of popular cultural bricolage glacially unconcerned with niceties of radical schools or purist debates. *Moonlighting*'s strength, originality and challenge to aspects of avant-garde (and/or alternative) media practice is in its subtle intertextualities and formal devices being produced for a popular TV audience, within its paradigms and with none of the cares of the avant-garde and no allegiance to any movement or practice beyond that of populism. (Hayward, 1990, p. 226; also cited by Feuer, 1995, p. 101)

The virtue of this, if there is one, may be that, as Robin Nelson (1997) suggests, the viewer can come to terms with the way that media culture constitutes its own subjectivities, or it may be that the post-modern simply encourages indulgence in the pleasure of freedom from inherited categories.

Adrian Page

RECOMMENDED READING

Collins, Jim (1992), 'Postmodernism and Television', in Robert C. Allen (ed.), *Channels of Discourse, Reassembled*, London and New York: Routledge.

Lavery, David (ed.) (1994), *Full of Secrets: Critical Approaches to 'Twin Peaks'*, Detroit: Wayne State University Press.

Nelson, Robin (1997), 'Coda – Critical Postmodernism: Critical Realism', in Robin Nelson, *TV Drama in Transition: Forms, Values and Cultural Change*, London: Macmillan.

SOAP OPERA

Studying Soap Opera

What is soap opera? What are its distinctive features as a narrative system and a way of addressing the viewer? The name itself gives us some clues. 'Soap' marks the genre's commercial origins. It refers to the fact that the format emerged from the radio sponsorship by detergent companies in 1930s radio; indeed, the immense popularity of the soap opera in the 1940s means that it must be viewed as a central force in the rise of broadcasting as a commercial institution. 'Opera' is a clue to the kinds of judgements often made about this genre, as well as an indication of its characteristic emotions, plots and performance styles. The word served as a way of ridiculing the high-blown sentiments of the programmes and their female audience signalling a vulgar taste for overdramatic excess. The term 'soap opera' thus communicates something of the cultural and economic status historically assigned to this particular genre, a status we need to take into account when we study it. Yet even though the formal characteristics of the genre and the institutional conception of its spectator stem from this consumer cultural framework, the uses of soap opera for both viewers and for media scholars extend into broader territory, as we shall see.

Soap opera is, most basically, serialised narrative in broadcasting. Definitions of soap opera's specific formal characteristics vary in scope and emphasis, but they generally share some core features. To begin with, all in one way or another centre on the concept of seriality. Seriality is a narrative structure that spans multiple media and storytelling genres. Its core feature is the distinctive packaging of the experience of fiction over an extended period of time, in segments; all serial narratives thus involve some form of interruption in the flow of the story. The serial form is closely aligned with the rise of fiction as a commodity form. It achieved ascendancy in the nineteenth century in England and America with the growth of a mass market for novels and magazines (Hayward, 1997; also see 'The Mini-series', p. 35).

As Jennifer Wicke notes in a study of Anglo-American consumer culture and literature in this period, the scheduled structure of the serial narrative, as a commodity and as a space for commercial speech, encouraged a close, readerly attention. Its regularised forms of interruption

and continuity rewarded readers who maintained an ongoing engagement with the text and its advertising inserts (Wicke, 1988, pp. 35, 51). The mass-market institutionalisation of serial fiction extended from magazines to motion pictures with the emergence of popular film serials in the early twentieth century. In this period the identification of serial fiction with women audiences was solidified, as ongoing film serials like *The Perils of Pauline* were actively marketed to young women consumers (Stamp, 2000).

By the time broadcasting came along, the commercial and textual conditions of serial narrative as a form directed towards a female audience were already largely in place. Radio, however, extended this narrative's reach, allowing serial drama to integrate itself into the rhythms and routines of the home and the (specifically female) labour associated with it. As a broadcast, domestic form, soap opera thus has some specific characteristics. Muriel Cantor and Suzanne Pingree note that seriality proliferates and expands in the broadcast versions of soap opera. The daily, decades-old soap opera narratives that appear today on American daytime television include characteristics such as 'competing and intertwining plot-lines', each developing at an independent pace and forestalling any final resolution of conflict: 'The completion of one story generally leads into others, and ongoing plots often incorporate parts of semi-resolved conflicts' (Cantor and Pingree, 1983, p. 22). A long history of feuds and alliances between characters establishes a deep 'backstory' for all ongoing arcs at any moment in soap opera, and makes dramatic reversals, revelations, and emotional reorientations a constant element of soap opera plotting. Built-in pedagogical structures of redundancy and summary ensure that fans who are at different levels of familiarity with the action and character relations may find a point of engagement. In addition, American soap opera narrative, particularly on daytime television, tends to focus on particular communities and family groups. Over the course of a show's run, the drama, emotion and intrigue that unfolds in these settings seems to happen at seemingly the same pace as the everyday life of the viewer.

Cantor and Pingree define the soap opera quite narrowly, restricting their definition (and the extreme form of seriality included in it) to the daytime soaps that air in five-day instalments on American television. However, soap is perhaps more accurately perceived as a flexible and adaptable narrative form, capable of many kinds of variation across temporal and national contexts (Feuer, 1994, p. 552). Prime-time soap operas such as *Dallas* (see box) or *Dynasty* are also serials, but their weekly schedules, more closely governed by the seasonal structure of the prime-time TV schedule in America, mean that they embody a different set of serial conventions. Indeed, as Jane Feuer has pointed out, over the course of the 1970s American prime-time television moved increasingly towards serial rather than episodic forms of narrative (Feuer, 1992). A series like *Melrose Place* (which refers in its title to one of the first prime-time soap operas, *Peyton Place*) might legitimately be called a prime-time soap opera in the tradition of *Dynasty*, *Dallas* and *Falcon Crest*. Yet at the same time it is important to point out that the serial plotting devices (cliffhangers, characterological reversals and last-minute plot twists) that link *Melrose Place* to these earlier forms are also increasingly characteristic of other forms of prime-time drama, from *LA Law* to *Chicago Hope* (see 'Hospital Drama', p. 23) to *NYPD Blue* (see 'The Police Series', p. 19).

These American examples should not obscure the fact that the conditions of seriality and the history of soap opera shift from one national context to another. In the UK, where commercial broadcasting did not exist until the mid-1950s, soap opera developed relatively late. BBC drama director Val Gielgud considered serial drama vulgar and opposed its production. It was not until after the war and the programme *Mrs Dale's Diary* that serial narrative entered British radio. It is somewhat ironic, in this light, that whereas radio soap opera died out in the early 1960s in the United States, replaced by daytime serial

Peyton Place: a place for melodrama in the prime-time schedule

drama on television, it continues in England – the popular programme *The Archers*, aired first in 1951 as a form of public education for the Ministry of Agriculture, maintains a devoted following of listeners to this day. Nor should the American origins of the genre prevent us from noting that definitions of soap opera themselves vary from one country to another. Whereas in America soap opera is a term associated primarily with daily daytime serials, in other countries programmes designated as 'soap operas' may air once a week, several times a week, or daily and at different times of day. Some, like the long-running British soap *Coronation Street*, might have started out as weekly or biweekly programmes but now broadcast more frequently as a result of changing institutional relations between advertisers, broadcasters, and other programming sectors.

However, one aspect of soap opera does seem consistent across national boundaries, and that is its historical association with female spectatorship. Soap opera's narrative characteristics and institutional forms are deeply rooted in a particular, and most certainly *gendered*, cultural history of the home as a target of consumer address. In the early 1930s, when the soap opera format first took shape, major transformations in consumer culture were in process. Alongside commercial radio came the rise of brand names, the increase in advertising and, by the late 1920s, the recognition of household markets dominated by female consumers – a recognition signalled in the titles of books such as Christine Frederick's 1929 marketing classic *Selling Mrs Consumer*. At the beginning of the next decade, radio became increasingly identified with female markets. Robert C. Allen (1985, p. 107) cites a 1932 study that found that 'the housewife in a majority of cases is the member of the family who has the most influence upon family purchases and is the one who spends the greatest amount of time in the home. She is therefore, the member of the family most easily reached by radio broadcasts.' Although it has attracted viewers from a range of demographics throughout its history, the image of the soap opera as a 'women's genre' persists to this day. As Laura Stempel Mumford points out, this persistence does not tell us much about 'actual' audiences, but it does call attention to the fact that soap opera narratives require of the viewer 'a set of knowledge and skills normally associated with women in patriarchal culture' (Mumford, 1995, p. 45).

Perhaps because of the perception of its audience as female, soap opera was also an early and important space for women and writers in American broadcasting. *Painted Dreams*, written by Irna Phillips, is generally described as the first soap (Allen, 1985, pp. 110–16). It aired locally, on a

Chicago radio station, but its popularity and the success of both Phillips and her protégés led to more and more serials for women. By the 1940s, soap operas were the dominant form of radio programming. As Michelle Hilmes and Ellen Seiter have shown, Phillips battled critics constantly. In her professional writings, Hilmes notes, Phillips 'tried to draw the serial back into the mainstream of radio practice and to reveal the falseness of the dichotomy between daytime/female audiences and nighttime/masculine ones so carefully drawn by the industry' (Hilmes, 1997, p. 157). Phillips's success was also the occasion for criticism; her career was marked by a constant battle with the characterisation of her work as 'unrealistic' and 'melodramatic'. As Allen points out, the cultural devaluation attached to soap opera in its heyday echoed a nineteenth-century conception of female authorship, voiced in Nathaniel Hawthorne's disparaging caricature of women authors as a 'damned mob of scribbling women' (Allen, 1985, pp. 140–1.) Furthermore, Hilmes points out, the institutional recognition of women both as a buying power and as authors of daytime programming had a double edge. In practice, it meant that women would be figured in radio's programming practices *primarily* as targets of a commercial address and as daytime listeners. Women listeners were rarely figured into assessments of the audience at other times of day and in other formats; and in the sphere of production they were graually excluded from 'non-feminine-designated areas of production and industry management' (Hilmes, 1997, p. 165).

Soap opera production 'crossed over' into other media before television; the radio serial *Stella Dallas*, for example, was made into a film with Barbara Stanwyck. However, with the arrival of television the institution of radio began to change, and soap opera moved from radio to TV. The first radio soap to be produced on television was *The Guiding Light*, a daytime soap that still airs to this day. These first broadcasts, like their radio counterparts, were fifteen minutes long. By the mid-1970s, daytime soap operas in America were an hour in length, a fact that led not only to extremely elongated narrative patterns but also to the development of detailed studio designs and techniques for shooting these narratives. Soap opera production since this period is a highly regimented industry. As Allen points out, the tremendous demands of the shooting schedule, in which one hour's worth of broadcast quality programme be produced per day, led to a rigid and detailed division of labour in soap opera production. Programmes are shot quickly in 'real time', in studios built especially to accommodate quick set changes. Scripts are written according to strict guidelines and are rewritten along a particular chain of command; directors, similarly, are allowed

'an extremely limited repertoire of visual flourishes' (Allen, 1985, pp. 48–54, 55).

The serial form associated with daytime soap opera in America travelled to prime-time television in 1964, with the twice-weekly series *Peyton Place*. The programme, based on a bestselling novel, featured a high-profile celebrity cast that 'showcased the expression of female sexuality, leading to its controversial reception as part of the new "single girl" phenomenon' (Luckett, 1999, p. 75). Peyton Place left the air in 1969, but it established a place for melodrama in the prime-time schedule. The popularity of *Dallas* (see box, p. 52) and *Dynasty* both in America and abroad in the 1970s and 1980s reflected the expansion of soap opera conventions beyond the daytime context, as well as their transformation within more high-society fantasies of wealth and power.

Anna McCarthy

RECOMMENDED READING

Allen, Robert C. (1985), *Speaking of Soap Operas*, Chapel Hill: University of North Carolina Press.

Brunsdon, Charlotte (2000), *The Feminist, the Housewife, and the Soap Opera*, Oxford: Oxford University Press.

Mumford, Laura Stempel (1995), *Love and Ideology in the Afternoon: Soap Opera, Women, and Television Genre*, Bloomington: Indiana University Press.

Realism and Soap Opera

We often judge fictions – novels, television programmes, films – on their degrees of realism and verisimilitude, but what does the word *realism* mean? The history of realist movements in art and culture is a history of diverse aesthetic forms and constructions of reality, from social realism to psychological realism. Realism originally arose as an aesthetic movement in the nineteenth century. Its aim, art historian Linda Nochlin writes, was 'to give a truthful, objective and impartial representation of the real world, based on meticulous observation of contemporary life' (Nochlin, 1971, p. 13.) As she points out, the sense of reality depicted in realist art was drawn from the philosophical and material resources of nineteenth-century networks of science, industry, and artistic practice. Paintings depicting the labour process and the urbanising working class, like Claude Murillo's *Young Beggar* or Courbet's *The Stone Workers*, gave aesthetic and political status to everyday life. Nochlin and other critics in a variety of disciplines emphasise that conceptions of the real have strong generic, national and historical boundaries. As a critical concept, an aesthetic strategy, a framework within which fiction is produced and consumed, realism is thus continually expanding. As John Fiske points out, 'Realism is not a matter of fidelity to an empirical reality, but of the discursive conventions by which and for which a sense of reality is constructed' (Fiske, 1987, p. 21 – see 'Documentary Realism', p. 126).

There are several reasons why realism is a useful category for the study of soap opera's textual forms and reception contexts. As Ien Ang showed in *Watching Dallas*, viewers use a working model of realism in their assessments of serial drama and its pleasures. As already noted, Ang found that a number of viewers judged *Dallas* to be 'realistic'. However, it was clear that this sense of reality did not emerge from the show's diegetic world, its settings, characters and plot elements; these aspects of the show were incommensurable with the reality of viewers' everyday lives. Rather, viewers derived a sense of realism from the show's apparently true-to-life depiction of psychological situations. Ang called this sensibility *emotional realism*, and concluded that 'what is experienced as "real" indicates above all else a certain structure of feeling which is aroused by the programme' (Ang, 1985, p. 47). This sense of the emotionally real does not require verisimilitude on the level of plot, character or setting. On the contrary, Ang discovered that these diegetic elements played quite a different role in viewers' engagement with the programme. She wrote that '[t]he external manifestation of the fictional world of *Dallas*' contributes to pleasure 'not because of its reality effect . . . but because of its stylisation' (see box, p. 52 and 'Soap Operas and their Audiences', p. 55).

Insisting on the specificity of emotional realism and distinguishing between different levels of realism that are made possible in serial television is crucial for feminist approaches to the study of soap opera as a genre. Popular representations often depict it as a fantasy genre and its viewers as deluded and gullible persons, unable to distinguish between reality and fiction. This stereotypical representation of women's reception practices has a long history, dating back at least to Jane Austen's *Mansfield Park* (see 'Costume Drama' p. 38); its resilience is indicated in the popularity of a film called *Nurse Betty*, which tells the story of a waitress who is deluded into thinking that she is a character in a soap opera. Ang's study, along with others such as those by Dorothy Hobson (1982) and Christine Geraghty (1991), contributes a richer understanding of the relationship between knowledge and belief in the viewing process. As such they offer not only a useful corrective to representations of women as deluded viewers, but also

allow us to see how viewers actively manipulate the boundary between fiction and reality for pleasurable purposes.

In addition, the responses of Ang's viewers introduce another reason why it can be helpful to focus on realism as a mode of address in the study of soap opera. This is the fact that variations in the production and reception dynamics of realist forms in soap opera tend to demarcate national differences within the genre, for both viewers and critics. When distinguishing *Dallas*'s emotional realism from its diegetic reality, Ang's respondents often focused on the latter's 'Americanness'. These viewers, like many consumers of prime-time American serial drama exported from the United States, linked the stylised elements of the programme's *mise en scène* to Hollywood production values and by extension to an 'unreal' and excessive imaginary world (Ang, 1985, p. 55; see also Morley, 1989, pp. 31–4). Similarly, Dorothy Hobson notes, British viewers of soap operas such as *Coronation Street* and *EastEnders* tended to oppose their 'native' soaps to American ones via the distinction between fantasy and realism (Hobson, 1989, p. 157). Such judgements signal a cultural recognition of social realism as an aesthetic strategy in British and Australian serial drama; often, they reflect a corresponding recognition of the settings and situations of American soap opera exports as hyperbolic and hence unrealistic.

Coronation Street has been singled out in particular as a paradigmatic example of realism in British soap opera. Focusing on conflicts and struggles in the lives of working people in a small urban community in the industrial north of England, the programme uses a range of visual and narrative techniques to convey a sense of the everyday lives of 'ordinary people'. As Marion Jordan explains, in *Coronation Street* as in social realism 'the settings should be commonplace and recognisable (the pub, the street, the factory, the home, and more particularly the kitchen) . . . the time should be the present . . . the style should be such as to suggest an unmediated, unprejudiced and complete view of reality' (1981, p. 28). This conventionality is not invisible, however: '*Coronation Street*, though deploying the devices of the soap opera realism upon which it is based, far from attempting to hide the artifice of these devices . . . asks us to take pleasure in its artistry' (p. 39). But whereas *Coronation Street* exploits verisimilitude as both a technical feat and an affective relationship for the viewer, American prime-time drama exports are less flexible. As Jostein Gripsrud notes in a discussion of the Norwegian reception of *Dynasty*, 'the historical experience with Hollywood films and TV shows made the "emotional realism" more or less the only realism expected from American screen entertainment' (1995, p. 258.)

Coronation Street: social realism in British soap opera?

Dallas

Created by David Jacobs, *Dallas*'s first five-episode pilot season was aired in April 1978 on CBS. Although it quickly received poor reviews, it had already reached the audience rating top ten by the end of its first limited run. Centred around a saga of lust, greed, power and sex, it was the first genuinely success-ful 'prime-time' soap opera since *Peyton Place*. As Sue Brower puts it, 'It was the complicated stuff of daytime melodrama, done with big-budget glamour – high-fashion wardrobes, richly furnished home . . . office interiors' and 'exteriors shot on location' (Brower, 1997, p. 453). At the height of its popu-larity *Dallas* was exported to ninety countries, reaching 200 million viewers each year, and would go on to produce 356 episodes. Such was its success that it quickly produced spin-offs (*Knots Landing*) and countless imitations (most notably *Dynasty*, *Flamingo Road* and *Falcon Crest*).

A modern rehash of the Romeo and Juliet story, *Dallas* centred around the conflict of two oil families (the Ewings and the Barnes), with Bobby Ewing (Patrick Duffy) and his wife Pamela 'Barnes' Ewing (Victoria Principal) as its 'star-crossed lovers'. However, as popular as both these characters were, it was J.R. Ewing (Larry Hagman – also executive producer) who really caught the public's imagination. As the unscrupulous heir to the Ewing empire, J.R. became an archetypical tele-vision villain and a character the public loved to hate. Kind to his mother Miss Ellie (Barbara Bel Geddes and later Donna Reed) and to his young son and heir John Ross, he was nonetheless shameless and underhand with anyone who came in his way of attaining the power and money he so desperately craved. The most regular victim of his continually abusive behaviour was his business rival Cliff Barnes (Ken Kercheval) and his long-suffering and alcoholic wife, Sue Ellen (Linda Gray). This fascination with the character and the serial reached a crescendo in the 1980 season when the by now regu-lar cliffhanger ended with the question, 'Who Shot J.R.?' With so many possible suspects, this conundrum became the talking point of the summer. When it returned in the following season 76 per cent of all American television sets (83 million American viewers) were tuned in to find out.

Despite its incredible success, *Dallas* has also become a byword for the unbelievable and sensational elements that,

Dallas viewers responded to its 'emotional realism'

critics argue, typify contemporary television. When a speed-ing car killed Bobby so that Patrick Duffy could leave the soap, the subsequent drop in ratings meant that drastic action needed to be taken. The following season when Duffy returned, Pam went to the shower to find Bobby standing there. It seems she had dreamt the entire season before! Such sensational storylines have meant that critics some-times talk about '*wall-to-wall-Dallas*' when criticising the 'dumbing-down' of television generally. However, as Ien Ang's (1982) ground-breaking study of the soap opera has shown, the way people watched it and the 'emotional real-ism' it produced for viewers was sometimes more important that the quality of the writing and the believability of the actual storylines (see 'Soap Operas and their Audiences', p. 55). As Ang puts it, 'It is in this world of the imagination that watching melodramatic soap operas like *Dallas* can be pleasurable: *Dallas* offers a starting point for the melodra-matic imagination, nourishes, makes it concrete' (Ang, 1982, p. 80). Its final melodramatic episode was aired on 3 May 1991.   *Glen Creeber*

These stark contrasts between national versions of the soap opera are reflected in the different ways critics approach soap opera's relationship to realism in different countries. Whereas British and European critics of soap opera generally pay more attention to realism as a strategy

for representing social realities of class and *habitus* in popular television, American soap opera criticism brings a quite different set of questions to bear on the genre's relationship to the real. Rather than focusing on the implicit opposition between reality and fantasy, or viewerly and textual constructions of an 'authentic' class experience via *mise en scène*, American scholars have addressed questions that arise from the particular form of the soap opera as a daytime and prime genre in the United States. In the case of the (non-export) daytime soaps, this means examining how the studio space and the serial form set parameters on the ways that soap operas create the ongoing impression of *perceptual* reality, and also (and more implicitly) the ways in which the genre relates to the lived realities of the spectator, often understood to be female and almost always considered to be a devoted watcher. Robert C. Allen (1985) addresses realism's textual dimensions in quite formal terms, focusing primarily on the evolution of a conventional audiovisual language for the coherent representation of sense of time and space in daytime soap opera studio production: 'soap opera style can be seen as a continuation, if not condensation, of Hollywood's stylistic practice, in which elements of style function in support of diegetic illusion' (p. 64; for a discussion of realism in theory construction, see pp. 225–6, n. 9).

In a more recent study of American daytime serial soap opera, Laura Stempel Mumford (1995) brings in similar comparisons with cinematic realism, focusing on the formal and political implications of soap opera's transformation of certain Hollywood realist structures, notably closure. She also points out that 'the fact that many soap opera events take the same amount of time they would occupy in viewers lives makes their depictions especially "realistic" ' (p. 29). This is compounded by the fact that soap operas tend to observe national holidays when they occur on weekdays – soap opera plots often feature Christmas dinner on Christmas Day, for example. Mumford also notes that production budgets of soap operas, permitting fewer retakes, shape actors performances so that characters' conversations often seem no smoother than viewers' (p. 38). Both Mumford and Allen thus address realism primarily as an issue of representational *style* or transparency, as a set of formal techniques that do not call attention to their own artifice.

However, as Mumford's interest in the serial form might suggest, the specificity of the daytime drama's ongoing, seemingly endless narrative structure in American television means that even when the term 'realism' is not literally used, many American soap opera critics are nevertheless very interested in the genre's relationship to 'the real'. This can be seen in two distinct lines of inquiry. One approaches the serial form by raising questions about the relationship between the cycles of the programme and the cycles of everyday life for the spectator. Tania Modleski, for example, shows in her classic study (1982) that the

ongoing, predictable schedules of American daytime soaps bring the texts of the soap opera into the conceptual orbit of everyday life and lived experience. A 'deeper' reality is thus discernible in the serial form of the soap opera, she suggests: the reality of housework, of domestic rhythms, and the endlessness of household routines for women. Similarly, Christine Gledhill (1992) implies that the ongoing, dialogical nature of soap opera narrative gives rise to strategies of representation more realist than melodrama, soap opera's filmic relative. She writes that instead of offering 'deus ex machina resolutions' typical of the latter form, soap opera's event structure provides a space for characters to explore 'the emotional, moral and social implications and consequences of the event' (p. 121; see also Mumford, 1995, p. 25). The seriality of daytime soap opera also shapes the ways in which it depicts certain political possibilities. As Joy Fuqua (1995) notes, writers for daytime soap operas in the 1990s found it difficult to include gay characters as ongoing, developing participants in the diegetic everyday. As one writer put it: 'It's one thing to explore homophobia. It's quite another to explore the life of a gay couple – a life that includes sex and such problems as whether or not to adopt children' (Michael Malone, quoted in Fuqua, 1995, pp. 208–9). As this indicates, gay issues were a way of injecting a sense of topical, political 'realism' into the narratives of soap operas, but institutional barriers prevented their presence in the more mundane diegetic reality of daytime serial dramas.

This example illustrates that there is no straightforward or singular relationship between realism and politics in soap opera. Rather, realist conventions and sensibilities are formed on different levels of the text and may raise political issues on one level while foreclosing upon them on another. Indeed, to refer to a previous example, American daytime soaps can present a realist and an anti-realist sense of the passage of time simultaneously. Although events seem to take place on the same calendar and seemingly at the same rate in as they might in 'real life', child characters in some soap operas can mature at a rapid rate, going from birth to adolescence (and romance plots) in a few years. Such fractured and contradictory modes of realist social identification and critique in various national contexts reflect, to a large degree, the limits imposed upon representation and narrative by the commercial broadcasting systems in which soap operas generally air. Political speech and the representation of alternative political or communitarian realities must necessarily exist within the boundaries established by an implicit sense of the mainstream. However, in other nations, where non-commercial broadcasting predominates or where commercial television is

Soul City

Soap opera is not generally thought of as a form in public and political education, but innovative serial television drama in the Republic of South Africa has been used for precisely this purpose. In 1994, after the collapse of the apartheid system, an Independent Broadcasting Authority (IBA) was created to introduce large-scale policy reforms into the once white-dominated South African Broadcasting System. Among these was a mandate that television serve the public not only as a source of entertainment but also as an agency of free information and education during the transition to democracy (see 'Educational Programming', p. 137). This mandate reflected the overall ethos of 'transparency' that governed the establishment of state and private institutions in the post-apartheid era, and that structured the unique system of disclosure and amnesty in the judicial process established with the Truth and Reconciliation Commission (TRC).

Soul City has been described as 'what might result if ER or General Hospital were set in a clinic serving a sprawling black South African township'. Like many prime-time and daytime dramas in the west, it is set in a medical facility. Indeed, Soul City is almost closer to a hospital drama (see p. 23) than a soap opera; it airs on television once a week over a fifteen-episode season, a broadcast schedule that excludes it from basic definitions of seriality. However, the programme is not only a television phenomenon. A fifteen-minute radio version, closer to the 'classic' soap opera form, also broadcasts daily. This accommodates a broader audience, given that, according to figures from 1998, only 60 per cent of the population has access to television sets (Department of Communications, 1998, Chapter 6). The programme's public health goals are also reinforced through tie-ins with other media: serialised health education booklets and weekly health-oriented contests run in newspapers each week.

Seriality in some form or another is thus crucial to Soul City's public health strategies, as it provides a way of reinforcing issues and interventions over an extended period of time. In this respect, the programme seems to affirm Gledhill's characterisation that the soap opera's ability to 'chew on' social realities in its narratives lies partly in the serial form and in the emphasis on dialogue. Its weekly situations, addressing ongoing health and workplace issues in the lives of its characters through dialogue, are clearly the root of Soul City's attempts to bridge dramatic enactment and the realities of the spectator's everyday life. The serial is distributed by California Newsreel on a compilation cassette entitled Prime Time South Africa.

Anna McCarthy

invested with a high level of political responsibility by government policy-makers, other possibilities for rendering the politics of everyday reality in soap opera become possible (see box).

A final issue that should be addressed in any discussion of soap opera and realism is the role of technological change, and the aesthetic paradigms associated with it, in constructing new horizons of 'the real' in television. Most obviously, the rise of 'real life' serial programme forms, like MTV's (see 'Music on Television', p. 89) popular and long-running programme The Real World, and the spate of surveillance-based reality dramas like Big Brother and Survivor (see 'Reality TV', p. 134), suggests that changes are under way with the emergence of non-fiction analogues of the soap opera form; indeed, when MTV launched The Real World, it promoted the show as 'a real-life soap opera'. Although, as Mumford notes (1995, p. 32), critical clarity requires that soap opera continue to be defined as a fictional form, it is clear that emotional and perceptual realism are the point of overlap between 'actual' soap opera and these new forms of serial documentary.

In such programmes the hyperbolic and 'unreal' conditions of the production process, analogous to social psychology experiments, produce a sense of immediacy and transparency. Similarly, the artificial social engineering through which such shows are 'cast' nevertheless leads to high degrees of emotional realism as the people on screen interact with each other over time. Even though they are not technically 'soap operas', such programmes are thus interesting to consider in relationship to the soap opera because they expose the dialectical and multiple relations between transparency and hyperbolic artifice that shape the genre's modes of realism across institutional and textual borders (see 'Docusoaps', p. 132, and 'Reality TV', p. 134).

Anna McCarthy

RECOMMENDED READING

Gledhill, Christine (1992), 'Speculations on the Relationship between Soap Opera and Melodrama', Quarterly Review of Film Studies, vol. no. 14, no. 1–2.

Fuqua, Joy V. (1995), 'There's a Queer in my Soap!', in Robert C. Allen (ed.), To Be Continued: Soap Operas Around the World, Chapel Hill: University of North Carolina Press.

Jordan, Marion (1981) 'Realism and Convention', in Richard Dyer et al. (eds), Coronation Street, London: British Film Institute.

Soap Operas and their Audiences

From the time of its construction and articulation among popular media genres in the 1930s, soap opera has been signified in public discourse via its 'audience'. On the one hand, for US soap companies, soap opera was fashioned as a direct route to women who controlled a household's consumption. In this domain, the most significant fact about the soap opera audience was its *quantity*. As Robert Allen says (1985, p. 30), 'Within nine years after the debut of the first network radio soap opera in 1932, the soap opera form constituted 90 percent of all sponsored network radio programming broadcast during the daylight hours … . This enormous audience today provides … one-sixth of all network profits.'

On the other hand, this clear embedding of the soap opera form and its (female) audience within the most overt aspects of capitalism led academic and other critics into a sustained rejection of the new genre. Soap opera and its audiences were swept along on cross-currents of critical discourses that, as Allen says, were to define its image for decades. He points to two 'superintending' discourses that, almost from the beginning, positioned the soap opera audience in a position of 'lack'. On one side, there was the deeply conservative aesthetic discourse of 'mass culture' thinking, which expressed itself in different forms (German Expressionism, the literary criticism of F.R. Leavis, and so on) in the new 'mass industrial' societies.

To the other side of this 'aesthetic' critique of the soap opera audience, there was the 'scientific' one. Allen explains the complex relationship between soap opera audiences and American social scientific research of the dominant Lazarsfeld Bureau of Applied Social Research, founded in 1939 with significant commercial funding. This commercial 'scientific' backing 'helped to "encrust" the meanings of soap opera within the discourse of mass communications research with a particular conception of its audience, which is felt even today' (Allen, 1985, p. 22). Lazarsfeld's research was in part designed to counter the 'anti-social' charges against soap laid by psychiatrists like Louis Berg, who claimed that broadcasters proffered a surfeit of daytime fare that 'pandered to perversity' and played out 'destructive conflict' (cited in Allen, 1985, pp. 21–2). A more 'pro-social' message about soap opera was needed, and this was provided by pioneering research within the Bureau: for example, by Herta Herzog's definitive 1942 study of the soap opera audience, which emphasised the

psychological and social *needs* that listening to soap opera fulfilled. However, the lack of comparable work on *other* popular genres, meant that:

> Despite the clear indication that soap opera listening pervaded all groups, the methodologies of the studies suggested that soap opera enjoyment had to be explained as some kind of lack on the part of listeners: the psychological need of women for advice, a social or emotional lack, educational deprivation, the inability to enjoy other types of programming, and so forth. (Allen, 1985, p. 25)

As Allen says, work in the Lazarsfeld Bureau defined the field of academic soap opera study for the next thirty years. But in the 1970s (as a result of the competing frameworks of uses and gratifications studies and screen theory) and particularly in the 1980s, the soap opera audience gained a more positive face. Most important here was the work of feminists in the field of soap opera audiences.

- Terry Lovell (1981), who deployed Gramsci's distinctions between 'good sense' and 'common sense' in her study of *Coronation Street* to argue that this soap opera offered viewers certain marginalised 'structures of feeling'. 'It offers women a validation and celebration of those interests and concerns which are seen as properly theirs within the social world they inhabit. Soap opera may be … a context in which women can ambiguously express *both* good-humoured acceptance of their oppression *and* recognition of that oppression, and some equally good-humoured protest against it' (Lovell, 1981, pp. 50–1).
- Charlotte Brunsdon (1981), who drew on her work on other television genres (such as her *Nationwide* study with David Morley, 1978) to resituate soap opera and current affairs in terms of gendered cultural competences. Brunsdon reassessed Bourdieu's work on class and cultural competence to point to practical and ideological knowledge systems internalised by young men and women that leads to greater attention to, and pleasure in, one popular television form than another. In the case of soap opera, programmes like *Crossroads* were engaging with, and extending, existing discourses of femininity.
- Dorothy Hobson (1982), whose own study of *Crossroads* may be said to have pioneered a new generation of 'ethnographic' (or at least empirical–qualitative) studies of the 'active audience'. Deliberately addressing 'the most maligned programme on British television' (p. 36),

Hobson challenged head-on the 'deficit/lack' model of soap opera audiences that had prevailed for so long. As she argues, 'It is criticised for its technical or script inadequacies, without seeing that its greatest strength is in its stories and connections with its audience's own experiences. The programme is a form of popular art precisely because it has a relevance to its audience' (pp. 170–1).

- Tania Modleski (1982), whose study of Harlequin romances and daytime soap opera argued for the relationship between these forms and a new, historically positioned, feminist aesthetic. 'Soap operas invest exquisite pleasure in the central condition of a woman's life: waiting ... [S]oap operas do not end. Consequently, truth for women is seen to lie not "at the end of expectation", but *in* expectation, not in the "return to order", but in (familial) disorder' (p. 88). Why, asks Modleski, given the post-structuralist emphasis on 'decentring the subject', do we not start by acknowledging women's pleasures in a popular television from where 'women are, in their lives, their work, and in certain forms of their pleasure, already decentred' (p. 105) – the soap opera?

- Ien Ang (1985), who, in her study of *Dallas*, drew (like Terry Lovell) on Raymond Williams's notion of 'structure of feeling' to argue for the notion of an emotional realism that is beyond the empiricist 'real' (see the *Dallas* box, p. 51 and 'Realism and Soap Opera', p. 49). Ang engages critically with both empiricist realism (where 'a text is realistic (and therefore good) if it supplies "adequate knowledge" of reality') and screen theory's concept of the 'classic realist text' (which is 'bad because it only creates an illusion of knowledge'). In both these notions of realism, 'a cognitive–rationalistic idea dominates: both are based on the assumption that a realistic text offers *knowledge* of the "objective" social reality ... . But the realism experienced by the *Dallas* fans ... bears no relation to this cognitive level – it is situated at the emotional level: what is recognised as real is not knowledge of the world, but a subjective experience of the world: a "structure of feeling".' (p. 45). Ang is marking here a profoundly important movement in post-structuralist feminist research against the 'cognitivist/rationalist' and instrumentalist biases of modernist thinking, and towards her own later elaboration of critical ethnography (Ang, 1995). 'It is emotions which count in a structure of feeling' (p. 45); and it is the pleasurable play of 'endless fluctuation between happiness and unhappiness' (p. 46) that marks soap opera's 'tragic structure of feeling'. For example, Sue Ellen's alcoholism is a potent metaphor for a woman

trapped in desperation, and her sexual affairs are a potentially appealing action with which women viewers can empathise in fantasy.

- Ellen Seiter et al. (1989), whose Oregon study also took up the 'critical ethnographic turn', discussing reflexively the 'discursive formation of women talking to women' in the research interviews conducted by Ellen Seiter, Gabriele Kreutzner and Eva-Maria Warth. Focusing on 'soap operas in the context of the everyday life for women working in the home' (p. 223), the Oregon study took to task Modleski's overtly 'textualist' analysis. Working-class women, in particular, rejected Modleski's analysis (of the 'ideal mother' inscription of the soap viewer) as middle class. Seiter et al. did, however, find 'fond admiration' (p. 237) for 'the supposedly despised villainesses' of soap opera – thus inadvertently supporting Modleski's argument that this perennial soap representation provides 'an outlet for feminine anger: in particular ... the spectator has the satisfaction of seeing men suffer the same anxieties and guilt that women usually experience, and seeing them receive similar kinds of punishment for their transgressions' (Modleski, 1982, p. 97).

- Mary Ellen Brown (1990, 1994), whose emphasis on soap opera and women viewers' talk took the 'resistance' line of feminist theory (which is so evident in the contributions described above) to its ultimate, 'everyday' position. Brown recognises that women are embedded in patriarchal culture, but they are not victims of it – especially when they talk to each other about soap opera. Brown's emphasis on 'emotional critique' and 'speaking with the body' extends Ang's post-structuralist critique of the 'cognitive–rationalistic' concerns with a 'knowledgable' reality. Her emphasis that 'talk is action' also quite directly opens the way to further feminist work in two important areas: the social constructionist discourse analysis of E. Graham McKinley (1997) in her study of *Beverley Hills 90210* (see 'The Teen Series', p. 41); and the critical ethnography of Marie Gillespie (1995) in her ethnographies of Indian-produced soap operas among a Punjabi Hindu family living in Southall, London.

- Michael Stewart (1999) has argued – rightly, in my view – that Gillespie's work (and also Lisa Rofel's (1995) study of the soap opera *Yearnings* in post-Tiananmen China) marks an important new phase of analysis of the soap opera audience. In Stewart's view, the feminist studies so necessary in the 1970s and 1980s were nevertheless considerably overdetermined by soap opera's negative historical inscription. This is entirely understandable, given the social weight and historical depth of the discourses of cultural value that have shaped soap opera's reception and within which soap opera continues to be understood. However 'in the [Modleski, Seiter et al. and Ang] studies . . . there's a danger that the recurring oppositions – between realism and pleasure, public and private, masculinity and femininity, activity and passivity – are inverted rather than undone' (p. 74). Speaking of Gillespie's *Mahabharata* study in Southall, Stewart says, 'The great value of Gillespie's study lies in the richness and detail of its ethnographic observation. Most noteworthy, perhaps, is how particular, binary ways of thinking about soap opera collapse when a specific cultural context is examined . . . . The programme's excessive, melodramatic structure does not transcend other restrictive or illusory realities; it very clearly *is* the reality, part of the "factual" history within which the Dhanis make sense of their lives' (p. 79).

Nevertheless, continuity with the feminist research of the 1980s needs to be maintained. Above all, the analysis of embodied emotionality (both in soap opera and in audience responses to it) needs to remain a central research focus. Ironically, that is where it started – in Louis Berg's psychiatry. We have come a long way from his description of the soap opera audience as victims of 'acute anxiety state, tachycardia, arrhythmias, increase in blood pressures, profuse perspiration, tremors, vasomotor instability, nocturnal frights, vertigo and gastrointestinal disturbances' (cited in Allen, 1985, p.21). But the importance of bodily and emotional responses to the soap opera 'event' is one that (as Ang and others have argued) has been almost entirely lost from view in instrumentalist academic discourse. The analysis of soap opera audiences – in relation to the emotions of risk and fear, as well as pleasure and anger – is still ahead of us.

John Tulloch

RECOMMENDED READING

Ang, Ien (1985), *Watching Dallas: Television and the Melodramatic Imagination*, London: Routledge.

Seiter, Ellen, Borchers, Hans, Kreutzner, Gabriele, and Wrath, Eva-Marie (eds) (1989), *Remote Control: Television, Audiences and Cultural Power*, London: Routledge.

Tulloch, John and Moran, Albert (1986), *A Country Practice: 'Quality' Soap*, Sydney: Allen & Unwin.

The Telenovela

The telenovela (or the television novel) constitutes one of the most important cultural expressions within contemporary Latin American popular culture. They are massively present in the everyday life of millions of Latin Americans, to a degree unseen in most other parts of the world. The most popular television channels show telenovelas in both daytime and prime-time broadcasting. In a small country like Nicaragua, for example, the largest television channel broadcasts eight daily Latin American telenovelas, five days a week. Latin America's largest TV network, Brazilian Rede Globo, broadcasts four telenovelas daily, six days a week (all in prime time – between 5.30 and 9.30 p.m. – only interrupted by thirty minutes of news). They run an average of 120–150 episodes, in some countries more, and they achieve ratings unseen in most other countries in the world (often surpassing the ratings of the daily TV news). Rede Globo's prime-time telenovelas reach about 50 per cent of the audience, and this in a highly competitive environment where many of the other channels compete by also transmitting telenovelas.

In addition to the cultural significance of telenovelas in Latin American societies, they are also big business on the Latin American media market (traditionally a commercial market), and have been exported to more than 130 countries worldwide. The main producers are Brazil, Mexico and Colombia, followed closely by Argentina, Venezuela, Peru and Chile. As Trinta (1998, p. 276) points out, their traditional characteristics can be found rooted in the dynamics of melodrama:

> Common elements include emotional entanglements involving well-established characters and the traditional romance plot with true love triumphing over adversity; characterisation is clearly subordinated to plot and spectacular physical action predominates. The plot is developed around a sad 'love story', whose end is reached by resolving a certain number of interwoven situations. In this way, affectionate and tender devotion always wins a victory over evil.

As a melodramatic art of storytelling, telenovelas have grown out of the history of popular culture, having historical matrices in ancient oral and literary storytelling (also reflected in more recent mass communicative narratives within newspapers, theatre, circus, radio and cinema). As such, a joint history can be traced together with the soap operas of the anglophone world. However, the particulari-

A Country Practice

Production analysis is another side of the soap opera/audience relationship that can provide the ethnographic 'richness and detail' that Stewart (1999) is looking for. Although serious ethnographies of television production in Britain were being published in the later 1970s and early 1980s, these were on the private eye (see 'The Action Series', p. 17), cop (see 'The Police Series', p. 19) and science fiction (see p. 26) genres, not soap opera. However, David Buckingham's important book on *EastEnders* (1987) and its audience did show the value of a *processual* analysis of production (via interviews with television personnel about 'creating the audience'), the 'audience in the text', the circulation of publicity and media comment about the series, and 'active audience' analysis. Like the feminists, Buckingham also engaged with 'pleasure', but situated socially and historically in individual viewers.

In 1986, Tulloch and Moran produced *A Country Practice: 'Quality' Soap*, based on several months' ethnographic study of Australia's longest-running and highest-rating, peak-viewing soap opera of the 1980s (which was also the first to open up the British market for Australian soaps). The intention here was to challenge the long history of dismissal of soap opera and its audiences in a different way from the feminist 'resistance' studies. A soap opera was chosen that was both very high rating *and* regarded as 'quality' professional work by all who worked on it (the series attracted Australia's best film writers, was regarded as their 'best work' by set designers, floor managers, sound and vision directors and so on at Channel 7, Sydney). Each professional worker on the series, from executive producer through actors and studio-floor staff to station scheduling managers and publicity, were working daily to put their particular economic and semiotic 'signature' on the show. Consequently, by

(a) studying several episodes through from pre-planning to post-editing meetings,
(b) examining the positioning of this particular product in a particular commercial channel, and
(c) conducting audience research on the episodes the researchers had followed,

they could explore the 'semiotic density' of the television text (with its *range* of inscribed audiences according to multiple and fragmented 'authorships'), and relate this to actual audience meanings.

On the audience side, it was possible to:

- Examine the meanings of both 'issues' (rural unemployment, HIV/AIDS) and 'romance' stories among different viewers, according to gender, class and age.

A Country Practice: 'quality' soap?

- Assess the effect of the 'halfway-house' style (which made *A Country Practice* (1981–93) a very 'traditional', naturalistic formula for some of its film-experienced writers). For example, one writer worried that the quick 'cutaway' style (between 'laughter' and 'tears') would lessen the 'impact' of his HIV/AIDS story: consequently the researchers assessed the meanings of differently edited versions of his episode with audiences.
- Explore the meaning of different audiovisual signatures on audiences: for instance, according to directors' different visual styles (in relation to the 'legalise heroin' insertion), or omitting (young/old addiction) 'balancing' information conveyed by the music and sound score in differently edited versions of the same episode.
- Examine differences in the meaning of 'pleasure' over 'romance' strands as between 'fans' and mixed family groups at home.
- Assess with audiences the executive producer's assertion that his needle-sharing, HIV/AIDS message would have more 'impact' if carried by a much-loved soap opera character than via a ninety-second public service advertisement.

Like the feminist audience research, this work responded to the long history of denigration of soap opera and its audiences, but in different ways: (1) It went to the 'everyday' of the TV industry for its own construction of 'quality'; (2) It traced the economy and semiotics of this 'quality' into the production and circulation of its 'texts'; (3) It examined the pleasures, meanings and (production-team intended) 'impacts' on different audiences of the show, drawing on both qualitative and quantitative methods. 'Pleasure', then, was traced both in the everyday working practices of TV professionals and in audience responses.

John Tulloch

Brazilian Telenovelas

The Brazilian telenovela is the telenovela of Latin America into which most resources are poured. They are the most expensive, they use the most locations, employ the best actors and tend to incorporate the most social critique within their narratives. The largest producer on the Brazilian market is Central Globo de Produção, part of the Globo corporation and owned by the legendary ninety-year old Roberto Marinho, honorary president of the Globo companies. In the early 1990s Globo was the world's largest producer of television fiction, producing simultaneously an episode a day for four different telenovelas. The Globo companies include all aspects of the culture industry and have also spread into several other industries (telecommunications, oil, agriculture, sports).

Two major trends influenced the genre from the mid-1980s, leading to the development of the 'post-realist' telenovela: first, the process of democratisation in Brazil, and second, the international orientation of Rede Globo. Democratisation in society led to an abundance of political criticism and social comment in telenovelas generally. From the mid-1980s the daily eight o'clock telenovela contained highly political subtexts, criticising corruption, nepotism and the fight for power and raising important issues (such as Catholic priests getting married, agrarian reform, racial questions and disappeared street children). These contemporary problems were massively visualised by the telenovela and transformed into issues discussed by almost all levels of society. *Roque Santeiro* in 1985, by Dias Gomes, was the first telenovela along this line (originally produced in 1974, but censored), and has become one of the most important telenovelas in the history of the genre.

In the 1990s, political subtexts were increasingly apparent in telenovelas, reflecting the freedom of speech and marking the post-military epoch in which Brazil now lives. Simultaneously, a certain generic innovation had emerged, based partly on a nostalgic turn and focusing on rural settings and plots that unfold in some of Brazil's many beautiful natural settings. *Pantanal* (TV Manchete, 1990) was a trendsetter in this respect. It evoked the nostalgia shared by many of the first- and second-generation migrants in the huge urban centres in Brazil. *Renacer* (*Reborn*, 1993) and *O Rei do Gado* (*The Cattle King*, 1996–7) were two other major examples.

O Rei do Gado brought a very polemic issue to the screen, that of agrarian reform and the social movement of the landless in Brazil (the 'Sem Terra' movement). This telenovela took up the agrarian reform issue in the midst of serious land conflicts in Brazil. Nineteen landless peasants were killed in a conflict with landowners shortly before the telenovela went on air. The narrative, telling the story of a rich landowner falling in love with a poor landless woman, became a direct comment on the contemporary conflict in Brazil – and, indeed, sought to place itself as close to the actuality of the contemporary climate as possible. It visualised on a massive scale the struggle for land that had been a growing social movement in Brazil, turning this issue into one of public knowledge and concern, and transforming this particular struggle into a legitimate political cause. It had a tremendous effect, significantly increasing public attention, media debate and political discussion, and even encouraging the passing of several laws on the issue. As such, it is arguable that the televnovela continues to play an important and crucial role in the development of democratisation within Latin America as a whole (see Trinta, 1998, pp. 281–4).

Thomas Tufte

ties of the Latin American telenovelas are obviously the result of forty to fifty years of genuine development as a Latin American genre. Furthermore, the telenovela can be distinguished by their national genre characteristics. Whereas the Brazilian telenovas tend to be more modern and socially aware, the Mexican have generally been regarded as more traditional and romanticised in tone. This has, however, been changing in recent years, not least with the growth of the Mexican TV company, TV Atzeca.

We also find subgenres in individual countries, characterised by significant differences in aesthetics, content and audience profile. This is the case in Brazil where Rede Globo has developed a six o'clock subgenre (mostly the historic epos or *novelas de epoca*); a seven o'clock subgenre (comedic, youth-oriented satire of a very national–domestic nature); and finally, the eight o'clock telenovela (usually the flagship programme of the evening, being the most expensive, often most socially oriented and almost always based on a contemporary narrative woven around a classical melodrama).

Dramaturgically, telenovelas are 'open' works; the narrative is not concluded when the telenovela goes on air, but unfolds in a process dependent on audience response. Typically, when a telenovela starts, between twenty and thirty episodes are filmed and ready, the author has written fifteen to twenty more, and thereafter seeks to keep about twenty episodes ahead of the episode on air.

Very roughly, three major genre developments can be

depicted in the history of the telenovela (the first screening in the early 1950s, as 'tele-theatre', with the daily telenovela emerging in the early 1960s). The 1950s and 1960s can be seen generally as the period of *romanticism*, being largely theatrical, thematically and aesthetically distanced from reality and primarily focused on a love story. In contrast, the late 1960s to the mid-1980s was the period of increased *realism*, when the tele-novela developed into a genuine national *and* Latin American genre, culturally and thematically reflecting contemporary issues, inherently more televisual, and with the gradual introduction of ordinary dialect and colloquial language. The language of the telenovelas (especially the Brazilian, of the late 1960s and onwards) reiterated this realism, further enhancing the close relationship between telenovelas and the everyday life of Latin Americans. *Beto Rockefeller* (Brazil, 1968) marked the major breakthrough of this realistic subgenre. Finally, from the mid 1980s (the beginning of this phase varying somewhat according to the political developments in each country) the genre developed into a *post-realist phase*, reflecting thematically the spirit of (re)democratisation and freedom of speech. However, all three subgenres still co-exist today.

Throughout their history, telenovelas have tackled some of the most important issues of the day, including migration, adaptation to urban life, managing rural nostalgia, struggling for social mobility and coping with and aspiring to modern consumer culture. During the years of military dictatorship in many Latin American countries it combined the dual role of being an attempted instrument of the military rulers, and at the same time respecting the audience demand for reflecting everyday contemporary life.

Today, freedom of expression is widespread and an integral element of the conditions upon which the media industries operate. Many contemporary issues are now taken up in the genre, parallel to and often woven together with the continued discourse of romantic and realist telenovelas. However, the emotionally abundant melodrama continues to be the overall rule of the game, often with the inclusion of a touch of fantasy or 'magic realism'. As such, telenovelas continue to predominate their national and regional markets, leaving American television series to more marginal broadcasting hours or to specialised television channels.

Thomas Tufte

RECOMMENDED READING

Fadul, A. (ed.) (1993), *Serial Fictions in TV: The Latin American Telenovelas, São Paulo*: ECA/USP.

Trinta, Aluizio R. (1998), 'News from Home: A Study of Realism and Melodrama in Brazilian Telenovelas' in Christine Geraghty and David Lusted (eds) *The Television Studies Book*, London, New York, Sydney, Auckland: Arnold.

Tufte, Thomas (2000), *Living with the Rubbish Queen – Telenovelas, Culture and Modernity in Brazil*, Luton: University of Luton Press.

COMEDY

Studying Comedy

Many analyses of comedy begin by noting the paucity of work in the field, and this will be no exception. Although the analysis of television is itself in its infancy, the discussion of television comedy has been categorised by fits and starts, exploring a diverse range of concerns, and arising out of conflicting histories and methodologies. Considering the sitcom's dominance of American prime-time television for nigh on thirty years now (see 'Situation Comedy, Part 1', p. 65), as well as the genre's central family entertainment status in Britain, it seems odd that sustained analysis has not been a mainstay of media studies.

This lack arises from a congruence of factors. Most visibly, comedy's low cultural status has meant that academics coming from a humanities or literature background have often chosen to focus on more 'serious' concerns; comedy has always played second fiddle to tragedy. In addition, humour is, on the whole, popular and popularist, and, although cultural studies' aims included broadening analysis out to popular forms, it is clear that much work is still carried out on 'quality' texts (see 'The Populist Debate' p. 76).

More subtly, however, other factors have prevented a sustained critique of broadcast comedy. The range of the field is enormous and complex, incorporating sitcom, sketch shows, stand-up, advertising and animation, as well as the role of comedy in other genres such as drama, news, chat shows and so on. Furthermore, variations within each of these genres are vast. Where to begin analysing comedy when it encompasses mainstream sitcoms such as *Friends*, surreal horror comedy like Chris Morris's *Jam*, thirty-second television adverts, and Jerry Springer's interjections on his talk shows (see p. 84)? The complex and ubiquitous nature of comedy is one of its clearest defining aspects: unfortunately, this makes it notoriously difficult to get to grips with.

Furthermore, the nature of comedy itself has remained annoyingly elusive. So, while humour theory (see box, p. 63) has attempted to define just what it is that makes us laugh, that theory's interdisciplinary nature and acknowledged failure in so far achieving its aims has meant that, on the whole, its work has not been taken up by media and cultural studies. This has resulted in studies of broadcast comedy that, bizarrely, almost fail to acknowledge humour at all.

In response, studies of comedy have chosen to focus on its other aspects. Predominant is the question of humour's subversive nature, representing a critique of dominant ideologies apparent within much of cultural studies. Comedy has been co-opted for such analysis precisely because of its assumed social role as a questioner of norms and a licence to say the unsayable. It is clear that Rowe's (1995) work (see 'Situation Comedy, Part 2', p. 67) on the 'unruly woman' legitimises certain representations and jokes precisely because they question not only the norms for comedy, but also those for society as a whole. This has also been explored in terms of representations of sexuality, in which a contradictory tone is often adopted: for example, although comedy was one of the first places to acknowledge that homosexuals exist, its predilection for camp portrayals has resulted in criticisms of stereotyping (Medhurst and Tuck, 1982). The question remains, of course, of whether we laugh *with* or *at* such portrayals.

Such analyses focus on the sitcom, and this has been a notable aspect of the study of broadcast comedy. The subsequent narrowing of the perceived role and nature of comedy has meant that, academically, it appears as if stand-up, satire, radio comedy, or anything other than sitcom does not exist. Furthermore, other aspects specific to comedy have yet to be adequately explored, such as audience readings, performance and stardom. And contemporary trends in cultural studies methodologies (particularly ethnography) have not, on the whole, been applied to comedy which, considering the social focus of both of these, would seem a fruitful collaboration.

This is not to say that valuable work does not exist. In the UK the field was kick-started by Cook's (1982) edited collection in which sitcom's structure, social role and forms of representation are thoughtfully outlined. Although the collection's tone is an obviously cautious one (perhaps the authors could not believe they were writing about sitcom either), it pinpoints a variety of aspects broader than many subsequent analyses. Neale and Krutnik (1990) explore both film and television comedy, citing humour's potentially subversive social role in accordance with much similar analysis. They employ a rare method in which the varieties of comedy (sketch shows, slapstick and the like) are not only explored but are a central concern of their thesis.

In the USA, much work on comedy has explored its socio-political nature. Hamamoto (1991) finds comedy to be a unifying, equilibrium-supporting form, noting this as different from its role in Britain. Similarly, Marc (1989, p. 118) argues that sitcom is 'a representational art committed to harmony and consensus'. These analyses are placed within work on broadcasting in the USA as a whole, in which attempts to coalesce a geographically and ideologically disparate audience are best achieved, it seems, by comedy. There is a concurrent concern with the industrial nature of television comedy that, because of syndication and global sales, represents a significant source of possible long-term revenue unmatched by other genres. Moreover, the production of comedy is notably different in the UK and the USA, with the former based around specific solo writers, while the latter depends much more on stand-up comedians and producers.

Such critiques are indicative of sitcom's central position within academic work on comedy. This is odd, for it ignores the political nature of satire (seen by Carpenter (2000) as responsible in Britain for the downfall of Macmillan's government in the 1960s), as well as the formal differences apparent in sketch shows and stand-up that surely offer sites for complex critiques of, and responses to, social ideologies and norms. Yet this very lack of formal structures (in both construction and reading) may be responsible for the deficiency of analysis of the full range of broadcast comedy. It appears that studying comedy is just too *difficult*. Yet that difficulty that has so far discouraged thorough long-term analysis of broadcast humour will, it is hoped, become its major focus and guiding principle.

Brett Mills

RECOMMENDED READING

Cook J. (ed.) (1982), *Television Sitcom*, BFI Dossier 17, London: British Film Institute.

Morreall J. (ed.) (1987), *The Philosophy of Laughter and Humour*, Albany: State University of New York Press.

Neale, Steve and Krutnik, Frank (1990), *Popular Film and Television Comedy*, London: Routledge.

Sketch Comedy

In both Britain and America, sketch comedy derives from the institutions and performance traditions associated with the professionalisation and commercialisation of theatrical entertainment in the nineteenth and early twentieth cen-turies. These included music hall in Britain, and minstrel shows, burlesque and vaudeville in America, all of them forms of variety entertainment containing a mix of music, comedy and other specialised acts and types of perform-ance: magic acts, acrobatic acts, animal acts and so on (Bailey, 1986; Bratton, 1986; Toll, 1976). From 1907 onwards (the year in which music halls in Britain were first legally permitted to present them), comic sketches with dialogue (which in America had always been allowed) became part of a repertoire of comic forms that also included solo stand-up comedy and double acts. As further sites for comic performance were developed during the course of the twentieth century, comic sketches and their performers found a home not just in variety theatre but also in radio, film and television. Sometimes the shows and films in which they appeared would be dedicated solely to comedy, sometimes to a range of variety forms (Scheurer, 1985, p. 307, distinguishes between 'general variety', 'musi-cal variety' and 'comedy variety'). Either way, and however tailored it was to the needs of these forms and the different media in which they appeared, sketch comedy, like solo stand-up and double-act comedy, continued – and con-tinues – to thrive (Crowther and Pinfold, 1987; Halliwell, 1987; Jenkins, 1992; Neale and Krutnik, 1990, pp. 176–208; Putterman, 1995; Toll, 1982, pp. 211–43; Took, 1976; Wertheim, 1979; Wilmut, 1980, 1985; Wilmut and Rosengard, 1989).

As the term implies, sketches are short, usually single-scene structures. They generally comprise a setting, one or more characters, and an internal time frame within which the comic possibilities of a premise of one kind or another – a situation, a relationship, a conversation and its topics, a mode of language, speech or behaviour, or some other organising principle – are either pursued to a point of climax and conclusion (sometimes called a 'pay-off'), or else simply abandoned (a device pioneered in Britain by Spike Milligan in *Q* – see box, p. 64). The brevity of sketches derives from their origins in variety, in which acts of any kind usually lasted no more than twenty minutes. (Most lasted around ten minutes and radio and television sketches are usually even briefer than this.)

Distinctions can be made between sketches that are visual in orientation (like Benny Hill's speeded-up chase sequences, in which the only sound is that of musical accompaniment) and those that focus largely or exclusively on dialogue (like the Smith and Jones 'head-to-head' sketches, where the only action is conversation and where the setting consists simply of a table and chairs). Wilmut (1985) further distinguishes between sketches and double acts (whose sketches are built around two equally billed

Humour Theory

Humour theory is a complex and relatively undefined area, whose application to broadcast comedy has only recently begun to be explored (see, for example, Morreall, 1987). It is truly interdisciplinary, coalescing linguistics, sociology, psychology, maths and performance, among others, which may explain its involved and sometimes confusing nature. A central concern is the unpicking of joke structure, as well as questioning the role of humour within society generally. Like much of cultural studies, it explores the possible subversive nature of communication, locating humour as a potential site for critiquing dominant ideologies. However, unlike media and cultural studies, humour theory positions its subject as an essential and significantly radical social phenomenon.

Humour theories have traditionally been split into three separate camps: superiority, incongruity and relief. Although these have been treated as separate and conflicting it is clear that they overlap, with varying degrees of relevance to media communication.

The superiority theory dates back to Plato (tr. 1975) and Aristotle (tr. 1925) in the fourth century BC, but was given its clearest form by Hobbes in the mid-seventeenth century. He suggests that humour arises from attaining a position of 'sudden glory' (1914, p. 27), in which laughter reinforces power positions and is inevitably defined as a negative social phenomenon. This is similar to many analyses of sitcom, in which jokes have been seen to confirm hegemonic ideologies (Lovell, 1982).

The incongruity theory is traced back to Kant in the late eighteenth century, in which 'Laughter is an affect resulting from the sudden transformation of a heightened expectation into nothing' (2000, p. 209). Here humour results from the clash of incompatible discourses, which are themselves socially constructed and learned. It is this theory that has been most taken up by media studies, with Palmer drawing complex distinctions between social humour, broadcast comedy, and jokes within narrative (1987, pp. 154, 167). Similarly, Morreall (1983) positions incongruity as essential not only to comedy but all social interactions, as one of the ways in which societies speak to themselves both socially and through media.

The relief theory is rooted in Freud (tr. 1976), in which humour functions socially and psychologically as a vent for repression and, by extension, questions social norms. Although it has proved difficult to relate such analysis to broadcast comedy, satire and a range of more socio-political comedians (Lenny Bruce, Bill Hicks, Ben Elton, Mark Thomas) could usefully be seen as lancing society's boils. The relationship between such a role and the debates on media effects are clear.

What has hindered the application of humour theory to broadcast comedy has, however, been its focus on jokes and joke structure. If cultural studies has increasingly noted the complex nature of media consumption (particularly its domestic mode and variable viewing patterns), the analysis of something as tiny as a joke seems like a backward step. Indeed, as contemporary analysis of broadcast comedy has focused on a narrow range of specifics to the detriment of a broader understanding, so has humour theory. It seems possible, then, that the developing relationship between the two is likely to open up a whole range of questions, methodologies and analyses, in which the study of both social and broadcast comedy will blossom.

Brett Mills

performers: the Smothers Brothers, Morecambe and Wise, Smith and Jones and the like). Since double-act sketches are still sketches, the usefulness of this particular distinction is perhaps open to debate. What is important is the range of comedy made possible by what may initially appear to be a restricted form.

In the early years of television after the Second World War, sketches (and other forms of comic performance) were broadcast live, usually in the context of revues and other kinds of variety shows. It was at this time that performers like Milton Berle and shows like *The Toast of the Town* became established in the USA. Even though programmes of all kinds were soon to be pre-recorded, the aura of 'liveness', of a 'here and now' performance before an audience, remained an important ingredient in variety, as witness subsequent shows such as *Sunday Night at the London Palladium* and *Saturday Live* in the UK and *Your Show of Shows* and *Saturday Night Live* in the USA. However, sketch comedy was always less dependent on this aura than stand-up. Sketches could therefore always make more overt use of recording, editing and other television techniques and could appear (whether in live, in would-be live, or in pre-recorded contexts) either as obvious inserts or as part of a pre-recorded package of items.

In the USA Ernie Kovacs and *Rowan and Martin's Laugh-In* and in the UK *Monty Python's Flying Circus* (see box) were among the first to explore the possibilities of these techniques during the 1960s and early 1970s. They were also among the first to explore (and to parody) the forms and conventions of broadcast TV and to adapt the

Monty Python's Flying Circus

The first episode in the first series of *Monty Python's Flying Circus* was broadcast in Britain on 5 October, 1969. Commissioned by the BBC, there were eventually four series overall (the last episode in the fourth series was first broadcast on 5 December 1974). The show's principal writers and performers were Graham Chapman, John Cleese (who left at the end of the third series), Eric Idle, Terry Jones and Michael Palin, with additional performances and animated titles, sketches and links provided by Terry Gilliam and regular appearances by Carol Cleveland, Ian Davidson and others.

Gilliam was American, and the show and its spin-off concerts, films and books were popular in the USA. However, most commentators have focused on the show's British (indeed, English) antecedents, sociocultural context, and institutional base. Aside from the TV and radio shows on which members of the *Python* team worked prior to the advent of *Python* itself (*The Frost Report*, *Not the 1948 Show*, *Do Not Adjust Your Set*, *I'm Sorry I'll Read That Again* and others), and in additon to the initial willingness of the BBC to sponsor a new generation of performers and writers at a time when established traditions, forms and values of all kinds were being challenged, commentators generally stress the team's background at Oxbridge and in Oxbridge revues and usually cite *The Goon Show*, *Beyond the Fringe* and *Q* as especially influential (Perry, 1983, pp. 9–56; Wilmut, 1980).

The humour in *The Goon Show* and *Q* in particular is often described as absurd or surreal, and this is the hallmark of *Python* as well: the elements of illogicality and playfulness to be found in most comedy are in *Python* stretched to the limit (hence the prevalence of 'silliness' as an accusation levelled at some of the sketches from within the programmes themselves). So overriding are these features that they tend to qualify those aspects of the *Python* programmes that might otherwise be viewed as straightforwardly satirical (the persistent lampooning of judges, accountants, doctors, politicians, TV announcers, military officers: all who claim, assume or aspire to institutionally established modes of authority, control and social status). Although satire, certainly, can be found in a number of otherwise similar or influential 1960s sketch shows (*That Was The Week That Was*, *Not So Much A Programme, More A Way of Life* and the like), the *Python* programmes themselves are perhaps best characterised by what Putterman (1995, p. 163) describes as 'a single level of burlesque that turned every manner of thought into some aspect of an all-consuming vaudeville show'.

What was distinctive about this particular show was that it

Monty Python's Flying Circus: illogicality and playfulness stretched to the extreme

encompassed a much wider range of 'thought' than had hitherto been the norm (including as it did references to Icelandic sagas, philosophers such as Jean-Paul Sartre and relatively obscure historical events) while persistently playing with the formats and forms of traditonal variety and its sketches, of popular culture and popular film, and, most notably, of TV itself (Neale and Krutnik, 1990, pp. 196–208; Wilmut, 1985, pp. 195–231). In combining these elements with a complex array of comic techniques and organisational features (repetition, interruption, digression and the like), the *Python* programmes appealed in particular to a generation of young, often university-educated audience willing to make a cult of its absurdities, and able to understand its references, to appreciate the uses it made of media formats and forms, and to identify with its comic attacks on institutional authority. As Miller points out, (2000, pp. 127–38) this was its appeal in the USA as well as in the UK.   *Steve Neale* presentation of their sketch material to its segmental rhythms and structures. *Rowan and Martin's Laugh-In* in particular was marked by the rapid-fire presentation of one-line gags, regular comic characters, recurrent catch-phrases and regular situations (not unlike an extended sequence of advertisements). Its sketch material was compressed, condensed and telegraphic, with variants produced across the span of a programme or series (not unlike a running gag). In all these respects, it set a precedent for later rapid-fire programmes such as *Three of a Kind* and *The Fast Show*.

Another type of innovation was the production of sketch and variety shows by women (Carol Burnett, Tracey Ullman, Victoria Wood, French and Saunders and others) and by ethnic minorities (*The Flip Wilson Show, The Real McCoy, Goodness Gracious Me*). However, alongside the additional innovations introduced by *The Muppet Show*, more traditional shows continued to be made. Morecambe and Wise, the Two Ronnies, Russ Abbot, Hale and Pace, Fry and Laurie and a number of others have all appeared in successful sketch shows in Britain since the 1960s. In America, on the other hand, whereas sitcoms (and stand-up) have flourished, new variety and sketch shows have been few and far between. Aside from the perennial *Saturday Night Live, SCTV Network* and the subsequent *The Dave Thomas Comedy Show* are obvious exceptions.

Steve Neale

RECOMMENDED READING

Neale, Steve and Krutnik, Frank (1990), *Popular Film and Television Comedy*, London: Routledge.

Scheurer, Timothy (1985), 'The Variety Show', in B.G. Rose (ed.), *TV Genres: A Handbook and Reference Guide*, Westport: Greenwood Press.

Wilmut, Roger (1980), *From Fringe to Flying Circus: Celebrating a Unique Generation of Comedy, 1960–1980*, London: Methuen.

Situation Comedy, Part 1

Situation comedy (sitcom) is one of the staples of mature broadcast television. On the genre-dial it sits between 'sketch comedy' (see p. 62) and 'situation drama', especially continuous serials and episodic series (see 'The Mini-series' p. 35 and 'Soap Opera', p. 47). It has had a remarkably stable semiotic history, migrating fully formed to TV from radio (does anyone remember *The Clitheroe Kid*?) and continu-ing to the present day with few fundamental changes (see Marc, 1989). The heyday of broadcasting was made just that by classics like *The Phil Silvers Show* and *I Love Lucy*, still revered by many as among television's best-ever creations, or *Hancock's Half Hour, Steptoe and Son* and *Till Death Us Do Part* in Britain.

American and British sitcoms have proved to be extremely exportable around the world, using a formula so 'transparent' that they could stand in for 'indigenous' programming for the local audience (see Olsen, 1999). This is especially true for English-speaking countries, or even for those countries where English-language programming is 'neutral' compared with, say, French programming in Germany, German in France or Holland, Dutch in Belgium, and so on. The genre has also led to an excess of 'fanship' with broadcasters mounting 'fests' of just one or two shows. In Australia, Foxtel opened a special cable channel during the Sydney 2000 Olympic Games, devoted to sixteen days of non-stop *Simpsons* (see 'Adult Animation', p. 73) twenty-four hours a day.

The sitcom format suited the Anglo-American industrial production of TV very well. It could use a studio with one or at most two sets, and few or no film inserts. With stable characters in a given situation it could be written and produced by an in-house team of screenwriters and production staff in industrial quantities at so many pages a day. It was also tolerant of commercial imperatives, allowing for segment-length acts, interrupted by commercial breaks, fitting into the TV hour (fifty-odd minutes) or half-hour. It was even productive enough to generate spin-off shows, such as *Rhoda* from *The Mary Tyler Moore Show, George and Mildred* from *Man About the House* or *Frasier* from *Cheers*.

Such shows were distinguished by combining comic talent with dramatic character and action. Sitcom could put seriously funny actors into fictional situations (like John Cleese in *Fawlty Towers* and Rowan Atkinson in *Blackadder* or *Mr Bean*) where the 'situation' in the sitcom was a vehicle for the comedic genius of a given actor, without whose services the show would be hard to imagine. Or it could feature an ensemble of less-well-known actors to bring out the comedic potential in a given situation, such as *Dad's Army* or *Taxi*. Naturally, producers liked it best when a sitcom developed a 'situation' and a star comic together, as in *Roseanne, I Love Lucy* (see 'Situation Comedy, Part 2', p. 67) or *The Cosby Show*. And of course, such shows made stars out of their performers, for instance Christina Applegate, who went on to a good Hollywood career after playing Kelly, the definitive 'gormless gorgeous' dumb-blonde teenager in *Married . . . With Children*.

There were two main types of sitcom: the drama of family comportment (often mixed with sibling rivalry) and the drama of sexual exploration. The former was routinely set in a *home* environment, the latter in the *workplace*:

Family sitcoms specialised in the drama of *family comportment*. They were distinguished from serials and drama series by their focus on internal family roles: usually parents, children and siblings, whether they were presented as blood family (*Roseanne*), melded family (*The Brady Bunch*), or metaphorical family (*Cheers*). Soap opera (see p. 47), on the other hand, focused on the drama of *neighbourly* comportment. It covered the street, neighbourhood or community. Sitcoms and soaps between them showed how families could get along internally (sitcom), and alongside each other (see Hartley, 1999, p. 172). Some sitcoms hybridised with soaps (see p. 47). The BBC's *The Vicar of Dibley* was really about neighbourliness, although it was also a 'workplace sitcom' (see below) with plenty of talk and funny business in the flirting and fancying department.

Family or domestic sitcoms were perhaps the bedrock of broadcast television. They were what you grew up on, gently and amusingly teaching two important skills: how to watch television (media literacy); and how to live in families with tolerant mutual accommodation, talking not fighting (life skills). Although the sitcom remained primarily an adult genre, its efficiency in the matter of family role play also made it a major component of children's TV (see p. 96).

One of the pleasures of watching sitcoms was to observe how bizarre some of the family set-ups were, no matter what their surface 'smileyness' suggested about 'family values'. It was rare indeed to get the traditional 'nuclear family' – so rare that it became a plausibly novel 'situation' for the BBC's *2.4 Children*. More likely was a non-standard family: solo father and boys in *My Three Sons*; father and girls in *Full House*; father and boys melded with mother and girls in *The Brady Bunch* – with never a sexual frisson among the whole lot of them, including aunt-cum-servant Alice.

There were monster families (*The Munsters*), vampire families (*The Addams Family*), witch families (*Bewitched*), alien families (*Third Rock from the Sun*), all of which tended to suggest that, like modernity, progress, science and reason themselves, the modern suburban family was shadowed by darker and mostly unspoken 'others' from pre-modern and irrational traditions (see Spigel, 1996). Within the sphere of everyday ordinariness, families were fractured at best. *Cybil* was divorced and menopausal, *Ellen* gay (see p. 70), *Murphy Brown* a single parent and Victor

Meldrew (in *One Foot in the Grave*) a grouchy old man. Even where families were intact they were dysfunctional, as in *Married . . . With Children*, *Absolutely Fabulous* or *Roseanne* (see box, p. 68).

Sitcoms' attention to the 'not-quiteness' of family life, and to some of the grittier issues lurking under suburban consumerism even as audiences lived in it and endorsed it at elections, made them capable of politics. Classic in this respect was *Till Death Us Do Part*, making a national hero out of a really ghastly old bastard, whose sexist, racist, xenophobic chauvinism and insularity were mercilessly lampooned by writer Johnny Speight. Speight thought he was inoculating the English against some of their nastier 'cultural heritage'. They perversely loved Alf Garnett in their millions, and made it hard for actor Warren Mitchell to play any other role. Alf Garnett, for his part, crossed the Atlantic to become Archie Bunker in Norman Lear's *All in the Family*, which also politicised both 'traditional family values' and the sitcom format.

In1992, the then Vice President Dan Quayle criticised *Murphy Brown* – 'it doesn't help' – for promoting single parenthood instead of 'family values'. Candice Bergen, who played Murphy Brown, got a 'right of reply' in the subsequent season of the series. The media throughout America spent several months debating family philosophy and national policy priorities via a fictional sitcom persona (whose own speech on the subject, however, as right-wing 'shock-jock' Rush Limbaugh commented at the time, 'wasn't funny'). Other 'political' sitcoms included *M*A*S*H*, making war less than noble in the Vietnam era, although it was set in Korea (see 'Hospital Drama', p. 25). *Ellen* sparked public debate about gay and lesbian issues in families just as *Murphy Brown* did about single parents. *Roseanne* put working-class life and non-standard body shapes into prime-time sitcom.

Using 'not-quite' family set-ups to teach about family comportment while attending to humourous situations and attractive characters obviously caused the format to cascade from regular TV to kids' TV. The family was intact in *Clarissa Explains it All*, but the perspective was that of the teenage daughter, not the parents (see Hartley, 1999, pp. 181–5). In *Sister Sister* the main characters were (and were played by) African-American twins who were supposed to have been brought up separately by different parents not married to each other. The white version of this was *Two of a Kind*, played by the Olsen twins (who debuted as 'the' baby in *Full House*), whose mother was absent. Then there was the highly successful *Sabrina the Teenage Witch* (Melissa Joan Hart), who lived with two witch aunts. *Moesha* featured an all-black leading cast, with a teenage girl (Brandy Norwood) having to deal with her father's new partner. These shows indicated that, for teenage-oriented sitcoms especially, there was a need to 'delete' the *mother* from the family in order to propel the 'situation'. The same was true for *My Three Sons, Full House, Father Knows Best* and the like.

Workplace sitcoms often developed characterisations and actions that undercut or even belied the 'situation' itself. Even allowing for the banal sociological fact that sexual partners are often selected from among workmates, workplace sitcoms seemed generically driven to be about sexual chemistry rather than occupational specificity. They routinely reverted to an almost obsessive focus on 'situations' that occurred in relationships rather than in workplaces as such, especially after a given sitcom had relaxed after a couple of seasons' ratings success. A camp, pioneering example of this format (workplace as pretext for risqué talk) was *Are You Being Served?* Long-running American sitcoms like *Taxi* and *Cheers* also used the device of flirting in the workplace.

British television's *Drop the Dead Donkey* was set in a TV newsroom, and initially developed characters associated with that environment. The unseen but brutal owner Sir Royston and his awful corporate-speak sidekick, the preening presenters with feet of clay (one of them clearly paying homage to a real newsreader, the late Reginald Bosanquet), and the reporter who'd stop at nothing to get a story (less obviously modelled on front-line war reporters of the period like Sue Lloyd Roberts). But pretty soon, with the success of the show, *characters* and *actions* took over the comedy, leaving the *situation* – newsgathering and its ethical dilemmas – increasingly in the background.

The character of Joy (Susannah Doyle), for example, was a great comic creation. Joy was young, lovely and smart, but low enough in the office food chain to attract sexist and patronising treatment from the main characters. Her wonderfully viperish responses, and her increasingly implausible revenges, were a delight of the show – but they had very little to do with the *situation* of a newsroom. The script began to pander directly to what Joy was 'about' in viewers' minds rather than in the diegetic world of the TV newsroom, putting her into situations (the gym, the Awards Night) where sexy clothes and extreme violence might coincide.

The emphasis of the show as a whole moved inexorably towards further sexual exploration: the predatory behaviour of the 'loveable rogue' larrikin reporter; the failing marriage of the wimpish hypochondriac editor; the love life of the lesbian big-sister editor; the predilection of the snooty female anchor for one-night stands with truck drivers. Eventually, *Drop the Dead Donkey* was not about TV news at all, it was about sex.

Some sitcoms seem to be hybrids, joining family comportment (living together, couch-centric) and workplace (sexual exploration, flirt-centric). *Friends* was classic here, as was *Seinfeld*. These twenty-something heterosexual home-building shows sometimes went all the way and put their characters in a relationship – *Mad About You* (Helen Hunt) did that, eventually producing another sitcom baby to join those in *Murphy Brown* and *Full House*. Many workplace sitcoms reproduced the *family* formula, while many domestic comedies required a novel 'situation'. For example, in the BBC's *Game On*, the 'family' comprised three flat-sharers. Samantha Janus was the potent force of the show, pretending to be a dumb but single blonde. She lived with two inadequate men, one disabled by unrequited love of an idealised partner who was cynically ripping him off, the other disabled by agoraphobia. They talked about sex all the time, as people did in workplace sitcoms, but they lived in an internally celibate household, albeit not in a classic family.

Some sitcoms seem so full of raw, new energy that they could be counted as R & D for the genre itself, renewing its very form for a new generation of writers, performers and audiences. *The Young Ones* and *Absolutely Fabulous* (see box, p. 68) did that in the UK, *Seinfield* and *The Larry Sanders Show* in the USA. More recently, *The Royle Family* achieved the same rare trick of being 'about' TV as well as 'life', testing its genre, and any vestigial faith we may have had in 'the' family, to destruction.

John Hartley

RECOMMENDED READING

Hartley, John (1999), *Uses of Television*, London and New York: Routledge.

Newcomb, Horace (1974), 'Situation and Domestic Comedies: Problems, Families and Fathers', in Horace Newcomb, *TV: The Most Popular Art*, New York: Doubleday.

Spigel, Lynn (1996), 'From Theatre to Space Ship: Metaphors of Suburban Domesticity in Postwar America', In Roger Silverstone (ed.), *Visions of Suburbia: Symptoms and Metaphors of Modernity*, London and New York: Routledge.

Situation Comedy, Part 2

As explained above, the workplace can provide a pseudo-family of co-workers who take the place of the traditional nuclear family. Sitcoms can alternate between the home and the office (beginning with *The Dick Van Dyke Show* (CBS, 1961–6)). The home and workplace can be one and

The Unruly Woman Sitcom (*I Love Lucy*, *Roseanne*, *Absolutely Fabulous*)

A subtype of the family sitcom – the comedy of the 'unruly woman' – has formed a persistent thread, running from *I Love Lucy* to *Roseanne* to *Absolutely Fabulous* and continuing in the more contemporary characters of Grace in *Will and Grace* (see box, p. 72); and Dharma in *Dharma and Greg* (see above). The term 'unruly woman' has been applied to the sitcom by Kathleen Rowe (1995) with particular reference to *Roseanne* and her image of the 'domestic goddess'. The term describes an icon of a grotesque female whose excesses break social boundaries. She is characterised by a body that is both 'excessive' and 'loose'. In the cases of Roseanne (Roseanne Barr) and Edina (Jennifer Saunders), the excess is represented by fat; but since the unruly woman is just as often tall, thin and attractive (Lucille Ball or Patsy (Joanna Lumley)), it may also take the form of excessive loudness (Roseanne's voice), excessive clothing (Edina's La Croix outfits), hairstyle (Patsy's beehive) and make-up (Lucy's mouth), excessive drinking and smoking (*AbFab*) or simply exceeding the norms of femininity at the time the character was popular.

In the 1950s, for example, Lucy could have been considered 'unruly' because she constantly sought an outlet from domesticity and because she was such a comic failure at domestic tasks. Similarly, looseness can consist in anything from Roseanne's loose tongue to Edina's tendency to lose control of her body and fall (down stairs, into graves, on to conveyor belts). The sitcom has always drawn on a tradition of physical comedy, and the unruly woman is often a female clown (Lucille Ball, Jennifer Saunders, Jenna Elfman). Yet the looseness and excess of her body is not merely funny; it represents an ideological field through which the unruly woman embodies a critique of more conventional notions of the proper behaviour for a sitcom wife.

This is why Rowe and others have viewed Lucy as the prototype for the unruly woman character in the sitcom. Rowe (1995, p. 80) believes that both Hollywood romantic comedy and the sitcom centre on the relationship between the sexes and provide a clearly delineated space for female 'disruptiveness . . . the unruly woman became anchored in the family like television itself, no longer a bride but a wife, a mother, a matriarch . . . taking up the woman's story after the high drama of courtship and the wedding that resolves romantic comedy, the domestic sitcom explores what follows'.

That is, marriage and the family act as social forces that 'contain' the 'transgressive' spirit of the unruly woman, to borrow some terms from Pat Mellencamp's discussion of

Absolutely Fabulous: feminine excess in the unruly woman sitcom

Lucy and Gracie Allen. Mellencamp (1986, p. 61) writes that 'containment' was not only a defensive, military strategy developed as US foreign policy in the 1950s; it was practised on the domestic front as well, and it was aimed at 'excluding women from the workforce and keeping them in the home'.

The issue becomes the following: just how 'transgressive' should we read these sitcom wives as being? Do their antics cause them to transcend the boundaries of their situations or does the domestic setting of the sitcom act to contain them at the end of each week's episode, sending them back to the situation of domestic imprisonment with which they begin each week? In other words, how we analyse the transgressive or critical potential of each unruly woman will determine our view of her position. If we merely look at the sitcom's 'narrative architecture', no sitcom can be transgressive because the episodic format forces us to return to the familiar status quo with which this week's episode began. In order to perceive subversion, we must look at something besides narrative closure. For instance, it is possible that the outrageousness of the physical 'gags' performed by Lucy et al. may transcend her return to being Mrs Ricardo each week. Indeed, these are the moments that one remembers from *I Love Lucy*, the comic peak of the series.

In this reading, because her gags have never been surpassed, Lucy could be read as the most subversive of all, given the constraints of her historical position. On the other hand, if we are looking to find a total critique of domesticity one must choose between *Roseanne* and *Absolutely Fabulous,* which would seem to go much further in presenting characters who lack all maternal instincts; this is exacerbated by the role reversal between Edina and Saffron according to which Saffron's place is in the kitchen whereas Eddie displays a surreal level of domestic ineptitude (see Kirkham and Skeggs, 1998, pp. 287–98). In this reading, farce and ideological subversion count for a lot; the exaggerated excess of the characters makes them radical. The fan culture that formed around *AbFab* would seem to indicate that many viewers identified with the bad mothers and therefore against the proper but dull daughter. Yet one can also read Eddie and Patsy as characters without any redeeming value, thus identifying with Saffron and against the lead characters. In this way a more 'realistic' sitcom such as *Roseanne*, with its proletarian setting and more lifelike characters, may be seen as providing a better critique of domesticity in its very believability.

Whereas few viewers, if any, would compare their family to the Monsoons, nearly every American could identify with the typical nuclear family populating *Roseanne*. Roseanne's acts of unruliness, that is to say, mean more to the audience than do the more outrageous antics of highly stereotyped characters such as Lucy or Edina. Thus when it comes to doing ideological analysis, the sitcom is far less simplistic than its structure would indicate. The situation of the unruly woman illustrates this truth about our most common form of television comedy.

Jane Feuer

the same, as in those sitcoms set in family-owned inns or resorts or in families who live 'above the store' (for example, *Fawlty Towers, Newhart*). Friends can provide a substitute family in shows intended for younger audiences (*The Young Ones, Seinfeld, Friends, Sex and the City*). The nuclear family often breaks down into odd combinations including single parents with children, step-families, even gay men and straight single women (see box). Yet in every case (even in a science fiction setting such as *Red Dwarf* – see p. 31), the sitcom seems to require the presence of a quasi-familial structure in order to satisfy the needs of the viewer. The TV viewer is always addressed by the sitcom as a member of a family – 'from our family to yours'; in fact, the familial mode of address permeates TV in general. In some ways, then, the title 'family sitcom' is redundant since all sitcoms involve some kind of domestic unit.

On the other hand, one could argue that the workplace or 'friends' situation is distinct from the nuclear family setting; that it appeals to a different (younger, hipper) audience; that it is ideologically more contentious. Such an argument is based on the fact that the nuclear family is considered an ideologically conservative social unit that supports the status quo of 'family values'. Therefore, to base a sitcom on a nuclear family is to affirm rather than question the status quo. Following this point of view, sitcoms that undo the nuclear family are in a sense critical of it as a social institution; the alternate families that develop are social alternatives to the nuclear family status quo. Thus *The Cosby Show*, a blockbuster sitcom coming along after a long line of successful workplace family sitcoms, could be read as an ideological regression to the traditional 'Father Knows Best' ideologies of the 1950s and thus reflective of a conservative turn (despite issues of race) in the sitcom taken during the Reagan/Thatcher era. On the other hand, a show that has been considered quite radically critical of family values – The Fox Network's iconoclastic *Married . . . With Children* – also uses a nuclear family setting.

The question of what counts as an innovative feature in the development of a sitcom is difficult because in some ways we are talking about a framework so simple and so easy to recognise that the sitcom is, literally, child's play. And yet the form shows no signs of being exhausted or of not being adaptable to all kinds of socially and comically complex circumstances. As David Marc has pointed out, the sitcom's 'narrative architecture' has remained directly traceable to the radio period. As he explains it, 'episode = familiar status quo ➔ ritual error made ➔ ritual lesson learned ➔ familiar status quo' (Marc, 1989, pp. 190–1).

This 'storytelling grammar', he remarks, has 'persisted across the stylistic revisions of four decades'. Marc goes on to show how episodes of different sitcoms from each decade (*I Love Lucy, Bewitched, All in the Family, Cosby*) illustrate this problem/resolution format. That is to say, that if we look at the sitcom in terms of what might be called its plot, we find little development or innovation. The situation has always been a simple and repeatable frame on which to hang all manner of gags, one-liners, warm moments, physical comedy and ideological conflicts.

In fact, one could say that it has been the *ideological flexibility* of the sitcom that has accounted for its longevity. The sitcom has been the perfect format for illustrating current ideological conflicts while entertaining an audience. What if, for example, a family of hillbillies struck oil and moved to the richest community in the USA? What if a working-class bigot father had to live with a leftist son-in-law? What if a family of liberals gave birth to a Republican son? What if the daughter of aging hippies in San Francisco were to marry the son of a ruling class corporate family? These are the comic premises of *The Beverly Hillbillies, All in the Family* (see 'Situation Comedy, Part 1', p. 66), *Family Ties,* and *Dharma and Greg*, respectively, and what is remarkable about this list is the wide range of ideological conflict the sitcom proves able to accommodate, even including political reversals to accommodate changing social and political norms (for instance, the premise of *Family Ties* is that of *All in the Family* reversed).

The US sitcom *Dharma and Greg* (1997–) well illustrates the ideological flexibility found in most of these 'divided family' premises. If we look at the first scene of the first (pilot) episode, we see the binary, dualistic structure so typical of the domestic sitcom. A young boy and a young girl find themselves on an underground train. The girl and her parents, coded to signify 'hippies', discuss astrological signs. The boy and his parents, dressed in preppy attire, discuss the health hazards associated with taking public transportation. Already (before Dharma and Greg even meet in their adult personas) the basic ideological oppositions of the show are set forth in this amusing fatalistic 'flashback'. The past three seasons of the series have merely served to flesh out the details. If Greg is a government attorney, then Dharma has to be a yoga instructor. If Greg is rigid and organised, Dharma must be laid back and spiritual. However, as the episodes progress, new weekly situations must be generated from this basic premise. That is why, increasingly, the parents of Dharma and Greg have served to carry the basic ideological oppositions between conservative and radical American lifestyles.

In particular, Dharma's father, Larry Finkelstein, has remained the static character signifying (warmed over and burnt out) 1960s radical hippie politics, whereas Greg's mother has served as a similar tentpole for high-society Republican gentility. This has freed up the other characters to indulge in more fluid and changeable behaviour, as when Greg leaves the law to become a 'free spirit' for a few episodes or when Dharma becomes increasingly materialistic. Since US sitcoms usually run much longer than British ones, the

basic dualism of such shows tends to thin out as time goes by and more and more situations are required. *Family Ties*, for instance, started out with a sharp contrast between 1960s liberal parents and neo-conservative children, but as the show continued it came to centre more and more on the popular son character played by Michael J. Fox; the ideological conflicts waned, and many believe the show was trivialised. For this reason, US sitcoms usually reveal their ideological frames much more clearly in the first season than in ensuing ones, and in studying the family sitcom, we often make generalisations based on the first season of the show's run.

Jane Feuer

RECOMMENDED READING
Marc, David (1989) *Comic Visions: Television Comedy and American Culture*, Blackwell.
Mellencamp, Patricia (1986) 'Situation Comedy, Feminism, and Freud: Discourses of Gracie and Lucy', reprinted in Charlotte Brunsdon et al. (eds) (1997) *Feminist Television Criticism: A Reader*, Oxford: Oxford University Press.
Rowe, Kathleeen (1995) *The Unruly Woman: Gender and the Genres of Laughter*, Austin: University of Texas Press.

The 'Gay' and 'Queer' Sitcom

If the family sitcom often begins with a strong ideological premise that gradually exhausts itself, the gay sitcom often goes the other way: beginning with an ambiguous or confused situation, it picks up steam as the gay characters 'come out' or as the show's 'camp' humour thereby takes over. This was demonstrated by *Ellen* (ABC, 1994–8) that floundered in its first seasons because the lead character, played by stand-up comedienne Ellen DeGeneres, was not convincing in a pseudo-heterosexual role. And the reason she was not convincing was that Ellen DeGeneres herself was a confirmed lesbian, a state that was always readable to her gay audience. For example, she wore trousers when she was a maid of honour at her friend Paige's wedding. This was read by lesbians in the audience as a giveaway signifier of her sexual identity. It was no doubt also read as 'off' the heteronormative path by non-gay-identified viewers.

As Ellen DeGeneres started to 'leak' news of her gayness to the media (by denying, for example, that she was 'Lebanese'), the show took on a clearer identity, culminating in the coming-out episode ('The Puppy Episode', 30

April 1997). This episode also illustrated how closely interwoven in the public's mind are the persona of a sitcom star (especially ones with a background in stand-up comedy) and the assumed life status of the actor portraying that character.

Contemporaneous with Ellen's coming out on US TV, other sitcoms started to make extensive use of jokes about gender-bending and gender confusion. Suddenly Susan (NBC, 1996–2000) did an episode ('A Boy Like That', 24 April 1997) in which a typical liberal statement about how 'we' need to tolerate homosexuals fronted an actually quite outrageous joke on its star, Brooke Shields. The episode traced a movement from rejection to acceptance of the gay brother of one of the supporting characters, a macho Latino male. This comic premise was not particularly humourous. But in the course of following the problem/resolution format, the brothers visited a gay country and western bar with Susan (Brooke Shields) and her female co-worker.

When a gay cowboy tried to pick her up (mistaking her for a drag queen), Susan/Brooke said to him, 'Sorry, I'm really a woman.' He replied, 'Not with those shoulders.' This flirtation with the possibility of 'troubling' Brooke Shields's gender is both the funniest and most radical moment of the show because it calls attention to the fact that Brooke Shields *could* represent a drag queen's image of a woman. It thus represented a form of 'queer' comedy that acted to unsettle our normative notions of masculinity and femininity. By 'queering' Susan, Brooke Shields's status as the perfect heteronormative cover girl was called into question by the joke.

Taking as our premise a distinction between comedy and humour (comedy being the overall form a show takes and humour being what makes the audience laugh), it is possible to categorise many presumably heterosexual sitcoms as possessing 'gay humour' or a 'queer sensibility'. Shows that fool around with gender identity often have a gay sense of humour, as does cult behaviour around *Absolutely Fabulous* when fans dress up as either Eddie or (more often) Patsy. The US show *Frasier* (NBC, 1993–) is widely read as a 'queer' sitcom, although the producers vehemently deny it.

This raises the issue of what humour means to gay versus straight audiences. Many well-meaning heterosexual viewers find it offensive that Frasier and his brother Niles are considered 'queer' because of their feminine tastes and preferences for opera, fine wine, designer clothing and the like. They consider this to be stereotyping and ask: why can't a man be heterosexual and effeminate? Although many gays and lesbians share this critique of

Ellen reacted to its star's 'coming out'

stereotyping, others take comic pleasure from reading Niles and Frasier as 'queer', thereby identifying with their effeminacy. A third viewing position here would be a homophobic one in which Frasier's effeminacy is also read as gay but the laughter is at his expense – not as an individual (for Frasier's and Niles's pretensions are certainly laughable) but as a 'fag'.

In this way, *Absolutely Fabulous* and *Frasier* (as well as that moment in *Suddenly Susan*) could be considered 'queer' sitcoms; whereas *Ellen* (final season) and *Will and Grace* as well as the short-lived *Normal, Ohio* (Fox, 2000) might be considered *gay* sitcoms since they began with already fully formed gay main characters. Although there has yet to be a sitcom on US television that is targeted entirely to a gay audience, *Ellen* came the closest in its fifth and final season (1997–8). Much of the humour during the final season consisted in gay 'insider' jokes that appealed to a gay or gay-friendly audience. For instance, 'Emma' (19 November 1997) featured a bizarre narrative in which Emma Thompson, playing 'herself', reveals to Ellen that she (Emma) is a lesbian. This plays against her well-known image as Kenneth Branagh's (ex) wife. In 'It's a gay, gay, gay, gay world' (25 February 1998), Ellen's straight cousin Spence has a dream episode in which he wakes up in a world wherein gayness is the norm and heterosexuality is aberrant. Many of the final season episodes dealt with the humour to be found in the more or less mundane events of a lesbian's life: coming out to friends and family, firing a gay but incompetent plumber, attending a women's music festival, dating and falling in love with a woman, being rejected by her lover's family.

In conclusion, we can distinguish between 'gay' and 'queer' sitcoms according to the relative specificity of the jokes and according to how much of an attempt the writers make to reach a heterosexual audience with their jokes.

Jane Feuer

Will and Grace

When his flaming homosexual pal Jack chides the more masculine but no less gay Will Truman for not dating enough, he
taunts Will by referring to him as 'Margaret Truman'. I want to
take this very simple joke from the sitcom to demonstrate
some of the issues surrounding 'queer' humour, using *Will and
Grace* (NBC, 1998–) as a case study. You do not have to know
who Margaret Truman was to laugh at this joke. The mere fact
that Jack refers to Will by a woman's name represents an
'insider' form of humour among gay men similar to the appel-
lation 'Miss' in front of a girl's name (as in calling another gay
man 'Miss Mary'). There is the simple acknowledgement that
this is a conversation between one gay man and another.
There is an acknowledgement as well of a shared historical
situation according to which effeminacy and gender transitiv-
ity were what united one gay man with another. For older
(American) viewers there is also the knowledge that Margaret
Truman, daughter of President Harry Truman and sometime
actress and mystery author, was a celebrity who possessed the
particularly minor form of fame so important to twentieth-
century gay male cultural experience.

Although the joke can be read and enjoyed on a number of
levels, it is in fact steeped in gay cultural experience. And yet
the gender-bending nature of that culture experience seems to
have penetrated sufficiently into the mainstream to allow *Will
and Grace* to be an equally successful sitcom for gay and
straight audiences. Just as in the earlier sitcoms, Jewish
humour became American humour; nowadays it might be
that 'queer' humour is American humour, that the 'camp' sensibility long cherished by closeted gay men has now become
part of mainstream American humour. Following a definition
of 'camp' as a 'gay sensibility', we can say that 'queer humour'
embraces both identification and parody, that it paradoxically
combines into one sensibility the most extreme feelings of
empathy and the bitchiest kind of detached amusement (Dyer,
1986, p. 154). This is the sense of humour that *Will and Grace*
so frequently invokes. Although Jack is the most overt 'campy'
character, even the relationship between Karen and her maid
Rosario combines feelings of intense devotion with an attitude
towards the Latina woman that is deeply politically incorrect.

Gender-bending is crucial to *Will and Grace*. In this regard
it shares the sensibility that one author has attributed to US
actress and comedienne Sandra Bernhard, saying that she
refuses to accept a static sexual identity (such as 'lesbian') and
that she is a woman who performs gay male drag (Williams,
1998, p. 148). Thus it is not surprising that Bernhard (perhaps best known to the general public for her supporting role
as a lesbian on *Roseanne*) should turn up as a guest star in an
episode of *Will and Grace* (11 January 2001) that deals
specifically with star worship as a manifestation of queer culture. Will and Grace are pursuing a hobby of photographing
themselves in celebrities' homes that they are pretending to
buy from estate agents. Masquerading as a heterosexual
couple, they get away with outlandish infertility jokes such as
Grace telling the world that Will has an 'undescended testicle'.
When Sandra Bernhard (playing 'herself', which is what she
usually does) comes home during their visit to her apartment, she immediately wants to sell to the 'happening gay guy
and the vivacious redhead'. She tells them that they are soul-
mates and Will is so overwhelmed that he makes a 'lowball'
offer of a million dollars on the apartment, which Bernhard
accepts. Then Will and Grace have to tell her they cannot
afford to buy it.

At this point, Bernhard's accompanist starts mixing drinks
in a blender whose sound drowns out the obscenities that
Sandra Bernhard is hurling at Will and Grace. She has
assumed her well-known abrasive persona and her routine
about being a megastar is implanted within the format of *Will
and Grace*. Like Cher, Sandra Bernhard is an appropriate guest
star for a show so rooted in gay cultural practices such as celebrity worship. The episode works not because of the jokes
(these are relatively few) but because of the situation and the
way Bernhard's stand-up persona lends itself to the inflation
and deflation of gay subculture's and now mainstream
American culture's obsession with the cultivation of celebrity.

In fact, many sitcom jokes in US sitcoms assume a deep
knowledge of show business on the part of the American
public. *Will and Grace* differs only in that the knowledge
invoked is gay subcultural knowledge. That is to say, any
sitcom can joke about Elizabeth Taylor's weight, but only Jack
can refer to Ricky Martin as the 'openly Latino pop singing
sensation'.

Jane Feuer

RECOMMENDED READING

Capsuto, Steven (2000), *Alternate Channels: the Uncensored
Story of Gay and Lesbian Images on Radio and Television,
1930s to the Present*, New York: Ballantine Books.

Doty, Alexander (1993), *Making Things Perfectly Queer:
Interpreting Mass Culture*, Minneapolis: University of
Minnesota Press.

Wagg, Stephen (ed.) (1998), *Because I Tell a Joke or Two: Comedy,
Politics and Social Difference*, London: Routledge.

Adult Animation

The importance of design, voice and music mark animated programmes' difference from the dominant conventions of mainstream cinema and television, eschewing the whole notion of 'realism' and embracing zany activities to keep the wandering attention of child audiences (see 'Children's Television', p. 96). Yet animation has also aimed at adult audiences, and in the 1990s there has been a proliferation of successful television cartoons aimed more at adults, or at least aimed less specifically at children.

The predominant form of animation has been drawn and painted. This is called cel animation, as originally an outline was inked on to a sheet of acetate, or cel, and then painted by hand. Thousands of these cels made up a cartoon, photographed painstakingly one by one in succession to give the impression of motion. Another form of animation that is noteworthy is clay animation, where models are constructed of clay or Plasticine and moved very gradually as successive frames of film are exposed. Both of these processes are most laborious. More recently, the use of computers has entered the field of animation. Although it is responsible for the kind of CGI (computer generated imagery) that graces live-action films, computers have aided the production process for traditional animation, allowing faster working through computerised camera movement and co-ordination.

What often is referred to as the classic period of animation took place under the Hollywood studio system (Wells, 1998, p. 208), and was led by such inspired animators as Chuck Jones and Tex Avery, and cartoon characters such as Bugs Bunny, Mickey Mouse and Road Runner. Until the 1960s, short animated comedies or cartoons were fillers on a cinema schedule that would have included a number of items. Cartoons such as those produced by Disney and Max Fleischer's *Betty Boop* (1930) were produced to fill cinema schedules yet had a far longer shelf life than expected. *Betty Boop* also included some very risqué moments. When cartoons were simply part of the cinema bill, there was a need to engage adults as well as children, but with the wholesale move of the television cartoon in the early 1960s, they aimed more directly at children. As the decade of the 1960s started, television began to require so much in the way of cartoons that more were made expressly for the small screen as the demand from the large screen waned with changing patterns of film exhibition. However, the quality of animation dropped as more programmes were made, at a faster rate and more cheaply than had previously been the case.

William Hanna and Joseph Barbera were paramount to developments in comedy animation on television during the 1960s and 1970s (Erickson, 1995, p. 22 – see 'Children's Cartoons', p. 105). Some of their shows recast adult live-action television programmes for children, such as the very successful *Top Cat* (1961–2), known as *Boss Cat* in the UK to avoid connection with a branded pet food, which was loosely based on the characters in *The Phil Silvers Show* (1955–9). Similarly, *The Flintstones* (1960) bore a distinct similarity to *The Honeymooners* (1955–6), with Fred Flintstone being reminiscent of Jackie Gleason's Ralph Kramden. Hanna–Barbera dominated the market for children's cartoons, producing only isolated adult fare. One show was *Wait Till Your Father Gets Home* (1972–3), which was similar to *All in the Family* (1971) (see 'Situation Comedy, Part 1', p. 65). It centred on Harry, wife Irma and their children, college drop-out Chet, overweight sixteen-year-old Alice and nine-year-old hustler Jamie. Adult cartoons seem to return perennially to the theme of family strife, and ultimate unity. Indeed, it is easy to see a direct line of descent from *The Flintstones* and *The Jetsons* (1963), through *Wait Till Your Father Gets Home* to *The Simpsons* (1989 – see box) and *Family Guy* (2000).

In the 1990s, a greater number of cartoons have aimed at a more adult market, sometimes through appealing to the juvenile in adults. MTV (see 'Music on Television', p. 89) produced animation such as Mike Judge's *Beavis and Butthead* (1993). It saw successful spin-offs in *King of the Hill* (1997) and *Daria* (1997), both of which lost the cruder edge of the original, through a focus on middle-aged men and young women respectively in place of juvenile males. *Beavis and Butthead* evolved from a short animation on MTV's seminal weekly *Liquid Television* slot in the early 1990s. This programme showcased animation with no limits and primarily courted an adult audience. Later MTV animation included such cult successes as *The Head* (1996) and *Celebrity Death Match* (1998). The latter evinced a cruel sense of humour, pitting clay models of well-known stars against each other in an arena, in a no-holds-barred fight to the death.

As this illustrates, sex and violence were often on the agenda in animations in the 1990s. *Ren and Stimpy* (1991–4) reinvigorated the classical style of crazy cartooning, and both *The Simpsons* and *South Park* (1997) broke new ground for television cartoons. British animation has never attained the success or volume of production of American products, although it has produced international successes such as the *Wallace and Gromit* short clay-animation films: 'A Grand Day Out' (1992), 'The Wrong Trousers' (1993), and

The Simpsons and South Park

The Simpsons and South Park inaugurated a new phenomenon, seeming in essence to be children's cartoons although
they were aimed more at adults, and both exhibiting witty storylines imbued with massive amounts of popular culture references. The Simpsons was a ground-breaking cartoon series.
One of its great strengths was that it worked on two levels: on
one it was a comic 'sitcom' (see 'Situation Comedy, Part 1', p.
65) about a family, while on the other it was a riot of popular
culture references and self-reflexivity. It was created by Matt
Groening (born 1954), and first appeared as a regular small
animated section in The Tracey Ullman Show in 1987. The
series debuted in 1989, and got massive ratings. It was shown
on prime time by the Fox network, becoming the first animated prime-time series in twenty years. In the UK, The
Simpsons was central to the expansion of BSkyB satellite television, which retained it and only later allowed it on to
national terrestrial television, where it found a home on the
BBC. In the UK it was nurtured for an audience that included
younger children, hence the significant number of more 'adult'
moments edited out of British broadcasts of the show by both
the BBC and Sky.

The Simpsons was premised upon a number of seemingly
universal attractions, based on a dysfunctional family, that
made it popular with diverse audiences. The father, Homer, is
selfish and ignorant, while mother Marge holds the family
together. Son Bart, like his father, is none too intelligent,
having trouble at school and being destructive in the home.
Daughter Lisa functions as the social conscience of the family
and is mentally gifted, although her parents rarely recognise
this. The final member of this nuclear family is Maggie, the
baby. Examples of shows include 'Natural Born Kissers', where
Marge and Homer's love life is reinvigorated by dangerous
situations, while Bart and Lisa discover the alternative ending
of Casablanca when using a metal detector. In 'Rosebud', parodying Citizen Kane, Mr Burns wants to find his childhood
teddy bear, which now belongs to Maggie Simpson. The
show's satire has included mutated fish caused by a nuclear
power plant, corrupt politicians and media manipulation.
Added to this is the propensity for rapid-fire cultural references and intertextuality, including appearances by media
mogul Rupert Murdoch (the owner of Fox network), Mulder
and Scully from The X-Files (another Fox show – see box,
p. 30). The Simpsons broke new ground for animated television shows, opening the way for South Park and King of the
Hill. Its place at the centre of American popular culture was
underlined when, in the 1992 election campaign, George Bush

South Park dealt with adult and controversial themes

declared: 'We're going to keep on trying to strengthen the
American family. To make them more like the Waltons and
less like the Simpsons.'

South Park appeared on television to voices raised in
protest by moral guardians everywhere. For parents with
young children, South Park represented a threat in that it was
about young children, looked like a cartoon for young children, yet dealt with adult and controversial themes such as
sex, Charles Manson, murder and suicide: material clearly for
an older audience. The show's originators, Trey Parker and
Matt Stone, created South Park to look like the most primitive
cartoon possible, with very simple character design, which
proved particularly suited to being made into tied-in products
like stuffed toys.

The show's protagonists are a group of third-grade children who live in a small Colorado town called South Park.
They are Stan, Kyle (the Jewish one), Cartman (the fat one)
and Kenny (the poor one). Although Stan and Kyle are the
'best friends' at the centre of many of the stories, the other two
proved more popular with audiences. Whereas Kenny always
wears a coat with the hood up so that his dialogue is muffled,
the obese and antisocial Eric Cartman proved very popular
with children, to their parents' chagrin. Apart from basic and
crude humour, the programme was very stylised. In each
episode, for example, Kenny has to die in some way or
another, prompting a repartee between Kyle and Stan: 'Oh my
God, they killed Kenny!'; 'You bastards!' Satire was more evident in other South Park characterisation. The children's
accomplice on many of their adventures is 'Chef', voiced by
soul singer Isaac Hayes, who serves them dinner at school.
School, and authority more generally, is represented in rather
negative terms. The children's neurotic teacher, Mr Garrison,

is always accompanied by and speaks with a vent glove puppet called 'Mr Hat'.

An example of the unpredictable trajectory of an episode is 'Pinkeye', where Russian space station Mir falls to earth, landing on Kenny's head. He dies but returns as a zombie, as the town is overwhelmed by zombies straight out of George Romero's film *Night of the Living Dead*. At the conclusion, Chef sings Michael Jackson's *Thriller* in a parody of the pop video. The show has a fine sense of popular culture references, as well as (usually spurious) celebrity cameos in unusual situations. Actual guests included George Clooney (voicing a dog), Jennifer Aniston, the band Korn and Elton John, and other celebrities have been crudely fabricated, including Streisand, Celine Dion and Saddam Hussein, not to mention Jesus who regularly appears with his own television talk show.

However, *South Park*'s roster of guests fades into insignificance in comparison with that of *The Simpsons*. Their show has included Bob Hope, singer Tom Jones, scientists Stephen Jay Gould and Stephen Hawking, artist Jasper Johns, basketball player Magic Johnson, and musicians such as Ringo Starr and Sting voiced by the stars themselves. A principal attraction of both *The Simpsons* and *South Park* is that they allow a kind of regression to childhood for their adult viewers. This is stronger in the case of *South Park*, where there is additional perverse enjoyment of the child characters' precociousness as well as their misunderstanding of the adult world. Although *The Simpsons* has become one of the most popular television cartoons ever, *South Park* has managed to gain more notoriety for its bad taste, often bordering on the insulting, although its success did lead to the production of a feature film.

Kevin Donnelly

'A Close Shave' (1995). Similarly, Japanese cartoon animation, called 'Animé', were very popular in the Far East and by the mid-1980s started to appear on western screens, although they ended up becoming a cult rather than a mainstream item (Erickson, 1995, p. 36).

Since the mid-1980s, animation was almost all contracted out to Asiatic studios, not only because of their expertise but also because of their cheap labour costs. European art-animation, such as three-dimensional work by Jan Svankmajer (*The Death of Stalinism in Bohemia*, 1990) and the Quay brothers (*The Street of Crocodiles*, 1986), received great acclaim. Art-animation never reached the degree of international impact exhibited by series like Fox's *The Simpsons*, for example, which was the first cartoon scheduled on US prime time for decades. The Cartoon Network was launched in the USA in 1992 and, despite commissioning the production of new cartoons, still relies heavily on reruns of the massive volume of cartoons from the past.

Kevin Donnelly

POPULAR ENTERTAINMENT

The Populist Debate

'Popular Entertainment' could be judged as a misleading title, in the sense that it might suggest that other TV genres are neither 'popular' nor 'entertaining'. This is clearly not the case. Soap opera, for example, is probably one of the most consistently *popular* forms of television *entertainment* the medium has yet to produce (see p. 47), and comedy is almost always based (at least, in the first instance) on its ability to entertain its audience and make it laugh (see p. 61). However, for the purpose of clarity and organisation alone (and not, we hope, any hierarchical undercurrent), the title seems to suit a number of different and assorted genres individually addressed here under this rather broad but useful umbrella heading. It could be argued that included here are a variety of different (and perhaps even miscellaneous) programmes that can be seen as sharing a number of inherent forms and characteristics – not least, their tendency to be downgraded and despised by critics for their unashamedly populist and frequently commercial aspirations.

At its most basic level, television is a scientifically managed institution for the mass production of entertainment, a bureaucratically organised regime of pleasure that systematically produces permutations of the everyday and the spectacular. These permutations are designed to capture audiences and deliver them to advertisers (see 'Advertising' p. 94), in the case of commercial networks, or government, in the case of public stations. Genres combine the memorandum and the commodity; one ensures standardisation, the other marketability. They also provide benchmarks for aesthetic taste and pedagogic direction.

The populist debate revolves around the question of pleasure and consumption. In particular, it centres on the issue of whether some forms of 'popular entertainment' purely pander to an audience's 'baser' tastes and desires (simply designed to keep advertisers happy); or whether programmes such as the quiz or talk show (see pp. 79, 81, 84) can actually provide audiences with more than simply 'standardised' and 'formulaic' fare. Central to this debate is the issue of whether television viewers are primarily 'passive' or 'active' in their viewing habits. Whether they passively accept television's commercial imperatives or whether they actively produce meaning and resistance in their complex production of pleasure and entertainment (also see 'Soap Operas and their Audiences', p. 55). Because certain programmes are judged to be inherently 'formulaic' or driven by *mass desires* (for instance, the consumerist imperative of the quiz show – see p. 79), particular genres face the wrath of public and critical scorn more than others. As a result, 'popular entertainment' on the small screen quickly came to the attention of politicians, academics and influential pressure groups, all eager to promote their particular ideological crusade.

One hundred and fifty years ago, it was taken as read that audiences were active, given their unruly and overtly engaged conduct at cultural events. But the emergence of public education in the west in the nineteenth century, allied to the disciplines of literary criticism and psychology, shifted critical rhetoric about audiences (Butsch, 2000, p. 3). Since the advent of the mass media, especially television, much energy has been devoted to evaluating the active versus passive sides to media audiences. Television programmes are 'symbols for time' (Hartley, 1987, p. 133), and the alleged misuse of time has become integral to the desire to police everyday television-watching (see 'Educational Programming', p. 137). Various critics have in turn defended audiences against these charges of inactivity, arguing that 'the people' engage in resistive readings of TV programmes that reference viewers' social struggles rather than adhering to television producers' preferred responses.

Widespread anxiety is expressed by social critics about the supposed lack of 'active choice' in watching television (Carson, 1983). This concern dates back a long way: the modernist American architect Frank Lloyd Wright called TV '[c]hewing gum for the eyes' (quoted in Kellner, 1990, p. 1). Today, communitarian philosophy and sociology rail against rampant individualism, secular selfishness and the absence of civic responsibility. An allegedly active public is contrasted with a putatively inactive TV audience:

> we are not happy when we are watching television, even though most of us spend many hours a week doing so, because we feel we are 'on hold' rather than really living during that time. We are happiest when we are successfully meeting challenges at work, in our private lives, and in our communities (Bellah et al., 1992, p. 49).

Hence the link to panics about education, violence and apathy supposedly engendered by (popular) television and routinely investigated by the state, psychology, Marxism, neoconservatism, the Church, liberal feminism and others. The audience as consumer, student, felon, voter and idiot engages such groups. Sometimes the criticisms are about particular genres, TV wrestling (see 'Sport' p. 87) is degrading, infotainment (see p. 118) is commercial, and talk shows (see pp. 81, 84) trivialise current affairs; in contrast, 'real' sport binds the nation and 'real' journalism informs the electorate. Sometimes the criticisms are about TV *as* a genre (its audiovisual form makes it inappropriate for education (see p. 137), or its commercialism/statism scar its democratic potential).

These anxieties have in turn drawn critique. In the 1960s, Harold Garfinkel (1992) developed the notion of the 'cultural dope', a mythic figure 'who produces the stable features of the society by acting in compliance with pre-established and legitimate alternatives of action that the common culture provides'. The 'common-sense rationalities . . . of here and now situations' used by ordinary people are obscured by this condescending categorisation (p. 68). When the audience is invoked as a category by the industry, critics, and regulators, it becomes such a 'dope'. This is often a gendered invocation, as Michèle Mattelart (1986, p. 65) explains:

> in the everyday time of domestic life . . . the fundamental
> discrimination of sex roles is expressed. . . . The hierarchy
> of values finds expression through the positive value
> attached to masculine time (defined by action, change
> and history) and the negative value attached to feminine
> time which, for all its potential richness, is implicitly dis-
> criminated against in our society, interiorised and lived
> through as the time of banal everyday life, repetition and
> monotony.

Quiz and talk shows (see pp. 79, 81, 84) are deemed inferior because they are associated (contradictorily) with both passivity and high emotion. These criticisms have supporters on both left and right, across both the social sciences and the humanities, and such denunciations continue to flourish.

The active-audience tradition picks up on Garfinkel's cultural-dope insight. Instead of issuing jeremiads, it claims that audiences are so clever and able that they outwit the institutions of the state, academia and capitalism that seek to control and measure them and their interpretations. In one sense, this position has a venerable tradition, via literary theorists like old Nazism man Hans

Robert Jauss's (1982) aesthetics of reception and old Marxism man Jean-Paul Sartre's (1990) philosophy of the mutual intrication of writer and reader in making meaning (Mattelart and Mattelart, 1998, pp. 119–20, 123). In communications and culture, especially television, the idea really spread with Umberto Eco's mid-1960s development (published in English in 1972) of a notion of open texts and processes of encoding–decoding. This was picked up by sociologists Frank Parkin (1971) then Stuart Hall (1980) on the left, and on the right by uses-and-gratifications functionalist Elihu Katz (1990). It is often associated today in television studies with John Fiske (1987).

This counter-critique attacks criticisms of television for failing to allot the people's machine its due as a populist apparatus that subverts patriarchy, capitalism and other forms of oppression (or diminishes the tension of social divisions, depending on your politics). Popular TV is held to be subversive/relieving because, almost regardless of content, its output is decoded by audiences in keeping with their own social situation (Seiter, 1999). The active audience is said to be weak at the level of cultural production, but strong as an interpretative community. Consider the special skills of cultish fans. They construct parasocial or imagined connections to celebrities or actants, who fulfil friendship functions or serve as spaces for projecting and evaluating schemas that make sense of human interaction. In addition to adoring the text, cult audiences domesticate the characters, removing them from the overall story and quoting their escapades and proclivities as if they were part of the fan's world, a world opened up to other followers through quizzes and rankings. References to favourite episodes, the behaviour of actants, or the qualities of stars, catalyse memories. Sequences and tendencies are disarticulated from screen time, reshaped and redisposed to contrast with one's own social circumstances (Leets et al., 1995, pp. 102–4; Harrington and Bielby, 1995, pp. 102–4, 110; Eco, 1987, p. 198). In addition, the despised genres listed earlier are recuperated: wrestling (see 'Sport', p. 87) becomes carnivalesque, infotainment legitimises the pleasures of shopping, and talk shows address hitherto suppressed topics of public debate.

Meaghan Morris (1990) glosses, enacts, and criticises the active-audience tradition in her account of *The Lucille Ball Show* as seen on 1950s Australian television. This isolated image of women evading patriarchal control had dramatic effects on the Morris household – mother and daughter revelled while father absented himself. But the programme was also a sign of political economy and diplomacy: it represented a resiting of Australian geopolitical culture away from Britain and towards the United

Lucille Ball: breaking the boundaries of female comedy

States (pp. 15–16). This captures the duality of television as a capitalist and governmental technology that is *also* populist. It follows that the idea of this apparatus as a sign of freedom is an ambivalent fable for cultural democracy. Popular TV is certainly amenable to a notion of localism, resistance and feminism working via the 'subversive pleasure of the female spectators' to produce an active engagement with both the text and the family. But this can become a critic's alibi for social speculation. Our suspicions should be aroused when academic theory cites 'the people' as demotic supports for its own preoccupations, because when 'the people' become one more text to be read and interpreted, they stand for the critic's own practice of reading. Far from being sources of information, 'the people' have been transmogrified into delegates that endow the critic's *own* account with a populist ring (Morris, 1990, pp. 21–3). Aberrant decoding by fans becomes a means of making the output of the culture industries isomorphic with a professor's anti-capitalist, anti-patriarchal, anti-racist politics.

Today, this active-audience position may be the most visible aspect of television studies. Virginia Postrel wrote a 1999 op-ed piece for the right-wing US financial newspaper the *Wall Street Journal* welcoming active-audience research, describing it as 'deeply threatening to traditional leftist views of commerce' because notions of active media consumption by fans were so close to the sovereign consumer beloved of the right: 'The cultural-studies mavens are betraying the leftist cause, lending support to the corporate enemy and even training graduate students who wind up doing market research.' Todd Gitlin (1997, p. 32) argues that some sectors of cultural studies are indeed in synch with neoclassical economics and the right: 'What the group wants, buys, demands is *ipso facto* the voice of the people. Supply has meshed with demand'. As Herbert I. Schiller puts it (1989, pp. 147–8, 153), the direct opposition that is frequently drawn between political economy (production matters) and active-audience theory (interpretation matters) assumes that the fragmentation of audience niches and responses nullifies the concentration and reach of economic power in mass culture – pluralism ensures diversity. But is this credible? Perhaps a 'shared interest in [a] show is an end in itself and seldom leads to some action beyond that interest, some larger political purpose' (Butsch, 2000, p. 291).

In reaction to both the cultural-dope and active-audience models, Alec McHoul and Tom O'Regan (1992, pp. 5–6, 8–9) criticise the idea that 'local instances' of people 'embracing' or 'refusing' the dominant interpretations preferred by global producers 'guarantee any general statement about textual meaning'. Instead, they propose a 'discursive analysis of particular actor networks, technologies of textual exchange, circuits of communicational and textual effectivity, traditions of exegesis, commentary and critical practice'. In other words, the specific 'uptake' of a text by a community should be our focus; but not because this reveals something essential to the properties of TV genres or their likely uptake anywhere else or at any other time. We can only discern a 'general outline' of 'interests', applied to specific cases 'upon a piecemeal and local inspection'. For television is an instrument of instruction and response that varies with place, time, genre and audience (O'Shea, 1989, pp. 376–7).

As Justin Lewis says (1991, p. 49), 'TV viewing is a cultural practice, and like all cultural practices, it involves not only "doing it" but "ways of doing it" '. For those of us schooled in pub talk or Leavisite talk, whether they be about sport, art, politics, literature, friends or television, there is nothing necessarily new or socially subversive about evaluations by fans. None of which is to say that, on the other side, the anti-populists are correct in their infantalisation of audiences. As Pierre Bourdieu suggests (1998, p. 48), 'paternalistic–pedagogical television' is 'no less opposed to a truly democratic use of the means of mass circulation than populist spontaneism and demagogic capitulation to popular tastes'. Dan Schiller (1996, p. 194) suggests a way beyond such graceless antinomies. TV production need not be thought of in opposition to consumption, with one practice 'productive' and the other not, or one side trumping the other. Instead, the work of television employees is one moment of labouring activity, and the work of television audiences is another moment. This suggests that rather than embarking on either active interpretation or passive reception, audience members' labour includes self-understanding – but that labour cannot and should not be conceptualized in isolation from their day jobs, or the work of others in bringing TV to them (Maxwell, 2001).

Toby Miller

Author's note: My thanks to Marie Leger and Richard Maxwell for their comments.

RECOMMENDED READING

Fiske, John (1987), *Television Culture*, London: Routledge.
Harrington, C. Lee and Bielby, Denise D. (1995), *Soap Fans: Pursuing Pleasure and Making Meaning in Everyday Life*, Philadelphia: Temple University Press.
Schiller, Herbert I. (1989), *Culture Inc.: The Corporate Takeover of Public Expression*, Oxford: Oxford University Press.

The Quiz Show

The quiz (or game) show genre has played an important and sometimes controversial role in the history of television in the United States and elsewhere. Legendary quiz show executive Mark Goodson, whose company has been responsible for over 22,000 hours of quiz show programming on US television, called quiz shows and soaps, 'the great indigenous television forms', and the two genres have several common features. Like soap operas, TV quiz shows in America grew out of a popular radio format of the 1930s; and both genres have been aimed principally at a daytime, and largely female, audience. Unlike the experience in many other nations, in the US only rarely have soaps (see p. 47) or quiz shows had a significant presence in network prime time. The chief exceptions for the US quiz show are the period between 1955 and 1958, when the *$64,000 Question* sparked a short-lived, high-stakes quiz show boom in prime time before revelations of fraud in many of the most popular programmes nearly killed the entire genre. The second exceptional period of prime-time game show popularity followed the phenomenal success of *Who Wants to Be a Millionaire?* as a summer replacement series in 1999, spurring the current proliferation of prime-time game shows in American TV network schedules.

The subject of little scholarly attention, the quiz show genre has endured long periods of critical disdain and indifference, interrupted by infrequent moments of generalised and often hyperbolic critical reaction to the spectacular success of a specific show or format, before the genre recedes again into fringe-time invisibility and *critical obscurity*. Unlike the soap opera, the subject of sustained and sophisticated scholarly attention over the past two decades (see p. 55), the critical literature on TV game shows remains dominated by fan tributes, sociological reflectionism and elitist scorn.

As John Fiske has pointed out, soaps and quiz shows share a climate of critical hostility, a tendency towards stylistic excess and parody (the precise differences between a straightforward quiz show and the many parodies of quiz shows across TV history are sometimes difficult to identify, and a popular image of their audience as highly – perhaps pathologically – involved in their viewing styles). Although Mark Goodson argued that the successful quiz show should have the viewer talking out loud to his or her TV set, the narrative and character structures of the genre are arguably the most distant from those of literary-based TV genres. As nearly authorless texts, the

Who Wants to be a Millionaire?: 'England's most successful cultural export in the last 30 years'

quiz show has frustrated traditional auteurist and generic methods of analysis imported from literature and film studies.

If neglected by critics, the quiz show has proved to be one of the most flexible and resilient of television formats. Cheap and easy to produce, the format has thrived at diverse levels of the television food chain, from low-budget, local, live origination and fringe-time syndication to network prime time and cable networks as diverse as Nickelodeon, the Playboy Channel, MTV (see box, p. 91), and the Food Network. It is not uncommon for a long-extinct quiz show from decades past to be revived with a new host or minor revision in format, or for a successful programme quickly to spin off multiple sequels and imitators. Quiz shows have run the gamut from the low-stakes, high-prestige contests of official knowledge of *Mastermind* in the UK and *GE College Bowl* in the USA, to the carnivalesque celebrations of consumer desire of *The Price is Right* and *Supermarket Sweep*. In the USA, the genre is robust enough to have supported a number of so-called 'misery shows', including *Queen for a Day* and *Strike it Rich*, where down-and-out contestants compete

for sympathy from members of the studio and home audiences.

The genre has also proved to be an extremely exportable one, less in the form of programmes themselves than in the licensing of programme formats. Indeed, the 1999 success of the UK programme hit *Who Wants to Be a Millionaire?* for the ABC network in the United States, followed by the similar success of *Survivor*, the following year, created a minor buying frenzy among US programmers for new game show formats. The exploding trade in programme formats, driven principally by the game show and 'Reality TV' genres (see p. 134), has at least temporarily weakened traditional US network hostility to foreign programming and American domination of global TV markets.

The quiz show genre is a highly diverse one, ranging from straight contests of knowledge, to audience-participation games featuring outlandish and sometimes humiliating stunts, to programmes built around stumping a panel of celebrities, where the emphasis is less upon a specific outcome than on the humourous or risqué banter between celebrity and civilian. Contests of knowledge range between 'official' and vernacular knowledge, from arcane facts of history or science to the prices of everyday commodities. Other popular shows, including *The Dating Game*, *The Newlywed Game*, and *Family Feud*, depend upon the success of contestants in correctly surmising the responses of others to a range of questions. Perhaps inevitably, the extremely popular high-stakes quiz shows of both the late 1950s and the late 1990s provoked widespread critical musings about how such get-rich-quick dramas reflect cultural attitudes about class, knowledge and upward mobility.

The various television quiz formats turn around differing calibrations of luck, knowledge and skill, and almost all offer the spectacle of ordinary people facing life-transforming decisions in extended real time. Indeed, although several episodes of a series are typically taped back-to-back some weeks before their air dates, contemporary high-stakes quiz programmes expend a great deal of effort to create a sense of 'liveness', supporting an analogy to televised sporting events (see 'Sport', p. 87). Most game show formats depend heavily on the figure of the host, almost always male (of the thirty-five national versions of the current global hit programme *Who Wants to Be a Millionaire?*, only three are hosted by women), who functions as something between the contestant's sympathetic helpmate and cruel inquisitor. The visual design of the game show ranges from the quotidian opposing tables and podiums of the school spelling bee to the video game and science fiction

Who Wants to Be a Millionaire?

Described by the *New York Times* as 'England's most successful cultural export in the last 30 years', the high-stakes quiz show *Who Wants to Be a Millionaire?* has demonstrated the power of a single programme to reshape prime-time schedules and broadcast competition around the world. After two years of fruitless pitches to British broadcast networks by its production company, Celador, *Millionaire* was picked up by ITV in the autumn of 1998 and became an immediate hit, gaining as much as 72 per cent of the television audience. By the end of 2000, the programme was on the air in thirty-five countries and sold as a format to forty-five more; Celador's managing director told a journalist, 'It's a bit like the old days of the British Empire. We've got a map of the world in the office coloured in pink where we've placed the show. Most of the world is pink.'

The British production company maintains tight control over the franchise, and the format of various national versions is identical: after being selected via a series of telephone and studio qualifying quizzes, individual contestants answer a series of fifteen questions of escalating difficulty while seated opposite the programme's host in the middle of a high-tech amphitheatre. Contestants may draw upon assistance three times, electing either to poll the studio audience, phone a friend for advice, or eliminate two of the incorrect answers. Top prizewinners are rare across the world, most frequently occurring in the USA, where six contestants have won $1,000,000 over two seasons of the programme. The show's Indian version, *Kaun Banega Crorepati*, broadcast five nights a week in the 2000 season, gained an 87 per cent audience share and was responsible for vaulting Rupert Murdoch's Star Plus satellite channel from third to first place across India; Star's profits from this one programme were more than the combined earnings from all the other Star TV channels in India.

The success of *Who Wants to Be a Millionaire?* in the USA since 1999 has been equally spectacular. Picked up for a limited-run summer replacement series in August 1999 by Disney–ABC, it reached as many as 22 million viewers per broadcast and was responsible for boosting the overall summer audience ratings of the largest four US networks by 9 per cent. In the 1999–2000 television season, it lifted ABC from third to first place in network competition, the first time that had been accomplished in US television history. For the February 2000 sweeps period, when advertising rates are set for the ensuing quarter, ABC filled 18 per cent of its entire prime-time schedule with multiple episodes of the show.

Its success at ABC brought many imitators, and by January 2000 quiz shows consumed six and a half hours of weekly prime time, more than at any point since the 1950s. By May 2000 it was among the top ten US network shows for each of its three weekly broadcasts, and ABC's overall audience figures were up 20 per cent for the season. ABC's revenues were up 30 per cent for the season, with the network demanding up to $400,000 per thirty-second commercial in the programme (production costs are estimated at between $500,000 and $1,000,000 per episode); industry estimates placed ABC's annual profits from the show between $400 million and $600 million, an amount greater than the typical total annual profits of an entire US TV network.   *William Boddy*

film inspired *mise en scène* of the contemporary big-budget *Who Wants to Be a Millionaire?* and *Winning Lines*. Indeed, it is not unusual for producers to spend more on the programme's set than upon any other element of the programme, including prizes.

William Boddy

RECOMMENDED READING
Fiske, John (1987), 'Quizzical Pleasures', in *Television Culture*, London: Routledge.

Goedkoop, Richard (1985), 'The Game Show', in Brian Rose (ed.), *TV Genres: A Handbook and Reference Guide*, Westport: Greenwood Press.

Schwartz, David, Ryan, Steve and Wostbrock, Fred (1999), *Encyclopedia of TV Game Shows*, New York: Checkmark Books.

The Celebrity Talk Show

The child of vaudeville and radio variety, TV celebrity talk shows have been a staple of American TV since *The Tonight Show* premiered in September 1954. Pat Weaver, the famed NBC producer in the 1950s, is credited with originating the genre. He changed the focus of late-night programming from a variety show emphasising performance to a talk show with a series of conversations interspersed with performances.

Since its start, the set on the stage replicates a living room with a desk for the host and a couch for the guests (with a curtained performance stage to the right). The format, too, has remained the same: an opening monologue by the host, a segment with the studio audience

The Tonight Show

The Tonight Show has aired uninterruptedly since 27 September 1954 on NBC as the pre-eminent late-night talk show. It remains the most profitable series on American television. It was never seriously challenged for its authority as the leading celebrity talk show until *Late Night with David Letterman* in 1993. The programme has gone through a number of hosts, but its success is most closely associated with Johnny Carson, a mild-mannered comedian who perfected the good-natured humour and light conversation that characterises American celebrity talk shows.

Nightly after the news, the programme would announce itself with the upbeat sound of swing music as Ed McMahon, the sidekick, would sing out 'Heeerrrrrrrrrrrrrre's Johnny!' Carson would appear from behind a curtain in a sports jacket to wild clapping and howls. After thanking them for their generous applause, he began his monologue, a humourous combination of joking about current events and interaction with the audience. His style reflected his Midwest background: cool, casual, and clean-cut but still mischievously charming,

which made going 'to bed with Johnny Carson' an American pastime. His humour was self-consciously fashioned on the work of Jack Benny, who emphasised comedic timing such as the pause and slow burn. Carson conversed with celebrities with the air of cocktail party repartee. He kept the conversation light assiduously avoiding confrontation and political controversy. But he also kept it flirtatious as he kidded his guests about their lives and work. The programme's popularity relied on the unerring uniformity of the programme and Carson's humour for over thirty years.

The various incarnations of *The Tonight Show* are distinguished by the personalities of the different hosts. The programme originally began under the title *Tonight!* in 1954 with Steve Allen as the host. Although he established the basic format of *The Tonight Show*, Allen as a musician created a more musical show with musical guests as regulars. His method was improvisation, and he would often jump up and run into the audience or out on to the street, invent narration to the imagery of a remote camera, or compose a song spontaneously based on audience suggestions. Jack Paar, the second host (1957–62), was not a comic but an

The Tonight Show with Johnny Carson: 'cool, casual and clean-cut'

expert conversationalist who could joke. As a result the pro-gramme was more issues-oriented and acerbic and ulti-mately controversial. When NBC censored a joke of his, he walked on stage the next night and announced his anger with NBC's decision and walked off the programme. In 1961 he took the show to West Berlin and filmed in front of the Berlin Wall, which was less than a month old. The Defense Department deployed a group of soldiers to stand between the Wall and the filming. The department launched an inquiry into Paar's action, leading ultimately to the host's resignation in 1962 when Carson came on.

In 1992 Jay Leno (a stand-up comic and frequent guest) took over after Carson's thirty-year stint. Although David Letterman a popular, but acerbic guest host, was the heir apparent to the permanent position, he lost out to the softer and warmer humour of Leno, a closer model to the light tra-dition of Carson. In 1994 Letterman was the first to compete successfully with his own celebrity talk show on CBS by carv-ing out a younger audience with his irreverent humour. By 1995 the late-night celebrity talk show audience split.

Jane Shattuc

(interviews and games), and a set of interviews and per-formances with well-known guests on stage. Each host is paired with a sidekick who functions as an announcer but also a foil for humour and an ideal listener. The pro-grammes are recorded with a live studio audience in the daytime and aired at night. *The Tonight Show* (1954– see box), *The Dick Cavett Show* (1969–86), *The Arsenio Hall Show* (1989–94), and *Late Night with David Letterman* (1982–) represent the most successful examples in the United States. The programmes have a cultural cachet, given their centrality in the late-night schedule of the net-works. They serve as important publicity venues, which have made the careers of guests by increasing the visibility of the individual or group. *The Mike Douglas Show* (1962–82) and *The Mere Griffin Show* (1965–86) were day-time celebrity talk shows and became the prototype for confessional talk shows (see p. 84) when the daytime genre began to shift in the 1970s and 80s to average Americans as the 'celebrity' guests and their social and personal issues as topics.

The genre focuses on interviews with entertainment luminaries (actors, musicians, popular artists and tele-vision personalities) but sometimes politicians, authors and average citizens whose lives merited public recog-nition. Each programme establishes a set list of celebrities who 'drop in' regularly much like neighbours for a chat. The host and guest (often with mugs of coffee) carry on a lively slightly rehearsed conversation focused around a specific object or media event that the guests want to pro-mote (film, TV programme, CD or tour). In exchange for the publicity, the guest usually divulges intimate details of their lives or work to please the audience. Much like domestic hospitality, the host treats the guest as if s/he is 'royalty' or a celebrity in the case of American culture. 'In this form, entertainment is sacred, providing viewers release from the frightening events and less-than-desirable

life conditions in their everyday experience. Fun is func-tional. Entertainers are elevated to the status of cultural heroes' (Himmelstein, 1994, p. 343).

The celebrity talk show is also marked by its interaction with the studio audience. After a five- to ten-minute humourous monologue that warms up the audience's response, the host often steps into the audience. The inter-action serves numerous functions. It allows for a seemingly 'democratic' moment as average people are given a similar treatment to the celebrity guests. The audience interaction also creates a more emotive response from the audience, and the rest of the programme becomes more dynamic. The audience members are frequently called on by name and asked to interact with the host. Although the studio audience is seen and called upon, it still functions similarly to a laugh track (although less predictable) as passive 'inscribed viewers' whose main role is to represent the at-home viewer by following the programme's rules of good viewership. They embody the immediate 'you' to whom the hosts refer in their monologues as they address the camera. They laugh and applaud to a degree voluntarily out of appreciation for the entertainment. Nevertheless, the pro-ducers attempt to prescribe the emotional tenor of the show through studio signals – flashing signs or gesturing personnel – telling the studio audience to laugh and applaud.

The history of celebrity talk shows is defined by slight variations in the prescribed formula of light entertainment established in the 1950s. *The Dick Cavett Show*, the ABC celebrity talk show of the late 1960s and early 1970s, posed as the 'intellectual' alternative to *The Tonight Show*. Partially because of Cavett's Yale University education and interest in language, the programme attracted a more high-brow audience and set of guests. It was famed for the verbal sparring between guests and sometimes host: bouts between Norman Mailer and Gore Vidal, Cavett and Lester

Maddox (a southern anti-civil rights politician) and TV actor Chad Everett and Lily Tomlin (who walked off the stage when Everett objectified his wife). The programme never retained a large viewership.

The Arsenio Hall Show in 1988 was the first to attract a younger audience than The Tonight Show. With the first black talk show host, the programme was able to book soul and rap groups on TV (McNeil, 1996, p. 58). David Letterman followed Hall's youth-orientation when he competed successfully opposite The Tonight Show in 1993. With his irreverent humour ('Top Ten Lists' and 'Stupid Pet Tricks'), ribbing of everyday New Yorkers (often working class and immigrant Americans), and sardonic sparring with women celebrities, Letterman offered an iconoclastic alternative to the staid slower style of Jay Leno's Tonight Show. By 1995 the late-night celebrity talk show audience split: Letterman's Late Show retained the all-important demographics of young viewers, but The Tonight Show regained its overall ratings lead as the voice of light entertainment in America (see box). However, Letterman's irreverent style quickly spread to the UK, 'borrowed' by presenters such as Jonathan Ross (The Last Resort) and Chris Evans (TFI Friday).

Jane Shattuc

RECOMMENDED READING

Himmelstein, Hal (1994), Television Myth and the American Mind, Westport: Praeger.

McNeil, Alex (1996), Total Television: A Comprehensive Guide to Programming from 1948 to the Present, New York: Penguin Putnam.

Munson, Wayne (1993), All Talk: The Talk Show in Media Culture, Philadelphia: Temple University Press.

The Confessional Talk Show

The confession or the baring of private feelings and acts in public is what most people associate with American talk shows between about 1980 and 2000. An Oprah Winfrey programme on 3 May 1994 typified this when a rape victim confronted her alleged rapist. On one level, Winfrey's graphic description of the rape relegated the topic to the cheap thrills or voyeurism of a tabloid. She carried on the tabloid tradition of exploiting these two people's misfortune for corporate profit. Yet on another level, the dramatic and individualised account on the pro-

gramme allowed ordinary citizens – in the studio and at home – to enter a debate about sexual power in their everyday lives. These confessional talk shows, whether the topic is transsexuality, incest, interracial sex or wife beating, took up the feminist slogan of the 'personal is political' and gave it a commercial forum. They gave feminine or race issues normally labelled private, personal or domestic a public airing, reaching women of all classes, races and ages. The tension between commercial tabloid exploitation and the politicisation of the private sphere stands as the central debate in the reception of these talk shows.

This talk show genre is more complex than a label such as 'confessional' or 'tabloid' reveals. The form is divided from the other types of talk shows by the following five distinct characteristics:

- it is 'issue-oriented'. I choose this term over 'confessional' to avoid the sensational inference involved in the word 'confession' (for example, revealing taboos). The content of these programmes emanates from social problems or personal matters that have a social currency, such as rape, drug use or sex change;
- it is distinguished by the centrality of active audience participation;
- the subgenre is structured around the moral authority and educated knowledge of a host and/or an expert who mediates between guests and audience;
- they are constructed for a female audience in that women were the overwhelming majority of viewers until the mid-1990s, when the producers created a more masculine, youth-oriented form;
- this kind of talk show is usually an hour-long syndicated programme produced by non-network production companies to be sold for broadcast to network-affiliated television stations in the United States.

The first generation of talk shows or four top A.C. Nielsen-rated programmes in the 1980s fit these generic traits: Geraldo (1987), The Oprah Winfrey Show (1984 – see box), The Phil Donahue Show (1967), and Sally Jessy Raphaël (1985). Such unanimity allows them to be characterised as a distinctive cultural group. The issue-oriented content of the first generation differentiates daytime talk shows from other interactive TV forms such as game shows (see 'The Quiz Show', p. 79) and other talk shows (see p. 81). Talk shows are not the news. But even at their most personal and emotional, the topics of these shows emanate from a current social problem or issue. They can be considered the fleshing out of the personal ramifications of a news

The Oprah Winfrey Show

Although Phil Donahue originated the genre of the confessional or issue-oriented talk show, *The Oprah Winfrey Show* is responsible for its international success. By 1993 it attracted a greater number of women viewers than network news programmes, night-time talk shows, morning network programmes and any single daytime soap opera in America. It was seen in sixty-four foreign countries. Over 15 million American people were tuning in daily to watch Oprah Winfrey and her female audience debate personal issues with as much fury as an old-time revival meeting. For its first nine years the programme typified the genre: a social issue was individualised as a personal problem at the top of the hour ('How do girls lose self-esteem?' 'Toxic Prozac?' or 'Violence in high schools'). A series of guests who characterised the issue, often representing two sides of the matter, were invited to discuss it with the host Oprah Winfrey, an expert and the studio audience. A debate would usually take place between various factions on stage and/or in the audience.

Winfrey's success as a host lay in her ability to posit herself as a 'typical' American woman in her beliefs and experiences (despite her $50 million yearly income). The *New York Times* described her as 'everywoman'. She continually called on her personal experience as a source of evidence, and in the process became famed for her confessions: being born out of wedlock, childhood sexual abuse, childhood poverty, HIV brother, and her own cocaine addiction. Her on/off battle with her weight evolved into a leitmotif for the talk show as she staged her weight problem with programmes on weight control, dieting, cooking and exercising. She carted in a wagonload of fat on stage to indicate her reduction, to the emotional applause of her studio audience. 'If Oprah can do it, you can do it', or self-empowerment, became a central theme. Yet such emphasis on self-help was often criticised in the press as masking the financial difference between Winfrey's and her average viewer's ability to be empowered.

More importantly, Oprah Winfrey was the first black woman to host a daytime talk show in America. Although the programme focused on the private sphere, it staged more women's and racial issues than the other talk shows. The degree to which one can consider these to be political debates depends on the definition of 'politics' used. Winfrey tended to focus on the personal problems emanating from current societal issues. Amid shows on celebrities and makeovers, typical feminine/feminist topics were rape, the glass ceiling, girls and self-esteem, and spousal abuse. A number of academics see the early years of *The Oprah Winfrey Show* as embodying populist

The Oprah Winfrey Show: 'a typical American woman'?

feminist politics as she staged the 'personal as political' (Carpignano et al., 1990; Livingstone and Lunt, 1994; Masciarotte, 1991). The power relations of the domestic or traditionally feminine world got a public airing. Average women of all colours were given a rare voice to complain about their treatment.

However, critics protested that the programme sensationalised social issues by revealing the private lives of unsuspecting guests. Other critics saw her programme as reproducing 'self-contained individualism' where the audience and guests depoliticise problems and can only change themselves personally (Peck, 1994, 1995; McLaughlin, 1993). Overtly race-based discussions were less common. In 1987 the programme went to a small town in Georgia to stage what became a famed debate about racism. The programme produced a thirteen-part series called 'Racism 1992'. Other episodes discussed issues about, for example, 'What colour are you?' and 'Why the black man is the most feared individual'. As a commercial product, the programme more often deflected the possibility of larger political change or movements. For all their airing of angry social debates, the programmes would end on Winfrey invoking the power of the individual and/or a 'higher power'.

In 1995 Winfrey went on air and renounced the tabloid nature of talk shows in general and her own talk show in particular. She pledged she would go on a 'spiritual quest of moral uplift' with her programme. As promised, the programme changed radically. The subjects became directed at personal self-improvement without a social connection with topics such as 'Tipping and gift-giving anxiety' and 'Advice to Oprah letter-writers'. Interviews with celebrity standard-bearers became routine. The programme also returned the bourgeois expert to central stage and created star new-age experts such as 'Dr Phil' McGraw and Gary Zukav (who is 'dedicated to the birth of a new humanity'). The programme began 'Oprah's Book Club' in order to get 'the country excited about reading'. Within months, Winfrey's monthly picks would make the books instant best-sellers – proof of the programme's ability to guide tastes.

Importantly, the role of the audience declined, switching from a town hall debater to deferential question-askers with this new top-down structure. The programmes focus on established 'bourgeois' authority, whether it is Winfrey, an expert, a celebrity or a novelist. The audience has evolved into a school of acolytes in this personal and moral self-improvement quest. The political dimension of social problems has moved to the background if not disappeared. Oprah Winfrey expanded this new-age media empire in 2000 by launching *O, the Oprah Magazine*, Oxygen.com and a cable network – all generically dedicated to a nebulous notion of 'a woman's view of the world' (Oprah.com).

Jane Shattuc

story: the human-interest story. There needs to be a cultural conflict around which the drama of the show is staged. The subjects are culled from current newspaper and magazine articles, viewer mail, and viewer call-ins. The producer deems whether the issue has opposing sides and is socially broad enough to be applicable to a large audience. In fact, local stations categorised them as 'informational' programmes for their licence renewals in the 1980s.

On one end you have programmes staging classic social policy or public sphere debates such as 'Mystery disease of the Persian Gulf War' with army personnel (*Phil Donahue Show*, 23 March 1994), 'Press actions on Whitewater' with reporters (*Phil Donahue Show*, 16 March 1994), 'Strip-searching in schools' with school administrators (*Sally Jessy Raphaël*, 14 March 1994), or even 'Do talk shows and self-help movements provide excuses?' with lawyers and cultural critics (*Oprah Winfrey Show*, 22 February 1994).

More typically, the social issue is placed in a domestic and/or personal context such as 'Arranged marriages' (*Oprah Winfrey Show*, 10 March 1994), 'When mothers sell babies for drugs' (*Geraldo*, 17 March 1994), 'Custody battles with your in-laws' (*Sally Jessy Raphaël*, 22 April 1994) and 'Domestic Violence' (*Phil Donahue Show*, 1 February 1994). Such domestic social issues are often further broadened to deal with perennial behaviour problems such as 'You are not the man I married' (*Geraldo*, 14 February 1994), 'Broken engagements' (*Oprah Winfrey Show*, 31 January 1994), 'Ministers who seduce ladies' (*Sally Jessy Raphaël*, 19 April 1994) or 'Jealousy' (*Phil Donahue Show*, 3 March 1994). These topics are still social; they involve the breaking of a cultural taboo (for example, infidelity, murder, seduction or non-procreative sex).

Because of the phenomenal popularity of *The Oprah Winfrey Show*, a second wave of programmes in the 1990s emerged from the historical need of commercial television to repeat success. These are what can be clearly classified as 'confessional talk shows'. To create a different market, the new programmes reached out to a younger audience and constructed a new form based on the sheer pleasure of breaking social taboos – especially those maintained by an older generation of 'serious' talk shows. Scores of new talk shows aired: *The Jerry Springer Show* (1991), *Maury Povich* (1991), *Montel Williams* (1991), *Jenny Jones* (1991), *Ricki Lake* (1993), *Gordon Elliott* (1994), *Carnie* (1995), *Tempestt* (1995), to name but a few.

With this shift, topics moved from personal issues connected with social injustice to interpersonal conflicts that emphasised the visceral nature of confrontation, emotion and sexual titillation. The expert disappeared as the number of guests proliferated, each programme staging a whirlwind succession of five-minute sound bites of conflict, crisis and resolution. Topics were more baldly about conflict: 'They're out of control . . . sex', 'Sister! Stop stealing my man', 'Women confront ex who cheated and warn new girlfriend', and 'Now that I slept with him, he treats me like dirt'. Fights between the guests, guests and audience members and audience members became a staple. Reacting to this shift towards greater 'tabloidisation', both the political left and right in America exploded in anger.

Liberal to left magazines (*Ms*, the *New Yorker* and the *Nation*) decried the lack of social consciousness of the programmes. William Bennett, the neo-conservative former Secretary of Education, launched a campaign against the new talk shows in October 1995. He labelled them as a form of 'perversion'. This controversy around the new talk shows caused them to be universally labelled 'confessional'. By January 1996 many talk shows were cancelled. Phil Donahue quit. *Geraldo* and *Oprah Winfrey* changed format under social pressure. Only *The Jerry Springer Show* succeeded in carrying on the tabloid banner by taking the conflict to extremes with ritualistic on-stage profanity and brawls. Any connection to the original claim of talk shows of staging the political issues of the identity rights movement had disappeared.

Jane Shattuc

RECOMMENDED READING

Carpignano, P., Andersen, R., Aronowitz, S. and Difazio, W (1990), 'Chatter in the Age of Electronic Reproduction: Talk Television and the "Public Mind"', *Sociotext*, 25/26.

Livingstone, Sonia and Lunt, Peter (1994), *Talk on Television: Audience Participation and Public Debate*, London: Routledge.

Shattuc, Jane M. (1997), *The Talking Cure: TV Talk Shows and Women*, London and New York: Routledge.

Sport

Sports television does not constitute a single genre, but rather a mix of different forms of television production practice. Firstly, television coverage of major sporting contests belongs to the category of *media events* (Dayan and Katz, 1992) alongside royal weddings and funerals, state occasions and live music concerts, sometimes sharing the same outside broadcast production facilities. The most important of these – the Olympics, the soccer World Cup, and the Super Bowl – play a role in encouraging a sense of national identification. Secondly, the news reports, interviews and discussion panels that are integral to television sports broadcasts represent a specialised form of *journalism*, framed by a distinctive set of news values shared with newspaper and radio sports journalism. Thirdly, sports television often performs an explicitly *promotional* role. Title sequences and video segments promote sporting events through constructing narrative conflicts between participants, using techniques that are similar to those used in advertisements (see p. 94), pop videos (see 'Music on Television', p. 89) and movie trailers.

SPORTS TELEVISION AS MEDIA EVENT

Although the first moments of live television sports coverage occurred before the Second World War – in the UK a Wimbledon tennis match in 1937, in the USA a college baseball game at Columbia University in 1939 (Barnett, 1990, pp. 5, 19) – it was not until the late 1940s and 1950s that the conventions of sports television that we now take for granted were established. In general, television presentation of many sports events continues to follow the rules of the 180° system: cameras are all positioned on one side of an imaginary line running from one end of the playing area to the other, as if to transgress this rule would disorientate the viewer. Whatever presentational changes there have been over the years – faster editing and the use of more camera positions and new technologies (mobile,

tracking, miniature and blimp cameras, for example) – this basic principle is still largely adhered to.

Sports television involves the deployment of a range of routines that have been developed to react to events as they unfold. The biggest disaster that can happen in sports broadcasting is to miss crucial moments in the action, and these techniques have developed to try to make sure that this does not happen. Accordingly, sports television production is based on a division of labour whereby editors, camera operatives and technicians are assigned specific, clearly defined tasks. Personnel are employed on the basis of their skills and experience in applying tried and tested conventions (Gruneau 1989; MacNeill, 1996).

Following radio, the conventions of television commentary have also developed to respond to uncertainty in the action. Commentary is organised around a distinction between a commentator (UK) or play-by-play announcer (USA), and a summariser (UK) or color announcer (USA). Typically, the former will be an expert in narrating the event and take responsibility for controlling the commentary, whereas the latter will be an ex-athlete and provide a participant's perspective. Although commentary is improvised and unscripted, commentators prepare through compiling extensive background notes, using information provided by sports journalism.

SPORTS TELEVISION AS JOURNALISM

Much of the content of sports telecasts is in the form of reports and interviews conducted by sports journalists. Sports journalism is a specialised branch of journalism with its own distinctive hierarchy of news values (see p. 114). The preoccupations of sports journalism routinely involve stories concerning sport issues exclusively: disciplinary issues, contract negotiations, levels of motivation and commitment, tactics, injuries and the like. Occasionally, stories relating to the financial or public policy aspects of sport will be covered, as will scandals around betting or drugs. Even more exceptionally major crime, sex or violence scandals involving sports stars will intrude, although these stories are less likely to be covered by sports journalists. However, most of the time sports journalism produces news that is predominantly about how sporting performance is directly affected by any of a limited range of predictable and routine matters.

SPORTS TELEVISION AS PROMOTION

In the context of the escalating costs of sports rights, broadcasters not only cover events, they also aggressively promote them. Title sequences and video segments typically set the scene for television coverage of major sporting

The Super Bowl

Since its inauguration in 1967, the National Football League's Super Bowl has provided the paradigm example of television's role in the increasing commodification of sport. In the USA many of the highest-rating television events ever are Super Bowls, the 1996 game between Dallas and Pittsburgh peaking at 138.5 million viewers. The Super Bowl has become a festive ritual linking households with the abstract community of the nation through a shared viewing experience, providing an ideal opportunity for the articulation of hegemonic representations of American values (Wenner, 1989). The Super Bowl provided a prestigious showcase for new advertisements from blue-chip companies. The fees that broadcasters have commanded have been estimated at $1million for a thirty-second spot in 1995, increasing to $2million in 2000. And competition for the broadcasting rights to the package of which the Super Bowl forms a part is fierce, the cost of rights escalating exponentially with each new contract negotiated. The package the NFL sold to ABC, CBS and Fox in 1998 amounted to $2.2 billion a year. American football also provides one of the earliest examples of how the rules of sport have been modified as a result of the growing economic power of television: it was as long ago as 1958 that the television time-out was introduced to provide extra spots for advertisers.

The Super Bowl broadcast exemplifies sports television as a hybrid genre. The build-up to the Super Bowl starts up to two weeks before the event. The NFL, the two participating teams, the host city's organising committee, sponsors and other interested parties all provide journalists with story material through press conferences, controlled access to the players, and other stage-managed events (Schwartz, 1997). This journalism provides many of the frames of reference for the ensuing promotion and coverage of the Super Bowl.

Promotion constitutes a crucial element of this coverage. Video segments are used to promote the Super Bowl through innovative use of editing, computer-generated effects, sound and music. By contrast, television presentation of the actual game typifies that of other sporting events in relying on conventional, tried and tested techniques, although American football is distinctive for its stop-start action – the ball is 'in play' considerably less than it is in similar sports (Real, 1989). Breaks are filled by detailed analysis of replays and statistics and, of course, advertisements (see p. 94). Close-ups of players are also regularly featured, although American football is different from other sports in that the protective headgear used prevents television from conveying the player's emotions through the demonstration of facial expressions; almost as if to compensate, the aggressive or celebratory gestures performed by the players appear exaggerated.

Rod Brookes

events through using a variety of post-production techniques. Slow-motion action, sound effects, computer-generated graphics and effects, music, voiceover, colourisation, all enhance the construction of narrative conflicts between the participants to be resolved, at least temporarily, in the contest to follow. Further, broadcasters promote those events where they own the rights through promos or spot advertisements in advance of the broadcast itself. This is as crucial for public service broadcasters needing to attract high ratings to justify the financial outlay of acquiring sports rights, as it is for pay-TV or pay-per-view broadcasters seeking to persuade viewers to subscribe to their services.

Additionally, frequent advertisement breaks are integral to commercial sports broadcasts as broadcasters seek to maximise, within regulatory constraints, the revenue that can be generated. In the case of major events the subject of advertisements is directly related to the event in the course of which the advertisements are scheduled – for example, for the 1998 World Cup Nike produced a series of skits featuring the stars of the tournament playing beach football.

The individualist values embodied in Nike advertisements accentuates the status of sports stars as celebrities, and tends to present even team sports as contests between star individuals.

Although sports television can be described as a *hybrid genre*, in practice it is impossible to identify clear boundaries between the different televisual practices that constitute it. A typical sports event broadcast will unfold seamlessly from introductory titles through an opening video segment, to a news feature segment on the teams or individuals involved, then perhaps to a pre-game ceremony, back to expert discussion panels, into the game proper, and finally interviews with the participants. Yet analysing sports television as a complex mix of different genres is useful in understanding the changing tensions that characterise its production and consumption. There has always been a conflict between television's role in purporting to *cover* or *report* sports events and television's role in *promoting* those events by enhancing their entertainment value through a variety of techniques (Whannel, 1992), but this conflict has intensified in the context of increasing commodification of sport since the 1980s.

Similarly, sports television has always had to reconcile serving the different interests of the knowledgeable sports fan and the uncommitted 'general viewer'. How these conflicts are resolved in different ways can be exemplified by comparing the BBC's and NBC's coverage of the 2000 Olympic Games. Whereas live coverage was prioritised by the UK public service broadcaster, even though this meant events were transmitted when many viewers were asleep or at work, the US commercial network withheld live coverage, preferring instead to provide extensively packaged recorded highlights during prime time in order to generate maximum revenue from advertisers.

An analysis of television sport as comprising a hybrid mix of genres is useful in addressing a range of contemporary issues: the changing relationship between media and sport, the significance of the processes of commodification and globalisation, and the role of sport in the construction of identities around nation, gender and 'race' (Brookes, 2001; also see 'The Globalisation of Television News', p. 122).

Rod Brookes

RECOMMENDED READING:

Barnett, Steven (1990), *Games and Sets: The Changing Face of Sport on Television*, London: British Film Institute.

Rowe, David (1999), *Sport, Culture and the Media*, Buckingham: Open University Press.

Whannel, Garry (1992), *Fields in Vision: Television Sport and Cultural Transformation*, London: Routledge.

Music on Television

Like its close sibling radio, television has always been part of the transmission of music, converting music from a live form into a recorded form, and stimulating the sales of recordings. The development of music on television broadly has seen the trajectory of a move from simple live performances of songs and musical pieces, to a situation where the music is accompanied by enhanced and often elaborate visuals. This spectrum includes performances enhanced by lights, camera effects, props and editing, although the proliferation of music television has inaugurated a new audiovisual form, the *pop video*, that has furnished a new style to television, seeping out of specialist channels and into commercials and action films.

Live television broadcasts relied upon the performance

of musical numbers as much as they relied upon other 'turns' from the stage, offering the opportunity for audiences to see stars from close quarters. With the arrival of rock'n'roll, popular music became more stridently visual, embodied by the impact (both real and imagined) of seeing Elvis swinging his hips. The visual aspect has always been tied closely to fashion, and the role of singers in influencing youth consumer choices has been a central way for pop musicians to differentiate their products in a very competitive market. The 'image' of the musician and the music spilt over into clothing, record covers, and later into pop videos.

In the 1950s, shows appeared that were based on popular music, such as *Your Hit Parade* and in its wake shows like *Soul Train* and *American Bandstand*. All music shows were based on having musicians appear in the studio and perform hit songs of the day. ABC's *American Bandstand* ran for three decades; it was hosted by Dick Clark and made its debut in May 1957, running until 1989. It had a live audience and featured live acts as well as filmed performances. With its neat teenagers and rather staid Dick Clark, *American Bandstand* was notable not only for making rock'n'roll acceptable to parents but also for its 'integrationism', including black musicians and audience members at a time when other shows refused. Other shows like *Your Hit Parade* played more 'adult' music, as did variety shows with occasional musical appearances. *The Ed Sullivan Show*, for example, famously would only show Elvis from the waist up, and the Doors contravened orders and persisted with the 'suggestive' lyrics to *Light My Fire*, although the show broke viewing records during the Beatles' appearance.

In the USA, radio was paramount for records reaching audiences, but in the UK television took on this function, as there were fewer radio stations. Television shows became a central means of marketing singles, and a record could be made a hit by simply managing an appearance on *Six-Five Special* (1957–8), *Oh Boy!* (1958–9), or later *Top of the Pops* (1964–) or *Ready Steady Go!* (1963–6). *Ready Steady Go!* was the first television programme to serve the new generation of 1960s youth in Britain (Hill, 1991, p. 103); presented by the young and fashionable Cathy MacGowan, it always commenced with the catchphrase, 'The weekend starts here!' (see 'The Teen Series', p. 41).

Pop musicians' appearances on television were important for publicity, directly stimulating record sales. Initial television appearances were nakedly about publicity. The Beatles made their first 'pop videos' in 1965 in order to facilitate multiple TV appearances but without the expense and effort of live performance in the TV studio (Neaverson, 1997, p. 120). This led the way forward,

Ready Steady Go!: 'the Weekend starts here!'

Top of the Pops: a central means of marketing singles

ultimately to music television's channels of pure pop promo. In the 1970s, there was a more diversified programming of music on television. 'Rock' programmes appeared that, as a symptom of progressive rock, were more 'serious' about their content. In the UK, *The Old Grey Whistle Test* became an institution, consisting of live studio performances as a reaction to the endemic lip-synch 'miming' on most pop shows. The range of groups appearing was far wider than the pop chart, and many appeared briefly before returning to obscurity. In its ethos of musical authenticity, the show was similar to the *MTV Unplugged* of the 1990s.

MTV (see box) started in the USA in 1981 and changed the whole landscape of music on television. Not only was it the first full television station dedicated to music, but it became the arena for a new form of stylistic combat between pop groups. Throughout the decade, pop videos often differentiated their product through a distinctive video, such as Madonna's *Like A Virgin*, which portrayed her individual fashion sense as well as her sensual image. Europe did not get MTV until 1 August 1987. In the UK at this time, an innovative music show called *The Tube* (1982–7) was bringing MTV's style to terrestrial television as well as proving inspiring to later music television generally.

1985 saw the musical television event of the twentieth century, the Live Aid concert in aid of the famine in

Music Television (MTV)

MTV went on the air for the first time on 21 August 1981 announcing itself with The Buggles' 'Video Killed the Radio Star'. The record had been released two years earlier, but audiences got the point. MTV, as a television station playing only pop music, had developed out of Warner's pop music shows such as *Pop Clips* and *Sight On Sound*, which allowed viewers to decide on the videos that would be screened on the programme. At first, it showed many promos by British groups (Rimmer, 1985, p. 71). One reason for this was that British and other European acts had already been producing videos, to take advantage of the opportunities for publicity on television that Europe had and the USA lacked. The British 'New Romantics' and 'new pop' broke into the American market at this point, and video and MTV were central in their success. New styles could be showcased by promos and the distinctiveness of British groups like Culture Club (featuring cross-dressing Boy George) and the bravura of videos like Duran Duran's *Rio* were compounded by the New Romantics' unique visual character.

The early 1980s simultaneously saw the proliferation of video technology, and the outlet of MTV inspired the use of the gamut of video processing effects, as well as offering almost limitless possibilities for imagination. The pop video allowed another dimension to pop music's product differentiation in a market that was increasingly competitive, and against a background of declining music industry sales over the long term. At first, record labels allowed pop videos to be shown by MTV at no cost. After all, they were simply a form of publicity or advertising, inspiring audiences to run out and buy records. Fairly quickly, however, the music industry worked out that promos were popular in their own right, and thus could be sold on video and MTV could be charged a licence fee for showing them.

Upon its inception, MTV had worked largely to the principle of keeping up a steady flow of pop videos, although in the later 1980s its slots became scheduled in a more traditional manner for a television station (Goodwin, 1992, p. 132). The channel has set the norms for pop and rock music, inspiring the notion of the 'MTV-friendly' video (Banks, 1996, p. 175), and certain types of musical genres, such as light heavy metal and adult-oriented rock, tended to dominate broadcasts. The channel's narrow marketing strategy simply ignored many musical genres. Local television started to exploit the areas of popular music not reflected by MTV, with rap, soul, country music and jazz having their own minority channels.

By 1985, Viacom, MTV's parent company, decided they wanted a channel to attract some of the older generation, specifically the baby boom generation, who had grown up with pop and rock music and wanted a diet of older 'classics' as well as more album-oriented material. This led to the introduction of MTV's sister channel VH-1 ('Video Hits One'). Despite increasing competition from other music television channels such as Video Jukebox Network's The Box, MTV is still massively successful and now has channels in Europe, Asia and Latin America.

Kevin Donnelly

Ethiopia. It was broadcast live all over the world, and cut between stages at Wembley in London and Philadelphia. The roster of stars was notably conservative, including a re-formed Led Zeppelin and Paul McCartney, the spectacle amplified by Phil Collins singing on the stage in London, then flying on Concorde to the USA to take the stage again. Probably the most memorable moment was a montage of starving Ethiopians accompanied by the Cars' song 'Drive'. This was very affecting, yet ambivalent in that the profound images were altered through their accompaniment by a banal pop song. Live Aid reinvigorated the flagging careers of a few older pop stars, and the music industry in the later 1980s reflected this turn to conservatism. In the 1990s, classical music has been the recipient of the same processes as pop music, with the Performance Channel on cable and satellite television showing operas, ballets and full classical concerts, as well as shorter pieces. The proliferation of channels made possible by digital television has already opened the gates to many specialist music stations, catering for very specific and fragmented audiences, unlike the mass audience that once sat enthralled in front of *American Bandstand* or *Top of the Pops*.

Kevin Donnelly

RECOMMENDED READING

Banks, Jack (1996), *Monopoly Television: MTV's Quest to Control the Music*, Boulder: Westview Press.

Goodwin, Andrew (1992), *Dancing in the Distraction Factory: Music Television and Popular Culture*, Minneapolis: University of Minnesota Press.

Rimmer, Dave (1985) *Like Punk Never Happened: Culture Club and the New Pop*, London: Faber & Faber.

Daytime TV

Classic daytime TV was a by-product of the successful establishment of the concept of 'prime time,' especially in the USA during the late 1940s and early 1950s. This was a period when sex-role stereotyping was all the rage. It was just after the Second World War, during which millions of women had been mobilised, not only to join the armed services but also to take up employment in factories and elsewhere. 'Rosie the Riveter' was a vital part of industrial and economic production. After the war, some ideological effort was made by government and commercial agencies alike to persuade women to be satisfied with home duties and domestic life – the rationale being partly a 'return to normal', partly to open up job opportunities for demobilising GIs. A commercial craze for domesticity was evident that had no precedent; certainly it had not occurred after the First World War.

Having established prime time as the default setting of television entertainment, daytime TV became a site of anxiety for programmers and audiences alike. The anxiety centred on the role of the housewife, and women more generally. They were cast as home makers, and that role was understood as productive (*not* leisure). Work included cleaning, both wet (laundry, dishes) and dry (polishing, vacuuming), cooking and, after that was done, parenting and 'wifely duties' – not only sexual, but also keeping the family mood up. But at the same time women were cast as consumers, in particular purchasing 'freedom' from housework drudgery, 'earning' leisure for themselves by choosing products that would, often as if by magic, cook and clean *for* them (see Spigel, 1992).

But being at home in the day was meant to be *productive*. Naturally, television executives wanted to capture larger audiences for their commercials, increasing capacity not least by extending the length of the broadcasting day (using programming that was dirt cheap compared with prime-time drama). There was no way of stopping daytime TV, which therefore had to promote the amelioration of housework while maintaining the housewife as a productive worker whose reward for wise consumption was leisure. What would they do with this leisure but watch TV? In this anxious, not-quite balancing act, daytime TV became somewhat different from its prime-time sibling. It was more *useful*.

The presumed audience profile (isolated suburban housewives at home, with children at school, husband at work, and a home to make) was not a mere demographic fact, although such people were available as audiences. More

to the point it was a *desire* both of television networks and of commercial organisations more broadly. The era of 'mass persuasion' was as much about trying to get people to take satisfaction from their *role* as domestic consumers as it was about selling individual brands and products. Hence, daytime television was not only a conduit through which domestic product could be promoted, chiefly *orificial* and *alimentary* items like food, cleaning agents for body and house, and capital items for the home such as fridges (Hartley, 1999, pp. 99–103). It was also the means by which the very 'ideology of domesticity' that would make such things acceptable and even attractive could be communicated on a society-wide scale.

What emerged from this was a psycho-profile of 'the housewife' and the desires projected on to her, which daytime TV then sought to satisfy. Homemaking and emotionality were the chief characteristics, leading very quickly to the broadcast forms that brought those characteristics together. Women at home could take time out from the pursuit of food and cleansing products through their loved ones' alimentary systems, and of germs and dust out of the home, then:

- put their feet up to enjoy soap opera's emotional dilemmas while relishing the vicissitudes of neighbourliness (see p. 47);
- prepare neat culinary and cleansing surprises for the family while watching help shows;
- take note of the hints offered by TV experts to make the household economy more efficient;
- reflect on the politics of the personal with talk shows (see pp. 81, 84);
- be updated on desirable products and their purposes in commercials and sponsors' segments;
- bring the children back into focus in the afternoon with shows aimed at pre-schoolers (later afternoon shows for older children would not assume a parental co-viewer; see 'Children's Television', p. 96).

These functions were mixed and matched through the daytime period, supplying it with an internal rhythm it may otherwise have lacked. Daytime TV became a kind of metronome, pacing the progress of the day. It also performed this function for viewers not directly addressed by the 'housewife' scenario, including seniors, unemployed workers, rich people and people in institutions and shops.

Here, then, was a textual system geared to TV viewing as domestic *work*. And hard work it was, for both sides of this Faustian bargain. Daytime TV was teaching people to devote themselves to a practice of self-definition and self-affirmation based on resolving anxiety about their status as housewives with desire for products. Those products were both semiotic (TV shows) and in the shops (advertised commodities and services). It was not easy for TV shows to 'interrogate' or address a viewer who was simultaneously watching TV and working, consuming and producing (no wonder they were 'distracted'). And perhaps it was not so easy for women to internalise the 'ideology of domesticity' required to sustain their domestic labour. Certainly daytime TV quickly attracted the critical attention of the resurgent feminist movement in the 1970s (see Lopate, 1976), and many women never recognised themselves in the 'imagined community' of daytime TV viewers even as they watched daytime TV (see Brunsdon, et al., 1997). The work of Lynn Spigel (see, for instance, 1992) is exemplary in tracing domestic fantasies of suburban consumption and isolation in television history.

Daytime TV eventually matured as just one segment of a 'family' programming schedule that was consciously constructed by the TV networks on both sides of the Atlantic, and wherever commercial television took hold in consumer cultures:

- breakfast TV for children preparing for school (and their carers);
- daytime for women (and unproductive persons);
- afternoon for children;
- early prime-time for family (channel choice exercised by children);
- late prime-time for family (channel choice dictated by 'dad');
- late-night television for men or non-family (single) adults.

This orderly sequence could be disrupted by sport (see p. 87), news events, specials ('telethons', for example) and blockbuster movies. But in general the 'family schedule' purported, over time, to address all members of 'the' family, making a composite 'normal citizen' anew every twenty-four hours, even though such a beast was never being addressed 'whole' at any one time. But the combination of daytime and prime-time TV left little room for conceptions of the audience other than the family (Paterson, 1980; Feuer, 1983).

The networks did not compete with each other by counter-programming against this scheduling regime until the 1980s, after the advent of BBC 2 and Channel Four in the UK and Fox in the USA. The family schedule's long-term supremacy was also threatened by cable, although some cable channels distended the daytime format further by stripping

particular soap operas (*Days of Our Lives, Dallas, Dynasty* – see 'Soap Opera', p. 47) over the whole week, or particular genres ('shopping') over the whole day (and night).

Daytime TV was for most of its heyday a 'despised' area of programming, little watched by politicians, academics and moral entrepreneurs. It was never policed for moral, political or sexual deviation quite as heavily as were news, current affairs or prime-time drama series. As a result, daytime TV was often able to address topics and debates that would not have found clear expression in prime time. Talk show guests (see pp. 81, 84), soap opera characters (p. 47), women presenters with strong characters, all were able from time to time to 'push the envelope' of the sayable and seeable (see Lumby, 1997).

Even in more routine sequences, daytime TV was often very close to the slower, more 'anthropological' rhythms of life, starting afresh each week on the perennial lack of fit between expectations and performance of the self, the family and interpersonal relations. It was an early mechanism for bringing private life into the public domain. Sooner or later the issues of gender, neighbourliness, personal identity and sexual politics in which it dealt would loom much larger in the 'public sphere' (see Lumby, 1999).

Daytime TV may not survive the post-broadcast era as a distinctive 'genre', although many of its elements will persist (not all of them during the day). But its dispersal into other forms can only mean that its counterpart – prime-time – is also facing radical changes. As interactive and multimedia applications mature, and view-on-demand becomes more available, there is no need for audiences to sit down together at one time in one country to see particular shows. They can view *whatever, wherever*, and *whenever* they can choose from digitised archives to which they subscribe. People may *prefer* to see 'women's' genres in big daytime swathes, in the knowledge that others in their imagined community are doing the same things to the same temporal rhythm. But they will not *have* to. They can watch them any time, or use the daytime for other things, like watching the shows that cable TV already offers throughout the day.

John Hartley

RECOMMENDED READING

Lopate, Carol (1976) 'Daytime TV: You'll Never Want to Leave Home', *Radical America*, vol. 11, no. 1.

Lumby, Catharine (1997), *Bad Girls: The Media, Sex and Feminism in the 90s*, Sydney: Allen and Unwin.

Spigel, Lynn (1992), *Make Room for TV: Television and the Family Ideal in Postwar America,* Chicago: Chicago University Press.

Advertising

Although TV advertising cannot directly be termed a form of 'popular entertainment', the commercial imperative behind many of the programmes included in this section clearly makes it an important part of this much wider category – although, of course, advertising exists at all points in the schedule. But in whatever category it is placed, advertising is clearly a type of television that has its own particular form, content and characteristics that clearly need to be addressed and studied like any other 'genre'.

Indeed, it could be argued that advertising is a form of television 'programming' that behaves like a genre in many respects. It is usually addressed to specific target audiences and defined by demographic markers such as age, gender and class. In addition, like other television genres, advertising comprises many 'subgenres' (the demonstration, the testimonial, the 'infomercial') that are shaped by recognisable conventions and that draw upon a shared body of knowledge on the part of the viewer. This sense of a familiar horizon of convention is evident in the fact that advertising is so easily parodied: a long tradition of humourous intertextual reference can be traced in the history of advertising and in film and broadcast comedy (see p. 61).

However, there are obvious differences between other television genres and advertising, no matter how much the latter seems to blur the distinction between fictional and commercial modes of address (as in infomercials, for example, or the famous Nescafé Gold Blend serial advertisements in the UK, which tell a soap-opera-like romance story over several years). The primary difference is the fact that advertisements and programmes occupy quite distinct positions within the revenue structure of commercial television systems.

It might seem to the casual viewer that the programming is the main 'fare' of television, whereas advertising is a supplemental interruption, but in fact (at least, from the perspective of political economy) the reverse is true. In purely revenue-based terms, programmes are supplemental necessities in the TV production sector. This is because their business purpose is to secure an audience for the advertisements that appear within and between them. Therefore, as Canadian communications researcher Dallas Smythe (1977) pointed out in a groundbreaking essay, the commodity that networks sell to advertisers is not a time slot within a programme but rather an audience. Advertising's relation to the economics of television is thus very distinct from that of the non-fiction genres in which it appears. Whereas the latter, in combination with the programmes that comprise them and the ratings that quantify their audiences, are involved in the *production* of the 'audience commodity' by attracting viewers, advertising can be thought of as the consumption of this commodity by the sponsor, that is, as a 'use value' purchased by a corporation and put to use in the act of airing.

Of course, manifestations of the commodity form in advertising extend beyond the audience. As a textual genre, advertising's central theme is the use value of the commodities it showcases. Though it is classically understood as the demonstration, or inculcation, of a need on the part of the viewer, advertising also has more specific goals, such as foregrounding a particular brand name in the buying behaviour of the spectator or even, more directly, to initiate the immediate or delayed exchange of money for the commodity. These factors suggests that, if one of advertising's goals is to achieve some kind of (consuming) effect on the body of the spectator, then it could be considered part of the genre category Linda Williams calls 'body genres'. According to Williams, genres like pornography, melodrama and horror are 'what may especially mark these body genres as low is the perception that the body of the spectator is caught up in an almost involuntary mimicry of the emotion or sensation of the body on the screen . . . [there is] an apparent lack of proper aesthetic distance, a sense of over-involvement' (Williams, 1995, pp. 143–4).

Critics have often noted the parallels between advertising's modes of address and the genres that Williams names. Sandy Flitterman-Lewis (1983), for example, explores the affiliation between advertising and melodrama, and Edgly (1988) argues that advertising and pornography have similar and reinforcing social effects. Further points of comparison between advertising and body genres can be discerned in the fact that overinvolvement and excess are often defined as the normative goals of commercials: advertising researchers' perceptions of the genre's effects are certainly based in a notion of mimicry. Moreover, despite the fact that it costs far more per minute to produce than most television programmes, advertising is consistently devalued in aesthetic terms, to the extent that we often refuse to watch it. And finally, just as body genres are highly gendered, often revolving around the display of the female body, so too is advertising – not only in the sense of the commonplace idea that advertising uses sex to sell things but also in the fact that women, considered primary household consumers, have historically played an important role in the development of advertising's modes of address (see 'Daytime TV', p. 92).

Within the history of advertising as a professional sphere, one can chart debates over *how* it might serve as a 'body genre', or in other words, over how exactly to change the behaviours of the consumer–viewers with commercial speech and images. As Merle Curti (1967) has noted, strategies of consumer persuasion changed several times over the course of the twentieth century, depending on whether the dominant definition of the consumer psyche was based in a rational or emotional paradigm. Television advertising, however, emerged at a moment when the 'motivation research' school of persuasion in advertising was coming into prominence. Under the leadership of Freudian psychologist-turned-adman Ernest Dichter, motivation research probed the embedded, irrational and primal urges that led consumers to identify positively with particular brands. Mary Beth Haralovich (1992, p. 126) notes that this could lead to some extreme claims, such as Dichter's discovery that 'women reacted with favorable emotions to [the] fresh, creamy surface of a newly opened shortening can'. Claims such as this formed the basis of Vance Packard's's best-selling exposé of motivation research as a sinister science, *The Hidden Persuaders*, published in 1957.

Advertising research has become a multimillion-dollar industry in the intervening years, and the Freudian methods developed by Dichter have largely given way to more behaviourist understandings of consumer motivation, ones that can be more easily verified through empirical techniques. Interestingly, however, despite the claims of the industry of advertising production and research, the actual effects of advertising on consumer behaviour are notoriously difficult to prove (Rothenberg, 1995).

This uncertainty about advertising's effects does not mean that advertising is not a powerful form of social communication. Using diverse methods, scholars from a number of disciplines have diagrammed the generic conventions of advertising. Sut Jhally (1987), for example, uses empirical social scientific techniques to discover the operations of commodity fetishism in TV commercials, using male and female subjects to discern their differential effects in gendered terms. The 'codes' of product presentation on which Jhally focuses in the texts of advertising fall into several categories. They include the representation of the commodity's role in interpersonal relationships, in the performance of everyday tasks, in the construction of romantic scenarios and fantasies, and the elevation of social status. Interpreted as a description of the generic themes of advertising, Jhally's typology shares much in common with the work of Wolfgang Haug (1986).

However, rather than using the experimental communications research methods favoured by Jhally, Haug explores the aesthetic foms of advertising on a larger scale, from a Marxist critical theory perspective. Haug defines the aesthetic conventions of advertising in terms of their commodification of intangibles, such as health, sensuality and happiness. Haug's analysis is helpful for understanding the specificity of advertising as a genre in that it seeks to link the aesthetics of advertising to the economic realities in which it is embedded, using the categories of value, circulation and surplus accumulation introduced by Karl Marx in the first volume of *Das Capital*. However, his approach neglects the actual economics of advertising as an industry that is involved not only in the distribution and valorisation of commodities produced in other industries, but also in the production of a commodity itself, namely, the audience it sells to the manufacturers of these advertised products.

Yet at the same time, as Graham Murdock charges, Smythe's discovery of the audience commodity neglects the aesthetic realm altogether, relegating it to the (in his view) exhausted research programme of western Marxism and its concern with advertising as primarily the reproduction of needs and the manipulation of consumers (Murdock, quoted in Smythe, 1978, p. 297; see also Smythe, 1977, p. 266). Smythe, however, claims that his materialist approach is designed to account for the fact that advertising is part of *both* the economic base and the ideological superstructure. Research into the conventions of advertising as a genre might therefore consider addressing *both* the relationship between the commodity form it sells (the product) and the commodity form it consumes (the audience) in order to avoid replicating the split between base and superstructure in the manner Smythe criticises. It might be possible, for example, to analyse the historical transformation and redefinition of consumer markets as niches in the post-war years as the refining of the production of audience commodities and the emergence of particular conventions for defining needs and use values (see Turow, 1997, for one example of such an approach).

Anna McCarthy

RECOMMENDED READING

Flitterman, Sandy (1983), 'The real soap operas: TV commercials', in E.A. Kaplan (ed.), *Regarding Television*, Frederick: University Publications of America.

Jhally, Sut (1987), *Codes of Advertising: Fetishism and the Political Economy of Meaning in the Consumer Society*, New York: Saint Martin's Press.

Smythe, Dallas (1977), 'Communications: Blindspot of Western Marxism', *Canadian Journal of Political and Social Theory*, vol. 1, no. 3. Reprinted in Thomas Guback (ed.) (1990), *Counterclockwise: Perspectives on Communication*, San Francisco: Westview Press.

CHILDREN'S TELEVISION

Studying Children's Television

'Children's television' is an unusual genre in that its title is defined by the people who watch it, rather than by the characteristics of the text. This section will discuss how programmes labelled as 'children's' can be generically distinguished from 'non-children's', and some of the implications of these distinctions.

The natural opposite of a 'children's' genre ought to be an 'adults' genre; but here, the grounds of definition shift. 'Adult' programming now usually means 'sexual' or 'pornographic'. Thus, one obvious definition of 'children's' as a genre is that there will be no sex in it. Sexuality portrayed in children's material will either be in coded form, or it will take the form of health education, designed to deter and protect the young from risk-taking behaviour: for example, storylines in the children's soaps *Grange Hill* and *Byker Grove* (BBC) about teenage pregnancy, or first sexual experiences. Producers of children's television, to a much greater extent than those of adult television, analyse storylines with a view to their didactic possibilities (Home, 1993).

This protectiveness as a characteristic of 'children's television' is institutionalised in regulatory documents dealing with possible 'harm'. Article 22 of the European Commission Broadcasting Directive (UK implementation, 1991), states that: 'Member states must prevent broadcasters under their jurisdiction from broadcasting programmes which might seriously impair the physical, mental or moral development of minors, particularly those involving pornography or gratuitous violence.' The other form of regulatory control that defines 'children's' is scheduling: in the UK, 'harmful' material should not occur in programmes shown before 9.00 p.m. ('the watershed'), although scheduling as a regulatory tool has become less effective with satellite and cable. Controls are concerned not only with sex and violence; they include not showing dangerous examples, and limitation of advertising content, to take account of the presumed susceptibility of children to persuasive techniques and copycat behaviour (see 'Advertising', p. 94).

A major aspect of regulation defining 'children's television' as a category is that it is seen as a public good that the state must provide. In the USA, commercial stations cannot be licensed unless they provide a minimum of three hours a week of 'educational' programming (a term that has been interpreted extremely loosely – see p. 137); in the UK, the provision takes the form of protected slots on the terrestrial airwaves in the afternoon. These blocks of programming (Children's BBC and Children's ITV) are expected to be diverse in genre, and appealing to children of different ages – producing further subdivisions of the generic label 'children's' into 'drama'; 'factual'; 'entertainment'; 'pre-school'; and 'animation' (see Davies and Corbett, 1997).

These requirements have come about as a result of a complex range of forces (for a historical overview of UK children's provision, see Buckingham et al. 1999; for a still-pertinent review of the rather different US situation, see Palmer, 1988), that continue to change as a result of new technology, more children's channels and the arrival of computers (Livingstone and Bovill, 1999). Such institutional changes could be seen as threatening to the concept of 'children's television' as a distinct programming category. Among the changes to the structure of the BBC announced in spring 2000 by its new Director-General, Greg Dyke, was the ending of a separate Children's Department within the BBC – an experiment tried, and failed, once before in the 1960s. Children's programming has been included under one of the four new 'adult' departments – not under 'Factual and Learning' (as it almost certainly would have been in the USA) but under 'Drama and Entertainment'.

The best children's schedules, whether on the BBC or within the commercial system, have traditionally attempted to provide a microcosm of adult schedules. As with adult programming, so with children's: drama is seen as a flagship genre, and a sign of the system's commitment to 'quality'. Children's drama schedules have displayed, in Caughie's terms (1991), the dual emphases of British broadcast drama: realistic authenticity, based on drama's origins in live studio production, and prestigious literary 'heritage' drama, as in costumed adaptations of classic books (see p. 38). Children's drama schedules have been one of the most favoured homes for classic serials; according to Buckingham et al. (1999, p. 36), this derives from an ideological 'core of values in which middle-class attitudes and universal moral principles had come to be seen as one and the same thing' – a view that overlooks the fact that many classic children's books have rather radical politics (for example, the stories of the Fabian Edith Nesbit). From the broadcasters' more pragmatic point of view, classic books are useful because out of copyright, and child audiences need to be sustained to help guarantee broadcasters' economic survival.

Outside the regulatory protected children's groupings, 'children's' is an extremely lucrative commercial proposition if the right formula (usually in the form of animation, and hence aimed at the younger end of the market) can be found and sold round the world. Examples are Teletubbies (see 'Teletubbies', p. 103), and toy-linked and merchandising-linked cartoons such as Smurfs, Ninja Turtles, (USA) and, more recently, Pokémon, (Japan). The most successful cultural business conglomeration of all time is a producer not of adults', but of children's products: Disney. Many writers, for example Kline (1993), have lamented the effect on narrative quality when merchandising becomes the primary focus, in order to lure children to buy linked products. Such programming, argues Kline, means that the whole field of childhood has now become commodified.

As with this case, writers on children's material tend to focus not on generic content features but on regulation, effects, ideological contamination, commodification and bad examples. Children's material is also expected to aid appropriate psychological and cognitive development and to stimulate youthful imaginations (Hilton, 1996). Little critical attention has been given to content, despite the fact that children's material has unique features worthy of critical notice. Children's drama is less bound by the constraints of realism than adults'; magic, fantasy, fairytale and slapstick humour are staple ingredients, which producers, writers and performers find liberating. Genuinely innovative, even avant-garde, material may be produced, for example the 1960s and 1970s programme for deaf children, *Vision On*, and the currently iconic *Teletubbies* (see box, p. 103).

A further creatively liberating aspect of children's material is its carnivalesque subversion of the respectabilities of adult authority. In children's comedy, such as *Welcome to Ourty Fou* (ITV), adults are the butt of children's humour, not the other way round (as in adult sitcoms like *The Cosby Show* – see p. 65). These subversions are also seen in more serious children's drama, such as *The Demon Headmaster*, a sci-fi story, with political subtexts about the necessity of resisting totalitarianism (see Davies and Machin, 2000; see also 'Science Fiction', p. 26). Animation, too, provides such subversions: series beloved by children, such as *Rugrats* and, above all, *The Simpsons*

(not strictly a children's programme, which exposes the ambiguity of the term), are characterised by the adult/child comic reversions that reveal the hypocrisies of adult social, commercial and political arrangements (see 'Adult Animation', p. 73 and Lurie, 1990).

Stylistically, the main distinction between children's films and family films is usefully made by Bazalgette and Staples (1995) as one of *point of view*. The children's drama, is told (and largely shot) from the point of view of the child protagonists. Other generic stylistic features signalling 'children's TV' include brightly coloured sets, vivid graphics, multimedia presentations (print, restless camera work, fast editing, computer graphics) and glamorous young presenters given frequent direct address to the audience (a privilege less available in adult programming) characterised by informality or 'wackiness' (see Buckingham, 1995). The most pervasive stylistic of all in children's television is animation, which, as Pilling (1999) has argued, has detrimentally been seen only as a 'kiddies' genre' because of the dominance of Disney (see p. 105).

Labelling a genre as belonging to its viewers, as in the case of 'children's', is a reminder that writers, artists and cinematic auteurs are in a cultural public sphere, writing to specific audiences who are likely to be influenced, inspired or disturbed by what these artists do (as regulatory arrangements surrounding 'children's' recognise). Classifying a branch of programming according to the group that uses it, also acknowledges that different audiences 'read' cultural material differently, and position themselves in multiple roles in relation to it (see 'Soap Operas and their Audiences', p. 55).

Máire Messenger-Davies

RECOMMENDED READING

Buckingham, David, Davies, Hannah, Jones, Ken and Kelley, Peter (1999), *Children's Television in Britain*, London: British Film Institute.

Home, Anna (1993), *Into the Box of Delights*, London: BBC.

Messenger-Davies, Máire (2001), '*Dear BBC': Children, Television Storytelling and the Public Sphere*, Cambridge: Cambridge University Press.

The Child Audience

For broadcasters in the UK, children are people aged between four and fifteen, who are assumed either to be in bed by 9.00 p.m. and thus 'safe' from any harmful influences of 'adult' programming or to be the responsibility of their parents after that time. This model of the child audi-

Goodnight Mr Tom

Goodnight Mr Tom, based on the 1982 children's novel by Michelle Magorian, was first transmitted on ITV in October 1998, and was a landmark production for 'children's television'. It was produced and financed by a children's department (in this case Carlton/Central for ITV), but was first transmitted during 'adult' viewing time, at 9.00 p.m. – a time when children are assumed to be in bed. It was repeated on ITV in spring 2000, in the early evening. As Nelson (see 'Costume Drama', p. 38) points out, children's drama schedules have always been one of the most favoured homes for classic 'teatime' serials, but *Goodnight Mr Tom* was a scheduling departure – an experiment to see whether children's programming could hold its own during adult viewing time. High ratings and a BAFTA award suggested that it could.

The programme was also unusual in being a full-length 'feature film', rather than an episodic serial. Otherwise, it had all the regular hallmarks of a generic children's drama: literary provenance; a historical setting (during the Second World War); a child as its central protagonist; impeccable period design – all signifiers, according to Charlotte Brunsdon (1997), of 'quality' television. Other guarantors of quality included location shooting in a picturesque English village; a prestigious director, Jack Gold; and the casting of a thoroughly bankable television star, John Thaw (*Morse, Kavanagh QC, The Sweeney* – see 'The Police Series', p. 19) as the gruff, elderly Tom Oakley who has a disturbed, eleven-year-old London evacuee billeted on him.

Children's drama set in the past (or future) can serve as a vehicle for distancing, and then safely examining, social issues that may (implicitly or, as in this case, very explicitly) be critical of the adult social order. *Goodnight Mr Tom* featured violent child abuse and neglect, mental breakdown, sexual dysfunction, the shortcomings of the welfare system, and the social collapse brought about by war. Admittedly, the child in *Goodnight Mr Tom* is rescued – and it is to Thaw's credit that at no point does the viewer share the suspicions of the story's professionals of him as an elderly man who should not be looking after a child. Further, there is no sense that what happened to William Beech in the Blitz, including the loss of a

Goodnight Mr Tom: a children's drama enjoyed by adults

Jewish friend, is anything other than appallingly traumatic. A central sequence – harrowing in the book, and unflinchingly translated by Carlton/Central's production – is the death of William's baby sister in his arms, and the final mental breakdown of his mother.

Goodnight Mr Tom was groundbreaking in its scheduling and brought the qualities of the best children's drama production into the adult television mainstream. The children's market for fantasies and literary adaptations is more favourable than the market for social-realist British drama (see p. 49), hence a current spate of international co-productions of stories about magic and witchcraft, once taboo in children's programmes (Home, 1993). *Goodnight Mr Tom* combined the social-realist tradition with literary 'heritage' qualities and has achieved a successful afterlife in the video market. Showcasing the best children's dramas such as *Goodnight Mr Tom*, at times when adults can see them too, would seem to be one of the best ways of guaranteeing public support for continued funding for high-quality children's programming, however 'quality' is interpreted. Most writers on children's television agree that 'quality' must include the kind of unsentimental, but ultimately reassuring (for a child audience), treatment of painful issues told from a child's perspective, as demonstrated in this film.

Máire Messenger-Davies

ence, if it were ever realistic, has been emphatically called into question by two features of contemporary children's media culture: one, the proliferation of TV satellite and cable channels, which do not observe the 9.00 p.m. watershed as strictly as terrestrial channels do, as well as the wide availability of video; and two, the growth of what

Livingstone and Bovill (1999) have called a 'bedroom' culture, in which unsupervised children have autonomous access to a wide range of media, including television and computers, in their own bedrooms, whether before or after 9.00 p.m.

Broadcasters in both the UK and the USA are required

by law both to provide material specifically for children, and to take account of the presence of children in adult audiences, at least up to 9.00 p.m. This is a major challenge to creativity because of the huge developmental range of the child audience. Four-year-olds have very little in common with fifteen-year-olds in terms of their interests, capabilities and experience, and even ten year-olds do not have much more. The age range does have some characteristics in common, such as the fact that they are all legal minors, subject to the authority of parents and of teachers and protected by law from 'harmful' experiences, such as sexual relations and the consumption of alcohol and tobacco. Such protectiveness is reflected in other regulations applying to the child audience.

RESEARCH ON CHILD AUDIENCES

Children as an audience are measured separately from adults in audience ratings conducted by BARB (Broadcasters' Audience Research Board) in the UK, and Neilsen in the USA. It is important for the industry to identify their child 'customers', since they are commmercially valuable for a number of reasons: first, in commercial television, they are key targets for toy, confectionery and convenience food advertising. Second, in public service terms, a children's service (no matter how skeletal or commercially driven) gives broadcasters public credibility, and in Britain and the USA, is one requirement for a commercial licence. Third, child audiences can bring adults with them, including their own care-takers while they are children, and in the sense that they grow up to be adults themselves, often retaining channel loyalty from their youth.

Child audiences have also been the subject of a very large number of academic studies in the past forty years, mainly by social scientists but some by educators. The first group has been particularly concerned with children as potential victims of harmful effects, such as copying violent behaviour. The second group is more concerned with how, and what, children learn from media. The harmful-effects school has had by far the most research money spent on it; in the 1960s and 1970s several experiments and surveys were carried out in the USA and the UK to see whether exposure to filmed violence led to children copying aggressive behaviour. Despite some evidence of short-term imitative effects in some children (mainly, though not exclusively, boys), and some evidence of weak statistical correlations between watching television and negative social attitudes, the effects-research tradition has never conclusively demonstrated to the rest of the academic community that media have direct, measurable, harmful effects

on the young. However, this has not prevented a continuing popular belief that they do.

The phenomenon of 'moral panic' surrounding the introduction of new communication technologies, especially with regard to children's access to hitherto taboo information, has been documented by Springhall (1998) and Starker (1991). Currently, such concerns are being expressed about the latest new technology, the Internet, including children's possible access to pornography. 'Moral panics' about technological change and its impact partly reflect genuine parental and pedagogic worries, and partly long-standing populist fears both of the new and of the young. It is sometimes translated into policy and legislation, as in the case of the 1994 Video Recordings Act in Britain.

Other, more positive, research traditions have arisen from the media education movement (see Kubey, 1997), where the concern is to establish the cultural contribution of mass media to children's learning and literacy in the broadest sense, including social attitudes and identity formation. Cognitive psychologists have also been interested in the new ways offered by audiovisual electronic media to understand children's intellectual functioning – for example, how they learn to 'read' the codes, conventions, signs and techniques of the media (Hodge and Tripp, 1986; Davies, 1997), a set of competencies sometimes called 'media literacy'. This tradition links with wider concerns in childhood studies about the relation of children to the social and political world; media literacy studies address children's understanding of reality and fantasy, their 'theories of mind' about intentionality and authorship, and their ability to distinguish differing degrees of realism, credibility and representational verisimilitude in different genres, fact and fiction.

The relationship of children to different forms of media has always been a site of cultural struggle where competing disciplines and ideologies clash. Allied to a desire on the part of many adults to keep their children safe and innocent for as long as possible, is an equally powerful tendency in growing children to want to try out taboo experiences and to explore adult 'secrets' through media. The relationship of children to culture is also part of a longstanding struggle about the kinds of messages and images that the whole of society should be allowed to have access to: hence the 9.00 p.m. watershed and the film and video classification system. Nevertheless, the child audience deserves to be seen, not just negatively, as people incapable of coping with adult material, but as a group with special interests, talents and needs of its own.

Máire Messenger-Davies

Pre-schoolers: A Special Audience

The biggest audiences in the four-to-fifteen age group usually go to adult programmes (with occasional exceptions, such as the 1996 series of *The Demon Headmaster*, BBC). This is not always true for the younger end of the age group, the under-tens, and it is never true for pre-school children, the under-fives. Catering adequately for this very young audience with programmes designed to stimulate learning, social skills and imagination has been characterised as one of the primary hallmarks of a public service system (Palmer, 1988; Blumler, 1992; Davies and Corbett, 1997). The conception of the pre-school audience has changed since the 1950s when the title 'Watch with Mother' assumed that very young children watching television would be at home with a full-time mother figure sitting with them. In the 1960s and 1970s, the producer of *Playschool* and *Playdays*, Cynthia Felgate, could assert: 'Our audience is one child in a room.' Nowadays, pre-school television addresses children on the assumption that they may also be in nurseries or with childminders. However, there is also an assumption that the child may be unaccompanied by an adult, for the adult presenters always address the child (through the camera,) not the accompanying adult(s). This is children's territory.

Pre-school television has a long and popular tradition in both British and American television. *Sesame Street*, aimed at the under-sevens, with (as its witty allusions to American popular and high culture make clear) an eye on accompanying older audiences, began in 1967 (see 'Educational Programming', p. 137). The slower, real-time, British *Playschool* began on the BBC in 1964, and was replaced by *Playdays* in 1985 and by *Teletubbies* in 1997 (see below). Both BBC and ITV have produced many programmes for pre-school children, including storytelling such as *Postman Pat* (BBC) and magazine-type shows such as *Rainbow* (ITV). Although the audience for them is small, in all senses of the

Playschool saw their audience as 'one child in a room'

Sesame Street prepared young children for formal school

word, such programmes can be an extremely worthwhile investment because, owing to the fact that turnover among the under-fives is rapid (obviously, the whole three-to-five population changes every two years) they can be repeated season after season – and, indeed, revived after decades (as the BBC's 1950s *The Flowerpot Men* have been). They can also have lucrative video spin-offs and toy-marketing deals. To the extent that this is so, the market, as distinct from the audience, for pre-school programmes will always be care-taking adults.

Traditionally, pre-school television assumed a linguistically competent child audience, capable of following narratives and appreciating jokes, that is primarily four-year-olds and over. This changed with the virtually inarticulate *Teletubbies*, and in 1998 a controversy broke out among children's producers, media educators and academics gathered at the second World

Summit on Television for Children in London, when this programme, despite its carefully researched origins, was accused of being exploitative and harmful to the very youngest children, because, unlike earlier pre-school programmes, it was aimed at pre-linguistic children who were deemed too young to be watching television; it is still, however, the most successful BBC export ever (see box, p. 103).

The case for specialised pre-school programming made by the originators of *Sesame Street* in the USA in 1967 is that, far from relying mainly on non-verbal material, it should include basic linguistic and numerical academic skills. This was seen as necessary in order to compensate the most disadvantaged children, who are most reliant on television, for a lack of pre-school experience (Palmer, 1988). *Sesame Street* consciously set out to prepare young children for formal school, by introducing them to classroom practices such as letter and number recognition, and the verbal expression of concepts such as size, height, distance and colour. All of this, plus a socially aware emphasis on different ethnic experiences and cultures, tended to imply an older audience than under-threes; it assumed that the watching children had some exposure to life outside the home, and some awareness of what 'school' is. In this, *Sesame Street*'s philosophy was different from that of British pre-school television, with its emphasis on play; it preferred a more directive approach and had much faster, more visually busy production styles, borrowed from American advertising techniques (see p. 94).

Despite their difference in styles, the common conception of the pre-school child audience underlying all these programmes is of a group with intelligence and interests of their own, but who lack experience and thus need to be gently introduced to basic information about the world, including life skills like teeth-cleaning and meeting new baby brothers and sisters. In all of them, the importance of learning is acknowledged – but so is the importance of play. Above all, the tone is one of kindliness and affection. In this, pre-school television's attitude to its audience is paternalistic (although it would be more correct to call it *maternalistic*, given the predominance of women in the field) in the best sense.

Máire Messenger-Davies

RECOMMENDED READING

Messenger-Davies, Máire and Corbett, Beth (1997), *The provision of children's programming in the UK between 1992 and 1996*, London: Broadcasting Standards Commission.

Palmer, E. (1988), *Television and America's Children: A Crisis of Neglect*, Oxford: Oxford University Press.

Starker, S. (1991), *Evil Influences: Crusades against the Mass Media*, New Brunswick: Transaction.

Moral Panics

Stanley Cohen's well-established paradigm concerning the emergence and maintenance of media-driven 'moral panics' finds special application in the always contentious field of children's programming. The media identifies a problem; its causes are simplified; its relevant participants are then stigmatised; a campaign accrues around the key issues that have emerged from this process; the programme-makers or the 'authorities' respond, and thereafter, a whole new frame of debate is created that perpetuates the 'panic'. From *Howdy Doody* to *Pokémon* (see below) in the United States to *Blue Peter* (see p. 104) and *Teletubbies* (see box) in Britain, programming for the children's demographic has been coloured by debates between parents, educationists, commercial enterprises and children themselves, largely focusing on the relationship between broadcasters as public service deliverers (even in the commercial sector) and parent advocacy groups, addressing the pedagogic and promotional agendas underpinning the broadcast remit.

Howdy Doody, which ran for 2,543 episodes between 1947 and 1960, alienated the establishment by playing out a mock presidential campaign in which the platform of 'two Christmases and one school day a year; more pictures in history books; double sodas for a dime; and plenty of movies' won more write-in votes than that of actual independent candidate Henry Wallace. The programme was one of the first children's programmes to provoke moral and ethical debates about its content, a consideration of the commercial factors potentially affecting editorial control, and the place of the programme within a more general debate about 'television as babysitter' – issues still relevant to the contemporary era. Arguably, *Howdy Doody* was advanced in its representation of Native Americans and women, and in its anti-war stance, a counterculture imperative taken up by *Sesame Street* (see box, p. 101), but ultimately it was a victim of the 'modernisation' of children's programming, largely symbolised by the impact of the Disney studio's television output (see 'Educational Programming', p. 137). *Disneyland* and *The Mickey Mouse Club* reconciled a populist ideology with commercial imperatives, promoting family values and new franchise operations alike. The American public readily engaged with the Disney ethos, and embraced the studio's theme parks with equal commitment.

This mode of quasi-vertical integration and its implications was challenged, however, by a New York PBS producer, Joan Ganz Cooney, who through her work with the Carnegie Corporation promoted the idea of pre-school entertainment for disempowered children. Empirical research conducted by the newly formed 'Children's Television Workshop' informed innovative approaches to production in the creation of *Sesame Street*, which included using advertising techniques to promote numeracy, and the exploitation of an assumed teleliteracy in children, where parody could be used to engage with educational and social issues.

Teletubbies

The BBC's attempt to speak directly to children as young as eighteen months old through the figures of Tinky Winky, Dipsy, Laa Laa and Po, four colourful, rotund, part-teddy, part-television creatures, in *Teletubbies*, provoked outrage among parents, educationists and tabloid journalists alike. The programme, part of the BBC's strategy to create a pre-school audience that would provide a platform for an older viewer demographic as the children aged, was underpinned by an unusually high £2 million budget, and was immediately seen as a vehicle for merchandising revenue. Inevitably, this provoked concern about what was seen as a conflict of interests between fulfilling the constitutional obligations of the BBC to educate, inform and entertain, and the commercial imperatives that required the programme to compete in a market environment.

The BBC stressed the credentials of Ragdoll Productions, the programme-maker, which was also responsible for the award-winning *Tots TV* (which features three puppets, one of which is a French-speaking girl), and the educational focus given to the merchandising, particularly the *Teletubbies* magazine. The 'Tubbyrage' that followed the release of the Teletubbie dolls and accessories at Christmas in 1997, however, undermined the programme's educational agenda, and prompted the *Sun* to scream 'Time for Tubby Buy Buy', and allege that the BBC had sacrificed its commitment to quality programme-making and the tradition epitomised by *Andy Pandy*, *Blue Peter* and *Grange Hill*.

The educational approach of the programme also received criticism. The verbal currency of the *Teletubbies* is in the delivery of partially formed words and sounds that echo the 'babble' of baby talk and seek to encourage increased expression in children through imitation and repetition. This strategy also informed the variety of live-action inserts projected through the stomachs of the Teletubbies themselves which are repeated twice in each episode to excited cries of 'Again ! Again !' These inserts have demonstrated a strong commitment to multicultural representation and the inclusion of a variety of previously marginalised models of the family and socio-cultural forms and practices.

Computer-animated sequences of dancing bears, sailing ships and marching animals also enhanced the contemporaneity of the programme. Concerns were raised, however, that charged the programme with encouraging poor diction and delivery, the corruption of language and learning, the creation of a context that was alienating and provocative, and knowingly seeking a cult-oriented adult audience. The latter charge was strenuously denied, but this did not prevent extensive debate about the alleged drug-culture connotations in the programme, its affiliation to quasi-apocalyptic science fiction (see p. 26), the gay iconography embodied in Tinky Winky, and the promotion of supposedly 'alternative' values in outlook and behaviour.

The global success of the programme may, however, speak to the view that 'moral panics' tend to be deliberately generated by specific interest groups to promote certain issues, are largely temporary, and (ironically) often generate new, curious and ultimately engaged audiences to programmes they might have otherwise ignored. *Teletubbies* has survived its moment of alarmist scrutiny, and exemplified a changing media environment in which the BBC has had to engage fully with the commercial sector while seeking to sustain its public service ethos.

Paul Wells

Despite receiving sustained criticism since it was first broadcast in 1969, *Sesame Street* still maintains its non-materialist, pro-environment, racially and generationally inclusive signature style, having overcome allegations that the programme did not teach children how to learn, but simply taught them how to watch more television. Similarly, the programme came under attack for its male orientation, its over-stated political correctness, its unrealistic, almost nostalgic air, and its alleged didacticism, something that saw it fall foul of the BBC, which would not broadcast the programme on these grounds. In 1996, at the Second White House Conference on Children and Television, hosted by President Clinton, however, the Markle Foundation endorsed *Sesame Street* as a significant aspect in the pre-school development of high school students who had achieved higher grades in English, science and maths courses (see above and 'Educational Programming' p. 137).

While the longevity alone of *Sesame Street* may offer testimony to its success, the overall quality of children's programming in the United States has been variable and subject to the consistent interrogation of the Action for Children's Television (ACT) committee, organised by Penny Charren. ACT campaigned against the proliferation of violence in children's shows, inappropriate advertising strategies for expensive toys and unhealthy foods, the use of popular celebrities in child-directed commercials, and the need for a minimum of fourteen hours per week of quality, monitored, children's programming. ACT petitions were highly effective in persuading the Federal

Communications Commission (FCC) and the American Advertising Federation (AAF) to modify broadcasting policy.

Parental bodies continue to engage with broadcasters about a range of issues, most notably how the representation of the family in popular programmes sits uneasily with the model children find in their own homes – a debate specifically contested in relation to the competing disparity between *The Cosby Show* and *The Simpsons*, both programmes having strong appeal to adult/child crossover audiences. Bill Cosby's advocacy of responsible programming promoting conscious role models was resisted by James Brooks, producer of *The Simpsons*, as 'pro-propaganda and anti-art' and predicated only on a singular and potentially misleading representation of children and childhood (see 'Adult Animation', p. 73.)

In Britain, broadcasters have been consistently preoccupied with this 'construction' of childhood as their programmes define it. Derek McCulloch, Head of Children's Broadcasting at the BBC between 1933 and 1951, sought to promote approaches that sought out the 'keen, fresh, unspoilt mind of the child', promoting activity over passivity, creativity over materialism, and integration and participation over mere imitation. In the spirit of this agenda and its public service ethos to educate, inform and entertain, the BBC created *Blue Peter*, which debuted in 1958. Extolling the creative virtues of 'sticky-back plastic', the care and consideration of tortoises, the worldwide effects of the annual *Blue Peter* appeal, and the globetrotting exploits of its enthusiastic presenters, the programme became a national institution for generations of children. Still the flagship of BBC children's broadcasting in the contemporary era, the programme has, however, struggled to maintain its ethos in the light of a changing social environment where 'activity' may now be reconfigured as 'anarchy', 'competition' or 'consumption' (see 'Educational Programming', p. 137). Changing worlds require new kinds of programming, which in turn potentially provoke new kinds of moral panic.

Pokémon, the $5 billion worldwide industry, incorporating the original Nintendo computer game, its affilated animated series and related playing card collectibles, has provoked a variety of moral panics. The challenge of the game in identifying, capturing and competing with a variety of 'pocket monsters', and the cajoling imperative whereby children 'gotta catch'em all', has proved highly appealing, and encouraged in children an empathy with the characters and the desire to collect and categorise. The Pokémon trading cards have provoked school bans because of their disruptive influence, which has included assaults and theft, while also enabling children with their literacy, numeracy and negotiation skills, and providing an inclusive culture for most children, instead of those determined by fashion, music or sport. The scale of intensity about these issues may be best measured, though, by the case of a Los Angeles schoolboy who sued a school for the loss of his confiscated trading cards and won $15,000.

Moral panic also attended the animated television series. Some 600 children were taken ill and some hospitalised during the broadcast of the now banned episode, 'Electronic Hero Porygon', in which a bright, pulsating, white light caused nausea and seizure. Further episodes have been banned in the United States because of their indigenous Japanese content (particular customs and holidays, for example) and the presence of potentially confusing sexual or violent imagery – most specifically, James, Team Rocket's camp male villain, a cross-dresser and occasional female impersonator. Ironically, these issues detract from the eco-friendly and quasi-spiritual agenda at the heart of *Pokémon*'s extended narrative, and that the *Pokémon* text has positively engaged with Japan's post-war concerns about the reconciliation of sacred traditions, the natural order, new technology and post-modern youth cultures.

Periods of 'moral panic' always reflect the desire for television to respect the needs, interests and culture of children in a non-exploitative way, while maintaining a quality output. At the World Summit on Children's Television in 1998, a 'Children's Television Charter' was drawn up to address these concerns. The summit articulated anxiety about the dispersion of televisions and personal computers within the domestic space, which, it was argued, encouraged anti-social, non-family-centred experiences, and implicitly demonstrated increasing fears about going outside. Further, concerns were raised about the escalating commodification of children's culture, especially with regard to the ways that private enterprise, in the guise of toy manufacturers, was funding the proliferation of programming for niche children's channels on satellite and cable. Inevitably, it was concluded that the public service ethos is ultimately neutered by competitive commercial agendas, and that quality thresholds were under threat. The Charter recognised, however, that children have a much more discriminating, active and critical relationship with television than is often thought, and that even the most commercially minded of producers and broadcasters recognise that making quality programmes requires conscience and commitment. Nickelodeon, the satellite and cable children's channel, for example, maintains that 'what's good for kids is good for business', and promotes social development rather than a specific curricular orientation.

Broadcasters realise that children are demanding viewers, and that their supposed passivity, and its negative effects is an overstated myth. Children for the most part move beyond the 'habit' of watching television and make choices; they know *how* they are watching: whether they are merely filling time, gaining reassurance and companionship, picking up ideas and cultural capital, overcoming boredom or moodiness, or simply having a pleasurable experience. Television remains a very important factor in many children's lives, and further 'moral panics' are inevitable, but should they provoke the degree of care and attention necessary to maintain high standards in children's programming, then for parents, broadcasters, academics and children alike, they will be embraced and understood (see 'The Child Audience', p. 97)

Paul Wells

RECOMMENDED READING

Buckingham. D. (ed.) (2000), *Small Screens: Television for Children*, London: Continuum.

Cohen, S. (1972), *Folk Devils and Moral Panics*, London: MacGibbon & Kee.

Gunter, B. and McAleer, J. (1997), *Children and Television*, London and New York: Routledge.

Children's Cartoons

Cartoons have played an intrinsic role in children's television programming on both sides of the Atlantic, and have become a significant aspect of its overall economy and profile. Since the early 1950s, the three dominant networks in the USA, ABC, CBS and NBC, have competed for the children's audience predominantly through the culture of cartoons. In Britain, the dominance of the BBC provided a platform for animated children's programming, most obviously in its 'Watch with Mother' and teatime strands, until the emergence of ITV in 1955 provided the context for both regular cartoon series and animated commercials (see 'Advertising', p. 94). The political economy of broadcasters and the aesthetic and thematic outcomes of cartoons are profoundly interrelated, and much that has been achieved in the television field has been about the buoyancy of the marketplace as much as the talents of the animation studios.

Faced with budgets *one-twentieth* of the amount used to produce a six-minute *Tom and Jerry* in the MGM studio era, Hanna–Barbera reconfigured the cartoon for television in the United States. After the initial effort of *The Ruff and Reddy Show* in 1957, *The Huckleberry Hound Show* debuted in 1958 and featured Huckleberry, Pixie and Dixie and Yogi Bear, some of Hanna–Barbera's most enduring characters. This type of 'reduced' or 'planned' animation necessarily prioritised its scripts, sacrificing any complex motion in the imagery to repeated cycles of movement and simple design strategies. Dialogue was more important than the visual elements, and the producers thus sought to create popular catchphrases – 'I'm smarter than the average bear' (Yogi Bear), 'I hate meeses to pieces' (Jinx the Cat), and so on – and focus on distinctive vocal idioms in performance that supported the verbal interplay between characters.

Voice artists like Daws Butler, Don Messick, June Foray and Mel Blanc were, in effect, the real stars of the shows. Children and adults clearly embraced this simplicity; its reward, ironically, the creation of *The Flintstones* for prime-time broadcast. The Hanna–Barbera series, from *The Huckleberry Hound Show* to *Scooby Doo, Where Are You?*, have proved, however, to be the high point of early TV animation, and the standard overall plummeted dramatically to the point that by the late 1960s the Action for Children's Television committee, led by Penny Charren, actively campaigned for better cartoons.

Significantly, in the British context, the 'cartoon' has not taken precedence, and its animation aesthetic has been much more informed by the three-dimensional puppet films of figures like Bura and Hardwick (*Trumpton, Chigley, Camberwick Green*), Oliver Postgate (*Bagpuss, The Clangers, Ivor the Engine*) and Ivor Wood (*The Herbs, Postman Pat, Paddington Bear*). Rather than embrace the 'gag' and 'chase' orientation of the American cartoon tradition, and its self-reflexive relationship to television and popular culture (still readily evidenced in *The Simpsons* and its imitators), British animation opted to create parochial, community-oriented vehicles that foreground benign paternalism, eccentric heroes, domesticised heroines and consensual modes of living. This kind of animation is grounded in more realist codes, and draws upon shared knowledge and nostalgic mythologies about 'localness', 'middle-England pastoralism', and 'ritual'. Whereas the American television cartoon paled against the graphic freedoms of its 'Golden era' antecedents at Disney, Warner Bros. and MGM, British animation drew upon its literary and artisanal arts traditions to create a distinctive kind of 'cartoon', one that explored the foibles and follies of character and situation rather than the open vocabulary of the cartoon idiom.

In the contemporary era, the overall boom in the production of animated feature films and quasi-sitcoms, and the emergence of niche children's channels and dedicated broadcast outlets like the Cartoon Network, has necessi-

Cartoon Controversies

Cartoons in the television era have often been subject to criticism, complaint and censorship. The Broadcasting Standards and Practices (BS&P) departments, drawing from the 1952 TV Code of Standards of the National Association of Radio and Television Broadcasters, have been the main arbiters of broadcast material in the USA. Advocacy groups such as the National Coalition on Television Violence and the National Federation for Decency, as well as sponsors and advertising agencies, have also been vigilant in monitoring graphic freedoms in animation, because of its assumed children's audience. The threat of 'anarchy' in the cartoon remains the enduring legacy of the studio era. Shorts produced for cinema exhibition, for example, were often re-cut for television, excising any contentious race representation, sexually provocative movement, scenes of excessive drinking or smoking, or unorthodox behaviour that might encourage imitation. Walter Lantz syndicated fifty-two theatrical cartoons to television and was required to cut twenty-five sequences.

Animators were fully aware of the constraints placed upon them by the medium within which they now worked, and practised self-censorship that was only further modified in the instance of justifiable complaint. Jay Ward's deliberately playful *Rocky and His Friends* challenged these boundaries, however, with satirical subject matter and 'smuggled' impropriety that attempted to provoke the censor. The *Mighty Mouse: The New Adventures* cartoons of the late 1980s, directed by Ralph Bakshi, also became a cause célèbre, when the Reverend Wildmon of the American Family Association alleged that one cartoon, *The Little Tramp* (1989), depicted drug abuse (the act of inhaling cocaine), though to more innocent eyes this may look like the sniffing of a crushed flower. This event did irreparable damage to the series, for in spite of the fact that the offending three and a half seconds were removed and, somewhat ironically, the series won an award from another parent watchdog group, the Action for Children's Television (ACT) body, *Mighty Mouse: The New Adventures* were cancelled. Later, in 1995, *Two Stupid Dogs* was subject to a small cut when a voice artist sought to include the word 'fuck' in a gabbled monologue.

Significantly, however, in the contemporary era, *The Simpsons*, *Beavis and Butthead*, *The Ren and Stimpy Show* and *South Park*, in uniformly challenging the consensual apparatus of institutional and utilitarian perspectives, have tested the arbitrariness of the BS&P guidelines (see 'Adult Animation', p. 73). In relaxing some areas of what may be addressed and represented, the BS&P departments have responded to changes in contemporary attitudes without sacrificing their responsibility. As recent Independent Television Commission studies in Britain have demonstrated, children are far more tele-literate and discriminating about the intended effects of cartoons than they have often been given credit for, and recognise the difference, for example, between that which frightens

The Simpsons: a dysfunctional American family

Beavis and Butthead: adult animation with few limits

them in an exciting and pleasurable way, and that which intimidates and alienates them. Further (and this is also supported by a number of American studies), children see the artifice and excess of cartoon language in a way that enables

them to distinguish between the harmlessness of Tom and Jerry's slapstick violence and the harmfulness of everyday brutalities in real life.

Paul Wells

tated a re-evaluation of the place of cartoons and animated films in aesthetic and commercial terms. The emergence of Nickelodeon, the Disney Channel and the Fox Network competing head-to-head against the majors in the children's market significantly reduced licence fees and production budgets for new work. Further, this necessitated new pre-sales and distribution agreements for animation houses worldwide. This has created an eclectic mix on all broadcast channels of 'classic' cartoons from the 1930s to the 1950s, previous 'home-produced' television animation, imported series from other countries (most notably Japan, but increasingly Britain has a foothold in overseas markets with programmes like *Noddy, Maisie, Kipper* and *Bob the Builder*), and new work produced in recent times on much reduced investment.

The Hanna–Barbera back catalogue and a range of Warner Bros. *Looney Tunes* and *Merrie Melodies* have found their place on the Cartoon Network, seeking its original audience of 'baby boomers' and, now, their children. Original series like *Jonny Quest* have been updated as *The Real Adventures of Jonny Quest* in order to accommodate computer-generated animation and 'modernise' the science fictional premise of the series (see 'Science Fiction', p. 26). A fully computer-generated series, *Starship Troopers,* contemporises this aesthetic further, echoing the graphic space and violent confrontational thematics of many computer games and their virtual environments. The often neglected *Reboot*, made in the United States by British artists, was a pioneer in this area by setting its narrative within a computer environment, aping Disney's feature film *Tron*. The popularity of mainstream Japanese feature anime is reflected in the presence of *Pokémon, Digimon* and *Dragonball Z* in the schedules, and may be traced in many elements of contemporary American cartoons. Ironically, many 'American' cartoons have often been made in Japanese production houses.

The popularity of these cartoons is well evidenced, and still speaks to the view that the graphic freedoms available in animated film are still profoundly innovative, even when potentially compromised by the production context. The 'cartoon' can facilitate the depiction of seemingly impossible actions, extraordinary metamorphoses, narrative acts of condensation (the maximum degree of suggestion and association in the minimum amount of imagery), and modes of caricature that offer insight, clarity and amusement in relation to complex ideas. This is self-evidently appreciated, but perhaps only partially understood, by the children and adults alike who embrace the form. Its very language, and its capacity to change with the sociocultural and economic conditions of its production, assures its longevity and continuity (see 'Adult Animation', p. 72).

Paul Wells

RECOMMENDED READING

Peary, D. and Peary, G. (eds) (1980), *The American Animated Cartoon*, New York: E.P.Dutton.

Pilling, J. (ed.) (1997), *A Reader in Animation Studies*, London: John Libbey.

Wells, P. (1998), *Understanding Animation,* London and New York: Routledge.

NEWS

Studying Television News

Television news generally presents itself as a 'window on the world', in which the events of the day are transparently revealed for all to see. Although we may praise or criticise television fiction for being realistic or unrealistic, many people assume that, in the case of news, such judgements are unnecessary. Thus news is not merely seen as *like* reality but as unmediated reality itself, beamed directly into people's homes. If this were really so, it follows that there would be little reason for anyone to study television news, since to study it would merely be to study the world it reveals. For us to analyse the news is therefore to assume that, like other television genres, the *news is a form of representation* (or, as it is called in semiology, signification) and that the images and words it uses are, like TV drama, the result of creative and interpretative processes. It is to assert that making television news is, in Philip Schlesinger's phrase, a matter of 'putting reality together' (Schlesinger, 1987).

Television news (and the news media in general) has been studied from a number of perspectives. Like many aspects of media studies, these perspectives range from more social-science-based approaches (in which, for example, news is examined in terms of the role it plays in *society*) to forms of analysis that come from the humanities (in which TV news is examined as a *text*). These approaches can be understood in sociological, epistemological, theoretical and methodological terms.

In general *sociological* terms, we can identify three broad frameworks that inform the analysis of the *social* role of television news.

The liberal pluralist model assumes that television news provides useful information and thus plays an important role in strengthening democracy and citizenship. Much of the scholarship and research into television news comes from and informs this approach. Within this framework, more news is good news, both in the sense that a range of different news organisations is needed to guarantee a healthy diversity of news providers, and because it is assumed that the presence of television news in TV schedules should be sufficient to guarantee wide access to serious news programming. It was in this spirit, for example, that Newton Minow, the US Federal Communications Commissioner in the 1960s, made increasing the length of network news broadcasts a priority. More recently, in 2000, the British Secretary of State for Culture, Media and Sport, Chris Smith, expressed concern about the BBC's decision to move their main evening news show from 9.00 p.m. to 10.00 p.m., on the basis that the move may decrease the overall number of viewers of television news.

From this perspective, structures that increase the range of outlets (such as the provision of public service broadcasting channels) are generally seen as positive. On the whole, however, the liberal pluralist approach assumes that news journalists and reporters have a certain degree of autonomy from the ownership or economic structures of television channels (see Curran and Seaton, 1991; Williams, 1998). So, for example, the demands of commercial television are not seen as incompatible with the objectives of news journalism. There is, nevertheless, a concern about what is often called the 'dumbing down' of television news reporting, with the increasing adoption of more parochial, *tabloid* news values at the expense of *hard* news stories informed by an international network of correspondents (see 'The Infotainment Debate' p. 118).

Two more critical approaches to television news see it as playing a more problematic ideological role. The **conservative approach** sees news journalists (particularly those working for public service channels) as a generally liberal or left-leaning social group, and therefore sees the news as a discourse that reflects a liberal or left-wing bias. This approach has often informed conservative political rhetoric, particularly in the United States, where the notion of the 'liberal media' is widely asserted and believed (Herman, 1999). Because of its emphasis on the individual views of journalists, this approach is not concerned with the influence of ownership and economic structures. Although the conservative approach often has powerful advocates, it does not constitute a significant presence in the academic literature. Its focus on the individual views of journalists (as the principal determinant of the content of news) is seen by many scholars as simplistic, and the claim that journalists lean to the left is highly contested (Gans, 1985; Naureckas and Jackson, 1996).

A more influential approach in terms of media research is what might be called **the critical framework** in which television news is seen as implicated in dominant social and ideological structures, and hence tends to represent the interests of the more powerful groups within society. This approach focuses on the influence of ownership structures and the economic pressures of commercial television, as well as on the day-to-day institutional structures of television news, such as its dependence on political, economic and cultural elites as the 'primary definers' of news events (see, for example, Cohen and Young, 1983; Hall et al., 1978; Herman and Chomsky, 1988; Kellner, 1990; Tuchman, 1978). Television news is thereby seen as playing an important ideological role in creating acquiescence or consent for elite agendas. One of the central implications of the critical framework is that *access* to the production of news, whether as a reporter, an expert or as a source of news, should be broadened to include a wider range of voices regardless of status or power.

In *epistemological* terms, the status of television news tends to be either understood as a *reproduction* of reality (albeit one that may privilege certain views over others), or else as a *form of social construction*. In the first instance, the relation between TV news and the reality it depicts is seen as unproblematic – particularly when journalists adopt principles of objectivity. From this perspective, news can be criticised if it distorts or fails to reflect reality. As a consequence, the degree to which news misrepresents or distorts the world has been a constant source of examination and study.

Approaches that regard news as a social construction see reality as something that is necessarily mediated through discourse: thus, the way we understand the world will depend upon the way we are taught or encouraged to understand it. From this perspective, for example, there is no single, essential reality that we could call 'the Middle East': for people who live in the region the meaning of the term is constructed by such things as religion and ideology, whereas for most of those outside the region the meaning of the Middle East is constructed by news broadcasts. This is not to say that there are not verifiably true or false claims that can made about the Middle East, since 'truth' and 'falsity' are evaluations based on socially constructed categories. So, for example, to say something is 'big' is to classify it within a socially constructed category of size, and to assume comparisons with other smaller objects.

Because, unlike fictional genres, TV news makes self-conscious claims about the relationship between the world outside and the world it reports, it makes a difference whether we see television news as a reproduction of reality or as a social construction. From a social constructionist framework, there is no one reality for news to capture or reproduce. Although it may still be possible to criticise the news in terms of its accuracy, the notion of objectivity becomes untenable. So, for example, a television reporter may cover a story in which representatives from the two main political parties are quoted in order to be 'objective'. And yet that reporter is, in so doing, inevitably privileging the views of political elites, and constructing a view of the world in which those views are seen as defining political debate (see, for example, Canham-Clyne, 1996, on the narrow frame of reference in which the healthcare debate in the United States was reported). To see television news as a social construction does *not* mean, however, that anything goes, and all accounts are equal. Within this framework questions about whose version of the world is being favoured or excluded are still at issue (see 'Objectivity and Television News', p. 117).

From within each of these perspectives or epistemological frameworks there are many ways of approaching the study of television news, using various theories and methods.

THE POLITICAL ECONOMY OF TELEVISION NEWS

In terms of the production of news, a number of studies have examined the political economy of television news. This involves exploring the role played by ownership and economic structures on news content. So, for example, the economic interests of the owner (or management board member) of a news broadcaster may be reflected in the kinds of stories that get told. On commercial television, the interests of advertisers, and the need for the news programme to deliver an audience to advertisers in a 'buying mood', may also be a powerful force in structuring the nature of a news broadcast (see box). Since advertisers are more interested in wealthier audiences, we might also expect to see news on commercial channels being tailored to more affluent audiences – favouring business news, for example (see Herman and Chomsky, 1988; McChesney, 1997; Murdock and Golding, 1973). The study of production has also involved examining the *institutional structures* within which news journalists operate (see, for example, Harrison, 2000; Tuchman, 1978; Schlesinger, 1987). This involves examining the professional codes that news journalists employ to make decisions about the news value of events and the routines used to construct news reports.

CONTENT ANALYSIS

The content of TV news has been examined both quantitatively and qualitatively. Quantitative forms of content analysis involve the systematic measurement of media content in order to provide a picture of the overall character of news coverage. A content analysis may, for example, look at which points of view are generally represented in the coverage of issues and which tend to be excluded. One of the best-known quantitative studies of television news is the series of studies carried out by the Glasgow Media Group on the TV news coverage of industrial disputes and related political and economic issues (Glasgow Media Group, 1976, 1980, 1982), which suggested a bias in the news media against the views of trade unionists. Overall, these forms of content analysis often suggest that television news is heavily reliant upon official or elite sources, in terms of both the issues covered and the patterns of coverage.

STRUCTURE AND NARRATIVE

More qualitative approaches to news content have focused on the structure and narrative of television news and current affairs. Work by Galtung and Ruge (1965, 1983) examined the structural imperatives, routines and rituals that inform news production, and the use of semiotics in media analysis has led to a number of detailed explorations of news programmes as *texts* (e.g. Brunsden and Morley, 1979; Hartley, 1982; Jensen, 1987). These approaches have stressed the importance of understanding how the form and content of television news programmes prefer certain meanings of the world over others (see also Morley, 1980).

AUDIENCES

Understanding the meaning of television news has also led to research on audiences. The influence of news on the way people think about the world has been a focus of media research for some time, and although questions of media influence were initially somewhat elusive, there is now a body of evidence to suggest that the news is influential on public opinion in a range of specific and measurable ways. So, for example, a number of studies have demonstrated that news clearly sets an agenda that is then reproduced in responses to surveys about people's priorities and opinions (see, for example, Iyengar et al., 1982; McCombs and Shaw, 1972).

Overall, audience studies focusing on television news in particular (now the dominant news source for most people) indicate that people watch television news more inadvertently and with less attention than other forms of television (see Lewis, 1991). This has led researchers to use various qualitative methods to explore in some detail the way in which television news does impact on viewers. So, for example, Iyengar's research suggests that what he calls

the 'episodic' framing of most news stories (which focus on events themselves rather than the causes or history of those events) makes it difficult to understand the social causes of issues like crime or poverty, and instead to attribute blame only to the individuals themselves (Iyengar, 1991); these findings are in keeping with studies by Lewis (1991) and Philo (1990), which suggest that television news can be important in creating or reinforcing fairly simple associations (such as Saddam Hussein with Hitler or striking workers with violence) that stick in people's minds.

Justin Lewis

RECOMMENDED READING

Cohen, S. and Young, J. (1983), *The Manufacture of News*, London: Constable.

Glasgow Media Group (1982), *Really Bad News*, London: Writers and Readers.

Iyengar, S. (1991), *Is Anyone Responsible?*, Chicago: University of Chicago Press.

Analysing Television News

The analysis of news requires us to begin by understanding the processes involved in making television news. Just as Hollywood producers decide that certain aspects of life are worth making films about whereas others are not, so news producers make, on a very basic level, decisions about what is news and what is not. Most TV news producers also share with Hollywood producers the need to entertain audiences – in order to gain viewers in a competitive market. Although this applies more clearly to commercial television companies, public service broadcasters such as the BBC also have indirect but tangible pressure to get respectable ratings in order to justify their level of funding (see 'The Infotainment Debate', p. 118).

Nevertheless, we still tend to *think* of news as an information rather than an entertainment service. Since most of us are well accustomed to the routines of television news programmes, and since news journalists often share a sense of which events have 'news value' and which do not, decisions about *what news is* often take on the air of inevitability. As a consequence, the first question we need to ask is this: why do some stories receive a great deal of coverage and others receive less, little or none?

Most people would agree that news coverage should bear some relation to the *importance* of an event, but the

'The Propaganda Model of News': Herman and Chomsky

In their book *Manufacturing Consent* (1988), Edward Herman and Noam Chomsky lay out what they call the 'propaganda model' of news production. The model suggests that the economic and ideological conditions in which news is produced means that only certain kinds of information filter through. These filters, they argue, tend to privilege information that suits the interests of powerful elites, while regularly filtering out things that might go against such interests. They identify, in particular, five filters involved in the manufacture of news.

The first filter involves media *ownership*. In an era where more news media are in the hands of a few large and wealthy corporations, they argue that we would expect aspects of that ownership structure to be reflected in news content. In brief, because owners of commercial news media are likely to be invested in a pro-business, corporate view of the world (especially on issues that directly affect their own business interests) we would expect the news divisions of these companies to be more likely to promote rather than question their owner's interests.

The second filter, which applies specifically to commercial news media, is *advertising*. On television, advertisers are paying TV companies to deliver an audience for their products. This can influence news coverage in three ways. First, because advertisers are interested in the more affluent sections of the population, news programmes that tailor broadcasts to the interests of that population are more likely to be profitable. Second, advertisers favour lighter, less disturbing kinds of programming that will keep audiences in a 'buying mood', making them more receptive to sales pitches. Third, advertisers are likely to withdraw support from current affairs programmes whose message conflicts with their corporate interests (see 'Advertising', p. 94).

The third filter involves what they call *sourcing*. Journalists working to tight deadlines are dependent upon their sources for the information they report. Powerful interests, whether in government or business, are aware of this, and are able to invest heavily in public relations geared to giving journalists well-packaged information designed to meet their needs. Although the provision of well-equipped press rooms, celebrity or 'authoritative' speakers, camera-friendly images, information packs and so on make the journalist's life much easier, they also make it easier for those with such resources to get their message across. This, they argue, exacerbates the tendency of news organisations to assume that government or business sources are more authoritative than, for example, citizen advocacy groups. This principle applies to news-shapers as well as news-makers. In particular, business support for various think tanks has produced a stream of corporate-friendly 'experts' who can offer 'informed' testimony on current events, whether global warming or policy on inflation.

The fourth filter they refer to as *flak*. When news threatens powerful interests, corporate-funded lawyers or advocacy groups are able to use their resources to make their voices heard. So, for example, a news story biased against poorer sections of society will tend to generate complaints from people with little power, whereas complaints from powerful interests (such as the tobacco industry) can lead to legal threats as well as creating publicity designed to discredit negative news stories.

The fifth filter they refer to is *ideological*. During the cold war, for example, this involved unquestioned assumptions about the superiority of capitalism over communist or socialist systems. Since then, these assumptions have evolved to a widespread belief among the more influential news media in the efficiency of market solutions and the inexorability of a global, capitalist, 'free trade' system.

(*Manufacturing Consent* is published by Pantheon (1988). A video explaining the propaganda model, *The Myth of Liberal Media*, is available from the Media Education Foundation, www.mediaed.org).

Justin Lewis

definition of importance will vary depending on who we are and how we view the world (see Galtung and Ruge, 1983). So, for example, should television news be concerned with the personal lives of public figures (whether politicians or celebrities) simply because they are in the public domain, or should such figures only be of news value when they do something that has an effect on significant numbers of people? How important is it for us to know about events in other countries, even if those events have little direct influence on our lives? Does TV news always have to be about an 'event', or can it be about trends or more general topics? Should television news reflect the unusual, such as plane or train crashes, or more typical events, such as car accidents?

Once we begin to think about these questions, it becomes clear that the decisions taken by news producers about news value are open to scrutiny. It may be that our notion of citizenship, and what it is important for citizens to know, is not adequately addressed by the norms of television news. So, for example, we may feel that it is important for citizens to know the details of things that affect them (whether it is changes in the environment, or debates around government policy on digital television) so that they might, as citizens, have some say on these issues. But we may feel it is less important to know about the personal lives or publicity stunts of politicians, if those matters have no significant influence on public policy or our understanding of issues. The consequences of such a judgement, needless to say, would involve a radical shift in the news values of much contemporary news programming (see 'The Infotainment Debate'. p. 118).

Once we have looked at *what* is included and excluded from television news, we should consider *how* stories are told. Whose point (or points) of view is represented in the story, and whose voice is excluded? Where there are different points of view, are these views given equal weight by the form or context in which they are represented? There are many ways to do this: for example,

- We can count who is quoted or able to speak on news programmes, in order to establish whether certain categories of people (who we can call 'primary definers') are more predominant than others. So, for example, who is quoted on stories about the economy? Is it, for example, government representatives, business representatives, or people representing consumers or wage earners?
- We can look at the *sources* of a news story. Does that source have an interest in promoting a certain point of view, and does the news programme point this out? So, for example, the release of a report by a business group is likely to reflect a business-oriented view of the world. Is this source balanced by an opposing view?
- We can examine whether the story itself tends to create a certain view of the world. So, for example, do crime stories reflect the real world of crime, or do they create an impression that unusual crimes are more prevalent than they really are?
- We can examine the *way* in which a story is told. Does the narrative construction of the story prefer some meanings over others? Does the use of visual information or live footage lead towards a certain impression? So, for example, if two different interpretations are presented, but only one of those interpretations is accompanied by visual information, does this make that interpretation seem more persuasive as an account?
- We can look at what information is presented in the story. Do the facts presented tend to favour some views over others, and, if so, is this a fair representation of the facts available?

Most of these forms of analysis demand not only a detailed examination of television news, they require us to know *more* about the topics represented than we are given in the newscast. In order to evaluate what is being represented, in other words, we need to know what information or perspective is being excluded from the story.

METHODOLOGY

We also need to consider a number of *methodological* questions. In particular, if we want to make any general observations, we need to ensure that the news programmes we look at are typical rather than unusual. This means gathering a *sample* of news programmes that is large enough to establish clear patterns, and to minimise the chance of examples we look at being untypical of news coverage as a whole. If we are looking at coverage of a particular event, it is helpful to look at coverage of other comparable events as a point of comparison. If we are looking at more general features of television news, then we need to ensure that our sample is spread across a reasonable period, so that the nature of the coverage will not be distorted by any one (possibly unusual) news event.

Once we have chosen a sample, we need to establish a *systematic* procedure for analysis. This may involve developing a *coding frame*, which comprises a set of criteria for categorising each news item or news programme. So, for example, if we are looking at who is represented, we might want to have various categories of appearance such as:

- quoted without being seen;
- quoted next to photograph;
- shown speaking on camera, etc.

and various categories of person such as:

- government representative;
- member of pressure group;
- business person;
- academic expert;
- member of think tank, etc.

Before we develop our coding categories, we should ensure that these categories are pertinent to the question or issue we are pursuing, as well as being a useful way of summarising news content. We might find, for example, that there are significant types of people or statements whose presence in television news we had not anticipated (and who therefore get coded or classified under opaque categories like 'other'). To limit this possibility, it is advisable to test the coding frame on a selection from your

How to Analyse a TV News Programme

As we have seen, television's dominant *generic* domains of actuality (including news) and drama have been studied by widely differing *methods*. Textual analysis, derived from literary/linguistic models, for instance, is applied to drama. However, news has tended to attract sociological approaches, dominated by 'content analysis'. Textual analysis was suited to analysing individual stories qualitatively, whereas content analysis was developed for quantitative research, seeking regularities and frequencies across many stories.

Textual analysis (humanities, criticism, critique) and content analysis (social science, research, policy) were used to investigate opposing realms:

- news: the public sphere, citizenship, political economy, truth;
- drama: the private domain, audiences, everyday life, emotion.

There was a gendered aspect to this distinction; news and social science seemed *'masculine'* compared with soap opera and textual criticism, but textual analysis of actuality genres has become an important component of TV studies.

How to do it (adapted from Hartley, 1999, pp. 229–31)

1. News as an industrial commodity

- *Journalism*: news values – conflict, importance, recency, nearness, human interest, novelty, celebrity.
- *Competition*: news as commercial commodity. Sources, agencies. Compare rival news media.
- *Entertainment*: how to retain viewers while telling them things they do not like. How does news appeal and appal simultaneously?
- *Regulation*: licensing, defamation, 'decency', 'self-censorship'. For example, violence may be shown (between strangers, not intimates), dead bodies may be glimpsed (but not in close-up).

2. News as a generic form

- *Visual elements*: studio anchor and decor; graphics and design; actuality footage.

- *Verbal/sound elements*: institutional voices (reporters, commentators, anchors); accessed voices ('real' people); effects (music, dubbed sounds).
- *Narration*: the 'plot' of stories; characters ('we' and 'they' personifications, heroes, villains, victims); action and dialogue within and between stories; sequence as a dramatisation of 'our democracy today.'
- *Differentiation*: how news is both *like* and *unlike* surrounding genres (advertising, talk shows, drama) and media (newspapers, radio, Internet).

3. News as a dramatisation of democracy

- *Our representatives*: talking heads (decision-making), visualised by *location* (reporters hanging around in doorways); celebrities (actions and comments), based on *bodily recognition*.
- *Vox pops*: 'ordinary' (i.e. anonymous) people's views – the grab and the sound bite as the chorus of politics.
- *National identity*: myths of who 'we' are; policing the boundary of the social ('we' have a government, 'they' have a regime; 'we' love children, 'they' are paedophiles; 'we' are free, 'they' are illegal immigrants).

4. News as a regime of truth

- *Impartiality versus bias*: how can you tell one from the other?
- *Conflict*: truth as a product of 'both' sides of a story; truth as violence.
- *Eyewitness ideology*: news stories are often based on reports, statistics, media releases. But trustworthy reporting is associated with *being there* in the thick of the action. In practice, the *information* comes from a 'handout,' while the *reporter* stands in front of something visually relevant.
- *Fact versus fiction*: news has eye contact but not music; drama has music but not eye contact.

5. Who wants to know?

- What are you looking for that you do not already know? The research question will shape your findings, and your methods will determine your results.

John Hartley

sample (often referred to as a 'pilot study'), and, if needs be, modify it accordingly.

Once we have studied television news as a *text*, we need to consider the *contexts* in which it is produced. The authorship of television programmes is complex and diffuse: there are a number of levels of decision-making and a variety of institutional, professional or ideological pressures on programme-makers (see 'Constructing News Values' p. 114).

In the case of television news, simply at the programme level, reporters, editors and other news professionals will all have some role in what gets produced, but in an environment in which political and corporate leaders are becoming increasingly skilled at anticipating what journalists want, news-makers also play a role in *constructing* the news. So, for example, Ronald Reagan's adviser Michael Deaver regarded himself as a news *producer*, because he knew the images he created would be perfectly targeted to the needs of television news (great pictures, good copy) and therefore irresistible to the makers of television news broadcasts. Thus, when Reagan started one of the best-known car races in the United States (the Daytona 500), it was the lead item on all three main US networks – even though the event itself had little effect on anyone.

There are also pressures that come from the ownership and control of a television channel. It is possible, for example, that Rupert Murdoch's various satellite news channels (such as Sky and Fox) may reflect Murdoch's conservative, pro-business ideology. Private newscasters may also have links (whether through ownership, directorships or shareholders) with other business interests, which may be influential in pressuring news companies not to jeopardise their corporate interests (see, for example, Herman and Chomsky, 1988 (see box' 'The Propaganda Model of News', p. 111); Lee and Solomon, 1990). Public service channels, such as the BBC, are less subject to pressure than privately owned media, but can also be influenced by political appointments (to Boards of Governors), and by the need to rely on government support in revenue-raising decisions (such as the level of the licence fee). The use of advertising as the main source of revenue on commercial channels may also be a source of pressure on TV news broadcasters.

Understanding the economic, social, institutional and cultural contexts in which television news is produced illuminates our study of the content of news, in the sense that it may illuminate patterns we discover in our study of the form and content of news. This understanding may also lead us to ask certain questions of the news programmes themselves: so, for example, we might ask whether commercial television news tends to play down negative news about companies linked to the TV channel, or that routinely advertise on that channel.

Finally, if we are concerned with the social impact of news, we might conduct an audience study. There are many ways to do this (see, for example, Lewis, 1991): we might adopt a more qualitative approach (interviewing small groups of people) or a more quantitative approach (in which surveys are used to reach larger numbers of people). In either case, as with content analysis, we need to be aware of the degree to which we can generalise from our audience sample. There are also ways in which we can explore the power of television news by comparing patterns of news coverage with data generated by public opinion polls (see Lewis, 2000; McCombs and Shaw, 1972). Since TV news is still one of the prime sources of information in the process of democratic decision-making, the study of the genre remains a critical issue.

Justin Lewis

RECOMMENDED READING

Cohen, S. and Young, J. (1983), *The Manufacture of News*, London: Constable.

Lee, M. and Solomon, N. (1990), *Unreliable Sources*, New York: Lyle Stuart.

McNair, B. (1999), *News and Journalism in the UK*, London: Routledge.

Constructing News Values

The ideological role of the news media can refer to the way that symbolic messages are used to establish and maintain power relations in society. In this sense the news media influence the way we perceive the world, they control what we see as 'natural' or 'obvious'. The journalist picks up cultural values in stories and presents them back to the audience. The media's production of news values is not necessarily deliberate or conspiratorial but is systematic and routine. Both the viewer and the journalist live in a social world of which they make sense via language and culture. Embedded in journalistic language, news values are taken-for-granted assumptions about the ways of life of a society within which journalism operates. As we have seen, mainstream news values are all constructed within a common framework of understanding, such as the legitimacy of a capitalist system or agreement on democratic government (see box 'The Propaganda Model of News', p. 111).

The construction of news values is also influenced by more tangible forces external to the news organisation, such as:

- the types of sources accessed by journalists for expert evaluations of events;
- the use of news agencies, which influence the news agenda;
- the importance placed by journalists on the output of other news organisations;
- the need to deliver large audiences to advertisers.

Many contemporary news organisations are therefore being forced to re-evaluate their news priorities and consequently their news values in the light of economic pressures, technological developments and the growing competition for audience share.

Audience needs are increasingly influencing the construction of news values. Because of ratings pressures, news organisations sometimes prioritise what they know audiences want to watch rather than always making the editorial decision for them. Technological developments and commercial pressures are also compromising the public service broadcasting remit in Britain and throughout Europe, forcing a re-evaluation of news values in most public service broadcasting organisations (see 'The Infotainment Debate', p. 118).

The audience tends to find stories interesting if they are human interest stories, show conflict or controversy, cover unusual happenings, cover events that are new and are happening now and are culturally and geographically relevant. These, and the news factors identified by Galtung and Ruge (1965) and others (see also Ostgaard, 1965; Sande, 1971; Tunstall, 1971; Bell, 1991) have been used to attempt to identify the properties of news stories that audiences will find appealing and are likely to want to watch. Television news events have 'news value' if:

- they contain good pictures;
- they contain short, dramatic occurrences that can be sensationalised;
- they have novelty value;
- they are open to simple reporting;
- they occur on a grand scale;
- they are negative or contain violence, crime, confrontation or catastrophe;
- they are either highly unexpected, or contain things that one would not expect to happen;
- they have meaning and relevance to the audience;
- similar events are already in the news;

- they contain elite people or nations or they allow an event to be reported in *personal* or *human interest* terms.

The construction of news values also depends on organisational values that usually differ between organisations. Different news organisations have different editorial approaches and house styles resulting in different news values. The BBC's *Ten O'clock News*, is clearly different from Britain's *Channel Five News* with the former concentrating more on international news and political issues and the latter producing more human interest stories, although news programmes can and do change their approach if necessary. The differences in approach can be related to the ownership of the organisation, its remit, its contractual obligations and the type and size of audience it needs to attract. These factors shape the organisation's news policy and its news values. In most organisations, although the key goal is to make a profit, there are other goals, such as to produce a quality product, serve the public and achieve professional recognition.

Within news organisations there has to be a mechanism in place to ensure that there is agreement among journalists about the type of news values the organisation or news programme holds. A study by Warren Breed in 1955 showed how agreement on news values is achieved by journalists through a process of socialisation. Often this occurs through assimilation of newsroom mythology that is communicated down by experienced journalists and by a general absorption of the organisation's remit and news policy.

A shared belonging to the profession should provide journalists with a clear and identifiable set of skills, practices, values, pressures, constraints and expectations within which they work. Gaye Tuchman (1997) revealed how journalists employ a set of routinised conventions in choosing and selecting news to cope with a variety of problems and pressures such as time and space limitations, financial, bureaucratic and legal restrictions, logistical difficulties and the particular constraints of the television medium itself, such as the continual need for visuals.

Journalists do not look everywhere for news but work in what Fishman (1997) called 'beats' and Tuchman (1997) refers to as 'news nets'. These are areas from which news is expected to arise at certain times and with some frequency. Fishman likens working on a beat to using a road map that helps a journalist to navigate through events successfully. Mastering areas of news such as council meetings, court reporting and news conferences indicates a basic acquisition of journalistic skills. These skills are driven by routine processes such as daily phone calls to the police, double-checking facts and figures, checking court lists, council

Gatekeeper Studies

'Gatekeeper studies' have played an important part in helping us to understand the way in which news values are constructed. David Manning White (1950) applied Kurt Lewin's (1947) term 'gatekeeper' to journalism practice to try to understand why a journalist chooses one story over another. White's US-based research centred on the role of an individual wire editor in a press newsroom. The wire editor, who White named 'Mr Gates', selected stories to be printed from the large amount of wire copy provided every day by three large news agencies. White believed him to be the most important gatekeeper of all, as he alone was able to reject the majority of stories coming into the newsroom, thus shaping and constructing the organisation's news values. Although his aim was to try to find a way of predicting journalistic behaviour, White's research raised more questions than it answered.

Snider (1967) used White's gatekeeper theory to see if Mr Gates's selection criteria had changed over time. His study showed that in 1949 Mr Gates chose more human interest material than any other type of story, followed by national politics, international politics, state politics, national farming and international war. In 1967 international war (due to Vietnam War coverage) was the most common story type, followed by crime, national economics, human interest and disasters. Snider concluded that in both 1949 and 1967 Mr Gates picked the stories he liked and believed the readers wanted, but by 1967 Mr Gates' news values had changed to include a wider variety of stories.

The concentration on individuals as gatekeepers, however, was challenged by studies that revealed that individual journalists were not actually the key characters in decision-making. Decisions were made, not on individual assessments of newsworthiness, but on other journalistic and organisational criteria and external pressures. The American study of the organisation of news selection at NBC by Bailey and Lichty (1972), showed that, in fact, news production involves a chain of journalistic activity from the initial event to the final news product, and that story selection does not lie solely in the hands of a specific individual. The organisation is the gatekeeper, not the individual journalist.

Further gatekeeping research has shown that journalists are only passive transmitters of information, as their work practice is routinised. Staab (1990) argued that it is not necessary to discuss separately the role of different gatekeepers in the news process, as there is little reason to believe that their perception of newsworthiness differs radically according to whether they are in the collecting, transmitting or presentation stage of the news process.

Gatekeeper research has made an important contribution to our understanding of the construction of news values, as it has shown that news selection does not take place on the basis of the whims of an individual journalist in an organisation but is built into an organisation's ethos and rationale. Journalists work together within organisational constraints to produce a news product that reflects a shared agreement on what has news *value*.

Jackie Harrison

notices, the parliamentary diary and the wires. A journalist has to able to recognise news value, a skill that is intrinsic to being a journalist. This lets them 'join the club' and excludes non-journalists.

However, it is not possible to explain the construction of news values simply in terms of monolithic issues. Such influences as:

- the ideological context within which journalism operates;
- the influence of sources, owners, advertisers and other news organisations;
- the needs of the organisation;
- the routine nature of journalistic practice;
- the importance of news factors as an explanation of the properties inherent in events;

are all important and relevant. No single one, however, will serve as a stand-alone explanation of the construction of all television news values.

Jackie Harrison

RECOMMENDED READING

Berkowitz, Dan (1997), *Social Meanings of News*, London: Sage
Harrison, Jackie (2000), *Terrestrial Television News in Britain: The Culture of Production*, Manchester: Manchester University Press.
Shoemaker, Pamela (1996), *Mediating the Message: Theories of Influences on Mass Media Content*, New York: Addison Wesley Longman.

Objectivity and Television News

In the UK, the requirement for both the BBC and ITN to produce impartial news is a legal one and is a part of the constitution of the two systems laid down by government from their inception. The news programming of the ITV system is regulated in terms of serving the public interest impartially. The Broadcasting Act 1990 states that 'any news given (in whatever form) in its programmes is presented with due accuracy and impartiality' (Broadcasting Act 1990, 6(1)6).

The Annex to the Licence and Agreement in 1964 states that the BBC accepts a duty 'to provide a properly balanced service which displays a wide range of subject matter . . . [and] to treat controversial subjects with due impartiality . . . both in the Corporation's news services and in the more general field of programmes dealing with matters of public policy' (BBC, 1996, p. 21). Regulation of television news content has an important implication for audiences. In the UK most people use television as their primary source of local and world news, and it is the most trusted source of news information (Gunter and Winstone, 1992). Audience trust has been gained via the application of journalistic objectivity norms.

However, many of the criticisms of objectivity and impartiality in journalism are generally underpinned by the assumption that objectivity and impartiality are always relative. In other words, ideas of what should be reported and in what way varies from society to society and from issue to issue. Those who argue that objectivity as a professional journalistic ideology is flawed believe that social reality is humanly produced and consequently is a social construction. Judith Lichtenberg (1991), however, argues that we cannot simply state that objectivity is impossible, and that critics of objectivity do not actually do so themselves. Although they appear to reject objectivity they are covertly relying upon it as a benchmark or ideal against which to assess deviations from it.

Completely objective television news is seen by many as impossible, owing to the subjective nature of journalistic value judgements, and by others as being undesirable, because it works against journalistic responsibility for content and against the watchdog role of the media (see box). However, despite the problems inherent in the meaning of objective news and the difficulty in achieving it, objectivity is an important professional aspiration and central to the task of television news as a whole. Indeed, journalists claim

to use a set of devices that ensures that they can argue that their reporting is unbiased, such as:

- use of verifiable facts;
- clear separation of fact from opinion;
- expression of professional judgement but not personal opinion;
- inclusion of opposing sides in a debate (or different truth claims of sources);
- separating different sources' views from the report by using either quotation marks in the press, or via sound bites on television;
- use of live television pictures or live two-ways where a journalist speaks live to a newsreader from a location, showing that something is actually happening or has happened and showing reports packed with facts and figures.

However, using these devices to achieve an appearance of objectivity has raised several concerns from critics, such as:

- the routine use of sources means that mainstream views are generally allowed greater access to television news than radical views, reducing the diversity of opinion;
- responsibility for the content of the news can be levelled at the sources, allowing journalists to be relatively free from the responsibility of justifying or defending the content of their stories;
- the use of sources as experts may allow journalists to avoid the acquisition of expert knowledge, while at the same time sources have become increasingly adept at information management and 'spin';
- the growth of live news reporting on location, which gives the appearance of more objectivity because the audience can see events unfold, may be confusing, deceptive and told out of context;
- the increasing use of live and often dramatic pictures means even relatively unimportant events are sensationalised making it more difficult for the audience to assess their significance.

Regulators aim to ensure that journalists do not unwittingly distort the news. However, the word 'objectivity' is rarely used by regulators, but is substituted by words such as 'impartiality', 'accuracy', 'balance' and 'fairness'. Here, impartiality implies a disinterested relationship to news content, whereas objectivity has broader demands than this.

However, objectivity remains valuable as an ideal against which bias can be evaluated, but is problematic as a method.

The BBC and Impartiality

Impartiality at the BBC originates from its founding principle of public service broadcasting: the detachment of the BBC from vested interests and government. The BBC is funded through the licence fee to ensure that it is free from direct governmental or direct commercial intervention. Its first Director-General, John Reith, believed that an impartial BBC could flourish and promote an enlightened and informed public only if it was not required to pass on the views of the government directly to the public. The role of the BBC is to act as interpreter of public affairs and arbiter of public tastes and standards. Over the years, however, the BBC has not been immune from political pressures. The General Strike of 1926 tested the relationship between the Government and the Corporation. The Government argued that the BBC should recognise the strike as illegal and not allow strikers' views to be heard on the radio, contradicting the BBC's requirement to be impartial.

Other governments have since tried to influence BBC content. In particular, the Thatcher Government tried to prevent the BBC from taking an impartial view during the Falklands War in 1982. In May 1982 a *Panorama* programme was heavily criticised for including dissenting views on the Conservative Party's war policy. BBC 2's *Newsnight* was accused by the Government of being too detached and not supportive of the British side. The BBC has defended its position on numerous occasions, arguing that conflicts such as the Falklands War, the Gulf War and the invasion of Kosovo are not total wars, and

consequently it is in the public interest to give an impartial account of events.

Impartiality is intended to be at the heart of all the BBC's programming, as it reflects two public service principles: serving all interests and ensuring that minority interests are represented. The BBC's public service broadcasting principles are codified in the BBC's *Producers' Guidelines*, which contains scrupulous requirements for news programming. The BBC is forbidden in Clause 13(7) of its Licence and Agreement from broadcasting its own opinions on current affairs and matters of public policy.

The BBC, however, is not always impartial when reporting terrorism or racism, and will only conduct interviews when it feels there is a public interest in doing so that outweighs the offence it would cause. In 1996 Martin Bell, then a BBC journalist, called for the abandonment of neutrality in war reporting and genocide in favour of a 'journalism of attachment'. Criticising the traditional form of BBC war reporting as 'bystander's journalism', Bell argued that journalists should show they care as well as know about the events they are covering. His view raised controversy; taking an impartial stance in news reporting is a central tenet of good journalism at the BBC. Its public service requirements mean that it must seek to serve the whole nation, reflecting and responding to differing tastes and views. At the BBC the maxim is that 'good journalism (which is impartial) will help people of all persuasions to make up their own minds' (BBC, 1996 p. 21).

Jackie Harrison

Any attempt to be objective impossibly implies the feasibility of somehow removing values from news content. Of concern is the compromise position that journalists take up between playing an active role in a democratic society and the attempt at 'objective' reporting using a variety of practical devices. The attempt at objectivity in broadcast journalism may also not be the best form of journalism as it serves broadcasters' interests rather than the public interest and reduces plurality of news information. Although it is important that television journalists continue to provide accurate and reliable news information, it is not necessarily the same as providing objective news reports.

Jackie Harrison

RECOMMENDED READING

Lichtenburg, Judith (1991), 'In Defence of Objectivity Revisited', in James Curran and Michael Gurevitch (eds), *Mass Media and Society*, London: Edward Arnold.

McQuail, Denis (1992), *Media Performance*, London: Sage.
Tuchman, Gaye (1999) 'Objectivity as Strategic Ritual: An Examination of Newsmen's Notions of Objectivity', in Howard Tumber (ed.), *News: A Reader*, Oxford: Oxford University Press.

The Infotainment Debate

The infotainment debate (as opposed to infotainment itself) is an argument about the relationship between television and public life. The debate, if not the phenomenon of infotainment itself, has been much more prominent in the UK and continental Europe than in the USA, largely because many European countries have maintained a commitment to what is known as 'public service broadcasting' as a national cultural policy (see box 'The BBC and

Impartiality', p. 118). Public service broadcasting in this context means television channels financed primarily from the public purse rather than from commercial (advertising) revenues. The purpose of such arrangements is to use broadcasting to *inform the public* and to *educate the citizen*, rather than to *entertain the consumer* (see 'The Populist Debate', p. 76).

The beginnings of the debate occurred during the 1980s and early 1990s, when the buzzwords of *deregulation* and *privatisation* swept across the Reagan–Thatcher political universe, from the airline industry to telecommunications. Applied to broadcasting, this political reform had two consequences:

- the privatisation of previously state-owned TV channels (e.g. ORTF in France and RAI in Italy);
- the relaxation of legislative controls over content.

Both led to what seemed to some observers to be a far too relaxed attitude to the presentation of public affairs on television.

TV overtook newspapers as the primary source of news for popular audiences in developed countries sometime in the 1970s. As an emergent medium, television news paradoxically had to grow out of a professional and cultural context that was suffused with the values and habits associated with the press, the very medium that TV was in the process of supplanting.

According to the prevailing wisdom, TV news ought to conform as much as possible to the existing generic format of a *serious newspaper*, and look as little as possible like *television*. This idea is as old as the press itself: it originated in the political philosophy upon which modern liberal democracies are said to be based. In countries where voting was universal, freedom of speech and access to information had to extend to the whole adult population in order for an 'informed citizenry' to make rational judgements and decisions about public affairs. The information communicated to them ought to be accurate, unbiased and impartial, on the model of the nineteenth-century broadsheet newspaper: the *Washington Post*, the *New York Times*, *The Times*, and so forth.

'Free press' advocates presumed that commercial TV companies were incapable of delivering such information unless they were under regulatory duress. Further, they thought that television was almost the binary opposite of the great civic freedoms: its appeal was to the *emotions* not to *reason*, its location was *private* not *public* life, and its purpose was *entertainment* not *decision-formation*. Indeed, television had some generic characteristics that were very challenging for a modernist understanding of what constituted good news reporting.

TV developed information formats along the following lines.

- *A talking medium*: words were heard one at a time, so a given current affairs show could only contain so many words, as opposed to a newspaper, where many more words could be printed, even if only a minority of them were read by any one reader.
- *A video medium*: moving pictures were more telegenic than talking heads. Having videotape of an event to hand tended to determine its inclusion in a news show, over and above any editorial assessment of its overall importance as a news story. Conversely, events of great significance for which there was no footage were less likely to reach the top of the news agenda.
- *A hybridising medium*: TV was very prone to evolution by spin-off. Successful formats were compulsively copied. In this very active semiotic environment, 'information' could never be 'pure' – it would always be presented via the techniques and generic formats that were regarded as most appealing at the time.
- *A porous medium*: TV contained an unusual mixture of incommensurable types of programming, especially fact and fiction, rubbing up against each other. Its formats were very porous to each other. News was constantly borrowing generic characteristics from non-news formats.

Television evolved its own time-based, audiovisual, hybridising aesthetic. Along the way it produced various conventions for generic differentiation whereby viewers could tell almost at a glance whether they were watching news or some other genre.

'Public service' news was especially committed to such distinctions. Semiotically, it was self-consciously authoritarian, often giving it a middle-aged male sort of feel, as opposed to the more energetic and 'feminised' genres around it. Journalists were often preferred as presenters, even rather than cute-looking personalities who nevertheless proliferated in children's, music, lifestyle and talk shows. News shows were often protected from advertising slots by 'news bumpers' (bits of continuity that ensured that a commercial did not lead straight into or out of a news story).

But news was never exempt from the imperatives of its semiotic surroundings. Throughout television and even print-media history, it has had to balance two contradictory necessities. Its mission to inform the public and educate the citizen meant that it had to give priority to the *facts* and to the due weight of stories on the day's news agenda. But simultaneously, the need to attract and retain large audiences of those same citizens (who were not compelled to attend) meant that news had to *appeal* to them, otherwise they would not watch it. This is an inescapable need in popular journalism (Hartley, 1996). Television had always to serve two masters – 'info-' and '-tainment', as it were.

Exactly how much should informational programmes appeal to their audience's desire just to 'watch TV'? Viewers were 'trained' by long habituation to accept that news might be boring but still be of some importance – hence their willingness to put up with the news staples of talking heads and people waiting outside doorways. But still editors had to decide just how much foreign news could be tolerated on a popular news show, as opposed to local crime, traffic and sport stories, or how many 'human interest', celebrity and showbiz stories to balance those about conflict, war and opposition.

Meanwhile, beyond the comparatively inflexible environment of the news, television experimented with presenting *information* in *entertaining* ways that suited its status as *television*. Many such infotainment formats were successful:

- *Lifestyle*: cooking, gardening, travel, house improvement, antiques (see 'Daytime TV', p. 92);
- *Reality*: traffic-camera shows, home-video shows, neighbours from hell, street-interviews. This format has evolved into 'survival' shows (see 'Reality TV', p. 134);
- *Tabloid*: consumer stories, crime, celebrities, scandal, hidden cameras and chequebook journalism;
- *Investigative*: most popular where the reporters put themselves in physical danger of assault by the subjects of the investigation;
- *Talk*: including celebrity chat shows, *Oprah* and *Springer*, late-night variety shows (see 'The Confessional Talk Show', p. 84);
- *Animal*: vet shows, nature documentaries; environmental stories.

On the fictional side of the divide, *drama series* were produced that exploited the documentary or informational mode of address to make satirical commentary (see 'The Police Series', p. 19, and 'Hospital Drama', p. 23). *Comedy shows* also made relentless use of news formats and personalities to send up people in public life and television itself (see 'Sketch Comedy', p. 62).

In such an environment, news and current affairs for-

mats inevitably hybridised. Editors tried to make their talking heads appealing. News anchors that could smile desirably and also carry descriptions of death, disaster and war were able to command high fees. Studio decor had to be appropriate – warm but not frivolous. Sometimes a newsroom staffed with eager newsgatherers could be glimpsed; other editors preferred the authoritative Big Desk. The format was occasionally revamped to maintain viewer interest. Thus, single newsreaders evolved to multiple anchors (especially older man/younger woman pairs), who moved from desks to sofas; then a vogue for single presenters returned, sometimes sitting casually *on* the desk. Singing or stripping news presenters were not entirely unknown (see 'The Uses and Limitations of Genre', p. 7).

In current affair shows the gravitational pull of infotainment was much more pronounced. Emotional scenes, such as a sporting victory or a homecoming, might be rendered with music and slow motion. Private conflicts were dramatised (often literally via 're-enactments') to produce public narratives. Facts were still routinely respected, but their status was subordinated to the mythic or symbolic resonance of a story.

Meanwhile, what happened to civil society? Some commentators lamented what they saw as 'dumbing down'. Infotainment was about identity and celebrity, not power and decision-making. Private life and personal emotion seemed to have triumphed over rational discourse about public affairs.

But this is not the whole story. Many of the criticisms levelled at infotainment formats were based on a cultural or taste hierarchy – a *preference for* modernist forms of political communication, and an equal but opposite *prejudice against* popular media. The idea that democracy might be conveyed and even extended by commercial and corporate means has been slow to gain acceptance among media theorists, even though commercial democracies have been manifest realities for a century or more.

Commercial communication – television is still the pre-eminent example – reaches citizens (including women, children, migrants and minorities) who have not been well served by the modernist communications technologies. Far from 'dumbing down' a once-knowledgeable populace, it could be argued that 'democratainment' extends the public sphere to places other media cannot reach (Hartley, 1999; Hartley and McKee, 2000). 'Infotainment' is just as active in public pedagogy and citizen-formation as was the serious press. The only difference is that its generic form belongs to television.

John Hartley

CNN (Cable News Network)

CNN pioneered the 'rolling update' format, where twenty-four-hour broadcasting required something different from the self-contained news bulletin of broadcast TV. 'Rolling update' news, in contrast, was generically innovative in three ways:

- *Distension.* Each new element of a running story was taken as a separate event in itself, thereby massively distending the story by prolonging the content of a paragraph to the length of a segment or even a show.
- *Repetition.* On the presumption that viewers watched CNN in segment-length chunks, rather than continuously, it was also able to recycle the same material relentlessly, often over several days.
- *News-talk.* CNN also pioneered 'news-talk', which was not the same as the established quasi-news format of *current affairs*. News-talk was the habit of introducing a story from the anchor's desk, perhaps with a brief throw to the scene via a taped report, but then returning (at length) to a studio discussion *about* the story, frequently with another CNN employee or journalist, and occasionally a professor from NYU or MIT. This way a one-and-a-half-minute item could fill an entire segment.

But what annoyed 'anti-globalisation' critics about CNN was not its generic endlessness, but its socio-economic provenance. Owned and controlled by entrepreneur Ted Turner until he sold it to Time Warner, CNN told its news stories from an American perspective for American subscribers. When the format was internationalised, via hotel chains and local cable providers, the content jarred for viewers habituated to their own national or state perspective on world events. From outside the USA, it seemed as if American national interests took precedence over an accurate impression of what may actually have occurred on the ground.

CNN was trusted (that is, tuned in) most at times of unfolding international crises, the paradigm instance being the Gulf War of 1990–1, when popular participation in the unfolding event, in all countries, was authenticated by watching it on CNN rather than on other providers. It was not just because CNN scooped the world with a reporter and camera in Baghdad; the very format suited the event (Wark, 1994). In Australia, which did not have widespread cable provision at the time, free-to-air broadcasters took CNN directly to bring the authentic experience of the continuously breaking story

CNN: the face of global news

to the home screen. Similarly, more recently, the political hiatus caused by the closeness of the vote in the 2000 American presidential election impelled viewers around the world to tune into CNN, not rivals such as Sky or the BBC. However, such trust was strictly limited: it extended only to seeking the authentic *American* perspective from CNN. That point of view needed triangulation with others, including one's own national carriers, before anything like understanding could be achieved.

Other providers, such as News Corp's Fox/Sky/Star and BBC World, began to compete directly with CNN as global providers of news in the 1990s. There was also competition between these corporations for the supply of satellite/cable news services to new markets such as India and China. In those markets, local political sensitivities came into play, often at the expense of the BBC, which was regarded as biased against the Chinese government in particular.

One of the ironies of the critique of 'globalisation' was that those who lamented the globalisation of news looked on its opposite, the localisation of news, with equal alarm. The tendency for television news to offer less foreign news in favour of more domestic, human interest and crime stories has been widely criticised as an instance of 'dumbing down' in the media. The alternative, to offer everyone news from everywhere, was already available via the Internet, but this innovation did not satisfy the critics, who saw it merely as evidence of a growing 'digital divide' in the information society. The same critics, however, organised themselves globally, using the Internet, to stage protests such as those in Seattle (1999) and Melbourne (2000) at the World Economic Forum. It seemed that globalisation was emancipatory when practised by political activists, but imperialist when practised by American corporations (see Andersen and Strate, 2000).

CNN's supremacy as the fastest source of news was brought to an end by the Internet. Funnily enough, the decisive moment was televised by CNN. Court decisions and news-sensitive information relating to the unfolding Monica Lewinsky affair were released on the Internet, for instance by Matt Drudge. On the publication of the Starr Report, TV viewers around the world saw CNN's own coverage reduced to pictures of a computer screen with a reporter scrolling down pages of Internet text to find newsworthy references to non-standard uses for cigars. The rolling update continuous 'breaking news' format of cable TV had become a mere servant of the instantaneous Internet. But in fact, CNN got into trouble even for this second-hand timeliness, as commentators expressed discomfort at seeing the unexpurgated account on a TV screen, although they seemed happy for the full text of the Starr Report to appear on the Net itself (Hartley, 2000, pp. 11–36).

Hence, 'globalisation' migrated to the next-fastest medium, where it could speciate and flourish for producers and consumers alike. Specialist providers such as Reuters Financial or Bloomberg.com could follow the movement of international capital itself, and consumers could buy books from Amazon.com, or wartime memorabilia via Yahoo, whatever local legislation decreed.

Finally, however, it is worth remembering that the most impressive 'globalisation' of all still belonged to television. No other medium gathered such immense populations as broadcast TV could. This was demonstrated every four years in the Olympic Games, which counted their audiences in the billions. During some moments – opening and closing ceremonies, perhaps, or an icon race such as indigenous athlete Cathy Freeman's gold-medal performance in the 400 metres in Sydney, 2000 – perhaps even a majority of the human population of the earth were watching the same thing at more or less the same time. The species reintegrated globally, 'prehistorically', as it were (see Hartley, 1999, pp. 8–11).

John Hartley

RECOMMENDED READING

Atkinson, Dave and Raboy, Marc (eds) (1998), *Public Service Broadcasting*, Paris: UNESCO.

Epstein, Edward Jay (2000), *News from Nowhere: Television and the News*, Chicago: Ivan R. Dee.

Hartley, John (1999), *Uses of Television*, London and New York: Routledge.

The Globalisation of Television News

Globalisation of everything is as old as the hills; it is the first thing *Homo sapiens* achieved, long before the invention of agriculture, cities, writing and thence history. Communication of commodities, money, spouses, and language across geodemographic boundaries, whether communal, civic, national or imperial, was of course a condition of those boundaries. More to the point, literally global exchanges of meaning have characterised every age and affected every region. In short, globalisation was not an invention of 'late capitalism', nor even of modernity.

Globalisation may be understood more narrowly as the exchange of capital and commodities across international boundaries by transnational firms trading for privately accumulated profit. In the sphere of information, even that narrow definition means that globalisation is at least as old as printing with moveable type. News has been global in terms of content since the first 'Intelligencers' and 'Mercuries' began to appear in the seventeenth century, to say nothing of 'news' conveyed by folk ballads and the like. Although they tended to be printed in and for the literate decision-makers of one country, newspapers brought to those readers' attention news from Tartary, Turkey and Timbuctoo, as well as from the local courts (see the contents of a 1736 English newspaper in Hartley, 1992, pp. 154–7).

So what's new? Not much – even the politicisation of globalisation derives from a century-old Marxist rhetoric of capitalist/worker adversarialism in social theory, and leftist opposition to liberal democratic commercial expansion (imperialism). Thus, those who worried about the international political hegemony of America worried also about the internationalisation of American firms. Military colonisation may not have been imminent, but 'Coca-colonisation' was widely feared.

The temporal coincidence of *technology* (e.g. satellite broadcasting capacity), *politics* (the collapse of the Soviet Union), the Clinton era *stock-market boom* in the knowledge economy (software, media and telecommunications), alerted critics to the internationalisation of technologically mediated information on a new scale. What was new about it may have been nothing more than the attention of these critics, but the political fact was that 'anti-globalisation' emerged in the 1990s as a new-left, new-radical slogan to replace the lost adversarialism of the cold war. Globalisation was criticised for inhibiting the economies of *developing countries*, deepening the '*democratic deficit*' in the accountability of transnational transactions (especially in a period when company law was still largely nation-based), and *environmental damage*, often of countries remote from multinational corporations' centres of profit or of consumption.

Globalisation in the context of news, however, is not quite the same as the more general socio-economic concept. In the television environment, it refers to the international deployment of news formats (not stories), on the model of CNN (see box). Actually, even formats had been traded or copied internationally over a long period in TV news: for instance, British television derived its news format from American models imported by ITN in 1955; competition soon obliged the antediluvian BBC to catch up. The chief generic features of broadcast network news were that it should (a) be dramatic but not be mistaken for drama, (b) be comprehensive while not exceeding half an hour, and (c) be distinguishable from, while closely resembling, the news shows of competing networks.

John Hartley

RECOMMENDED READING

Boyd-Barrett, Oliver, and Rantanen, Terhi (eds) (1998), *The Globalization of News*, London: Sage.

Wark, McKenzie (1994), *Virtual Geography: Living with Global Media Events*, Bloomington: Indiana University Press.

Miller, Toby, Lawrence, Geoffrey, McKay, Jim and Rowe, David (2001), *Globalization and Sport: Playing the World.*, London: Sage.

DOCUMENTARY

Studying Documentary

The study of documentary has only recently become an established feature of film and media studies programmes internationally. Film studies has always, and understandably, had as its primary concern the study of cinematic fictions, chiefly the 'art cinema' of European cinema and the popular cinema of Hollywood. Media studies has also been very interested in fiction too, but its concern with television non-fiction has been dominated by a focus on news (see p. 108). In order to understand what studying documentary might currently involve and what developments we might expect, it is helpful to look at three different contexts for academic interest. We can then move on to look at some key ideas and approaches.

Perhaps the oldest strand of interest in documentary history and analysis is that displayed by vocational film schools in various parts of the world. Here, the engagement is governed by a wish to learn techniques of production and to develop the craft and creative skills for making successful documentary films and programmes. Any form of study that cannot be seen to contribute to the ends of practice has figured only marginally, if at all, within this perspective. However, a great deal of clear and focused thinking about the nature, form and function of documentary work has developed from such teaching. The wish to make good documentaries has been a great motivator of analysis and criticism (Rabiger, 1998, is a notable example).

A second strand of interest emerged from within film studies, where this label describes a body of study more closely connected with literary and dramatic analysis than with training in film practice, although there are often interconnections. In film studies, the chief if not exclusive concern is with questions of aesthetics and textual form. A highly developed and often dense analytic agenda surrounding the organisation of the image, narrative structure, *mise en scène* and the symbolic and imaginary conditions of spectatorship provides the focus of study. Some of this analytical apparatus is carried over from the study of fiction, some of it was generated around the specific circumstances of documentary practice (see Nichols, 1976, for an early outline and Nichols, 1991, for a major, influential commentary; Renov, 1993, is an excellent collection centred within film scholarship). Film studies has tended to regard documentary film as constituting a special case of 'realism' (see 'Reality TV', p. 133), one in which complex questions of ontology and epistemology (the status of the filmed image and its use as a means of knowledge) are linked to particular political and social intentions. Both British and American writers within film studies recognised the creative achievement of documentary (Hiller and Lovell, 1972, is a pioneering text). Moreover, the lively strand of independent cinema in the United States allowed many American writers to see it not only as a project with a 'classic' past but one with continuing social potential. This view was in some tension with the move towards a more sharply anti-realist approach in film studies, coinciding with the rise of a Marxist perspective in the whole subject field. This gave prominence to questions about 'ideology' and the means of its reproduction. From such a position, documentary was interesting in so far as it was yet one more device of illusion and misinformation. For a while, the dominant tone became denunciatory. As I shall suggest below, this is now changing quite rapidly.

The third strand of study we can identify is that which comes out of interdisciplinary media studies and therefore, in part, from cultural studies. Here, the emphasis is more on documentary as a media product, to be considered in relation to other widely circulated products such as the news (see p. 108) and (more recently) soap opera (see p. 47). Film studies had almost entirely ignored television documentary, but within media studies, where documentary figured (it was still a marginal interest), it was in its television forms. These importantly included fly-on-the-wall formats (see 'Observational Documentary', p. 129) as well as the full variety of documentary journalism, including the current affairs series. The connection with journalism opened up a whole set of questions not asked much, if at all, within the film studies perspective. These questions concerned the institutional order of television, the professionalisation of its practices, the development of its generic system and, possibly most important of all, its routine requirement (both social and economic) to engage with popular audiences.

Kilborn and Izod (1997) provide a good introduction to documentary from within a media studies perspective, and the analytic commentaries in Corner (1996) largely draw on media studies approaches. In the UK, the sense of documentary achievement was supported, not so much by work in the independent film sector, as by the long and distinguished tradition of public service broadcasting. Discussion of documentary was thus an aspect of the developing debates, throughout the 1990s, about the future of public service broadcasting in an increasingly commercialised broadcasting ecology. More recently still, the emergence of the forms of reality television and docusoap (see p. 132 and see, for instance, Dovey, 2000 on this) have put questions of documentary form and value right at the centre of the debate about 'infotainment' (see p. 118) and the risks of 'dumbing down'.

We have, then, three broad strands of study, each with its different intellectual character but all of them considerably reinvigorated by changes in the nature of audiovisual documentation itself (of which the 'reality television' phenomenon is just one notable part – see p. 134). Although the study of documentary is showing stronger signs of interconnection across the three areas (there are many courses, for instance, that try to relate both to the film tradition as well as to television work and then to the development of practical video skills), it is not yet possible to talk of a coherent 'documentary studies'. One of the reasons for this is the particular way in which study of documentary raises the question of the relationship between form and content.

John Corner

Form and Content in Documentary Study

Documentary has always been defined in a loose, contingent kind of way (Winston, 1995, is the best historical account). 'Documentary' is an adjective that has been turned into use as a noun and, although the term still gives a useful indication of an area of practice and a range of programme types, it escapes any tight generic specification. What we understand by 'documentary' is always dependent on the broader context of the kinds of audiovisual documentation currently in circulation. For John Grierson in the 1920s, this presented a very different setting for his documentary ambitions than that within which a television producer today has to work; consequently, the word now points to something rather different both in its forms and its purposes. However, one common feature has been an interest in using images and sounds to provide an exposition or argument about the real world. This directness of address to something outside the 'text', this special level of referentiality, is one of the things that distinguishes documentary from fiction, that also points outside itself but much more indirectly. In fiction, the imagined world of the story is primary.

One of the consequences of this characteristic is that study of documentary, any documentary, has to engage directly with what the documentary is *about*. It has therefore to consider the question of, for instance, health policy on AIDS, international arms smuggling, labour relations in Japan, loneliness in the student population, the history of forensic science or whatever else a documentary chooses as its topic. The precise extent to which enquiry pursues this engagement will vary with the motivation of the researchers but it will also vary, predictably, with the kind of documentary under scrutiny. Here we can distinguish between 'thick text' and 'thin text' documentaries. A 'thick text' documentary is creatively dense. This is as a result of its mode of use of such features as narrative design, subjective voice, symbolic suggestiveness and the dynamics of depicted action (including dramatisation). Its status as an authorial artefact can, in analysis, be given primacy over its status as an intervention in a specific field of knowledge or debate.

'Thin text' documentaries, however (and this would include many television documentaries), work with a more directly reportorial and observational discourse. Analysing these documentaries requires that the subject matter itself be given close attention in a manner that can route the analysis out of strictly discursive matters quite quickly. Often, such extra-textual inquiry is necessary in order to say anything useful about the text, let alone about the terms of its production and its function for audiences. In some ways, the first kind of analysis described above is close to that applied to screen fictions, and the second kind is close to that applied to the news. The interplay between the discursive–aesthetic and sociological poles, their respective aims and methods of enquiry, is a significant variable in documentary study.

Analysis of documentary, simply because of the referential character of the material under scrutiny, has on the whole resisted a tight formalism of approach. But it has often been unsure as to how best to proceed with enquiry into contexts. For instance, it might seem that study of different documentaries addressing the same topic could often be more productive than study organised according to different documentary modes or production settings. However, the question of how far to take investigation into the non-televisual world of documented topics and events, and then of what kind of analytic relationship to set up between representation and represented, has been a challenge. Quite apart from the difficulties sometimes involved in collecting detailed and accurate extra-textual data, most critics have wanted to avoid any kind of 'reflectionism' whereby a documentary is judged chiefly by its correspondence with an independent account of external events and circumstances. Such a view would run counter to the whole swing towards a view of mediation as involving a good deal more than a 'relay' process. But commentators have also wanted, particularly in more recent writing, to locate documentaries more firmly in both their discursive and their material settings, and to trace their function as referential and knowledge-yielding practices. There is a new extra-textual, empirical ambition at work in documentary study, complementing its theoretical liveliness.

Corner (1995, pp. 79–81) outlines a view of documentary as a series of transformations. This is not by any means an original view but it can help in organising both study and research. First of all there is the transformation by which a particular topic in the world becomes, in the planning process, a given range of locations, interviews, archive clips and thematic emphases. Then, there is the shooting process itself and the whole range of audiovisual decisions that go into crafting footage from various kinds of settings, circumstances, events, actions and speech. Following this, there is the editing process, when the combinatory logics of documentary are variously applied, narrative coherence is achieved, evaluations are established, emphases marked, closures made, moods set. Finally, there is that transformation by which viewers take the screened material and turn it into sense and significance, which will be broadly social and yet at that same time, depending on the topic, quite closely personal too. It is across these transformations, here only sketched, that the real magic of documentary as what I have called 'the art of record' (Corner, 1996) is to be found. It is here that its classic controversiality lies too, in the apparent fusion of index (recorded image and sound) and rhetorical and aesthetic ambition.

There is no doubt that study of documentary practice is becoming popular and that it is widening its scope too, if sometimes cautiously (the references list some of the more recent additions to the literature). It is taking on questions of pleasure more directly and examining the links between pleasure and knowledge. It needs to retain its strong sense of history, including the history of photography as well as of film. At the other end, it cannot afford to ignore the way in which the Internet is reconfig-

uring the possibilities of documentation, both in form and mode of use.

'Documentary' as a category has always been leaky and unstable, but there are good reasons for thinking that it is now in a stage of radical dispersal. There will continue to be 'core' work, certainly, but there will be an increasingly wide range of television, video and Net-based practice that does not fit easily under the label even though it has strong 'documentary' elements. The new and sometimes messy depictive energies now at work in televising the real will be a stimulus to documentary study, and at the same time they will encourage us to rethink the generic assumptions that underpin both practice and critical inquiry.

John Corner

RECOMMENDED READING
Corner, J. (1996), *The Art of Record*, Manchester: Manchester University Press.
Dovey, J. (2000) *Freakshow: First Person Media and Factual Television*, London: Pluto.
Kilborn, R. and Izod, J. (1997), *An Introduction to Television Documentary*, Manchester: Manchester University Press.

Documentary Realism

'Realism' is a central and much-contested notion in painting, literature, theatre and in both film and television drama (see Corner, 1992, for a critical review). Essentially, it points to how what are essentially 'fictions' can seem, in different ways, to reproduce dimensions of the real as a result of their procedures of depiction or their mode of engagement with real-world issues. There is much confusion about the use of the term 'realism' in the arts, but this sense of 'real-seemingness' and of how an effect of the real is produced is generally a primary. Clearly, there will be major differences between how a painting, a novel and a television play achieve 'realism'. Moreover, the capacity of photography, film and television to 'show things realistically' as a function of their nature as visual recording systems is something that simply cannot be paralleled in the concerns of literature (see 'Realism and Soap Opera', p. 49).

'Realism' is also a term that has a long attachment to work in documentary, but here we have to be very careful in our application, for it is clear that most documentaries make quite direct and serious claims as to the reality of what they represent. They frequently do this both at the level of the image (this *is* the ship that brought survivors back, this *is* the captain of the ship) and at the level of general exposition (these *are* the known facts relating to the shipwreck, this *is* the judgement it is most sensible to make as to what happened). Their 'display' of the real world is frequently accompanied by spoken propositions about it (in commentary, voice-over or in-shot talk).

Although the point has not been noticed quite as much as it deserves to be, this means that the business of making a 'realistic' television play is likely to be very different from that of making a 'realistic' documentary. We may slip into a number of confusions if we do not recognise this from the outset.

It can help matters if we distinguish between two forms of realism in documentary practice. First of all, there is what we can call *observational realism* (see p. 129). This is essentially a set of formal markers that confirm to us that what we are watching (which might be in a 'fly-on-the-wall' documentary or a sequence from, say, a current affairs programme) is a record of an ongoing, and at least partly media-independent, reality. Important here will be a sense of spontaneity of action and a movement of camera that presents us with something which is perceptually coherent but which is following developments beyond the control of the crew. Some observational sequences will be shot in a 'raw' style, gaining their realism from their lack both of smoothness and of immediate significance when compared with television fiction. However, others may be shot in such a way as to imitate at least some of the scopic range and lucid continuity of fictional sequences (many early film documentaries had scenes like this, primarily because the 'fly-on-the-wall' effect was not then a technological option). We would not expect a documentary to look precisely like a scene from fiction (subjective point-of-view shots, shot reverses, and so on) except at the cost of undermining its credibility. Of course, a documentary shot entirely in 'dramatised' mode (see 'Drama-Documentary', p. 31) is likely to conform much more closely to the principles of dramatic realism as part of its general strategy.

It is important to notice that in both the above examples, any 'realist' effect is working to confirm what we have already been asked to assume by the more general claims made by documentary work. The 'realism' does not itself generate this assumption, as it does in dramatic fiction.

The second kind of realism we can call *expositional realism*. This is even less like the realism of fiction. It might be best to see it as a 'rhetoric of accuracy and truth' that many television documentaries variously draw on. Here, we are talking about the way in which an overall exposition and/or argument is structured across the various components of image and sound. We might think of a current affairs documentary claiming to expose the operation of international arms smugglers. What is the fit between what we see and what we hear? How are contesting interpretations of the evidence organised and weighed? How does the symbolic dimension of what we see bear on our emotional responses and our evaluations? In what ways are particular scenes offered as 'typical' of more general circumstances? What different relations of proximity and distance do we have to what we see and what we hear? Questions such as these will direct us to a close analysis of the way in which particular pictures and words combine to 'win the viewer' for the particular case that the documentary is making. This is a case that might be explicit (and that, rather than enforce a judgement, might encourage viewers to exercise critical independence), but it will often have an implicit level of working too.

One way of broadly distinguishing between realism in screen fiction and realism in documentary is to see the former as essentially provoking a distinctive kind of *imaginative* relationship between screened events and viewing consciousness. We can then see the latter as essentially provoking an *inferential* relationship between the two. What this means is that the narrative of the realist fiction is designed to engage imaginatively (and selectively) with viewers' perceptions of the real world and what can happen in it. There is often a pleasing play-off here between fantasy and reality. In the documentary, we are offered bits of evidence and argument and we have to construct truths from them, truths of fact and perhaps truths of judgement. However, we should remember that imagination plays a part here too.

The specific conventions of 'realism' in television drama are always changing (which is why the idea of 'realisms' is sometimes to be preferred). The particular ways of relating the viewer to the real in documentary are changing too, and the rise of popular factual entertainment (as in the emergency services series and the 'docusoap' – see p. 132) has increased the rate of change.

The special kinds of linkages with the real to which documentaries aspire ensure that the question of 'realism' will continue to surround work under this heading. Kilborn and Izod (1997) draw out the main factors and their interconnections usefully. But in addressing these issues we should be alert to how documentary practice differs from fictional practice, however fashionable it may have become to underplay or even to ignore this difference.

John Corner

Documentary Fakes

The question of 'faking' in documentary has recently received a lot of press attention in Britain, largely because of the greatly increased range of 'reality TV' formats, often shot on limited budgets and with an imperative to be visually entertaining (see p. 133). However, the issue of fraud and deception in documentary goes right back to the early days of documentary film-making, since it has always been clear that a degree of 'staging' is often a necessary part of giving coherence and continuity to documentary accounts. Winston (1995) is excellent on developments in practice and in principle here. In shooting a sequence of fishermen unloading their catch, for instance, what could be considered wrong with giving some directions as to their positioning and movement with respect to the camera? And, perhaps causing more pause for thought, why not reshoot it with their co-operation if it does not quite work first time? The sheer technical limitations on early actuality filming made such choices easy. In the classic 1930s documentary *Night Mail*, for instance, the need for good shots required that the travelling post office depicted was actually a studio set, not part of the train that we see in other shots. This is a move towards what one can see as part-dramatisation, extensively used in many film documentaries.

It is helpful, at least provisionally, to think of a sliding scale of fakery. At one end of this scale there are the minor bits of intervention and fiddling that go to produce a satisfactory shot and a nice level of depictive coherence. This may mean a degree of direction and repeat shooting. At the other end there is the wholesale fabrication of persons and events, still offered within a 'documentary claim'. In between, there are a number of practices (for instance, combining shots from two separate events to give the impression of a single event; cross-cutting between two events shot at different times to suggest their simultaneity; specifically requesting people to perform actions that, in the camera's absence, they would not have performed on that occasion). These remain the subject of debate, often in relation to specific contexts and programme aims.

Two strands of documentary raise the issue of faking in an especially sensitive way. First of all, the tradition of 'fly-on-the-wall' film-making (with its roots in cinéma vérité) has set up a number of expectations about its 'direct truth' to the events portrayed (see 'Observational Documentary', p. 129). There is sometimes a purist literalism about the claims made by this kind of project – everything you see really happened just as if the camera was not there at all. Again, Winston (1995) provides a useful discussion, with a strong historical perspective. This grounds the question of the integrity of the programme at a very demanding level of primary truth, one that has to take in the self-consciousness of the people being filmed. It is not surprising that 'breach of trust' becomes an ever-present concern here. Many of the new 'reality' formats, including docusoap, base themselves on this observational technique, with its distinctive, often rather voyeuristic, character (see 'Reality TV', p. 134). This has undoubtedly contributed to the intensified concern about unacceptable faking.

The second strand that needs special attention is journalistic documentary. A large number of television documentaries are still made within one version or another of journalistic investigation, perhaps with a reporter in shot, perhaps with only voice-over commentary. Broadcast journalism has its own protocols in relation to accuracy, truth and the scope for 'creativity'. These are problematic and often loosely applied, but they are different from those shaping the main development of documentary, even if the two modes are related. The journalist, usually the employee of a broadcasting organisation, occupies a public role. The claims, often explicit, made about circumstances, events and people in journalism work within tougher criteria than those surrounding documentary per se, even allowing for the difference between 'news' and 'feature' journalism. This point has sometimes been forgotten in recent debate in the newspapers, where, for instance, fakery in a docusoap about driving instruction has been placed alongside its presence in serious investigative programmes (see 'Docusoaps', p. 132).

Once we have moved beyond the minor, 'technical' level of fakery designed to produce coherence and continuity at the level of the shot, a key question will concern the extent to which the viewer is made aware of the status of what they are watching vis-à-vis 'the real'. If we take the example of recent docusoaps, the indications are that many viewers fully realise the extent to which high levels of self-conscious performance are an intrinsic part of the speech and action in such formats. As a condition of this performance, there is often likely to be some 'rigging' of the circumstances in which filmed people find themselves. This may be acceptable but, even within docusoap, if it is found that the people are not who they claim to be and did not 'in reality' do anything like they are seen to do on the screen, then there is likely to be a popular feeling of resentment against bad practice. In a current affairs programme, such deception would be extremely serious.

At the present time, as documentary energies disperse across a whole range of innovative and hybridised formats, the question of faking will be raised more often, renewing discussion about what is legitimate and what is not across different kinds of documentation. Winston (2000) and

Dovey (2000) are two recent and thoughtful attempts to debate this issue.

There is one kind of faking that has developed its own respected place in film and television. This is what is often now called the 'mockumentary', in which documentary devices are imitated and/or parodied for comic effect. The fun of 'mockumentary' usually comes from the subversive delight gained from aping documentary's discourse of seriousness, combined with an engagement with a particular topic thought ripe for comic exploration in its own terms. Rob Reiner's brilliant *This is Spinal Tap* (1983) mixes spoof rock-vérité with a hilarious exploration of band culture across a number of years and fashions. More recently, the wonderful New Zealand film *Forgotten Silver* (Costa Botes and Peter Jackson, 1995) spoofs historical documentary techniques with a comic sideswipe at film scholarship. On television, there has been a whole range of comic/parodic developments, ranging from the level of the sketch through to entirely faked programmes. The fact that documentary discourse is now seen as a fit subject for parodic attention is a healthy sign for television culture as a whole, and it will certainly do no harm at all to have the newer, more duplicitous formats exposed to ridicule in this way.

John Corner

RECOMMENDED READING

Corner, J. (1996), *The Art of Record*, Manchester: Manchester University Press.

Dovey, J. (2000), *Freakshow: First Person Media and Factual Television*, London: Pluto.

Kilborn, R. and Izod, J. (1997), *An Introduction to Television Documentary*, Manchester: Manchester University Press.

Observational ('Fly-on-the-Wall') Documentary

Stephen Mamber (1972a, p. 79) described direct cinema, the American observational documentary movement of the 1960s, as 'real people in undirected situations'. The idealism and impossibility contained within Mamber's definition of observational cinema at its zenith no doubt now seems quaintly outmoded: how can a filmic representation ever be 'undirected'? How can that film ever just be a 'way of looking' as opposed to a way of altering or manipulating the reality it is looking at? These are problems that have vexed both the history and the theorisation of observational cinema since its emergence as a documentary genre in the late 1950s to its multiple current refigurations in contemporary television.

The first problem facing anyone attempting an overview of observational documentary is that of naming. 'Observational' is the catch-all but 'unsexy' term for several substrands. 'Direct cinema' (equally unattractive and really rather nebulous) refers specifically to the film-making of Robert Drew, Richard Leacock, Donn Pennebaker, the Maysles, Fred Wiseman and their protégés working in America in the 1960s and after; *'cinéma vérité'* derives from Dziga Vertov and refers specifically to the reflexive, anthropological work of, for example, Jean Rouch in France, again in the early 1960s; 'fly-on-the-wall', a term universally disliked, is the term most readily applied to observational work in British television by, among others, Roger Graef and Paul Watson (see below).

Although 'direct cinema', 'cinéma vérité' and 'fly-on-the-wall' possess certain essential differences, the conflation of the terms is principally a matter of convenience that arose out of a recognition of a common root to films otherwise as dissimilar as *Chronique d'un été*, (1961), *Salesman* (1969) and *The Fishing Party* (1986). The attribution of the term 'cinema' in this context is also problematic as, apart from Rouch's *Chronique*, the notable examples of observational documentary have been made for television. There were also distinguishing cultural and historical differences between the American, French and British observational documentary movements; they derived from different national documentary traditions, possessed different antecedents and dealt with different subject material. The assimilation of direct cinema, cinéma vérité and 'fly-on-the-wall' into the generic term 'observational cinema' is arguably the result of documentary theory perceiving form to dominate history or content.

The pre-eminence of form is upheld by the fact that all 1960s strands of observational documentary share a unique technical–historical moment, namely the advent of lightweight 16mm cameras and portable, synch-sound recorders. Despite Annette Kuhn having argued that 'certain types of equipment were developed and marketed expressly to make a specific type of film-making possible' (Kuhn, 1978, p. 75), this is to put the cart before the horse. Instead, it seems logical to conceive of such technical advancements proving the necessary catalyst to a new type of documentary rather than vice versa. A comparable set of

New Reflexive Documentary – 'The Broomfield Film'

Nick Broomfield is the 'star' director of British documentary – perhaps more famous than the films or programmes he makes. So much so that in 1999 he appeared in a series of television advertisements for the Volkswagen Passat in which he performed a pastiche of what journalists readily refer to as the 'Broomfield film'. The essential ingredients of this by now caricatured formula are: Broomfield as sound recordist brandishing boom and sporting 'Mickey Mouse' earphones, a rambling investigative quest of an elusive subject, the unconventional but often compromising interview with the protagonists, a relaxed camera style and an ironic, retrospective voice-over. Along with other documentary-makers such as the American Michael Moore, the British Molly Dineen and Louis Theroux, Broomfield has helped create a sub-genre of the observational mode: the 'fly-in-the-ointment' or reflexive documentary in which the director appears (part investigative journalist, part nemesis, part comic turn) to prise the truth out of unwilling subjects.

Broomfield began far more conventionally with straight-forward observational films such as *Tattooed Tears* (1978) and *Soldier Girls* (1981), both of which he made with Joan Churchill, his then partner, who had worked as camerawoman on *An American Family*. His debt to vérité techniques is, however, clear from more recent statements such as: 'Feature films may be taken more seriously as works of art and as pieces of entertainment, but only the documentary can really capture the spontaneity and immediacy of real life' (Macdonald and Cousins, 1996, p. 364). At a recent question and answer session at the London Film Festival, Broomfield directly acknowledged his debt to direct cinema, naming Pennebaker, the Maysles and Wiseman as the greatest influences on his work.

In these early Broomfield documentaries, with their emphasis upon detailed observation and character, it is easy to see this legacy, particularly in the films' interest in the workings of institutions and the fraught situations the confrontations in such institutions promote. Both *Tattooed Tears* (about the California Youth Training School correction centre) and *Soldier Girls* (about the women US Army recruits of Charlie Company, South Georgia) are intensely moving in their sympathy for and empathy with the inmates and trainees. However, in retrospect, the documentaries hint at Broomfield's frustration with the traditional 'fly-on-the-wall' form. This frustration was cogently expressed in relation to the later and aptly named *Driving Me Crazy*: 'I'd become sort of disenchanted with the narrow parameters of this style of film-making. All too often what you look at on TV is very cleaned up and dishonest' (Paterson, 1989, p. 53).

It was during the making of *Driving Me Crazy* that Broomfield first appeared on camera, exasperated by his planned film beginning to implode. From this moment on, his films changed from 'fly-on-the-wall' to hybrid 'anti-documentaries' in which the conventional observational documentary coexisted with the anti-film elements that most documentary producers would leave on the cutting-room floor: abortive phone calls, chats with marginal characters, Broomfield and crew setting up. The coexistence of the conventional and the reflexive observational documentary illustrates Broomfield's predilection for dismantling the form itself. In doing this, Broomfield further forces his audience to reassess the whole notion of what constitutes a documentary. However, perhaps the radical has now become the mainstream, not only in the case of Broomfield but also in his imitators, not least Louis Theroux who in 2000 made a film about Eugene Terreblanche using remarkably similar tactics to those found in Broomfield's *The Leader, his Driver and the Driver's Wife* (1991).

Stella Bruzzi

innovations (DVC cameras, digital editing suites) proved equally significant factors in the 1990s revival of observational documentary in Britain in the form of the populist 'docusoap' (see p. 132), but it would be perverse to argue that docusoaps created the need for DVC.

Observation documentary tends to deal with current events, events that are unfolding in front of the camera and to which the makers of the programme do not know the outcome. Likewise, the new observational style has led to a greater interest in the *personal* and the *intimate*: people-based documentaries that are less preoccupied with the staple content of more didactic documentaries such as historical analysis. A charge levelled at many obser-

vational documentaries, therefore, is that they are superficial and apolitical. One can challenge this view in two ways: by following the lead of the editors of *Cahiers du Cinéma* who argued in the aftermath of 1968 that all films are political, even those that on the surface appear not to be, or by suggesting that the focus upon personality and character in many observational films simply offers political insight of a different, covert kind (see Comolli and Narboni, 1976).

The hidden or masked ideology of observational documentary remains one of the movement's more significant traits: the criticism through exposure of a class-riddled British society in Watson's *The Fishing Party*, the brutality of

1960s psychiatric care in Wiseman's *Titicut Follies* (1967), the severity of America's army training regime in Broomfield and Churchill's *Soldier Girls* (1981) (see box). It is always tempting to ignore the more naive protestations of the key direct cinema exponents when professing to have no substantial influence upon the events they filmed and to look instead at the truth that results from the very interventions these film-makers so studiously repress. Robert Drew and his followers believed they were striving for (and able to create) a *pure documentary*: that is, one that remained faithful to its subject matter through its responsive as opposed to proactive editing, camera and sound and through its eschewal of voice-over and interview (see Waugh, 1985).

The observational documentary movement has developed enormously since its conception in 1960, and yet the legacy of direct cinema is substantial. In Britain the style has continued to dominate, in a variety of modified forms, television output in particular. Out of direct cinema, *cinéma vérité* and its British contemporary Free Cinema (films such as Lindsay Anderson's *Every Day Except Christmas* and Karel Reisz's *We Are the Lambeth Boys*) came the use of observational techniques for the purposes of drama in films (for both cinema and television). *Cathy Come Home* (see 'Drama–Documentary', p. 33), directed by Ken Loach, was just one of several 'kitchen sink' or gritty realist dramas to emerge out of British cinema and television that adopted and adapted the techniques of direct cinema. In the 1970s and 1980s Paul Watson made *The Family* (1974) and Roger Graef made *Police* (1982). Both series derived from or were reminiscent of earlier American predecessors: *The Family* was based on *An American Family* (1972), while *Police* echoed the concerns of Fred Wiseman's institutions films. In the 1980s, the BBC 2 strand *40 Minutes* was dominated by observational documentaries, and even its more style-conscious replacement *Modern Times* conformed to many observational ideals. With the genre's proliferation and diversification throughout the 1990s, stylisation and reflexivity have increasingly crept into the observational documentary form (see box).

What is distinctive about the manner in which British observational documentary has evolved is its ability to assimilate widely differing and frequently contradictory conventions. Having started as an anthropologist, filmmaker Chris Terrill, for example, continued the 'fly-on-the-wall' tradition with series such as *HMS Brilliant* (BBC 1, 1995) before being a pioneer of the most popular and long-lasting reincarnation of the observational mode in Britain: the docusoap (see overleaf). In the series *Soho Stories*, *The Cruise* or *Jail Birds*, however, reflexivity and self-consciousness (the clear integration of the camera, Terrill's voice and presence or the subjects' performances for that apparatus and director) have burst into 'fly-on-the-wall' formats (see box). With British television's continued prioritisation of observational documentary comes the realisation that, if the genre is to be sustainable, it needs to acknowledge both the impossibility of direct cinema's aim and the essential voyeuristic impulse that still make observational documentary universally appealing.

If one thinks briefly of the British 'fly-on-the-wall' tradition, one senses immediately that what is most interesting about the films of Watson, Graef or those that came in their wake are the moments of disruption that no amount of observation can suppress. Watson has said that 'when I made *The Family*, I had an agenda, my own voice, a point of view . . . I made the films with a clear idea of the story I wanted to tell and in the hope of providing genuine insights into the human condition' (cited by Bruzzi, 2000, p. 79). This interaction between Watson's point of view (or 'manipulation' as Fred Wiseman contentiously put it during an interview at the National Film Theatre) and the documentary subject is what realistically constitutes observational documentary. Andrew Bethell, talking about his series *The House* (BBC/Double Exposure, 1995) commented that, after an initial observation period in which the subject matter dictated the filming, he developed a sense of what he wanted to capture in the series and so arrived for later filming 'with a shopping list' of confrontations, events, insights he needed and would seek out if not directly engineer.

The problem remains, however, of how unbiased 'fly-on-the-wall' can be and whether or not 'observational' can ever be synonymous with 'objectivity'. The work of Graef, Watson and Broomfield (see box) would, in their different ways, suggest that it can never be. What direct cinema ignored was precisely the value of the author's voice to observational documentary (a 'voice', ironically, that was there even in the films that ostensibly eschewed authorial intervention). One of the men featured in *The Fishing Party*, for example, had an injunction placed on the BBC film when he realised that even an observational documentary (that traditionally 'leaves the driving to us', as Bill Nichols has characterised it) could offer an intensely critical portrait of its subjects. Observational documentary is as full of bias and subjectivity as any other form of documentary; it is only recently coming to terms with integrating this realisation formally into the films themselves. Indeed, it could be argued that its spontaneity is but a useful masquerade for achieving its aims.

Stella Bruzzi

RECOMMENDED READING

Bruzzi, Stella (2000), *New Documentary: A Critical Introduction*, London & New York: Routledge.

Macdonald, Kevin and Cousins, Mark (eds) (1997), *Imagining Reality: The Faber Book of Documentary*, London: Faber & Faber.

Winston, Brian (1995), *Claiming the Real: The Documentary Film Revisited*, London: British Film Institute.

Docusoaps

Docusoaps were the television documentary find of the 1990s. For the first time factual programmes, put out in prime-time slots, could rival their popular drama counterparts. At its peak *The Cruise* achieved approximately 11 million viewers per episode, and *Driving School* peaked at 12.5 million. Even long-running series such as *Vet School* and *Vets in Practice* have retained audiences of around 8 million. The term 'docusoap' itself was coined by journalists keen to dismiss this new brand of factual television that, in their estimation, contaminated the seriousness of documentary with the frivolity of soap operas (see p. 47).

In certain respects, docusoaps resemble their more conventional 'fly-on-the-wall' antecedents. For example, like the films of Wiseman, Graef or Watson, they feature the lives of ordinary people sharing a common experience. The difference between docusoaps about ordinary lives and a Wiseman film about equally mundane existences is not essentially one of subject, although people having driving lessons is perhaps a less inherently 'worthy' subject than patients on a ward for the terminally ill; the real difference is one of tone. What truly sets docusoaps apart from their predecessors is their prioritisation of entertainment over social commentary. This is in part a formal issue. One docusoap convention borrowed from drama is the focus on 'characters', usually known by their first names and introduced during jocular opening title sequences. Allied to this is that docusoaps, like soaps (that also putatively tackle serious contemporary issues), are more interested in characters' personalities than in their social roles or profession.

Also reminiscent of soap opera is the docusoap's fast-paced editing style, chopping together short sequences and alternating between a limited number of narrative strands per episode. However, this bias towards drama and sensationalism has frequently got the genre into trouble. There were, for instance, the substantiated allegations that Ray

The Family: a precursor of the modern docusoap

Brown, the 'star' clamper of *Clampers* (1998) was no longer a clamper when the series was being made, but instead worked in the office of Southwark Council and had been picked for the series on the basis of his potential appeal to audiences. Likewise, some sequences in *Driving School* were shown to be faked for dramatic effect (see 'Documentary Fakes, p. 128).

Docusoaps, like earlier forms of observational documentary, were made possible by specific technological advances. By their very nature, observational series are bound to amass a higher-than-average shooting ratio, and working on 16mm film (for so long the preferred choice of television as well as cinema documentary film-makers) was becoming prohibitively expensive. With the arrival of new digital cameras and editing suites it has become at once easier and cheaper to film and cut material, thus allowing for the needs of observational documentary once more. In 1998, Paul Hamann, as head of BBC Documentary Features, commented that docusoaps could be produced three times as cheaply as comparable light entertainment. Coupled with the fact that, for the first time in British television history,

'Accidental Footage'

Linda Williams has detected, in what she terms the 'new' (that is, more reflexive) documentary, a loss of faith in 'the ability of the camera to reflect objective truths of some fundamental social referent' (Williams, 1993, p.13). Television's ability to represent the truth in the way that observational documentary film-makers argued it could, has recently been replaced by an acceptance of the medium's limitations and an awareness that, as Williams puts it, what can be shown is a series of 'competing truths' rather than one overarching one. This has become so much the way in which factual representation is interpreted that Andrew Britton states, as if it is a foregone conclusion, that 'there can be no such thing as a representation of the world which does not embody a set of values' (Britton 1992, p. 28).

However, the subject of this section is a form of factual film-making that is, by its very nature, less prone to distortion than others, and that is 'accidental footage'. By this I mean film or video material collated by individuals who do not set out to record the events they find themselves filming, which thereby lack premeditation and hence 'authorship' in any conventional sense. Examples of 'accidental footage' would be Zapruder's 8mm film of the death of President Kennedy, the assassination of Kennedy's brother Robert in 1968, George Holliday's home-video footage of the beating of Rodney King, live transmission of the Shuttle disaster or Concorde aflame seconds before crashing.

These examples are strictly speaking newsreel (see page 108) as opposed to 'documentary', the latter, as Soviet film-maker and pioneer of the compilation film Esther Shub argued, being the consciously, subjectively conceived final film into which raw material might be placed (Leyda, 1996, p. 59). The important factor linking the above cases of 'accidental footage' is that they were not premeditated or prepared for except in the split second it takes to turn a camera on and point it. Because of this, all possess an amateurish intensity even if, as in the case of Robert Kennedy's death, the cameras were operated by news professionals.

In the case of someone such as Abraham Zapruder, what he immortalised on 8mm on 22 November 1963 was entirely unexpected. 'The Zapruder film' (as it is commonly known) exemplifies the uniqueness of film as accidental record. Its most significant feature is the discrepancy between technical quality and the importance of its content. Zapruder is not an adept cameraman, and at one point, just before Kennedy receives the fatal shot to his head, threatens to lose the President from view altogether. His iconic twenty-two seconds of home-movie footage, however, have captured for posterity one of the most monumental events of the last century. The significance of the 8mm film is not simply its content, however, and 'Zapruder' became shorthand in New York film schools of the 1960s for a piece of film of extremely low technical quality whose content was nevertheless of great significance. Zapruder's film lacks 'value' as defined by Britton but has an impact upon its audience that any documentary film-maker craves by seeming as unadulterated as the moving image can be. The few frames of film offer no perspective on or understanding of the day's events in Dallas. In fact, it is deeply, tantalisingly ironic that this most graphic of material is incapable of yielding the answer to the most important question of all: who killed Kennedy?

Although it is these home movies that best deserve the tag 'cinema of truth', it is the very 'authenticity' of such material that also renders accidental footage inconclusive. To return to Shub's distinction between newsreel and documentary: such material as the Zapruder or the Concorde and Shuttle disasters are more often than not recontextualised within, for example, a news bulletin or documentary. The representational world is forever making sense of and explaining the real world, and the instinct is not to leave raw footage alone but to attempt to explicate it. Conversely, the dual impetus now is towards being wise to the inauthenticities of documentaries as Williams et al. are, while revering the most 'authentic' types of factual image-making. The two (the reflexively self-conscious and the spontaneous) have, in a further irony, become formally synonymous, as both fictional and factual television have adopted the shorthand of wobbly cam, blurred shots, crash-zooms and inaudible dialogue to signify greater truthfulness. The logical conclusion to the conundrum of the factual image is a series such as *Big Brother*, filming ten down to two contestants, twenty-four hours a day, for a prize of £70,000. The boundaries between the 'real' and the 'reel' no longer seem to hold much interest (see 'Reality TV', p. 134).

Stella Bruzzi

factual programmes regularly obtained a higher share of the viewers than drama, docusoaps proved irresistible to channel controllers and commissioners alike. It is also significant that the docusoap's similarity to popular drama has enabled it to retain much of the same audience.

There are several series that are repeatedly named as the direct precursors of docusoaps, the most commonly named being *The Family* (1974) or Watson's later *Sylvania Waters* (1993), *HMS Brilliant* and *The House* (both 1995). These more traditional BBC 'fly-on-the-wall' series (see

p. 129) were all relatively costly to make, but all proved unexpectedly popular. *The House* stands apart in this quartet and most explicitly paved the way for docusoaps in general. The series was more proactive than reactive, giving priority to drama and crisis over serious commentary; it was clearly intrusive and meddlesome and was swathed in an arch, forceful commentary narrated by Jancis Robinson. Although the film-makers did not manufacture crises (as they later did with *Driving School*), they did appear voyeuristically interested in them. This detail in itself spawned several imitators, most notably *Hotel*, Lion Television's series about the Adelphi in Liverpool, which almost exclusively revolved around crises and arguments among the staff, usually involving the manageress Eileen Downey or the chef Dave Smith. In every case, the reason for these heated confrontations is marginalised in favour of capturing a protracted 'slanging match' on screen. The producers of *Driving School* similarly admitted that Maureen and Dave Rees were chosen as the series' star couple because their naturally argumentative relationship would transfer well to a thirty-minute prime-time slot.

The docusoaps' penchant for drama has manifested itself in a variety of forms, the clearest being its reliance upon stars and performers. Again, however, this echoes concerns of earlier direct cinema documentaries about performers and the vérité preoccupation with the performances of their subjects in front of the cameras. The Adelphi, immediately following the transmission of *Hotel* on BBC1, became immensely popular as people wanted to see the 'real' Eileen and Dave; Maureen Rees got an agent, cut a record and appeared on *This is Your Life*, and Jane McDonald, the cabaret singer featured in *The Cruise*, has become an immensely successful recording artist and television presenter.

What clearly sets docusoaps apart from their immediate predecessors is their open acknowledgement of the importance of performance to factual as well as fictional programmes. So, in *The Cruise*, Jane McDonald chats to director/cameraman Chris Terrill while he is filming her, pushing the series beyond impersonal observation. One of the paradoxes of docusoaps is that they purport to be interested in the excessively ordinary, while at the same time having reached the level of success and notoriety they have done by the discovery and promotion of 'stars'. In this context, the stars of docusoaps are hyper-ordinary people, those who can transcend and achieve an identity beyond the series that created them. Consistent with this contradiction is the docusoap's reluctance to engage with what could be termed the theoretical permutations of the

relationship between factual broadcasting and performance. Latterly, docusoaps have become a caricature of themselves: vehicles for larger-than-life performers who have intentionally sought the new fame that factual television can offer.

It is this perceived 'shallowness' that has prompted much of the media criticism of the genre. The journalist Allison Pearson comments that, 'In the hands of its most serious practitioners – directors such as Molly Dineen and Roger Graef – documentary aspires to tell us something about the human condition. The docusoap, by contrast, tells us something only about the condition of human beings who know they're on television' (Pearson, 1998). Interestingly, Graef himself has vigorously defended docusoaps in the press, and Paul Watson has argued that 'there is no analysis, no insight . . . their only function seems to have been to turn the rest of us into peeping Toms' (McCann, 1998). At a time when documentary is more popular than ever, it has also come in for the sharpest criticism.

Stella Bruzzi

RECOMMENDED READING

Bruzzi, Stella (2000), *New Documentary: A Critical Introduction*, London and New York: Routledge.
Macdonald, Kevin and Cousins, Mark (eds) (1997) *Imagining Reality: The Faber Book of Documentary*, London: Faber & Faber.
Winston, Brian (1995), *Claiming the Real: The Documentary Film Revisited*, London: British Film Institute.

Reality TV

As already noted, the 1990s saw 'factual' television became one of the most dynamic, successful and rapidly evolving fields of production. In genre terms it is now characterised by a very high degree of hybridisation between what would formerly have been discrete programme types. This new mix is often referenced by the idea of 'infotainment' television, in which the primary public service goals of entertainment and the provision of socially useful information are assumed to dissolve into one another (see p. 118). Across the schedules of British TV the proportion of factual television increased between 1989 and 1999, often in prime-time pre- and post-watershed slots, mainly at the expense of sitcoms (see p. 65), game shows and quizzes (see 'Popular Entertainment', p. 76, and Dovey, 2000, p. 18).

'Reality TV' has become the description used by both popular and academic critics to describe some of the most high-impact examples of the new factual television. The precise use of the term 'reality TV' has shifted since it was first applied to news magazine programmes based round emergency service activities. It has subsequently also been used to describe talk shows (see p. 84), docu-soaps (see p. 132) and now 'constructed' documentaries such as *Castaway,* shown by the BBC in 2000.

As a descriptive term it was first used in the early 1990s to describe the particular genre of magazine-format pro-grammes based on crime, accident and health stories, what we might call 'trauma TV' (See Kilborn, 1994; Dauncey, 1996; Nichols, 1994). Reality TV is generally historically located as beginning in the USA with NBC's *Unsolved Mysteries* in 1987 (Kilborn, 1994, p. 426), followed closely by other networks' imitation and reproduction of the form with CBS's *Rescue 911, Real Life Heroes,* and the Fox ver-sions *Cops* and *America's Most Wanted.* In the UK the BBC's *Emergency 999* (1992–) is widely regarded as a reproduc-tion of the US *911* format but also has its own spin-off in the form of *999 Lifesavers.* Also in the UK, *Crimewatch UK* (BBC, originally started in 1984) has been seen as central to the development of the form, particularly in respect of debates around criminology and the media (see Schlesinger and Tumber, 1994). The UK also has a range of other police and emergency service programmes such as *Police Camera Action* (ITV) and *Blues and Twos* (ITV, 1993–), as well as its proportion of happenstance accident pro-grammes such as *Caught On Camera* (ITV). Through the early years of the 1990s the genre made inroads into TV schedules all over North America and Europe, running in prime-time pre- and post-watershed slots achieving fiction and variety show audience ratings. In the UK programmes such as *Crimewatch UK, 999, Blues and Twos* and *Police Camera Action* regularly attract audiences over the 10-mil-lion mark (Hill, 1999).

Reality TV is a compelling mix of apparently 'raw', 'authentic' material with the gravitas of the news magazine package or informational programme, combining the commercial success of tabloid content within a public serv-ice mode of address. At the level of construction, reality TV is characterised by:

- camcorder, surveillance or observational 'actuality footage' (see above);
- first-person participant or eye-witness testimony;
- reconstructions that rely upon narrative fiction styles;
- studio or to-camera links and commentary from 'authoritative' presenters;

- expert statements from emergency services personnel or psychologists.

These elements are often framed by a magazine format in which a number of stories will be covered in each pro-gramme, varying from the in-depth emergency service programmes in the UK such as *999,* often featuring just one dramatic rescue story per fifty-minute episode. The more explicitly observational *Blues and Twos* usually offers three stories per half-hour. The relentless pace of *Police Camera Action* offers an average of around thirty individual video clips in a TV half-hour, loosely grouped into different com-mentary-led sections.

The way the material is packaged is essential: the dis-parate elements are strongly narrativised in ways that con-form to conventional fictional police dramas (see p. 19) or to the form of melodrama (see p. 49). In turn, the individ-ual stories are structured within an overarching public serv-ice narrative address. In the case of 'trauma TV' we are given to understand that our viewing pleasures are safely con-tained by an explicit appeal to a communitarian logic of security (that is to say, how to *avoid* becoming a victim of crime or how to *participate* in crime-detection processes). Hill (1999) has argued that this narrative structure is reflected strongly in audience responses to reality TV pro-grammes based in the work of the emergency services. Here the fear occasioned by exposure to crime or ill health is bal-anced by the resolution offered in the outcomes of the fea-tured cases. In the case of programmes constructed around the drama of everyday life we may be offered the interpret-ation of psychologists to lend general insight into the par-ticular experiences being represented (for example. *Big Brother,* Channel Four, 2000; *Castaway,* BBC 1, 2000). In either case, the 'public service' utility of the programme is often awkwardly at odds with the entertainment-based drive of the narrative structure.

Since the first wave of ratings-friendly factual program-ming based on the emergency services, usage of the term 'reality TV' has widened somewhat. Popular use of the term 'reality TV' may also refer to programmes that use 'ordi-nary people' framed within a variety of 'first-person' or confessional modes of speech, such as the chat shows and docu soaps dealt with elsewhere in this volume. The differ-ent kinds of programme described as 'reality TV' are uni-fied by the attempt to package particular aspects of everyday life as entertainment.

'Reality TV' is now used as a genre description of any factual programme based on an aesthetic style of apparent 'zero-degree realism' – in other words a direct, unmedi-ated account of events, often associated with the use of

Big Brother

Footage from surveillance cameras or from covert taping have been a mainstay of the 'reality TV' programmes described in this section, such as *Crimewatch* or *Police Camera Action.* Concealed cameras have also formed the basis for a number of investigative documentary programmes, including *Undercover Britain,* (Channel Four, 1993), *Private Investigations* (Granada, 1994) and *MacIntyre Undercover* (BBC, 1999). These programmes have used undercover reporters equipped with hidden mini-cams to entrap subjects such as bad employers, bad landlords, sex workers and so on. This dissemination of surveillance-type images across the factual TV schedules is based on a widespread acceptance of the idea of CCTV as visual evidence. The CCTV image appears to simply calibrate visual perception: it is operated by machine, and no human mediation is involved in its production of 'pure' evidence. It has the additional power of a kind of voyeurism, in that its broadcast on television allows the viewer to see things that were never intended to be seen.

By 1999 there was already a widespread acceptance of CCTV footage as a 'natural' part of television output. The stage was set for the triumph of the global broadcasting phenomenon of *Big Brother*. Created in 1999 by the European transnational entertainment group Emdemol, *Big Brother* was first and foremost a brilliant marketing phenomenon for the way in which it combined a number of different elements into a seemingly unassailable combination. Firstly, it took the 'ordi-nary people' aspect of 'reality TV', exploiting the appeal of watching ordinary people interacting, with the permanent possibility of intimacy revealed. Secondly, it used CCTV tech-niques: the subjects were under constant camera observation, producing the impression of an indexical representation of reality with a chaser of voyeuristic pleasure. These two pre-existing elements were combined with three genuine innova-tions: firstly, the game show format (see p. 79). This was indeed a piece of factual television, though very few 'facts' or information were imparted: this was pure entertainment, a game, a competition. Secondly, it was a game with a peculiar psychological twist in that the participants were called upon to act as a team: the idea of the team was constantly invoked by the participants themselves, yet they were simultaneously called upon to 'betray the team' by voting out some of its members. This combination of collectivity and competition created the drama.

To the innovation of the game show the producers added the elements of interactivity. This functioned in two ways. The first and most obvious was through the telephone voting system that the public used to make the weekly eviction decisions. The revenues from the phone lines were enormous and made Emdemol an even bigger profit on their investment. (If television was once about delivering audiences to advertis-ers, it may soon be about delivering callers to phone lines.) The second element of interactivity that Emdemol utilised was the Internet, in so far as the user could log on to video streamed camera feeds from the house, plus audio, at any time

Big Brother: a combination of reality TV and the Quiz Show

of the day or night. However, the programme itself is perhaps the first example of a genre crossover from online to broadcast: since the first Web cams came on stream in 1996, the Internet has been the place where this surveillance of the everyday has truly developed. Web cams had already proved that the public performance of the intimacies of everyday life could be a revenue-earning hit. This use of the Net by *Big Brother* created a core of user involvement with the programme, points of activity and identification for the audience that in turn fed into the most important marketing network of all – the word-of-mouth network.

For *Big Brother*, although often excruciatingly boring to watch, provoked conversation, argument and intense investment on the part of its audiences. This fascination proved to be the basis for the first truly international new TV genre of the twenty-first century: the programme has now succeeded in the Netherlands, Spain, the UK and the USA.

Jon Dovey

video and surveillance-imaging technologies. During the 1990s the low-gauge video image, grainy, under-lit and often unsteady, became the pre-eminent televisual signifier of truthfulness. After a hundred years of moving-image culture we can now understand how each epoch has its own privileged style for the delivery of visual evidence. For the first 'actuality' audiences, the flickering images of everyday street scenes were astonishingly truthful and accurate. Later the Griersonian documentary tradition, very formal, constructed and poetic, became the standard for the portrayal of the everyday. This tradition in turn was overthrown by the observational film-makers of the 1960s and 1970s with their lightweight cameras and their mission to 'convey the feeling of being there'. The new standard for visual evidence within factual television is the video image itself. It is worth noting that the widespread success of programmes based in this appeal to authenticity occurs at the same time as the widely acknowledged triumph of simulation and spectacle, (see, for example, Baudrillard, 1983). An image-saturated culture appears to have produced a greater hunger than ever before for an astringent aesthetic of visual realism.

Jon Dovey

RECOMMENDED READING

Kilborn, Richard, (1994), 'How Real Can You Get? Recent Developments in Reality Television', *European Journal of Communication*, vol. 9, no. 4. See also, Kilborn, R. and Izod, J. (1997), *An Introduction to Television Documentary*, Manchester: Manchester University Press.

Hill, Annette, (1999), 'Crime and Crisis: British Reality TV in Action' in Ed Buscombe (ed.), *British Television: A Reader*, Oxford: Oxford University Press.

Nichols, Bill (ed.) (1994), 'At the Limits of Reality (TV), in *Blurred Boundaries*, Bloomington: Indiana University Press.

Educational Programming

The Roper Starch 1995 Global Consumer Survey found that 'educational' was the second most important description by respondents (after 'interesting') to describe the attributes of the television programmes they watched (Taylor, 1997, p. 56). The notion of 'educational' television is not at first as self-explanatory as it seems. Television has always had a consistent current that has seen its social function as being an educational tool, and this persists, even in the face of hard-nosed commercial interests, although it has caused radical changes to its form, moving away from traditional education 'from the top' (Quinn, 1997, p. 14).

The whole notion of public service broadcasting rests partly on the idea of education. Whereas television in the USA developed along commercial lines with only marginal public service, in the UK public service was at the centre of the BBC's remit. The whole conception of education has changed over the years along with television itself. Arguably, a large part of children's television is educational one way or another, and children clearly now receive a large part of their social education from television (see 'The Child Audience', p. 97). In a related development, the proliferation of 'infotainment' has increasingly become the preferred form of educational television, or informational television at the turn of the millennium (see pp. 118).

In the early 1950s, the Ford Foundation sponsored many small educational channels in the USA, granting them money to set up the Program Production Center in 1952 (which later became national Educational Television). By 1956, there were only two educational stations, mostly broadcasting British programmes and Canadian Broadcasting Corporation programmes, despite the Federal Communication Commission (FCC) reserving 242 channels for educational television in the early 1950s. The Carnegie Commission of 1965 looked into the possibilities for an educational television service and, concluding that

The Discovery Channel and *Walking with Dinosaurs*

The Discovery Channel was founded in the USA in 1987 by John Hendricks. Early on, the channel struggled. Its central aim was to merge learning and enjoyment, unlike the traditional form of education embodied by schools (Taylor, 1997, p.58). Discovery also owns the Learning Channel and has a worldwide reach to sixty countries, including over 11 million homes in Europe (Taylor, 1997, p. 55). Discovery is a niche channel, providing high-quality, factual and accessible programming. Its schedules rely heavily on documentaries, commonly on subjects such as the natural world, history (including war), people's lives (from surfers to firemen to famous celebrities), anthropology (such as the programme *Disappearing World*) and instructional programmes (telling audiences how to fish, cook or travel). The channel tends to have very repetitive scheduling, showing similar things at the same times each night, thus ensuring a regular audience. Some of the documentaries are produced by other channels and are repeated on Discovery, others are co-productions between Discovery and other channels.

One such co-production was *Walking with Dinosaurs*, made as a junior partner with the BBC and billed as 'the biggest thing on television in 160 million years'. On the one hand it was clearly a signpost to the future capabilities of television, but on the other it was simply a further evolutionary stage in the television nature programme. It strictly followed the strategies of this genre, although it harked back to age-old desires for humanity to commune with dead and mythological creatures.

Through the use of a computer graphics interface (CGI), the programme was able to bring the dead back to life, animating dinosaurs against a background of actual landscapes. Not only were the images diverting by their very spectacular nature, but the programme aimed to induce empathy in the audience through establishing certain 'characters' we could follow, and dramatising and narrativising their existence. Its format was based explicitly on this television genre, with the programme constructing a vista upon various dinosaurs' lives, as if they were living animals today being portrayed in a nature documentary like any other.

Each episode of *Walking with Dinosaurs* had a distinct theme and was set in a particular era, some of them aeons apart. The opening episode was about the start of the dinosaurs' ascendancy in the Triassic period, and was called 'New Blood'. The final episode was called 'Death of a Dynasty' and focused on the Tyrannosaurus Rex in the Late Cretaceous period. While unity was ensured by the voice-over declaring a 'scientific' analysis of the activities on screen, the narratives followed individual animals, constructing them as distinctive characters in order to elicit the audience's empathy and provide dramatic continuity to the events of each episode. *Walking with Dinosaurs* may never have existed without Steven Spielberg's *Jurassic Park* (1993) and its sequel *The Lost World* (1997). The irony was that *Walking with Dinosaurs* created the very theme park that is never completed in the films.

Kevin Donnelly

the networks could not be displaced, conceived the new Public Broadcasting Service (PBS) as an add-on to the current system. The Corporation for Public Broadcasting (CPB) was formed as the administrative body that would unify and protect the new stations, while overseeing the whole system. PBS was formally inaugurated in November 1969, with the CPB administering and co-ordinating the network of local stations.

The 'big five' educational broadcasters in the USA are WGBH (Boston), KCET (Los Angeles), WNET (New York), WETA (Washington, DC) and WTTW (Chicago). These supply most of the American programmes that appear on PBS stations, as well as exporting many programmes overseas. Some of the most successful PBS-produced programmes include *Sesame Street* (first televised 1969 – see p. 101), *Vietnam: A Television History* (1985), *The Civil War* (1993) and *Savage Skies* (1997). *Savage Skies*, a series about weather, was a co-production between WNET (New York) and the British broadcaster Granada. WGBH (Boston) has gone in for a number of international co-productions, particularly of the sort that adapts a literary classic. *Nostromo* (1997) was a co-production between WGBH, the BBC and RAI (Italian television). Similarly, WGBH has co-financed many British costume dramas, such as the BBC's *Great Expectations* (1998; see 'Costume Drama', p. 38). PBS programmes have also included *American Playhouse* and *Front Line* (a current affairs programme). In the 1990s, there have been calls for PBS to be disbanded, and its future has long been precarious (Katz, 1989, p. 203).

The provision of educational television has always targeted children. Children's educational television is embodied in *Sesame Street*, a programme that always had an entertainment aspect despite nominally being about teaching children spelling and simple maths (see p. 101). British productions included the 'Watch with Mother' slot (1950–80), with puppet or animated dramas broadcast immediately after lunchtime, extensive programming for schools on weekday mornings and youth television shows such as *Blue Peter* (1958–). The latter was hosted by presenters who resembled parents or scout leaders, and this same programme format and strategy was evident in programmes that addressed both children and adults. A good example from Britain is *Tomorrow's World*, a popular science and technology programme where, it could be argued, adults are regularly addressed *as if* they were children.

Formal education on television in the UK expanded with the advent of BBC 2 in 1964. More recently, the BBC has endeavoured to sell its 'educational' television abroad, discovering that there is a massive international market for high-quality programming. The BBC used to be satisfied with brief public information films, targeting children crossing roads, AIDS and drug abuse. It began a partnership with the Open University that involved extensive showings of its programmes, although in 'graveyard slots': first after midnight and more recently on Saturday mornings on BBC 2. The range of BBC educational programming for adults went from adult literacy programmes of the 1970s such as *On the Move* and *Your Move*, to the high-prestige intellectually inclined BBC 2 series *The Ascent of Man* (1973), presented by Jacob Bronowski, and John Berger's *Ways of Seeing* (1972).

Educational programmes that court a general audience, of both adults and children, have adopted the modes of 'infotainment', marking the union of informational and entertainment programming. Programmes are made as engaging as possible, and in an audiovisual language that spectacularises what a few years earlier might have been fairly dry discourses of information. The final product is educational television that uses an audiovisual language originally associated with mainstream entertainment television, such as sensationalism, fast pace, spectacle, enhancing music and narrativisation.

The BBC has reinvented its public service remit through the production of 'quality drama', usually based on a literary 'classic' (see 'Costume Drama', p. 38), and infotainment (see p. 118) culminating in the landmark series *Walking with Dinosaurs* (1999). This merged the tradition of the nature documentary with the spectacle of prehistoric monsters, conjoining adult and child audiences. The co-producer of *Walking with Dinosaurs* was cable/satellite Discovery Channel (see box). Along with the History Channel, it has developed a provision dominated by documentaries. Archive material used for historical programmes and documentaries is often cheap, and programmes relying on such material are certainly made more cheaply than drama shows of similar length. The success of the Discovery Channel and the History Channel parallels the perceived decline in education, certainly a decline in its status and prestige, in Britain. As television now provides large amounts of integrated information, perhaps education's principal functions have been absorbed by television as a whole.

Kevin Donnelly

RECOMMENDED READING
Katz, Helen (1989), 'The Future of Public Broadcasting in the US', in *Media, Culture and Society*, vol.11.

Quinn, Jane (1997), 'Getting Closer to Audiences: The BBC Experience', in Manfred Meyer (ed.), *Educational Television: What Do People Want?*, Luton: John Libbey Media/Luton University Press.

Taylor, Joyce (1997), 'Success in Cable Networks: The Discovery Channel', in Manfred Meyer (ed.), *Educational Television: What Do People Want?*, Luton: John Libbey Media/Luton University Press.

BIBLIOGRAPHY

INTRODUCTION: WHAT IS GENRE?

Allen, Robert C. (1989), 'Bursting Bubbles: "Soap Opera", Audiences, and the Limits of Genre', in Ellen Seiter, Hans Borchers, Gabriele Kreutzner, Eva-Maria Warth (eds), *Remote Control: Television, Audiences and Cultural Power*, London and New York: Routledge.

Alley, Robert S. (1985), 'Medical Melodrama', in B.G. Rose (ed.), *TV Genres: A Handbook and Reference Guide*, Westport: Greenwood.

Altman, Rick (1984), 'A Semantic/Syntactic Approach to Film Genre', *Cinema Journal*, vol. 23, no. 3.

Altman, Rick (1987), *The American Film Musical*, Bloomington: Indiana University Press.

Altman, Rick (1996), 'Cinema and Genre', in G. Nowell-Smith (ed.), *The Oxford History of World Cinema*, Oxford: Oxford University Press.

Altman, Rick (1999), *Film/Genre*, London: British Film Institute.

Ang, Ien (1991), *Desperately Seeking the Audience*, London and New York: Routledge.

Barson, Michael (1985), 'The TV Western', in B.G. Rose (ed.), *TV Genres: A Handbook and Reference Guide*, Westport: Greenwood.

Blakemore, Diane (1992), *Understanding Utterances: An Introduction to Pragmatics*, Oxford: Blackwell.

Butler, Jeremy G. (1994), *Television: Critical Methods and Applications*, Belmont: Wadsworth.

Cawelti, John (1971), *The Six-Gun Mystique*, Bowling Green: Bowling Green University Press.

Cawelti, John (1976), *Adventure, Mystery and Romance*, Chicago: Chicago University Press.

Cohen, Ralph (1986), 'History and Genre', *New Literary History*, vol. 17, no. 2.

Davis, Steven (1991), *Pragmatics: A Reader*, Oxford: Oxford University Press.

Derrida, Jacques (1990), 'The Law of Genre', in D. Attridge (ed.), *Acts of Literature* (trans. Avital Ronell), New York: Routledge.

Edgerton, Gary (1985), 'The American Made-for-TV Movie', in B.G. Rose (ed.), *TV Genres: A Handbook and Reference Guide*, Westport: Greenwood.

Ellis, John (1982), *Visible Fictions: Cinema, Television, Video*. London: Routledge & Kegan Paul.

Feuer, Jane (1992), 'Genre and Television', in R. Allen (ed.), *Channels of Discourse, Reassembled: Television and Contemporary Criticism*. London and New York: Routledge.

Freadman, Ann (1998), 'Untitled: (On Genre)', *Cultural Studies*, vol. 2, no. 1.

Frith, Simon (1996), *Performing Rites: On the Value of Popular Music*, Oxford: Oxford University Press.

Frye, Northrop (1957), *The Anatomy of Criticism*, Princeton: Princeton University Press.

Goedkoop, Richard (1985), 'The Game Show', in B.G. Rose (ed.), *TV Genres: A Handbook and Reference Guide*, Westport: Greenwood.

Hartley, John (1992), *Tele-ology: Studies in Television*, London and New York: Routledge.

Hoffer, Thomas W., Musburger, Robert and Nelson, Richard Alan (1985), 'Docudrama', in B.G. Rose (ed.), *TV Genres: A Handbook and Reference Guide*, Westport: Greenwood.

Jancovitch, Mark (2001), 'Genre and Audience: Genre Classifications and Cultural Distinctions in the Mediation of Silence of the Lambs', in R. Maltby and R. Stokes (eds), *Hollywood Spectatorship*, London: British Film Institute.

Jauss, Robert Hanns (1982), *Toward an Aesthetic of Reception*, (trans. T. Bahti) Brighton: Harvester.

Kapsis, Robert E. (1991), 'Hollywood Genres and the Production of Culture Perspective', in B.A. Austin (ed.), *Current Research in Film: Audiences, Economics and the Law*, vol. 5, Norwood: Ablex.

Lacey, Nick (2000), *Narrative and Genre: Key Concepts in Media Studies*, London, Macmillan.

Lukow, Gregory and Ricci, Stephen (1984), 'The "Audience" Goes "Public": Inter-textuality, Genre, and the Responsibilities of Film Literacy', *On Film*, no. 12.

Neale, Steve (1980), *Genre*, London: British Film Institute.

Neale, Steve (1990), 'Questions of Genre', *Screen*, vol. 31, no. 1.

Neale, Steve (2000), *Genre and Hollywood*, London: Routledge.

Newcomb, Horace (ed.) (1976), *Television: The Critical View*, New York and Oxford: Oxford University Press.

Norden, Martin F. (1985), 'The Detective Show', in B.G. Rose (ed.), *TV Genres: A Handbook and Reference Guide*, Westport: Greenwood.

Pratt, Mary Louise (1977), *Towards a Speech-Act Theory of Literary Discourse*, Bloomington: Indiana University Press.

Pratt, Mary Louise (1981), 'The Short Story: The Long and the Short of It', *Poetics*, no. 10.

Robards, Brook (1985), 'The Police Show', in B.G. Rose (ed.), *TV Genres: A Handbook and Reference Guide*, Westport: Greenwood.

Roberts, Thomas J. (1990), *An Aesthetics of Junk Fiction*, Athens Ga.): University of Georgia Press.

Rose, Brian G. (ed.) (1985a), *TV Genres: A Handbook and Reference Guide*, Westport: Greenwood.

Rose, Brian G. (1985b), 'Preface', B.G. Rose (ed.), *TV Genres: A Handbook and Reference Guide*, Westport: Greenwood.

Rose, Brian G. (1985c), 'The Talk Show', in B.G. Rose (ed.), *TV Genres: A Handbook and Reference Guide*, Westport: Greenwood.

Ryall, Tom (1975/6), 'Teaching through Genre', *Screen Education*, no. 17.

Schatz, Thomas (1981), *Hollywood Genres: Formulas, Filmmaking, and the Studio System*, New York: Random House.

Selby, Keith and Cowdery, Ron (1995), *How to Study Television*, London: Macmillan.

Threadgold, Terry (1989), 'Talking about Genre: Ideologies and Incompatible Discourses', *Cultural Studies*, vol. 3, no. 1.

Todorov, Tzvetan (1975) *The Fantastic: A Structural Approach to a Literary Genre* (trans. Richard Howard), Ithaca: Cornell University Press.

Todorov, Tzevtan (1977), *The Poetics of Prose* (trans. Richard Howard), Ithaca: Cornell University Press.

Todorov, Tzvetan (1981), *Introduction to Poetics* (trans. Richard Howard), Brighton: Harvester Press.

Tolson, Andrew (1996), *Mediations: Text and Discourse in Media Studies*, London: Arnold.

Tudor, Andrew (1976), 'Genre and Critical Methodology', in Bill Nichols (ed.), *Movies and Methods: An Anthology*, Berkeley: University of California Press.

Turner, Graeme (1989), 'Transgressive TV: From In Melbourne Tonight to Perfect Match', in John Tulloch and Graeme Turner (eds) *Australian Television: Programs, Pleasures and Politics*, Sydney: Allen & Unwin.

Vane, Edward T. and Gross, Lynne S. (1994), *Programming for TV, Radio and Cable*, Boston (Mass.) and London: Focal Press.

Williams, Alan (1984), 'Is a Radical Genre Criticism Possible?', *Quarterly Review of Film Studies*, vol. 9, no. 2.

Williams, Bruce and Delli Carpini, Michael X. (2000), 'Unchained Reaction: The Collapse of Media Gatekeeping and the Clinton–Lewinsky scandal', *Journalism*, vol. 1, no. 1.

Wright, Judith Hess (1986), 'Genre Films and the Status Quo', in B.K. Grant (ed.), *Film Genre Reader*, Austin: University of Texas Press.

Wright, Will (1975), *Sixguns and Society: A Structural Study of the Western*, Berkeley: University of California Press.

DRAMA

Altman, Rick (1999), *Film/Genre*, London: British Film Institute.

Anderson, Christopher (1994), *Hollywood TV: The Studio System in the Fifties*, Austin: University of Texas Press.

Ang, Ien (1985), *Watching Dallas; Television and the Melodramatic Imagination*, London: Routledge.

Ang, Ien (1991), *Desperately Seeking the Audience*, Routledge: London.

Barnouw, Erik (1975), 'Television Theatre' in *Tube of Plenty: The Evolution of American Television*, New York and Oxford: Oxford University Press.

Barr, Charles (1997), ' "They Think It's All Over": The Dramatic Legacy of Live Television', in John Hill and Martin McLoone, (eds), *Big Picture, Small Screen: The Relations Between Film and Television*, Luton: University of Luton Press.

Barrett, Michèll and Barrett, Duncan (2001), *Star Trek: The Human Frontier*, Cambridge: Polity.

Barson, Michale (1985), 'The TV Western', in B.G. Rose, (ed.), *TV Genres: A Handbook and Reference Guide*, Westport: Greenwood.

Baudrillard, Jean (1988), *Selected Writings*, (ed. Mark Poster), Oxford: Polity.

Baxter, John (1970), *Science Fiction in the Cinema*, New York: Paperback Library.

BBC (1995), *'Pride and Prejudice': From Page to Screen* (Videocassette), London: BBC Worldwide.

BBC Education (1994), *Middlemarch: A Viewer's Guide*, London: BBC Education.

Bennett, Tony et al. (eds) (1981), *Popular Television and Film*, London: British Film Institute/Open University Press.

Benjamin, Walter (1977) 'The Author as Producer', in Walter Benjamin, *Understanding Brecht*, London: New Left Books.

Bernardi, Daniel Leonard (1998), *'Star Trek' and History: Racing Toward a White Future*, Piscataway: Rutgers University Press.

Boddy, William (1993), *Fifties Television: The Industry and its Critics*, Urbana and Chicago: University of Illinois Press.

Boddy, William (1997), 'Senator Dodd Goes to Hollywood: Investigating Video Violence', in Lynn Spigel and Michael Curtin (eds), *The Revolution Wasn't Televised: Sixties Television and Social Transition*, New York: Routledge.

Boddy, William (1998), 'Sixty Million Viewers Can't Be Wrong: The Rise and Fall of the TV Western', in Ed Buscombe and Roberta Pearson (eds), *Back in the Saddle: New Approaches to the Western*, London: British Film Institute.

Bondebjerg, Ib (1992), 'Intertextuality and Metafiction: Genre and Narrative in the Television Fiction of Dennis Potter', in M. Skormand and K.C. Schroder (eds), *Media Cultures: Reappraising Transnational Media*, London: Routledge.

Bourdieu, Pierre (1992), *Distinction*, 1979, trans. R. Nice, (1992), London; Routledge.

Boyd-Bowman, S. (1984), '*The Day After*: Representations of the Nuclear Holocaust', *Screen*, Vol. 25, nos. 4–5.

Brandt, George (ed.) (1981), *British Television Drama*, Cambridge: Cambridge University Press.

Brandt, George (ed.) (1993), *British Television Drama in the 1980s*, Cambridge: Cambridge University Press.

Brunsdon, Charlotte (1998), 'Structure of Anxiety: Recent British Television Crime Fiction', *Screen*, vol. 39, no. 3.

Buckingham, David (1987), *Public Secrets: 'EastEnders' and Its Audience*, London: British Film Institute.

Butler, Jeremy G. (1994), 'Narrative Structure: Television Stories', in Jeremy Butler (ed.), *Television: Critical Methods and Applications*, Belmont: Wadsworth.

Caldwell, John Thornton (1995), 'Excessive Discourse in the Mini-Series', in John Thornton Caldwell. *Televisuality: Style, Crisis, and Authority in American Television*, Piscataway: Rutgers University Press.

Carpenter, Humphrey (1998), *Dennis Potter: The Authorized Biography*, London: Faber & Faber.

Cassidy, Jane and Taylor, Diane (1997), 'Doctor, doctor, where can I get an aspirin?', *Guardian*, 12 December.

Caughie, John (1991), 'Before the Golden Age: Early Television Drama', in John Corner, (ed.), *Popular Television in Britain: Studies in Cultural History*, London: British Film Institute.

Caughie, John (2000), *Television Drama: Realism, Modernism and British Culture*, London and New York: Oxford University Press.

Cawelti, John G. (1975), *The Six-Gun Mystique*, Bowling Green: Bowling Green University Press.

Chion, Michel (1995), *David Lynch*, London: British Film Institute.

Clarke, Alan (1986), ' "This Is Not the Boy Scouts": Television Police Series and Definitions of Law and Order', in Tony Bennett, et al, *Popular Culture and Social Relations*, Milton Keynes: Open University Press.

Clarke, Alan (1992), ' "You're Nicked!": Television Police Series and the Fictional Representation of Law and Order', in Dominic Strinati and Stephen Wagg (eds), *Come On Down? Popular Media Culture in Post-War Britain*, London: Routledge.

Clute, John and Nicholls, Peter (1999), *The Encyclopedia of Science Fiction*, London: Orbit.

Collins, Jim (1992), 'Postmodernism and Television', in Robert C. Allen (ed.), *Channels of Discourse, Reassembled*, London and New York: Routledge.

Cook, John R. (1995), *Dennis Potter: A Life on Screen*, Manchester and New York: Manchester University Press.

Corner, J. (1996), *The Art of Record*, Manchester: Manchester University Press.

Corrigan, Timothy (1991), 'Music from Heaven, Bodies in Hell: The Singing Detective', in Timothy Corrigan (ed.), *A Cinema Without Walls: Movies and Culture after Vietnam*, London: Routledge.

Coward, Rosalind (1987), 'Dennis Potter and the Question of the Television Author', *Critical Quarterly*, vol. 29, no. 4.

Creeber, Glen (1996), ' "Banality with a Beat": Dennis Potter and the Paradox of Popular Music', *Media, Culture and Society*, vol. 18, no. 3.

Creeber, Glen (1998), *Dennis Potter: Between Two Worlds, A Critical Reassessment*, London and New York: Macmillan.

Creeber, Glen (2001a), ' "Taking Our Personal Lives Seriously": Intimacy, Continuity and Memory in the Television Serial', *Media, Culture and Society*, vol. 23, no. 4.

Creeber, Glen (2001b), 'Cigarettes and Alcohol: Investigating Gender, Genre and Gratification in *Prime Suspect*', *Television and New Media*, vol. 2, May.

D'Acci, Julie (1987), 'The Case of Cagney and Lacey', in Helen Baehr and Gillian Dyer (eds), *Boxed In: Women and Television*, London: Pandora.

D'Acci, Julie (1994), *Defining Women: Television and the Case of Cagney and Lacey*, Chapel Hill: University of North Carolina Press.

Day-Lewis, Sean (1998), *Talk of Drama: Views of the Television Dramatist Now and Then*, Luton: University of Luton Press.

Dean, Jodi (1997), 'The Truth is Out There: Aliens and the Fugitivity of Postmodern Truth', *Camera Obscura*, no. 40–41.

Delaney, Paul (1988), 'Potterland', *Dalhousie Review*, vol. 68, part 4.

Delaney, Sean, Forbes, Tess, Keramos, Anastasia, Laffey, Erinna and Ormsby, Andrew (1996), 'Mary Shelley's *Frankenstein*; *Northern Exposure*; *The Vicar of Dibley*: Information Source Pack, London: BFI Library and Information Services.

De Moras, Lisa (1997) '*The Sound and the Fury*', *The Hollywood Reporter 1997–98 TV Preview*, September.

Dickenson, Roger, Harindranath, Ramaswami and Linné, Olga (1998), *Approaches to Audiences: A Reader*, London: Arnold.

Donald, James (1985), 'Anxious Moments: *The Sweeney* in 1975', in Manuel Alvarado and John Stewart (eds), *Made for Television: Euston Films Limited*, London: British Film Institute.

Dyer, Richard (1992), *Only Entertainment*, London: Routledge.

Eaton, Mary (1995), 'A Fair Cop? Viewing the Effects of the Canteen Culture in *Prime Suspect* and *Between the Lines*', in David Kidd-Hewitt and Richard Osborne (eds), *Crime and the Media*, London: Pluto.

Ellis, John (1989, orig. pub. 1982), *Visible Fictions: Cinema, Television, Video*, London and New York: Routledge.

Epstein, Michael (1996), 'Spaced Out: The Star Trek Literary Phenomenon: Where no TV Series has Gone Before', *Television Quarterly*, vol 28, no 1.

Esslin, Martin (1961), *The Theatre of the Absurd*, New York, Doubleday.

Felperin, Leslie (1999), 'Genre: Teenpics', in P. Cook and M. Bernink (eds), *The Cinema Book* (2nd edition), London: British Film Institute.

Feuer, Jane (1986), 'Narrative Form in American Network Television', in Colin MacCabe, (ed.), *High Theory/Low Culture*, Manchester: Manchester University Press.

Feuer, Jane (1995), 'Serial Form, Melodrama, and Reaganite Ideology in Eighties TV', in Jane Feuer, *Seeing Through the Eighties: Television and Reaganism*, London: British Film Institute.

Fish, Stanley (1980), *Is there a text in this class?: The Authority of Interpretive Communites*, Cambridge (Mass): Harvard University Press.

Fishbein, Leslie (1983), '*Roots*: Docudrama and the Interpretation of History', in Leslie Fishbein, (ed.), *American History/American Television: Interpreting the Video Past*, New York: Frederick Ungar.

Fiske, John (1987), *Television Culture*, London: Methuen.

Fitzpatrick, Michael (2000), *The Tyranny of Health: Doctors and the Regulation of Lifestyle*, London: Routledge.

Forrest, Emma (1998) 'Inside Story: The Future is Female', *Guardian*, 16 December.

Fuller, Graham (ed.) (1993), *Potter on Potter*, London: Faber & Faber.

Fuller, Graham (1996), 'Cautionary Tale', *Sight and Sound*, vol 6, no. 3.

Fulton, Roger and Betancourt, John (2000), *Encyclopedia of TV Science Fiction*, London: Boxtree.

Gardner, Carl and Wyver, John (1983), 'The Single Play: From Reithian Reverence to Cost-accounting and Censorship', *Screen*, vol 24, nos. 4–5.

Geraghty, Christine (1987), 'The Continuous Serial – A Definition', in Richard Dye, Christine Geraghty, Jordan Marion, Terry Lovell, Richard Paterson, John Stewart, BFI Television Monograph *Coronation Street*, London: British Film Institute.

Gibberman, Susan (1991), '*Star Trek*: An Annotated Guide to Resources on the Development, the Phenomenon, the People, the Television Series, the Films, the Novels and the Recordings*, Jefferson: McFarland.

Giddens, Anthony (1979), *Central Problems in Social Theory: Action, Structure and Contradiction*, London, Macmillan.

Giddings, Robert Selby (1990), *Screening the Novel*, London, Macmillan.

Gilbert, Stephen W. (1995), *Fight and Kick and Bite: The Life and Work of Dennis Potter*, London: Hodder & Stoughton.

Goodwin, A., Kerr, P. and Macdonald, I. (eds) (1983), *Drama-documentary* (BFI Dossier 19), London: British Film Institute.

Gras, Vernon W. (2000), 'Dennis Potter's *The Singing Detective*: An Exemplum of Dialogic Ethics', in Vernon W. Gras, and John R. Cook (eds), *The Passion of Dennis Potter*, New York: St Martin's Press.

Gray, Chris, Figueroa-Sarriera, Hiedi and Mentor, Steven (eds) (1995), *The Cyborg Handbook*, London: Routledge.

Greenwald, Jeff (1998), *Future Perfect: How 'Star Trek' Conquered Planet Earth*, Harmondsworth: Penguin.

Gregory, Chris (1997), *Be Seeing You: Decoding 'The Prisoner'*, Luton: University of Luton Press.

Gregory, Chris (2000), '*Star Trek*': Parallel Narratives*, London: Macmillan.

Hanely, Richard (1997), *The Metaphysics of 'Star Trek'*, New York: Basic Books.

Harraway Donna (1995), 'Cyborgs and Symbionts: Living Together in the New World Order', in Chris Gray et al. (eds), *The Cyborg Handbook*, London: Routledge.

Harrison, Taylor, Projansky, Sarah, Ono, Kent and Helford, Elyce (eds) (1996), *Enterprise Zones: Critical Positions on 'Star Trek'*, Oxford: Westview.

Hayward, Phillip (1990), 'How ABC Capitalised on Cultural Logic – The "Moonlighting" Story', reprinted in Manuel Alvarado and John O. Thompson (eds), *The Media Reader*, London: British Film Institute.

Hey, Kenneth, (1983) 'Marty: Aesthetics vs. Medium in Early TV Drama', in Leslie Fishbein (ed.) *American History/American Television: Interpreting the Video Past*, New York: Frederick Ungar.

Hilfer, Anthony (2000), 'Run Over by One's Own Story: Genre and Ethos in Dennis Potter's "The Singing Detective"' in Bignell, Jonathan, Lacey, Stephen, MacMurraugh-Kavanagh, Madeeine (eds), *British Television Drama: Past, Present & Future*, London and New York: Palgrave.

Hill, A. (forthcoming), 'Fearful and Safe: Audience Response to Popular Factual Entertainment', in R. Kilborn and J. Izod (eds), *Crossing the Boundaries*, Luton: University of Luton Press.

Hockley, Luke (2000), *Spectacle as Commodity: Special Effects in Feature Films in Multimedia: A Critical Introduction*, London: Routledge.

Holland, Patricia (1997), 'Narrative Television', in Patricia Holland, *The Television Handbook*, London and New York: Routledge.

Hollingsworth, Mike and Norton-Taylor, Richard (1988), *Blacklist*, London: Macmillan.

Hudson, R. (1972), 'Television in Britain: Description and Dissent', *Theatre Quarterly*, vol. 2, no. 6.

Hunningher, Joost (1993), 'The Singing Detective: Who done it?', in George Brandt, *British Television Drama in the 1980s*, Cambridge and New York: Cambridge University Press.

Hurd, Geoffrey (1981), 'The Television Presentation of the Police', in Tony Bennett, et al (eds), *Popular Television and Film*, London: British Film Institute/Open University Press.

Hutcheon, Linda (1989), *The Politics of Postmodernism*, London: Routledge.

Jacobs, Jason (1998), 'No Respect: Shot and Scene in Early Television Drama', in Jeremy Ridgman (ed.), *Boxed Sets: Television Representations of Theatre*, Luton: University of Luton Press.

Jacobs, Jason (2001), *The Intimate Screen: Early British Television Drama*, New York and Oxford: Oxford University Press.

Jacobs, Jason (2001), *Body Trauma: New Television Medical Dramas*, London: British Film Institute.

Jameson, Fredric (1993), *Postmodernism or the Cultural Logic of Late Capitalism*, London:Verso.

Jencks, Charles (1989), *What is Postmodernism?*, London: Academy Editions.

Jenkins, Henry (1992), *Textual Poachers: Television Fans and Participatory Culture*, New York: Routledge.

Jenkins, Steve (1984), 'Hill Street Blues', in Jane Feuer, Paul Kerr and Tise Vahimagi (eds), *MTM – 'Quality Television'*, London: British Film Institute.

Johnson, William (ed.) (1972), *Focus on the Science Fiction Film*, New York: Prentice-Hall.

Kaleta, Kenneth C. (1993), *David Lynch*, New York: Twayne.

Karpf, Anne (1988), *Doctoring the Media*, London: Routledge.

Kavanagh, James H. (1990), 'Feminism, Humanism and Science in *Alien*', in Annette Kuhn (ed.), *Alien Zone: Cultural Theory and Contemporary Science Fiction Cinema*, London: Verso.

Kellner, Douglas (1999), 'The X-Files and the Aesthetics and Politics of Postmodern Pop', *Journal of Aesthetics and Art Criticism*, vol. 57, no. 2.

Kerr, Paul (1984), 'Drama at MTM: Lou Grant and *Hill Street Blues*', in Jane Feuer, Paul Kerr, and Tise Vahimagi (eds), *MTM – 'Quality Television'*, London: British Film Institute.

Kilborn, R. and Izod, J. (1997), *An Introduction to Television Documentary*, Manchester: Manchester University Press.

Kingsley, Hilary (1993), *Casualty: The Inside Story*, London: BBC Books.

Kisseloff, Jeff (1995), 'The Golden Age' in *The Box: An Oral History of Television 1920–1961*, Harmondsworth: Penguin.

Kozloff, Sarah (1992), 'Narrative Theory and Television' in Robert C. Allen (ed.), *Channels of Discourse, Reassembled: Television and Contemporary Criticism*, London and New York: Routledge.

Krauss, Lawrence (1995), *The Physics of 'Star Trek'*, London: HarperCollins.

Kuhn, Annette (ed.) (1990), *Alien Zone: Cultural Theory and Contemporary Science Fiction Cinema*, London: Verso.

Laing, Stuart (1991), 'Banging In Some Reality: The Original *Z Cars*', in John Corner (ed.), *Popular Television In Britain: Studies In Cultural History*, London: British Film Institute.

Lavery, David (ed.) (1995), *Full of Secrets: Critical Approaches to 'Twin Peaks'*, Detroit: Wayne State University Press.

Lavery, David, Hague, Angela and Cartwright, Marla (eds) (1996), *Deny All Knowledge: Reading 'The X-Files'*, London: Faber & Faber.

Leman, Joy (1991), 'Wise Scientists and Female Androids: Class and Gender in Science Fiction', in John Corner (ed.), *Popular Television in Britain: Studies in Cultural History*, London: British Film Institute.

Lewis, Jon E. and Stempel, Penny (1999), *The Ultimate TV Guide*, London: Orion.

Lichenstein, Therese (1990), 'Syncopated Thriller: Dennis Potter's "The Singing Detective" ', *Artforum*, May.

Lyotard, Jean-Francois (1987), *The Postmodern Condition: a Report on Knowledge*, Manchester: Manchester University Press.

MacDonald, Fred J. (1987), *Who Shot the Sheriff? The Rise and Fall of the Television Western*, New York: Praeger.

McKinley, E.G. (1997), *'Beverley Hills 90210': Television, Gender and Identity*, Philadephia: University of Pennsylvania Press.

McLean, Adrienne (1998), 'Media Effects: Marshall McLuhan, Television Culture, and *The X-Files*', *Film Quarterly*, vol. 5, no. 4.

Macmurraugh-Kavanagh, Madeleine K. (1997), 'The BBC and the Birth of "The Wednesday Play", 1962–66: Institutional Containment versus "Agitational contemporaneity" ', *Historical Journal of Film and Television*, vol. 17, no. 3.

MacMurraugh-Kavanagh, Madeleine K. (2000), 'What's All This Then?: The Ideology of Identity in *The Cops*', in Bruce Carson and Margaret Llewellyn-Jones (eds), *Frames and Fictions on Television: The Politics of Identity Within Drama*, Exeter: Intellect Books.

Marc, David and Thompson, Robert J. (1992), *Prime Time/Prime Movers: America's Greatest TV Shows and the People Who Created Them*, Boston, Toronto and London: Little, Brown.

Matthews, Peter (1996), 'Reviews: *Emma*', *Sight and Sound*, vol. 6, no. 9.

Miller, Jeffrey S. (2000), *Something Completely Different: British Television and American Culture*, Minneapolis: University of Minnesota Press.

Miller, Toby (1997), *The Avengers*, London: British Film Institute; Bloomington: Indiana University Press.

Moir, Jan (1996), 'Oh, what a lovely ward!', *Observer*, 11 February.

Montgomerie, Margaret (1997), 'MiniSeries', in Horace Newcomb, (ed.), *Encyclopedia of Television*, Chicago and London: Fitzroy Dearborn.

Morley, David (1980), *The Nationwide Audience*, London: Britsh Film Institute.

Morley, David (1986), *Family Television: Cultural Power and Domestic Leisure*, London: Comedia.

Morley, David (1992), *Television Audiences and Cultural Studies*, London: Routledge.

Nelson, Robin (1997), *Television Drama in Transition: Forms, Values and Cultural Change*, London: Macmillan.

Nelson, Robin (2000), ' "Flexi-Narrative" Form and a "New Affective Order" ' (case study *Ally McBeal*) in Eckart Voights-Virchow (ed.), *Mediated Drama/Dramatized Media*, Frankfurt: Wissenschaftlicher Verlag Trier.

Newcomb, Horace (1974), *Television: The Most Popular Art*, New York: Anchor.

Nicholson, Martha (1997), *David Lynch*, Austin: University of Texas Press.

Page, Adrian (2000), *Cracking Morse Code: Semiotics and Television Drama*, Luton: University of Luton Press.

Okuda, Michael and Okuda, Denise (1999), *The 'Star Trek' Encyclopedia: A Reference Guide to the Future*, New York: Pocket Books.

Owen, Susan A. (1999), '*Buffy the Vampire Slayer*: Vampires, Postmodernity and Postfeminism', *Journal of Popular Film and Television*, vol. 27, no. 2.

Paget, D. (1998), *No Other Way to Tell It: Dramadoc/ Docudrama on Television*, Manchester: Manchester University Press.

Pearson, Roberta and Uricchio, William (eds) (1991), *The Many Lives of the Batman: Critical Approaches to a Superhero and his Media*, London: Routledge.

Penley, Constance (1997), *Nasa/Trek: Popular Science and Sex in America*, London: Verso.

Pines, Jim (1995), 'Black Cops and Black Villains in Film and TV Crime Fiction', in David Kidd-Hewitt and Richard Osborne (eds), *Crime and the Media*, London: Pluto.

Plummer, Laura (1997), 'I'm Not Laura Palmer: David Lynch's Fractured Fairy Tale', in *Literature/Film Quarterly*, vol.25, no. 4.

Porter , Jennifer and McLaren, Darcee (eds) (1999), '*Star Trek' and Sacred Ground: Explorations of 'Star Trek', Religion, and American Culture*, New York: Suny Press.

Presnell, Don and McGee, Marty (1998), *A Critical History of Television's 'The Twilight Zone', 1959–1964*, Jefferson: McFarland.

Purser, Philip (1981), 'Dennis Potter', in George Brandt, (ed.), *British Television Drama*, London: Cambridge University Press.

Radio Times (1996), 'Official Collector's Edition, *Star Trek* 30 Years', London: BBC.

Radway, Janice (1987), *Reading the Romance*, London: Verso.

Richards, Thomas (1997), *The Meaning of 'Star Trek'* (published in Britain as '*Star Trek' in Myth and Legend*), New York: Doubleday.

Roberts, Robin (1999), *Sexual Generations: 'Star Trek, The Next Generation' and Gender*, Urbana and Chicago: Illinois University Press.

Rosenthal, A. (1988), *New Challenges for Documentary*, Berkeley: University of California Press.

Rosenthal, A. (ed.) (1999), *Why Docudrama?*, Carbondale and Edwardsville: Southern Illinois University Press.

Ross, Karen (1996), *Black and White in Media: Black Images in Popular Film and Television*, Oxford: Polity.

Schiller, Herbert (1996), *Information Inequality: The Deepening Social Crisis in America*, London: Routledge.

Scounce, Jeffrey (1997), 'Science-Fiction Programs', in Horace Newcomb (ed.), *Encyclopaedia of Television*, Chicago and London: Fitzroy Dearborn.

Skovmand, M. and Schroder, K.C. (eds) (1992), *Media Cultures*, Routledge, London.

Self, David (1984), *Television Drama: An Introduction*, London: Macmillan.

Shubik, Irene (1975), *Play for Today: The Evolution of Television Drama*, London: Davis-Poynter.

Silver, Rachel (1988), *Casualty: Behind the Scenes*, London: BBC Worldwide.

Sobchack, Vivian (1987), *Screening Space: The American Science Fiction Film*, Piscataway: Rutgers University Press.

Sontag, Susan (1991), *Illness as Metaphor and AIDS and its Metaphors*, Harmondsworth: Penguin.

Sparks, Richard (1993), 'Inspector Morse: The Last Enemy', in George Brandt (ed.), *British Television Drama in the 1980s*, Cambridge: Cambridge University Press.

Spigel, Lynn (1991), 'From Domestic Space to Outerspace: the 1960's Fantastic Family Sit-com', in Constance Penley et al. (eds) *Close Encounters: Film Feminism and Science Fiction*, Minnesota: University of Minnesota Press.

Stark, Steven D. (1997), 'The Miniseries as History: Did *Roots* Change America?', in *Glued to the Set: The 60 Television Shows and Events that Made us Who we Are Today*, New York: Face Press.

Stead, Peter (1993), *Dennis Potter: Border Lines Series*, Bridgend: Seren Books.

Strinati, Dominic (1995), *An Introduction to Theories of Popular Culture*, London: Routledge.

Taylor, Don (1990), *Days of Vision, Working With David Mercer: Television Drama Then and Now*, Fulham (NH): Methuen.

Thomas, Howard (ed.) (1959), *The Armchair Theatre*, London: Weidenfeld & Nicolson.

Thomas, Lyn (1997), 'In Love With Inspector Morse', in Charlotte Brunsdon, Julie D'Acci, Lynn Spigel (eds), *Feminist Television Criticism: A Reader*, Oxford: Oxford University Press.

Thompson, Robert J. (1996), *Television's Second Golden Age: From 'Hill Street Blues' To 'ER'*, New York: Syracuse University Press.

Tulloch, John (1990), *Television Drama: Agency, Audience and Myth*, London and New York: Routledge.

Tulloch, John (1997), '*Doctor Who*', in Horace Newcomb (ed.), *Encyclopaedia of Television*, Chicago and London: Fitzroy Dearborn.

Tulloch, John and Alvarado, Manuel (1983), *Doctor Who: The Unfolding Text*, London: Macmillan.

Tulloch, John and Alvarado, Manuel (1990), 'Send-up: Authorship and Organization', in Tony Bennett (ed.), *Popular Fiction: Technology, Ideology, Production, Reading*, London and New York: Routledge.

Tulloch, John and Jenkins, Henry (1995), *Science Fiction Audiences: Watching 'Dr Who' and 'Star Trek'*, London: Routledge.

Turow, Joseph (1989), *Playing Doctor: Television, Storytelling and Medical Power*, Oxford: Oxford University Press.

Wagner, Jon and Lundeen, Jan (1998), *Deep Space and Sacred Time: 'Star Trek' in the American Mythos*, Westport and London: Praeger.

Wayne, Mike (1998), 'Counter-Hegemonic Strategies in Between the Lines', in Mike Wayne (ed.), *Dissident Voices: The Politics of Television and Cultural Change*, London: Pluto.

Wheale, Nigel (1985) 'Recognising a "human-thing": Cyborgs, Robots and Replicants', in Nigel Wheale (ed.), *The Postmodern Arts: An Introductory Reader*, London: Routledge.

Wheen, Francis (1985), *Television: A History*, London: Century.

Wolff, Janet (1981), *The Social Production of Art*, London: Macmillan.

Worland, Rick (1998), 'Captain Kirk: Cold Warrior', *Journal of Popular Film and Television*, vol. 16.

Wright, Elizabeth (1989), *Postmodern Brecht: a Re-Presentation*, London: Routledge.

Wright, Will (1975), *Sixguns and Society: A Structural Study of the Western*, Berkeley: University of California Press.

SOAP OPERA

Allen, Robert C. (1985), *Speaking of Soap Operas*, Chapel Hill: University of North Carolina Press.

Allen, Robert C. (1995), *To be Continued . . . Soap Operas Around the World*, London: Routledge.

Ang, Ien (1985), *Watching 'Dallas': Television and the Melodramatic Imagination*, London: Routledge.

Brower, Sue (1997), '*Dallas*' in Horace Newcomb, (ed.), *Encyclo-pedia of Television*, Chicago and London: Fitzroy Dearborn.

Brown, Mary Ellen (1990), *Television and Women's Culture: The Politics of the Popular*, London: Sage.

Brown, Mary Ellen (1994), *Soap Opera and Women's Talk*, Thousand Oaks: Sage.

Brunsdon, Charlotte (1981), '*Crossroads*: Notes on a Soap Opera', *Screen*, vol. 22, no. 4.

Brunsdon, Charlotte (2000), *The Feminist, the Housewife, and the Soap Opera*, Oxford: Oxford University Press.

Brunsdon, Charlotte and Morley, David (1978), *Everyday Television: Nationwide*, London: British Film Institute.

Buckingham, David (1987), *Public Secrets: EastEnders and its Audience*, London: British Film Institute.

Cantor, Muriel G. and Pingree, Suzanne (1983), *The Soap Opera*, London: Sage.

Dyer, Richard, Geraghty, Christine, Jordan, Marion, Lovell, Terry, Paterson, Richard and Stewart, John (1981), *Coronation Street*, London: British Film Institute.

Emmanuel, Susan (1992), 'Ien Ang, Watching *Dallas*', in Martin Barker and Ann Beezer (eds), *Reading into Cultural Studies*, London and New York: Routledge.

Fadul, A. (ed.) (1993), *Serial Fictions in TV: The Latin American Telenovelas*, São Paulo: ECA/USP.

Feuer, Jane (1992), 'Genre Study and Television', in Robert C. Allen (ed.), *Channels of Discourse, Reassembled*, Chapel Hill: University of North Carolina Press.

Feuer, Jane (1994), 'Melodrama, Serial Form, and Television Today', in Horace Newcombe (ed.) *Television: The Critical View*, New York: Oxford University Press.

Fiske, John (1987), *Television Culture*. New York and London: Routledge.

Fiske, John (1989), 'Moments of Television', in Ellen Seiter, Hans Borchers, Gabriele Kreutzner and Eva-Marie Warth (eds), *Remote Control: Television, Audiences, and Cultural Power*, London: Routledge.

Fuqua, Joy V. (1995), 'There's a Queer in my Soap!' in Robert C. Allen (ed.) *To Be Continued: Soap Opera Around the World*. Chapel Hill: University of North Carolina Press.

Geraghty, Christine (1991), *Women and Soap Opera*, Cambridge: Polity.

Gillespie, Marie (1995), *Television, Ethnicity and Cultural Change*, London: Routledge.

Gledhill, Christine (1992, 'Speculations on the Relationship between Soap Opera and Melodrama', *Quarterly Review of Film Studies*, vol. 14, nos. 1–2.

Gripsrud, Jostein (1995), *The 'Dynasty' Years: Hollywood Television and Critical Media Studies*, London: Routledge.

Hackett, Pat (ed.) (1991), *The Andy Warhol Diaries*. New York: Warner Books.

Hayward, Jennifer Poole (1997), *Consuming Pleasures: Active Audiences and Serial Fictions from Dickens to Soap Opera*, Lexington: University Press of Kentucky.

Herold, C.M. (1998), 'The "Brazilianisation" of Brazilian Television: A Critical Review', *Studies in Latin American Popular Culture*, vol. 7.

Hilmes, Michelle (1997), *Radio Voices: American Broadcasting, 1922–1952*, Minneapolis: University of Minnesota Press.

Hobson, Dorothy (1982), *'Crossroads': The Drama of a Soap Opera*, London: Methuen.

Hobson, Dorothy (1989), 'Soap Operas at Work' in Ellen Seiter et al. (eds) *Remote Control*, London: Routledge.

Jordan, Marion (1981), 'Realism and Convention' in Richard Dyer, Christine Geraghty, Marion Jordan, Terry Lovell, Richard Paterson and John Stewart (eds), *Coronation Street*, London: British Film Institute.

Lovell, Terry (1981), 'Ideology in *Coronation Street*' in Dyer et al. (eds), *Coronation Street*, London: British Film Institute.

Luckett, Moya (1999), 'A Moral Crisis in Prime Time: *Peyton Place* and the Rise of the Single Girl', in Mary Beth Haralovich and Lauren Rabinovitz (eds), *Television, History, and American Culture: Feminist Critical Essays*, Durham (NC): Duke University Press.

McKinley, E.G. (1997), *'Beverley Hills 90210': Television, Gender and Identity*, Philiadephia: University of Pennsylvania Press.

Martin-Barbero, Jesus (1993), *From Media to Mediations*, Minneapolis: University of Minnesota Press.

Mattelart, M. and Mattelart, A. (1990), *The Carnival of Images: Brazilian Television Fiction*, New York: Bergin & Garvey.

Modleski, Tania (1982), *Loving with a Vengence: Mass-Produced Fantasies for Women*, Hamden: Shoestring.

Morley, David (1989), 'Changing Paradigms in Audience Studies', in Ellen Seiter et al. (eds), *Remote Control*, London: Routledge.

Mumford, Laura Stempel (1995), *Love and Ideology in the Afternoon: Soap Opera, Women, and Television Genre*. Bloomington: Indiana University Press.

Nochlin, Linda (1971), *Realism*, Harmondsworth: Penguin.

Rofel, Lisa (1995), *Other Modernities: Gendered Yearnings in China after Socialism*, Berkeley: University of California Press.

Seiter, Ellen, Borchers, Hans, Kreutzner, Gabriele, and Wrath, Eva-Marie (eds) (1989), *Remote Control: Television, Audiences and Cultural Power*, London: Routledge.

Shelley Stamp, Lindsay, (2000), *Movie-Struck Girls: Women and Motion Picture Culture after the Nickelodeon*. Princeton: Princeton University Press.

Stewart, Michael (1999), *Television Soap Opera*, Block 3, Popular Genres, Popular Pleasures and Cultural Values Masters Programme, Milton Keynes: Open University Press.

Straubhaar, J. D. (1982), 'The Development of the Telenovela as the Pre-eminent Form of Popular Culture in Brazil', *Studies in Latin American Popular Culture*, issue 1.

Straubhaar, J. D. (1988), 'The Reflection of the Brazilian Political Opening in the Telenovela, 1974–1985', *Studies in Latin American Popular Culture*, issue 7.

Trinta, Aluizio R. (1998), 'News from Home: A Study of Realism and Melodrama in Brazilian Telenovelas', in Christine Geraghty and David Lusted, (eds), *The Television Studies Book*, London: Arnold.

Tulloch, John (2000), *Watching Audiences: Cultural Theories and Methods*, London and New York: Arnold.

Tulloch, John and Moran, A. (1986), *'A Country Practice': 'Quality' Soap*, Sydney: Allen & Unwin.

Tufte, Thomas (2000), *Living with the Rubbish Queen – Telenovelas, Culture and Modernity in Brazil*, Luton: University of Luton Press.

Wicke, Jennifer (1988), *Advertising Fictions: Literature, Advertisement, and Social Reading*, New York: Columbia University Press.

COMEDY

Aristotle (trans. Ross, W.D., 1925), *Ethica Nicomachea*, London: Humphrey Milford.

Bailey, Peter (ed.) (1986), *Music Hall: The Business of Pleasure*, Milton Keynes: Open University Press.

Bergson, H. (trans. Brereton C. and Rothwell R., 1911), *Laughter: An Essay on the Meaning of the Comic*, London: Macmillan.

Bowes, M. (1990), 'Only When I Laugh' in A. Goodwin and G. Whannel (eds), *Understanding Television*, London and New York: Routledge.

Bratton, J.S. (ed.) (1986), *Music Hall: Performance and Style*, Milton Keynes: Open University Press.

Capsuto, Steven (2000), *Alternate Channels: the Uncensored Story of Gay and Lesbian Images on Radio and Television, 1930s to the Present*, New York: Ballantine.

Carpenter H. (2000), *That Was Satire That Was: The Satire Boom of the 1960s*, London: Victor Gollancz.

Chambers, S., Karet, N. and Samson, N. (1998), *Cartoon Crazy?*, London: ITC.

Cohen, S. (1997), *Forbidden Animation*, Jefferson: McFarland.

Cook J. (ed.) (1982) *Television Sitcom*, BFI Dossier 17, London: British Film Institute.

Crowther, Bruce and Pinfold, Mike (1987), *Bring Me Laughter: Four Decades of TV Comedy*, London: Columbus.

Doty, Alexander (1993), *Making Things Perfectly Queer: Interpreting Mass Culture*. Minneapolis: University of Minnesota Press.

Dyer, Richard (1986), *Heavenly Bodies: Film Stars and Society*, London: British Film Institute/Macmillan.

Eaton, M. (1981), 'Television Situation Comedy', in Tony Bennett, et al. (eds), *Popular Television and Film*, London: British Film Institute/Open University Press.

Erickson, Hal (1995), *Television Cartoon Shows: An Illustrated Encyclopedia, 1949–1993*, Jefferson: McFarland.

Feuer, Jane (1992), 'Situation Comedy' in Robert Allen (ed.), *Channels of Discourse*, London and New York: Routledge.

Freud S. (trans. Strachey, J., 1976), *Jokes and their Relation to the Unconscious*, Harmondsworth: Penguin.

Halliwell, Leslie (1987), *Double Take and Fade Away*, London: Grafton.

Hamamoto D. (1991), *Nervous Laughter: Television Situation Comedy and Liberal Democratic Ideology*, New York: Praeger.

Hartley, John (1999), *Uses of Television*. London and New York: Routledge.

Hobbes, T. (1914), *Leviathan*, Letchworth: Aldine Press.

Jenkins, Henry (1992), *What Made Pistachio Nuts? Early Sound Comedy and the Vaudeville Aesthetic*, New York: Columbia University Press.

Kant, I. (trans. Guyer P. and Matthews E., 2000), *Critique of the Power of Judgment*, Cambridge: Cambridge University Press.

Kirkham, Pat and Skeggs, Beverley (1998), 'Absolutely Fabulous: Absolutely Feminist?', in Christine Geraghty and David Lusted (eds), *The Television Studies Book*, London: Arnold.

Lenburg, Jeff (1981), *The Encyclopedia of Animated Cartoons*, New York: Da Capo.

Lovell, T. (1982), 'A Genre of Social Disruption?' in J. Cook (ed.) *Television Sitcom*, BFI Dossier 17, London: British Film Institute.

Marc, David (1989), *Comic Visions: Television Comedy and American Culture*, New York: Blackwell.

Medhurst, Andy and Tuck, Lucy (1982), 'The Gender Game', in J. Cook (ed.) *Television Sitcom*, BFI Dossier 17, London: British Film Institute.

Medhurst, Andy and Tuck, Lucy (1996), 'Situation Comedy and Stereotyping', in John Corne and Sylvia Harvey (eds), *Television Times: A Reader*, London: Arnold.

Mellencamp, Patricia (1986), 'Situation Comedy, Feminism, and Freud: Discourses of Gracie and Lucy', reprinted in Charlotte Brunsdon et. al. (eds), *Feminist Television Criticism: A Reader*, Oxford: Oxford University Press.

Miller, Jeffrey S. (2000), *Something Completely Different: British Television and American Culture*, Minneapolis: University of Minnesota Press.

Mills, B. (forthcoming), *No Laughing Matter: The Constraints upon Television Sitcom in Britain*, Berlin and New York: Mouton de Gruyter.

Morreall J. (1983), *Taking Laughter Seriously*, Albany: State University of New York Press.

Morreall, J. (ed.) (1987), *The Philosophy of Laughter and Humor*, Albany: State University of New York Press.

Neale, Steve and Krutnik, Frank (1990), *Popular Film and Television Comedy*, London: Routledge.

Newcomb, Horace (1974) 'Situation and Domestic Comedies: Problems, Families and Fathers', in Horace Newcomb, *TV: The Most Popular Art*, New York: Doubleday.

Olson, R. Scott (1999), *Hollywood Planet: Global Media and the Competitive Advantage of Narrative Transparency*, New York: Lawrence Erlbaum Associates.

Palmer, J. (1987), *The Logic of the Absurd: On Film and Television Comedy*, London: British Film Institute.

Peary, D. and Peary, G. (eds) (1980), *The American Animated Cartoon*, New York: Dutton.

Perry, George (1983), *Life of Python*, London: Pavilion.

Pilling, J. (ed) (1997), *A Reader in Animation Studies*, London: John Libbey.

Plato (trans. Gosling, J.C.B., 1975) *Philebus*, Oxford: Clarendon Press.

Putterman, Barry (1995), *On Television and Comedy: Essays on Style, Theme, Performer and Writer*, Jefferson: McFarland.

Rowe, Kathleeen (1995), *The Unruly Woman: Gender and the Genres of Laughter*, Austin: University of Texas Press.

Sandler, K. (ed.) (1998), *Reading the Rabbit*, Piscataway: Rutgers University Press.

Scheurer, Timothy (1985), 'The Variety Show', in B.G. Rose (ed.), *TV Genres: A Handbook and Reference Guide*, Westport: Greenwood.

Selby, Keith and Cowdery, Ron (1995), 'The Sitcom: *Fawlty Towers*' in Keith Selby and Ron Cowdery, *How to Study Television*, London: Macmillan.

Spigel, Lynn (1996), 'From Theatre to Space Ship: Metaphors of Suburban Domesticity in Postwar America', in Roger Silverstone (ed.), *Visions of Suburbia: Symptoms and Metaphors of Modernity*, London and New York: Routledge.

Taylor, Ella (1989), *Prime-Time Families: Television Culture in Post-War America*, Berkeley: University of California Press.

Toll, Rober C. (1976), *On With the Show! The First Century of Show Business in America*, New York: Oxford University Press.

Toll, Robert C. (1982), *The Entertainment Machine: American Show Business in the Twentieth Century*, Oxford: Oxford University Press.

Took, Barry (1976) *Laughter in the Air*, London: Robson/BBC.

Wagg, Stephen (ed.) (1998), *Because I Tell a Joke or Two: Comedy, Politics and Social Difference*. London: Routledge.

Wells, Paul (1998), *Understanding Animation*, London and New York: Routledge.

Wells, Paul (2000), *Animation and America*, Edinburgh: Edinburgh University Press.

Wertheim, Arthur Frank (1979), *Radio Comedy*, New York: Oxford University Press.

Williams, Frances (1998), 'Suits and Sequins: Lesbian Comedians in Britain and the US in the 1990s', in Stephen Wagg (ed.), *Because I Tell a Joke or Two: Comedy, Politics and Social Difference*, London: Routledge.

Wilmut, Roger (1980), *From Fringe to Flying Circus: Celebrating a Unique Generation of Comedy, 1960–1980*, London: Methuen.

Wilmut, Roger (1985), *Kindly Leave the Stage! The Story of Variety, 1919–1960*, London: Methuen.

Wilmut, Roger and Rosengard, Peter (1989), *'Didn't You Kill My Mother-in-Law?': Alternative Comedy in Britain from the Comedy Store to Saturday Live*, London: Methuen.

Woolery, George W. (1989), *Animated TV Specials: The Complete Directory to the First Twenty-Five Years, 1962–1987*, Metuchen: Scarecrow.

POPULAR ENTERTAINMENT

Anderson, Kent (1978), *Television Fraud: The History and Implications of the Quiz Show Scandals*, Westport: Greenwood.

Andrews, David (1998), 'Feminizing Olympic Reality', *International Review for the Sociology of Sport*, vol. 33, no. 1.

Banks, Jack (1996), *Monopoly Television: MTV's Quest to Control the Music*, Boulder: Westview.

Barnett, Steven (1990), *Games and Sets: The Changing Face of Sport on Television*, London: British Film Institute.

Bellah, Robert N., Madsen, Richard, Sullivan, William M., Swidler, Ann and Tipton, Steven M. (1992), *The Good Society*, New York: Knopf.

Blaine, Allan (1994), 'Music Television' in Jeremy G. Butler, *Television: Critical Methods and Applications*, Belmont: Wadsworth.

Boddy, William (1990), 'The Seven Dwarfs and the Money Grubbers: The Television Quiz Show Scandals Revisited', in Pat Mellencamp (ed.), *Logics of Television: Essays in Cultural Criticism*, Bloomington: University of Indiana Press.

Bourdieu, Pierre (1998), *On Television* (trans. Priscilla Parkhurst Ferguson), New York: New Press.

Brookes, Rod (2001), *Representing Sport*, London: Arnold.

Brunsdon, Charlotte, D'Acci, Julie and Spigel, Lynn (eds) (1997), *Feminist Television Criticism: A Reader*. Oxford: Clarendon Press.

Brunsdon, Charlotte, Johnson, Catherine, Moseley, Rachel and Wheatley, Helen (2000), 'Factual Entertainment on British TV: The Midlands TV Research Group's 8–9 Project', *European Journal of Cultural Studies*, vol 4, no 1.

Butsch, Richard (2000), *The Making of American Audiences: From Stage to Television, 1750–1990*, Cambridge: Cambridge University Press.

Carpignano, P., Andersen, R., Aronowitz, S. and Difazio, W. (1990), 'Chatter in the Age of Electronic Reproduction: Talk Television and the "Public Mind"', *Sociotext*, nos. 25/26.

Carson, Tom (1983), 'Homage to Catatonia'. *Village Voice*, 19 April.

Cook, Guy (1992), *The Discourse of Advertising*, London and New York: Routledge.

Curti, Merle, (1967), 'The Changing Concept of Human Nature in the Literature of American Advertising', *Business History Review*, no. 41.

Dayan, David and Katz, Elihu (1992), Media Events. *The Live Broadcasting of History*, Cambridge (Mass): Harvard University Press.

DeLong, Thomas (1991), *Quiz Craze: America's Infatuation with the Radio and Television Game Show*, Westport: Praeger.

Dyer, Gillian (1982), *Advertising as Communication*, London and New York: Routledge.

Eco, Umberto (1972), 'Towards a Semiotic Inquiry into the Television Message' (trans. Paola Splendore), *Working Papers in Cultural Studies*, no. 3.

Eco, Umberto (1987), *Travels in Hyperreality: Essays* (trans. William Weaver), London: Picador.

Edgley, Charles (1988), 'Commercial Sex: Prostitution, Pornography and Advertising' in Kathleen McKinney and Sue Sprecher (eds), *The Social Context of Human Sexuality*, New York: Ablex.

Feuer, Jane (1983), 'The Concept of Live Television: Ontology as Ideology', in E. Ann Kaplan (ed.), *Regarding Television: Critical Approaches – an Anthology*, Frederick: University Publications of America/American Film Institute.

Fisher, David and Davies, Michael P. (eds) (1999), *Who Wants to Be Millionaire?*, New York: Hyperion.

Fiske, John (1987), *Television Culture*, London: Routledge.

Flitterman-Lewis, Sandy (1983), 'The Real Soap Operas: TV Commercials', in E. Ann Kaplan (ed.), *Regarding Television*, Frederick: University Publications of America.

Forest, Emma (1998), 'Inside Story: The Future is Female', *Guardian*, 16 December.

Garfinkel, Harold (1992), *Studies in Ethnomethodology*, Cambridge: Polity.

Gitlin, Todd (1997), 'The Anti-Political Populism of Cultural Studies', in Marjorie Ferguson and Peter Golding (eds), *Cultural Studies in Question*, London: Sage.

Goedkoop, Richard (1985), 'The Game Show', in Brian Rose (ed.), *TV Genres: A Handbook and Reference Guide*, Westport: Greenwood.

Goodwin, Andrew (1992), *Dancing in the Distraction Factory: Music Television and Popular Culture*, Minneapolis: University of Minnesota Press.

Gruneau, Richard, (1989), 'Making Spectacle: A Case Study in Television Sports Production', in Lawrence Wenner (ed.), *Media, Sports and Society*, Newbury Park: Sage.

Hall, Stuart (1980), 'Encoding/Decoding', in S. Hall, D. Hobson, A. Lowe and P. Willis (eds), *Culture, Media, Language*, London: Hutchinson.

Haralovich, Mary Beth (1992), 'Sitcoms and Suburbs', in Lynn Spigel and Denise Mann (eds) *Private Screenings: Television and the Female Consumer*, Minneapolis: University of Minnesota Press.

Harrington, C. Lee and Bielby, Denise D. (1995), *Soap Fans: Pursuing Pleasure and Making Meaning in Everyday Life*, Philadelphia: Temple University Press.

Hartley, John (1987), 'Invisible Fictions: Television Audiences, Paedocracy, Pleasure', *Textual Practice*, vol. 1, no. 2.

Hartley, John (1996) *Popular Reality: Journalism, Modernity, Popular Culture*, London and New York: Arnold.

Hartley, John (1999), *Uses of Television*, London and New York: Routledge.

Haug, Wolfgang Fritz (1986), *Critique of Commodity Aesthetics: Appearance, Sexuality, and Advertising in Capitalist Society*. Minneapolis: University of Minnesota Press.

Hill, John (1991), 'Television and Pop: the Case of the 1950s', in John Corner (ed.), *Popular Television in Britain: Studies in Cultural History*, London: British Film Institute.

Himmelstein, Hal (1994), *Television Myth and the American Mind*. Westport: Praeger.

Jauss, Hans Robert (1982), *Toward an Aesthetic of Reception* (trans. T. Bahti), Minneapolis: University of Minnesota Press.

Jhally, Sut (1987), *Codes of Advertising: Fetishism and the Political Economy of Meaning in the Consumer Society*, New York: St Martin's Press.

Katz, Elihu (1990), 'A propos des médias et de leurs effets', in L. Sfez and G. Coutlée (eds), *Technologies et symboliques de la communication*, Grenoble: Presses Universitaires de Grenoble.

Katz, Helen (1989), 'The Future of Public Broadcasting in the US', *Media, Culture and Society*, vol. 11.

Kellner, Douglas (1990), *Television and the Crisis of Democracy*. Boulder: Westview.

Knopf, Alfred A. (1992). *The Good Society*, New York: Tipton.

Leets, Laura, de Becker, Gavin and Giles, Howard (1995), 'Fans: Exploring Expressed Motivations for Contacting Celebrities', *Journal of Language and Social Psychology*, vol. 14, nos. 1–2.

Lewis, Justin (1991), *The Ideological Octopus: An Exploration of Television and its Audience*, New York: Routledge.

Livingstone, Sonia and Lunt, Peter (1994), *Talk on Television: Audience Participation and Public Debate*. London: Routledge.

Lopate, Carol (1976), 'Daytime TV: You'll Never Want to Leave Home', *Radical America*, vol. 11, no. 1.

Lumby, Catharine (1997), *Bad Girls: The Media, Sex and Feminism in the 90s*, Sydney: Allen & Unwin.

Lumby, Catharine (1999), *Gotcha: Life in a Tabloid World*, Sydney: Allen & Unwin.

McHoul, Alec and O'Regan, Tom (1992), 'Towards a Paralogics of Textual Technologies: Batman, Glasnost and Relativism in Cultural Studies', *Southern Review*, vol. 25, no. 1.

McLaughlin, Lisa (1993), 'Chastity Criminals in the Age of Electronic Reproduction: Reviewing Talk Television and the Public Sphere', *Journal of Communication Inquiry*, vol. 17, no. 1.

McNeil, Alex (1996), *Total Television: A Comprehensive Guide to Programming from 1948 to the Present*, New York: Penguin Putnam.

MacNeill, Margaret (1996), 'Networks: Producing Olympic Ice Hockey for a National Television Audience', *Sociology of Sport Journal*, no. 13.

Masciarotte, Gloria-Jean (1991), 'C'mon Girl: Oprah Winfrey and the Discourse of Feminine Talk', *Genders*, no. 11.

Mattelart, Armand and Mattelart, Michèle (1998), *Theories of Communication: A Short Introduction* (trans. Susan Gruenheck Taponier and James A. Cohen), London: Sage.

Mattelart, Michèle (1986), 'Women and the Cultural Industries' (trans. Keith Reader) in Richard Collins (ed.), *Media, Culture and Society: A Critical Reader*, London: Sage.

Maxwell, Richard (ed.) (2001), *Culture Works*, Minneapolis: University of Minnesota Press.

Miller, Jeffrey S. (2000), *Something Completely Different: British Television and American Culture*, Minneapolis: University of Minnesota Press.

Miller, Toby (1997), *The Avengers*, London: British Film Institute; Bloomington: Indiana University Press.

Moras, Lisa De (1997), 'The Sound and the Fury', *The Hollywood Reporter 1997–98 TV Preview*, September.

Morris, Meaghan (1990), 'Banality in Cultural Studies', in Patricia Mellencamp (ed.), *Logics of Television: Essays in Cultural Criticism*, Bloomington: Indiana University Press; London: British Film Institute.

Munson, Wayne (1993), *All Talk: The Talk Show in Media Culture*, Philadephia: Temple University Press.

Neaverson, Bob (1997), *The Beatles Movies*, London: Cassell.

O'Shea, Alan (1989), 'Television as Culture: Not Just Texts and Readers', *Media, Culture and Society*, vol. 11, no. 3.

Parkin, Frank (1971), *Class Inequality and Political Order*, London: MacGibbon & Kee.

Paterson, Richard (1980), 'Planning the Family: The Art of the Television Schedule', *Screen Education*, no. 35.

Peck, Janice (1994), 'Talk About Racism: Framing a Popular Discourse of Race on Oprah Winfrey', *Cultural Critique*, Spring.

Peck, Janice (1995), 'TV Talk Shows as Therapeutic Discourse: The Ideological Labor of the Televised Talking Cure', *Communication Theory*, vol. 5, no. 1.

Postrel, Virginia (1999), 'The Pleasures of Persuasion', *Wall Street Journal*, 2 August.

Real, Michael (1975), 'The Super Bowl: Mythic Spectacle', *Journal of Communication*, vol. 25, no. 1.

Real, Michael (1989), 'Super Bowl Football versus World Cup Soccer: A Cultural–Structural Comparison', in Lawrence Wenner (ed.) *Media, Sports and Society*, Newbury Park: Sage.

Rimmer, Dave (1985), *Like Punk Never Happened: Culture Club and the New Pop*, London: Faber & Faber.

Rothenberg, Randall (1995),*Where the Suckers Moon: The Life and Death of an Advertising Campaign*. New York: Vintage.

Rowe, David (1999), *Sport, Culture and the Media*, Buckingham: Open University Press.

Sartre, Jean-Paul (1990), *What is Literature?*, London: Routledge.

Schiller, Dan (1996), *Theorizing Communication: A History*, New York: Oxford University Press.

Schiller, Herbert I. (1989), *Culture Inc.: The Corporate Takeover of Public Expression*. Oxford: Oxford University Press.

Schwartz, David, Ryan, Steve and Wostbrock, Fred (1999), *Encyclopedia of TV Game Shows*, New York: Checkmark.

Schwartz, Dona (1997), *Contesting the Super Bowl*, New York: Routledge.

Seiter, Ellen (1999), *Television and New Media Audiences*. Oxford: Clarendon Press.

Shattuc, Jane M. (1997), *The Talking Cure: TV Talk Shows and Women*, London and New York: Routledge.

Smythe, Dallas (1977), 'Communications: Blindspot of Western Marxism', in *Canadian Journal of Political and Social Theory*, vol. 1, no. 3. Reprinted in Thomas Guback (ed.) (1990) *Counterclockwise: Perspectives on Communication*, San Francisco: Westview.

Smythe, Dallas (1978), 'Rejoinder to Graham Murdock', *Canadian Journal of Political and Social Theory*, vol. 2, nos. 1–2.

Spigel, Lynn (1991), 'From Domestic Space to Outer Space: The 1960s Fantasic Family Sit-com', in Constance Penley et al. (eds), *Close Encounters: Film, Feminism, and Science Fiction*, Minneapolis: University of Minneapolis Press.

Spigel, Lynn (1992), *Make Room for TV: Television and the Family Ideal in Postwar America*, Chicago: Chicago University Press.

Stone, Joseph and Yahn, Tim (1992), *Prime Time and Misdemeanors: Investigating the 1950s TV Quiz Scandal – A DA's Account*, Piscataway: Rutgers University Press.

Taylor, Joyce (1997), 'Success in Cable Networks: The Discovery Channel', in Manfred Meyer (ed.), *Educational Television: What Do People Want?*, Luton: John Libbey Media/Luton University Press.

Trujillo, Nick (1995), 'Machines, Missiles and Men: Images of the Male Body on ABC's Monday Night Football', *Sociology of Sport Journal*, no. 12.

Tulloch, John (1976), 'Gradgrind's Heirs – the Quiz and the Presentation of "Knowledge" by British Television', *Screen Education*, no. 19.

Turow, Joseph (1997), *Breaking Up America*, Chicago: University of Chicago Press.

Wenner, Lawrence (1989), 'The Super Bowl Pregame Show: Cultural Fantasies and Political Subtext', in Lawrence Wenner (ed.), *Media, Sports and Society*, Newbury Park: Sage.

Whannel, Garry (1992), *Fields in Vision: Television Sport and Cultural Transformation*, London: Routledge.

Williams, Linda (1995), 'Film Bodies: Gender, Genre and Excess', in Barry Grant (ed.), *Film Genre Reader II*, Austin: University of Texas Press.

Williamson, Judith (1978), *Decoding Advertisements*, London: Marion Boyars.

CHILDREN'S TELEVISION

Bazalgette, Cary and Staples, Terry (1995), 'Unshrinking the Kids: Children's Cinema and the Family Film', in Cary Bazalgette and David Buckingham (eds), *In Front of the Children: Screen Entertainment and Young Audiences*, London: British Film Institute.

Bianculli, D. (1992), *Teleliteracy*, New York: Simon & Schuster.

Blumler, J. G. (1992), *The Future of Children's Television in Britain: an Enquiry for the Broadcasting Standards Council*, London: Broadcasting Standards Council

Blumler, J. (1998), *The Integrity and Erosion of Public Television for Children*, London: Broadcasting Standards Commission.

Brunsdon, Charlotte (1997), *Screen Tastes: Soap Opera to Satellite Dishes*, London: Routledge.

Buckingham, David (1995), 'On the Impossibility of Children's Television: The Case of Timmy Mallet', in Cary Bazalgette and David Buckingham (eds) *In Front of the Children: Screen Entertainment and Young Audiences*, London: British Film Institute.

Buckingham, David (ed.) (2000), *Small Screens: Television for Children*, London: Continuum.

Buckingham, David, Davies, Hannah, Jones, Ken and Kelley, Peter (1999), *Children's Television in Britain*, London: British Film Institute.

Caughie, John (1991), 'Before the Golden Age: Early Television Drama', in John Corner (ed.), *Popular Television in Britain: Studies in Cultural History*, London: British Film Institute.

Chambers, S., Karet, N. and Samson, N. (1998), *Cartoon Crazy?*, London: ITC.

Cohen, K. (1997), *Forbidden Animation*, Jefferson: McFarland.

Cohen, S. (1972), *Folk Devils and Moral Panics*, London: MacGibbon & Kee.

Gunter, B. and McAleer, J. (1997), *Children and Television*, London and New York: Routledge.

Hilton, Mary (ed.) (1996), *Potent Fictions: Children's Literacy and the Challenge of Popular Culture*, London: Routledge.

Hodge, B. and Tripp, D. (1986), *Children and Television*. Cambridge: Polity.

Home, Anna (1993), *Into the Box of Delights*, London: BBC.

Kline, Stephen (1993), *Out of the Garden: Toys and Children's Culture in an Age of TV Marketing*, London: Verso.

Kubey, R. (ed.) (1997) *Media Literacy in the Information Age, Current Perspectives Information and Behavior* (volume 6), New Brunswick: Transaction.

Livingstone, Sonia and Bovill, Moira (1999), *Young People, New Media: Report of the Research Project: Children, Young People and the Changing Media Environment*. London: London School of Economics.

Lurie, Alison (1990), *Don't Tell the Grown-ups: Subversive Children's Fiction*, London: Bloomsbury.

Messenger-Davies, Máire (1997), *Fake, Fact and Fantasy: Children's Interpretations of Television Reality*, Mahwah: Lawrence Erlbaum Associates.

Messenger-Davies, Máire and Corbett, Beth (1997), *The Provision of Children's Programming in the UK between 1992 and 1996*, London: Broadcasting Standards Commission.

Messenger-Davies, Máire and Machin, David (2000), 'Children's Demon TV – Reality, Freedom, Panic: Children's Discussions of *The Demon Headmaster*', *Journal of Media and Cultural Studies*, vol. 14, no. 1.

Messenger-Davies, Máire (2001) *'Dear BBC': Children, Television Storytelling and the Public Sphere*, Cambridge: Cambridge University Press.

Palmer, Edward (1988), *Television and America's Children: A Crisis of Neglect*, Oxford: Oxford University Press.

Peary D. and Peary G. (eds) (1980), *The American Animated Cartoon*, New York: Dutton.

Pilling, Jayne (ed.) (1997), *A Reader in Animation Studies*, Sydney: John Libbey.

Sandler, K. (ed.) (1998), *Reading the Rabbit*, Piscataway: Rutgers University Press.

Springhall, J. (1998), *Youth, Popular Culture and Moral Panics: Penny Gaffs to Gangsta Rap, 1830–1996*, New York: St Martin's Press.

Starker, S. (1991), *Evil Influences: Crusades against the Mass Media*. New Brunswick: Transaction.

Wells, P. (1998), *Understanding Animation*, London and New York: Routledge.

Wells, P. (2000), *Animation and America*, Edinburgh: Edinburgh University Press.

Young, Brian M. (1990), *Television Advertising and Children*, Oxford: Clarendon Press.

NEWS

Andersen, Robin and Strate, Lance (eds) (2000), *Critical Studies in Media Commercialism*, Oxford: Oxford University Press.

Atkinson, Dave and Raboy, Marc (eds) (1998), *Public Service Broadcasting*, Paris: UNESCO.

Bailey, George and Lichty, Lawrence (1972), 'Rough Justice on a Saigon Street: A Gatekeeper Study of NC's Tet Execution Film', *Journalism Quarterly*, no. 49.

BBC (1996), *Producers' Guidelines*, London: BBC.

Bell, Allan (1991), The Language of News Media, Oxford and Cambridge (Mass.): Blackwell.

Blumler, Jay and Gurevitch, Michael (1995), *The Crisis of Public Communication*, London: Routledge.

Boyer, J. (1981), 'How Editors View Objectivity', *Journalism Quarterly*, no. 58.

Boyd-Barret, Oliver and Newbold, Chris (1995), *Approaches to Media*, London: Arnold.

Boyd-Barrett, Oliver and Rantanen, Terhi (eds) (1998), *The Globalization of News*, London: Sage.

Breed, Warren (1997), 'Social Control in the Newsroom: A Functional Analysis' in Dan Berkowitz (ed.), *Social Meanings of News*, London: Sage.

Broadcasting Act (1990), London: Stationery Office.

Broadcasting Act (1996), London: Stationery Office.

Brunsden, C. and Morley, D. (1979), *Everyday Television – Nationwide*, London: British Film Institute.

Canham-Clyne, J. (1996) 'When Both Sides Aren't Enough: The Restricted Debate over Health Care Reform', in J. Naureckas and J. Jackson, (eds), *The FAIR Reader: An Extra Review of Press and Politics*, Boulder: Westview.

Carter, Cynthia, Branston, Gill and Allan, Stuart (eds) (1998), *News, Gender and Power*, London: Routledge.

Cohen, S. and Young, J. (1983), *The Manufacture of News*, London: Constable.

Corner, John (1995), *Television: Cultural Form and Public Address*. London: Arnold.

Cumberbatch, Guy (1999), *Television: The Public's View*, London: ITC.

Curran, James and Park, Myung-Jin (eds) (1999), *De-Westernizing Media Studies*, London: Routledge.

Curran, J. and Seaton, J. (1991), *Power Without Responsibility*, London: Routledge,

Dholakia, Ruby Roy, Mundorf, Norbet and Dholakia, Nikhilesh (eds) (1996), *New Infotainment Technologies in the Home: Demand-Side Perspectives* (Lea's Communication Series), Boston (Mass.): Lawrence Erlbaum Associates.

Edelman, M. (1988), *Constructing the Political Spectacle*, Chicago: University of Chicago Press.

Eldridge, John (ed.) (1995) *Glasgow University Media Group Reader, Volume 1*, London: Routledge.

Epstein, Edward Jay (2000), *News from Nowhere: Television and the News*, Chicago: Ivan R. Dee.

Fishman, Mark (1997), 'News and Non-events: Making the Visible Invisible', in Dan Berkowitz (ed.), *Social Meanings of News*, London: Sage.

Fowler, Roger (1992), *Language in the News*, London: Routledge.

Franklin, Franklin (1997), *Newszak and News Media*, London: Arnold.

Galtung, Johan and Ruge, Mari (1965), 'The Structure of Foreign News', *Journal of Peace Research*, no. 2.

Galtung, Johan and Ruge, Mari (1983), 'Structuring and Selecting News' in S. Cohen and J. Young (1983), *The Manufacture of News*, London: Constable.

Gans, H. (1979), *Deciding What's News*, New York: Vintage.

Gans, H. (1985), 'Are US Journalists Dangerously Liberal?', *Columbia Journalism Review*, November/December.

Gibbons, Tom (1998), *Regulating the Media*, London: Sweet & Maxwell.

Glasgow Media Group (1976), *Bad News*, London: Routledge & Kegan Paul.

Glasgow Media Group (1980), *More Bad News*, London: Routledge & Kegan Paul.

Glasgow Media Group (1982), *Really Bad News*, London: Writers & Readers.

Gripsrud, Joestine (ed.) (1999), *Television and Common Knowledge*. London: Routledge.

Gunter, Barrie and Winstone, Paul (1992), *TV: The Public's View*, London: John Libbey.

Hall, S., Critcher, C., Jefferson, T., Clarke, J. and Roberts, B. (1978), *Policing the Crisis: Mugging, the State and Law and Order*, London: Macmillan.

Harper, Christopher (2000), *And That's the Way it Will Be: News and Information in a Digital World*. New York: New York University Press.

Harrison, J. (2000), *Terrestrial Television News in Britain: The Culture of Production*, Manchester: Manchester University Press.

Hartley, John (1982), *Understanding News*. London: Routledge.

Hartley, John (1992), *The Politics of Pictures: The Creation of the Public in the Age of Popular Media*, London and New York: Routledge.

Hartley, John (1999), *Uses of Television*. London and New York: Routledge.

Hartley, John (2000), 'The Frequencies of Public Writing: Tomb, Tome and Time as Technologies of the Public'. Media in Transition Conference Articles, http://media-in-transition.mit.edu/articles/, Cambridge (Mass.): Massachusetts Institute of Technology.

Hartley, John and McKee, Alan (2000), *The Indigenous Public Sphere: The Reporting and Reception of Aboriginal Issues in the Australian Media*. Oxford: Oxford University Press.

Held, David (2000), *Globalizing World?*, London: Routledge.

Herman, E. (1999), *The Myth of the Liberal Media*, New York: Peter Lang.

Herman, E. and Chomsky, N. (1988), *The Manufacture of Consent*, New York: Pantheon.

Iyengar, S. (1991), *Is Anyone Responsible?*, Chicago: University of Chicago Press.

Iyengar, S. and Kinder, D. (1987), *News That Matters*, Chicago: University of Chicago Press.

Iyengar, S., Peters, M. and Kinder, D. (1982) 'Demonstrations of the "Not-so-minimal" Consequences of Television News Programs', *American Political Science Review*, no. 81.

Jensen, K.B. (1987), 'News as Ideology: Economic Statistics and Political Ritual in Television Network News', *Journal of Communication*, Winter.

Kellner, D. (1990), *Television and the Crisis of Democracy*, Boulder: Westview.

Lee, M. and Solomon, N. (1990), *Unreliable Sources*, New York: Lyle Stuart.

Lewin, Kurt (1947), 'Frontiers in Group Dynamics, II. Channels of Group Life: Social Planning and Action Research', *Human Relations*, vol. 1, no. 2.

Lewis, J. (1991), *The Ideological Octopus: Explorations into the Television Audience*, New York: Routledge.

Lewis, J. (2000), *Constructing Public Opinion*, New York: Columbia University Press.

Lichtenburg, Judith (1991), 'In Defence of Objectivity Revisited', in James Curran and Michael Gurevitch (eds), *Mass Media and Society*, London: Arnold.

Lumby, Catherine (1999), *Gotcha! Life in a Tabloid World*, Sydney: Allen & Unwin.

McChesney, R. (1997), *Corporate Media and the Threat to Democracy*, New York: Seven Stories.

McCombs, M.E. and Shaw, D. (1972), 'The Agenda-setting Function of the Mass Media', *Public Opinion Quarterly*, no. 36.

McNair, Brian (1995), *An Introduction to Political Communication*, London: Routledge.

McNair, Brian (1999), *News and Journalism in the UK*, London: Routledge.

McNair, Brian (2000), *Journalism and Democracy: An Evaluation of the Political Public Sphere*, London: Routledge.

McQuail, Denis (1992), *Media Performance*, London: Sage.

Miller, Toby, Lawrence, Geoffrey, McKay, Jim and Rowe, David (2001), *Globalization and Sport: Playing the World*, London: Sage.

Mohammadi, Ali (ed.) (1997), *international Communication and Globalization: A Critical Introduction*, London: Sage.

Molotoch, Harvey and Lester, Marilyn (1977) 'News as Purposive Behaviour: On the Strategic Use of Routine Events, Accidents and Scandals', in Dan Berkowitz (ed.), *Social Meanings of News*, London: Sage.

Morley, D. (1980), *The Nationwide Audience*, London: British Film Institute.

Morley, D. (1992), *Television, Audiences and Cultural Studies*, London: Routledge.

Mosley, Ivo (ed.) (2000) *Dumbing Down; Culture, Politics and the Mass Media*. London: Academic Press.

Mowlana, H., Gerbner, G. and Schiller, H. (1992), *Triumph of the Image: The Media's War in the Persian Gulf – A Global Perspective*, Boulder: Westview Press.

Murdock, G. and Golding P. (1973), 'For a Political Economy of Mass Communications', in R. Milliband and J. Saville (eds), *Socialist Register*, London: Merlin.

Naureckas, J. and Jackson, J. (eds) (1996), *The FAIR Reader: An Extra Review of Press and Politics*, Boulder: Westview.

Ostgaard, Einar (1965), 'Factors Influencing the Flow of News', *Journal of Peace Research*, no. 2.

Peterson, Sophia (1979), 'Foreign News Gatekeepers and Criteria of Newsworthiness', *Journalism Quarterly*, no. 56.

Philo, G. (1990), *Seeing and Believing: The Influence of Television*, London: Routledge.

Ritchie, Jean (2000), *'Big Brother': The Unseen Story*, London: Channel 4 Books.

Rock, Paul (1973), 'News as Eternal Recurrence', in Jock Curran and Stanley Young (eds), *The Manufacture of News*, London: Constable

Sande, Oystein (1971), 'The Perception of Foreign News', *Journal of Peace Research*, no. 8.

Schiller, H. (1989), *Culture, Inc.: The Corporate Takeover of Public Expression*, New York: Oxford University Press.

Schlesinger, P. (1987), *Putting Reality Together*, London: Methuen.

Schudson, Michael (1995), *The Power of News*, Cambridge (Mass.): Harvard University Press.

Shoemaker, Pamela (1991), *Gatekeeping*, San Mateo: Sage.

Shoemaker, Pamela (1996), *Mediating the Message: Theories of Influences on Mass Media Content*, New York: Addison Wesley Longman

Snider, Paul (1967), 'Mr Gates Revisited: A 1966 Version of the 1949 Case Study', *Journalism Quarterly*, no. 44.

Staab, Joachim Friedrich (1990), 'The Role of News Factors in News Selection: A Theoretical Reconsideration', *European Journal of Communication*, vol. 5, no. 4.

Tracey, Michael (1997), *Decline and Fall of Public Service Broadcasting*, Oxford: Clarendon Press.

Trinta, Aluizio R. (1997), 'News from Home: A Study of Realism and Melodrama in Brazilian Telenovelas', in Christine Geraghty and David Lusted (eds), *The Television Studies Book*, London: Arnold.

Tuchman, Gaye (1978), *Making News*, New York: Free Press.

Tuchman, Gaye (1997), 'Making News by Doing Work: Routinizing the Unexpected', in Dan Berkowitz, (ed.), *Social Meanings of News*, London: Sage.

Tuchman, Gaye (1999), 'Objectivity as Strategic Ritual: An Examination of Newsmen's Notions of Objectivity', in Howard Tumber (ed.), *News: A Reader*, Oxford: Oxford University Press.

Tunstall, Jeremy (1971), *Journalists at Work*, London: Constable.

Vervliet, Hendrik D.L. (ed.) (1972), *The Book Through 5000 Years*. London and New York: Phaidon. Originally published (1972) as *Liber Liborum – 5000 ans d'art du Livre*, Brussels: Éditions Arcade.

Wark, McKenzie (1994), *Virtual Geography: Living With Global Media Events*. Bloomington: Indiana University Press.

Waters, Malcolm (2000, 2nd edn), *Globalization*. New York: Routledge.

White, David Manning (1950), 'The Gatekeeper: A Case Study in the Selection of News', *Journalism Quarterly*, no. 27.

Williams, K. (1998), *Get Me A Murder a Day! A History of Mass Communication in Britain*, London: Arnold.

Wilson, John (1996), *Understanding Journalism*, London: Routledge.

DOCUMENTARY

Baudrillard, J. (1983), 'The Ecstasy of Communication', in Hal Foster (ed.), *Postmodern Culture*, London: Pluto.

Britton, Andrew (1992), 'Invisible eye', *Sight and Sound*, vol. 1, no. 10.

Bruzzi, Stella (2000), *New Documentary: A Critical Introduction*, London and New York: Routledge.

Comolli, Jean-Luc (1980), 'Machines of the visible', in Teresa de Lauretis and Stephen Heath (eds), *The Cinematic Apparatus*, London: Macmillan.

Comolli, Jean-Luc and Narboni, Jean (1976), 'Cinema/Ideology/Criticism', in Bill Nichols (ed.), *Movies and Methods I*, Berkeley: University of California Press.

Corner, J. (1986), *Documentary and the Mass Media*, London: Arnold.

Corner, J. (1992), 'Presumption as Theory: Realism in Television Studies', *Screen*, vol. 33, no. 1.

Corner, J. (1995), *Television Form and Public Address*, London: Arnold.

Corner, J. (1996), *The Art of Record*, Manchester: Manchester University Press.

Dauncey, Hugh (1996), 'French Reality Television: More Than a Matter of Taste?', *European Journal of Communication*, vol. 11, no. 1.

Dayan, David and Katz, Elihu (1992), *Media Events. The Live Broadcasting of History*, Cambridge (Mass.): Harvard University Press.

Dovey, J. (2000), *Freakshow: First Person Media and Factual Television*, London: Pluto.

Fetveit, A. (1999), 'Reality TV in the Digital Era: A Paradox in Visual Culture', *Media, Culture and Society*, vol. 21, no. 6.

Gruneau, Richard (1989), 'Making Spectacle: A Case Study in Television Sports Production', in Lawrence Wenner (ed.), *Media, Sports and Society*, Newbury Park: Sage.

Heath, S. and Skirrow, G. (1977), 'Television: A World in Action', *Screen*, vol. 18, no. 2.

Hill, Annette (1999), 'Crime and Crisis: British Reality TV in Action'. in Ed Buscombe (ed.), *British Television: A Reader*, Oxford: Oxford University Press.

Hill, A. (forthcoming), 'Fearful and Safe: Audience Response to Popular Factual Entertainment' in R. Kilborn and J. Izod (eds), *Crossing the Boundaries*, Luton: University of Luton Press.

Hiller, J. and Lovell, A. (1972), *Studies in Documentary*, London: Secker & Warburg.

Katz, Helen (1989), 'The Future of Public Broadcasting in the US', *Media, Culture and Society*, vol. 11.

Kilborn, Richard (1994), 'How Real Can You Get? Recent Developments in Reality Television', *European Journal of Communication*, vol. 9, no. 4.

Kilborn, R. and Izod, J. (1997), *An Introduction to Television Documentary*, Manchester: Manchester University Press.

Kuhn, Annette (1978), 'The Camera I: Observations on Documentary', *Screen*, vol. 19, no 2.

Leyda, Jay (1996), 'Esther Shub and the Art of Compilation', in Kevin Macdonald and Mark Cousins (eds), *Imagining Reality: The Faber Book of Documentary*, Faber & Faber.

Macdonald, Kevin and Cousins, Mark (eds) (1996), *Imagining Reality: The Faber Book of Documentary*, Faber & Faber.

McCann, P. (1998). 'ITV Gives New Docusoap Prime Billing', *Independent*, 23 February.

Mamber, Stephen (1972a), 'Cinéma Vérité in America', *Screen*, vol. 13, no. 2.

Mamber, Stephen (1972b), 'Cinéma Vérité in America, Part 2: Direct Cinema and the Crisis Structure', *Screen*, vol. 13, no. 3.

Nichols, W. (1976), 'Documentary Theory and Practice', *Screen*, vol. 17.

Nichols, Bill (1985), 'The Voice of Documentary', in Bill Nichols (ed.), *Movies and Methods II*, Berkeley: University of California Press.

Nichols, W. (1991), *Representing Reality: Issues and Concepts in Documentary*, Bloomington: Indiana University Press.

Nichols, Bill (1994), 'At the Limits of Reality (TV)', in Bill Nichols (ed.), *Blurred Boundaries*, Bloomington: Indiana University Press.

Paget, D. (1998), *No Other Way To Tell It: Dramadoc/Docudrama on Television*, Manchester: Manchester University Press.

Paterson, Elaine (1989), 'Heller let loose', *Time Out*.

Pearson, Allison (1998), 'All the World's a Soap Set', *Daily Telegraph*, 28 May.

Plantinga, C. (1997), *Rhetoric and Representation in Non-Fiction Film*, Cambridge: Cambridge University Press.

Quinn, Jane (1997), 'Getting Closer to Audiences: The BBC Experience', in Manfred Meyer (ed.), *Educational Television: What Do People Want?*, Luton: John Libbey Media/University of Luton Press.

Rabiger, M. (1998), *Directing the Documentary* (2nd edition), London: Focal Press.

Renov, M. (ed.) (1993), *Theorizing Documentary*, New York and London: Routledge.

Rosenthal, A. (1988) *New Challenges for Documentary*, Berkeley: University of California Press.

Rosenthal, A. (ed.) (1999), *Why Docudrama?*, Carbondale and Edwardsville: Southern Illinois University Press.

Schlesinger, P. and Tumber, H. (1994), *Reporting Crime – Media Politics of Criminal Justice*, Oxford: Oxford University Press.

Taylor, Joyce (1997), 'Success in Cable Networks: The Discovery Channel', in Manfred Meyer (ed.), *Educational Television: What Do People Want?* (Luton: John Libbey Media/University of Luton Press.

Vaughan, D. (1983), *Portrait of an Invisible Man*, London: British Film Institute.

Waugh, Thomas (1985), 'Beyond Vérité: Emile de Antonio and the New Documentary of the 1970s', in Bill Nichols (ed.), *Movies and Methods II*, Berkeley: University of California Press.

Williams, Linda (1993), 'Mirrors without Memories: Truth, History and the New Documentary', *Film Quarterly*, vol. 46, no. 3.

Winston, Brian (1993), 'The Documentary Film as Scientific Inscription', in Michael Renov (ed.), *Theorizing Documentary*, London: Routledge.

Winston, B. (1995), *Claiming the Real: The Documentary Film Revisited*, London: British Film Institute.

Winston, B. (2000), *Lies, Damned Lies and Television*, London: British Film Institute.

LIST OF ILLUSTRATIONS

Whilst considerable effort has been made to correctly identify the copyright holders, this has not been possible in all cases. We apologise for any apparent negligence and any omissions or corrections brought to our attention will be remedied in any future editions.

Introduction: *Friends*, Warner Brothers International Television; *ER*, Warner Brothers International Television; **Drama:** *Heartbeat*, Yorkshire Television; *Marty*, National Broadcasting Company; *Bonanza*, NBC TV; *The Avengers*, Canal+; *The Man from UNCLE*, Arena Productions; *Cagney and Lacey*, MGM Television Distribution; *Z Cars*, BBC; *Dr Who*, BBC; *Star Trek*, Norway Productions/Desilu; *X Files*, 20th Century Fox International Television; *Singing Detective*, BBC/Australian Broadcasting Corporation; *Roots*, Wolper Productions; *Buffy the Vampire Slayer*, Warner Brothers International Television; *Twin Peaks*, Frost/Lynch Productions/

ABC; *Ally McBeal*, David E Kelley Productions; **Soap Opera:** *Peyton Place*, ABC; *Dallas*, Lorimar Productions; *Coronation Street* Granada Television; *A Country Practice* JNP Films Pty Ltd; **Comedy:** *Monty Python* BBC; *Ellen* ABC; *Absolutely Fabulous* BBC; *South Park* Comedy Central; **Popular Entertainment:** *The Lucy Show* Desilu Productions, Inc.; *Who Wants to be a Millionaire?* Celador Productions for Carlton Television; *The Tonight Show* National Broadcasting Company; *Oprah Winfrey Show* King World International; *Ready, Steady, Go!* Associated-Rediffusion Production; *Top of the Pops* BBC; **Children's Television:** *Goodnight Mr Tom* Carlton Television; *Play School* BBC; *Sesame Street* Sesame Workshop; *Beavis & Butthead* MTV; *The Simpsons* Gracie Films/20th Century Fox Television; **Documentary:** *The Family* BBC; *Big Brother* Bazal Productions; **Jacket:** *The X-Files* 20th Century Fox International Television

Index

Page numbers in **bold** signify detailed treatment in a 'grey box' case study; Page numbers in *italic* signify illustrations.

Schaffner, Franklin 11
Scooby Doo, Where Are You? 105
Scott, Gerry 38
Scounce, Jeffrey 31
Scream films 43
SCTV Network 65
Scum 13
The Secret World of Alice Mack 41
Seinfeld 5, 67, 69
Sense and Sensibility (film, 1996) 40
Serling, Rod 11
Sesame Street 100, *101*, **101–2**, 102–3, 138
Sex and the City 69
Shatner, William 28, 31
Shaw, Irwin 38
She's All That 41
Shields, Brooke 71
Shub, Esther 133
Sight On Sound 91
Silva, Frank 44
Silverman, Fred 36
Simpson, O.J. 36
The Simpsons 65, 73, **74–5**, 75, 97, 104, 105, *106*
Singin' in the Rain 1
The Singing Detective 36, *37*
Sister, Sister 41, 66
Six-Five Special 41, 89
The Six Million Dollar Man 16
The $64,000 Question 79
Smith, Chris, MP 108
Smothers Brothers 63
The Smurfs 97
Soho Stories 131
Soldier Girls 130, 131
The Sopranos 35
Soul City **54**
Soul Train 89
South African Broadcasting System 54
South Park 73, *74*, **74–5**, 106
Space Precinct 31
Speight, Johnny 66
Springer, Jerry 7, 61, 86, 120
St Elsewhere 25
Stanwyck, Barbara 49
Star Trek (and sequels) 26, 27, **28**, *29*, 30–1
Star Wars 2

Stargate SG-1 (TV series) 31
Starr, Ringo 75
Starr Report 121
Starship Troopers 107
Starsky and Hutch 22, 23
Steiger, Rod 11
Stella Dallas 49
Steptoe and Son 65
Sting 75
Stingray 31
Stone, Matt 74
Stranger from Space 27
Strike it Rich 80
Suddenly Susan 71
Sunday Night at the London Palladium 63
77 Sunset Strip 14, 17
Super Bowl 87, **88**
Supercar 31
Supermarket Sweep 80
Survivor 54, 80
Svankmajer, Jan 75
The Sweeney 17, 22
Sweet Valley High 41
Sylvania Waters 133

'tabloid TV' *see* 'dumbing down'
Takei, George 28
The Talk of the Town 63
A Tap on the Shoulder 13
Tarantino, Quentin 24
Target Luna 28
Tattooed Tears 130
Taxi 65, 67
Taylor, Don 13
Teaching Mrs Tingle 43
Teletubbies 97, 100, 102, **103**
Tempestt 86
Ten Things I Hate About You 41
Terreblanche, Eugene 130
Terrill, Chris 131, 134
That Was the Week That Was 64
Thatcher, Margaret 118
Thaw, John 98
theatre, influence of 8, 9–11, 43–4
Theroux, Louis 130
Third Rock from the Sun 66
This Is Spinal Tap 129
This Is Your LIfe 134
This Life 24

Thomas, Mark 63
Thompson, Emma 39, 40, 71
The Thorn Birds 38
Three of a Kind 65
Thunder on Sycamore Street 11
Thunderbirds 31
Till Death Us Do Part 65, 66
The Time Machine (TV, 1949) 27
Tinker, Tailor, Soldier, Spy 38
Titicut Follies 131
Tom and Jerry 105, 107
Tomlin, Lily 84
Tomorrow's World 139
The Tonight Show 81–4, *82*, **82–3**
Top Cat 73
Top of the Pops 89, *90*, 91
Tots TV 103
A Touch of Frost 23
Tron 107
Truman, Margaret 72
Trumpton 105
The Tube 90
Tuchner, Michael 13
Tulloch, John **10–11**
Turner, Ted 121
Twelve Angry Men (TV play) 11
The Twilight Zone 12, 35
Twin Peaks 36, 38, **44**, 46
Two of A Kind (US sitcom) 66
Two Point Four Children 66
The Two Ronnies 65
Two Stupid Dogs 106

Uggans, Leslie 36
UK/US TV, contrasted 25, 50–3, 105, 118–19
Ullman, Tracey 45, 65, 74
Unsolved Mysteries 135
Up the Junction 13

V 27
Vaughan Williams, Ralph 39
Vereen, Ben 36
Vertov, Dziga 129
Vet School 132
Vets in Practice 132
The Vicar of Dibley 66
Vidal, Gore 11, 84
Vietnam: A Television History 138
violence *see* objections

DATE DUE
